# Bhagavad-Gita: The Ambrosial 'Sat-Song' of Sri Krishna

Sajohn Daverly

# Some Appreciations For This Work (Continued from back cover)

"Your commentary on the Gita hits the essence of the Gita."
—Baba Hari Dass, Inspiration for and Spiritual Leader of Mount Madonna Center and author of *Silence Speaks: From the Chalkboard of Baba Hari Dass*

"Having read several commentaries on the Bhagavad Gita through the years, I am impressed with the author's skill in translating the text and the consistency of his insightful commentary. New readers of the Gita will have much spiritual nourishment to assimilate, and those who are already devotees will be inspired and motivated in their meaningful spiritual practices." —Roy Eugene Davis, Founder/Director of the Center For Spiritual Awareness and author of *The Science of Self-Realization*

"Sajohn Daverly's passion for the Bhagavad-Gita is apparent on every page. This is no intellectual endeavor, but a personal sojourn through territory of new discovery, making ancient wisdom come alive with contemporary meaning. Particularly refreshing is the social activism interwoven throughout the commentary. Women are included among the awakened ones that Krishna speaks about, not merely to. This offering makes the sacred text accessible to scholar and novice alike. Accept this invitation into the heart of the Bhagavad-Gita." —Rev. Deborah L. Johnson, Founder of Inner Light Ministries and author of *The Sacred Yes* and *Your Deepest Intent*

"Sajohn has delved deeply into expressing the inexpressible, and his love shines through." —Isaac Shapiro, spiritual teacher and author of *It Happens By Itself*

"This presentation of the Bhagavad-gita is erudite and straightforward in its clarity. It is a working treatise that goes deeply into the essence of the great teachings and avoids the tapestry of so many commentaries that tend to confuse rather than reveal. The carefully crafted translations illustrate the wisdom, devotion, and essential truth contained in this timeless text, and steer the reader in a straight path to understanding." —Norman Gilbert, Ph.D., Professor of Political Philosophy, Rollins College

"Sajohn's enlightened commentary is clearly the product of a lifetime devoted to understanding and experiencing this text in the core of his being. Thank you, Sajohn, for this gift to humanity. Your lovingly crafted Bhagavad Gita awakens a remembering of the omnipresent and deep truth within."
—Annie Elizabeth Porter, Co-founder of The River Sanctuary and author of *Affirmations for Everyday Living*

"Truly a remarkable and worthy translation." — Jonathan Wichmann, Assistant Editor, New World Library

"Sajohn Daverly brings a depth of insight and understanding to the Bhagavad-Gita. His clear and concise commentaries exhibit an intelligence born from years of study and a lifelong dedication to serving truth. The resulting work is fluid, elegant, and lucid. Very well done." — Doug Andrews, Founder/ Director of Ananda Sangha of the Redwoods and educator at the Living Wisdom School of Palo Alto

"Impressive." — Dilip K. Basu, Professor Emeritus, Departments of History and Asian Studies, University of California, Santa Cruz

"Sajohn Daverly's presentation of the Gita is unique in its consistent adherence to the universal truth of ever-present oneness. This beautiful interpretation of the Gita fully encourages and supports opening to one's own perennial innocence and direct experience, and offers alternative perspectives that are conducive to the releasing of any long-held beliefs that may be postponing that opening. It offers wise guidance for those desiring to see through the trance of the dreamforms to the experiencing of their true nature." — Roxanne Howe-Murphy, Ed.D., Founder of the Deep Coaching Institute and author of *Deep Coaching: Using the Enneagram As a Catalyst for Profound Change*

"Daverly's dedication to the Gita is unquestionable. His meticulous translation of its divine words from Sanskrit to English is a gift to us all, most importantly because his longstanding love of Spirit and spiritual realization is evident on every page. I couldn't recommend a read more highly."
— Joe Sousa (Mokshananda), MA, psychotherapist and spiritual teacher

"This new Bhagavad-Gita with commentary is a powerful work of scholarship paired with the deepest understanding of the way of Nonduality. Sajohn Daverly leads us on a journey through the Gita with a profound respect for its depths, and with a tender, clear, and learned heart-mind, helps us to touch into its flesh, its bones, and its spirit. We witness a graceful dance between the knowable and the unknowable, the visible and the invisible, the way of wisdom and the way of love. We are beautifully shown that there is nothing to hold on to, no one to do any holding, and yet at the same time no end to our discoveries as we explore the eternally unfolding mystery of existence."
— Robert Weisz, Ph. D., clinical psychologist and Director of the Milton Erickson Institute of New Mexico

Other Books by Zen Publications

- Heaven and Hell
- Am I - I Am
- May It Be As It Is
- Redemption Stories: Unwasted Pain
- Reflections From Lao-Tzu's Tao Te Ching
- A Duet of One
- May It Be As It Is
- Calm Is Greater Than Joy
- Pursue 'Happiness' And Get Enlightened
- Celebrate the Wit & Wisdom: Relax and Enjoy
- Pointers From Ramana Maharshi
- Enlightened Living
- A Buddha's Babble
- A Personal Religion of Your Own
- The Essence of The Ashtavakra Gita
- The Relationship Between 'I' And 'Me'
- Seeking Enlightenment –Why?
- Nuggets of Wisdom
- Confusion No More
- Guru Pournima
- Advaita and the Buddha
- Sin and Guilt: Monstrosity of Mind
- The Infamous Ego
- Who Cares?!
- The Essence of the Bhagavad Gita
- Your Head in the Tiger's Mouth
- Consciousness Strikes
- Consciousness Writes
- Consciousness Speaks
- The Bhagavad Gita – A Selection
- Ripples

# Bhagavad-Gita: The Ambrosial 'Sat-Song' of Sri Krishna

Translation and Commentary by
Sajohn Daverly

With a Foreword by Adyashanti

ZEN
PUBLICATIONS

PUBLISHED BY
ZEN PUBLICATIONS
60 Juhu Supreme Shopping Centre,
Gulmohar Cross Road No. 9, JVPD Scheme,
Juhu, Mumbai 400 049, India
Tel: +91 22 32408074
eMail: zenpublications@gmail.com
Website: www.zenpublications.com


Cover design and color illustration by Alixandra Mullins
and Melanie Gendron

Front cover concept and art direction: Sajohn Daverly

Back cover line drawing: Sanjay Kumar Chatterjee

Back cover photo: Brian Feaster

Production assistance: Donna Gervich

Printed by DeHart's Media Services Inc. in Santa Clara, California


ISBN 10 81-88071-97-8
ISBN 13 978-81-88071-97-5

Library of Congress Control Number 2012908508

Dedicated to
Swami B.R. Sridhar Maharaj,
Roy Eugene Davis,
Ramesh S. Balsekar,
and Adyashanti
...Guiding luminaries and beloved friends, all.

# Contents

Foreword by Adyashanti.................................................................xiii
Preface  .......................................................................................xvii
Invocation..................................................................................... xx

**Chapter One: Arjuna-vishada-yoga**
Verses   1-20: Preparing for Battle ............................................ 1
         21-35: Arjuna Surveys the Armies on the Battlefield............... 11
         36-47: Arjuna's Perspective of Dharma................................. 17

**Chapter Two: Sankhya-yoga**
Verses   1-10: Arjuna's Refusal to Fight ...................................... 23
         11-30: The True Nature of the Spirit-Self................................ 28
         31-38: The Duty of a Kshatriya........................................... 37
         39-53: Alignment With Universal Intelligence .......................... 40
         54-61: Indications of Insight-Wisdom................................... 50
         62-72: Recognition of Divine Inner Peace.............................. 54

**Chapter Three: Karma-yoga**                                              61
Verses   1-9: Working Without Attachment.................................... 62
         10-19: Turning the Wheel of Reciprocation............................. 66
         20-33: Perceiving Correctly, Living Holistically....................... 71
         34-43: The Nature of Desire ........................................... 80

**Chapter Four: Jnana-yoga**
Verses   1-15: The Reestablishment of Dharma ............................ 89
         16-23: Action, Inaction, and Mis-action ............................... 98
         24-33: Different Types of Sacrifice ................................... 102
         34-42: From Approach To Absorption In Truth ..................... 109

**Chapter Five: Karma-sannyasa-yoga**
Verses   1-13: Abiding At Ease In the Body............................... 115
         14-22: Flawless Equilibrium........................................... 122
         23-29: Cessation of the Imagined Self ............................. 127

**Chapter Six: Dhyana-yoga**
Verses   1-9: Freedom From Misidentification............................ 131
         10-32: True Meditation ............................................... 137
         33-47: Arjuna's Concerns Regarding Failure ..................... 153

## Chapter Seven: Jnana-vijnana-yoga

Verses 1-15: Nature and the 'I'-Sense ........................................ 163

16-23: Different Types of Worshippers ........................... 170

24-30: Freedom From Confusion ....................................... 174

## Chapter Eight: Akshara-brahma-yoga

Verses 1-15: The Art of Remembrance .................................... 179

16-22: The Unmanifest ......................................................... 187

23-28: Two Pathways After Death .................................... 191

## Chapter Nine: Rajavidya-rajaguhyam-yoga

Verses 1-15: The Origin of Beings ........................................... 197

16-25: To Heaven and Back ................................................ 204

26-34: The Supreme Refuge ................................................ 211

## Chapter Ten: Vibhuti-yoga

Verses 1-11: The Source of Creation ...................................... 217

12-18: Further Inquiry by Arjuna ...................................... 224

19-42: Infinite Variety Within Infinite Consciousness ........... 227

## Chapter Eleven: Vishvarupa-darshana-yoga ..................... 241

Verses 1-8: Arjuna Receives Supernal Vision ....................... 242

9-34: Beholding the Unity in Diversity ......................... 245

35-55: Arjuna's Revelation ................................................. 256

## Chapter Twelve: Bhakti-yoga

Verses 1-7: Two Approaches in Worship ............................... 267

8-12: Spiritual Practices ..................................................... 270

13-20: Valued Characteristics of the Devoted Ones ............... 273

## Chapter Thirteen: Kshetra-kshetrajna-vibhaga-yoga

Verses 1-11: Authentic Wisdom ............................................. 277

12-18: A Description of Reality .......................................... 283

19-26: The Intimacy of Spirit and Nature ....................... 286

27-34: True Seeing .............................................................. 291

## Chapter Fourteen: Gunatraya-vibhaga-yoga ..................... 295

Verses 1-10: Nature's Influences On Attention ...................... 296

11-18: Symptoms and Effects of Predominating Influences .. 301

19-27: Transcending the Captivity of Attention ..................... 304

## Chapter Fifteen: Purushottama-yoga

Verses 1-6: The Vedic 'Tree of Life'........................................................ 309

7-11: Affiliation With a Body ........................................................ 314

12-20: Presence of the Absolute.................................................... 316

## Chapter Sixteen: Daivasura-sampad-vibhaga-yoga

Verses 1-5: Celestial Qualities .................................................... 323

6-11: Enemies of the World........................................................ 325

12-24: Three Entranceways To Darkness.................................... 327

## Chapter Seventeen: Shraddha-traya-vibhaga-yoga

Verses 1-10: Ways and Means and Food Preferences ........................ 335

11-22: Sacrifice, Austerity, and Charity-Giving........................ 339

23-28: Invoking the Eternal ........................................................ 345

## Chapter Eighteen: Moksha-yoga

Verses 1-12: Conclusions Regarding Abandonment........................... 349

13-18: Five Causes of Any Action .............................................. 354

19-28: Perspectives, Performance, and Agents ........................ 357

29-40: Intelligence, Application of Will, and Happiness........ 361

41-49: Perfection in Allocated Work-Responsibilities ........... 366

50-54: The Culmination of Higher Knowledge ...................... 370

55-66: Love is the Highest Law .................................................. 372

67-78: Benedictions of the Gita .................................................. 380

A Closing Offering to Sri Krishna ........................................................ 387

Govindashtakam........................................................................................ 389

References.................................................................................................... 393

# Foreword

The Bhagavad-Gita is more than a profound Vedic scripture; it is a song of liberation. But this song is no nursery rhyme or lullaby to be sung to your children before bedtime. For all of its beauty and lyricism, the Bhagavad-Gita presents its readers with a great spiritual challenge. The opening scene of the Gita finds the warrior prince Arjuna and his charioteer Krishna situated between two armies readied for war. Arjuna has come to get a better look at his enemies, and:

> There Arjuna saw,
> Stationed within the ranks of both armies,
> Fathers and grandfathers,
> teachers, maternal uncles,
> brothers, sons, grandsons,
> And cherished friends as well.

Overwhelmed by the sudden realization of who he is about to go to war with, Arjuna cries out in despair. How can he sound the call to war when he sees that the enemy is made up of friends, family, and noblemen? What kind of man would set out to destroy that which he loves most? It is here that his charioteer Krishna, who is actually the personification of God, tries to convince Arjuna to throw himself into battle.

The whole subtext of the Gita is what Arjuna saw out there on the battlefield, why Krishna wants him to go into battle, and whether or not Arjuna can rise to the occasion. What is easy to misunderstand, though, is not only why Krishna wants Arjuna to go into battle, but what it is that Arjuna is being asked to conquer. The Gita is not something that you can read from a distance if you want to understand what it is trying to communicate.

Sajohn Daverly's Bhagavad-Gita is a real delight, and will be a treasure to anyone who reads it. His presentation is profound not only in its scholarly precision of translation, but also in its particularly insightful commentary. It is Sajohn's commentary that helps to draw us into the Gita and close the distance between the text and the reader. For if the Bhagavad-Gita is to open us to the richness of its treasure, we must enter into it as we would enter a forest or a stream.

The Gita is not simply a story about ancient kings, warriors, battles, and Krishna's exquisitely beautiful descriptions about the nature of Reality. It is much more than what it appears to be — about something of far greater urgency, something so important that your very life depends on it. It's about something that humanity tries with all its might to ignore, and which all of our tightly-held ideas try to protect us from. But even with all of our walls of protection and efforts to avoid, we will all sooner or later find ourselves in exactly the same position that Arjuna is in. And we will be asked to do exactly what he is being asked to do by Krishna.

At each moment we are but a breath away from our liberation, from God. Not even a breath away, but less than a breath. We are also on a battlefield between two immense armies, both containing people we love. The armies are symbolic, a metaphor for all that we are attached to, all that we love and hold onto to protect us from Reality. We have been told long ago not to cling to the things that hurt us. But here on this battlefield something else is being said, although we most likely won't hear it. We don't want to hear it. But the Gita is saying it anyway: What holds us fast in the bonds of illusion is the love we have for the people, things, and ideas which we hold most dear. That's what Arjuna saw. That's why he fell into despair. That's what the Gita is about.

Does that mean that we need to kill all that we love? No. That would be insane, and the Gita is about waking up from insanity, not perpetuating it. Nor is the Gita suggesting that we abandon loving and valuing people. The Gita is saying that we are held captive by our sticky attachment to our illusory ideas and beliefs about love and life. What we *think* love is actually turns out to be the cause of immense sorrow, greed, hate, and separation. The Gita is suggesting that if we want to wake up to Reality, we first have to see what Arjuna saw. Not simply read about it, but see it for ourselves. And although it may at first be disturbing to see, as it was for Arjuna, we need to see it nonetheless. Then the question for us will be whether we move forward and slay our illusions about love and life, or instead retreat into the cold comfort of our familiar darkness. This brings to mind one of the opening sayings in the Gospel of Thomas where Jesus says: "The seeker should not stop until he finds. When he does find, he will be disturbed. After having been disturbed, he will be astonished. Then he will reign over everything."

In a certain sense we are all Arjuna, and our true nature — Krishna, Reality — is waiting to reveal Itself to us on our own particular battlefield. Liberation is at hand. Losing our cherished notions can be very disturbing, especially when we begin to see that much of what we cherish is holding us in the bonds of illusion. It is not that we need to get rid of people, or things, or events. That would be to completely miss the point. What we need to dispel are deluded ideas and sticky attachments to people, things, and events. But in order to so, we must first see what Arjuna saw, and then see if we have the courage to continue.

Krishna is urging us on as he did Arjuna. Get up. Grab your sword. Face your illusions. Give your life to what is worth living for.

Adyashanti

# Preface

*Gita* means song, a *bhagavan* is an august personage, and the Bhagavad-Gita, contained within the ancient epic Mahabharata, is probably the most widely read of all Vedic scriptures. Its author is said to be India's great sage Vyasa, on whose illustrious resumé we also find the Vedas, the *Brahma-Sutras*, and the Puranas as well. Since the time of the Gita's initial recital, said to be at least three thousand years ago, revered masters from among India's many different schools of spiritual ideology have certainly presented a multitude of diverse approaches to Self-realization. Yet there seems to be unanimous agreement among them that the unique gift of the Bhagavad-Gita is its especially potent ability to illuminate the receptive heart with pointers toward divine awakenment of one's true nature.

The Mahabharata describes how the Pandava brothers' cruel cousin Duryodhana usurped their kingdom by deceitful means, consigned them to thirteen years' exile, and subjected them to profuse miseries in his many attempts to murder them. Yet even after all of that, he refused to honor his promise to return their kingdom upon their return from exile, saying that he would not give them 'even as much land as would fit on the head of a pin.' Krishna first acted as an ambassador of peace to try to prevent a war, but despite numerous appeals by Krishna and others for a kinder decision, Duryodhana's obstinacy ordained that war was inevitable. Unlike most wars, however, this particular one was prefaced by a discourse to one of the Pandava princes, Arjuna, regarding the nature of living beings, the universe, and the Absolute, which has since become a source of continual inspiration and hope for truth-seekers everywhere.

In regard to the nature of the Absolute, there is a wonderful verse in the Srimad Bhagavata Purana which states: *vadanti tat tattva-vidas, tattvam yaj jnanam advayam / brahmeti paramatmeti, bhagavan iti shabdyate* (1.2.11) — "Those who are knowers of the truth refer to the same one nondual Reality as Brahman, Paramatma, and Bhagavan." What this is saying is that although the human intellect prefers that things be either one way or the other, Reality has no reservations about being a complete paradox. It is completely content to simultaneously be without form (Brahman), with form (Bhagavan), and the witnessing Presence animating all life-forms (Paramatma). As Krishna's message in his Gita is that our true nature *is* That which effortlessly accommodates all paradoxes or apparently polaric opposites, the orientation in this particular rendering of the Gita is that Self-realization is not a process of getting somewhere later, but is rather a discovery of what is here right now.

In contrast to the spiritual approach marked by the struggle to achieve by pushing forward with more and more complex *doing*, one is herein offered the invitation to instead calmly step back into alert stillness so as to allow a natural opening into the simplicity of purely *being*.

It has been experienced that this opening is often preceded by sincere Self-inquiry and *satsang*. *Sat* means truth, a *sangha* is a community, and a *satsang* is a communal gathering for exploring the truth of one's own being utilizing the language of the undefended heart. Down through the ages, millions have joined Arjuna in attending *satsang* with Sri Krishna by deeply listening with the heart to his '*sat*-song,' his song communicating the truth of what we are prior to all philosophies and learned beliefs. Among those who deeply listened, many later spoke of experiencing a penetrating resonance which gradually ushered in profound transformation at every level of functioning. This energetic movement occurs most effectively after an initial 'throwing down of weapons,' meaning a spontaneous relinquishing of all strategies which are utilized to perpetuate the mythology of the egoic self. Whenever this type of surrender happens and we find ourselves totally vulnerable and thoroughly transparent, just as Arjuna did at Kurukshetra, those are the times when internal openings are most likely to occur.

By remaining open and available for Truth to reveal Itself at Its own pace, in Its own space, through Its own ways, by Its own grace, clarity dawns. It becomes clear that Self-realization does not imply self-reinvention, and that *yoga* does not involve a 'uniting' of things as much as a recognition of what was never separated to begin with. It becomes clear that *samadhi* is not a monumental experience of the assumed self for a period of time, but rather a space of timelessness wherein the dream of being the assumed self is altogether forgotten. Clarity reveals that variety or diversity is not a problem to be solved — that the polarizing of differences based on inherited beliefs may produce suffering, but diversity itself is a creative expression of the boundless Love which pure Spirit is. And clarity reveals that awakening to the truth of oneself is not a final endpoint heralding a transcendence which excludes the world. Rather, it is the beginning of a dynamic ongoing unfoldment in which truth is not merely realized, but lived and served even more authentically, lovingly, and compassionately within the body and within the world.

The intention behind this edition of the Gita is to present its teachings in a way that vitally beckons that clarity through consistent adherence to the truth of the always-already-existing unicity within the diversity. To that end there are two areas in which I humbly beg the indulgence of all those who are seasoned students of Sanskrit. First, phonetic spelling has been preferred over the use of diacritical markings in order to facilitate reading and recitation of the text for the broadest section of readers. An exception to this would be in the cases of words such as *jnana* and *prajna*, wherein the letters *j-n* are pronounced like the combined letters *g-y* in the phrase 'long yarn' to sound like 'gyana' and 'pragya.' Secondly, some concise and sensitive bracketed elucidations have been incorporated into the translations where it was felt to be genuinely helpful so as to avoid more frequently interrupting the flow of dialogue between Krishna and Arjuna with additional explanatory notations.

Readers may also notice that there are two distinct levels of communication presented in the Gita which are interwoven throughout the text — one by Krishna as the Absolute, and one by Krishna as Arjuna's dear friend and spiritual advisor. It is for this reason that the personal pronouns used for Krishna herein are sometimes capitalized and sometimes not, based upon the context within which Krishna is being referred to, or the standpoint from which he is speaking. We are indeed reminded of this distinction by Krishna's use of the words *mat-parah*, 'regarding Me as the Absolute,' in verses 12.6 and 18.57.

I am deeply grateful to all of the kind friends who provided continuous encouragement and support for this work both throughout its progress and in regard to its publication, especially Adyashanti, who graciously read through the entire manuscript and offered comments, Rob Koenig, Amritanand, Dana Tosta, Dr. Don Davies, Harley Matsil, Darlene Barbieri, and Deborah Turnor.

May the results of this work serve to kindle within us a greater sense of natural conductivity and connectivity with all of life — that any ambition for personal 'mastery' may yield to an appreciation for the perennial Mystery.

Sajohn Daverly
July 3rd, 2012 (Guru Purnima)
Santa Cruz, California

# Invocation

---

"Within my heart I meditate upon the lotus feet of Lord Sri Krishna,
Whose body is dark blue like clouds full of rainwater,
Whose eyes are like lotus petals,
Who wears a garland of forest flowers, a crown, and other ornaments,
Who has a radiant face like the full moon of the autumn season,
Who holds a flute,
And who, being embraced by the throng of milkmaids,
is anointed with their vermillion powder.

"O my Lord of captivating beauty who appeared in the Yadu dynasty,
Please come to my heart from Your island abode in the ocean of milk,
and adorn this golden throne resplendent with clusters of valuable jewels.
With holy water I wash Your lotus feet which are marked
with all auspicious symbols,
And, O enemy of the demon Mura, I place before You an offering
of fresh *durva* grass,* pure drinking water, and sweet ripe fruits.
Please accept it.

"Dear Lord of the universe, I am Your servitor,
So if any of the worship performed by me has been incomplete,
kindly forgive that and make it complete...."

— Adi Shankara, *Bhagavan Manasa-Puja Stotram*, verses 1, 2, and 9

---

\* Cynodon dactylon, used in traditional homage ceremonies.

# Chapter One

---

# Arjuna-vishada-yoga
### (Arjuna's Approach To the Recognition of Divine Unicity By Way of Despair)

"At the conclusion of the journey, the awakened one finds freedom from the fever of cravings; and in that boundless freedom, all tethers are severed. ...Even the celestials admire that wise charioteer who has tamed the horses of the senses and is devoid of pride and other such mental maladies. As all-accommodating as the earth, as reliable as a stone pillar, and as pristinely clear as an unmuddied lake, such a one is indeed free from the illusion of repeated births."   — The Dhammapada 7.90, 94, 95

"When the eye of the awakened one observes sentient beings, it sees that despite the coming and going of bodies throughout the various realms, there is a great treasure within those bodies which is eternal and unchanging. Upon seeing this, the awakened one teaches for the benefit of all beings, enabling them to discover the immeasurable wealth of wisdom and of widely caring for one another."   — *Tathagatagarbha Sutra*

"I fervently wish no misery ever came near anyone; yet it is that alone that gives us an insight into the depths of our lives, does it not? In our moments of anguish, gates barred forever seem to open and let in many a flood of light. ...That is a lesson for all life: face the terrible, face it boldly. Like monkeys, the hardships of life fall back when we cease to flee before them."
— Swami Vivekananda

"Keep quiet by knowing you are not the ego that has to keep quiet. ...The stirring thought 'I' creates an entire universe, but the Truth does not move. Keep vigilant of where and how this 'I' arises. This is Satsang and it is your own nature."   — Sri H.W.L. Poonja

### 1
*dhritarashtra uvacha:*
*dharma-kshetre kurukshetre / samaveta yuyutsavah*
*mamakah pandavash chaiva / kim akurvata sanjaya*

*dhritarashtrah* > Dhritarashtra ('holder of the kingdom,' the son
of Vyasa's brother Vichitravirya and uncle of the Pandavas);
*uvacha* > said; *dharma-kshetre* > in the place where righteousness dwells;
*kuru-kshetre* > the field of the Kurus (located in India's Punjab district
north of Delhi); *samavetah* > assembled; *yuyutsavah* > desiring to fight;

*mamakah* > my sons (the Kauravas); *pandavah* > the Pandavas (Yudhisthira, Arjuna, Bhima, Nakula, and Sahadeva, the five sons of Dhritarashtra's brother King Pandu); *cha* > and; *eva* > exactly; *kim* > what; *akurvata* > did they do; *sanjaya* > O Sanjaya (Dhritarashtra's minister, 'the fully victorious one').

**King Dhritarashtra said:**
**O Sanjaya, exactly what did my sons and the sons of Pandu do**
**when, desiring to engage in battle,**
**They [initially] assembled at Kurukshetra,**
**that place where righteousness dwells?**

This conversation between the blind king and his minister endowed with mystical vision took place on the tenth day of the eighteen-day war at Kurukshetra after the fall of Bhishma, the Kauravas' commander-in-chief. Bhishma was succeeded by Drona.

**2**
*sanjaya uvacha:*
*drishtva tu pandavanikam / vyudham duryodhanas tada*
*acharyam upasangamya / raja vachanam abravit*

*sanjayah uvacha* > Sanjaya said; *drishtva* > after seeing; *tu* > indeed; *pandava-anikam* > the army of the Pandavas; *vyudham* > arranged in a battle formation; *duryodhanah* > Duryodhana (cousin of the Pandavas, chief among the sons of Dhritarashtra and commander-in-chief of the Kaurava army whose name means 'one who employs foul tactics in fighting'); *tada* > at that time; *acharyam* > the master (Drona, the military teacher whose name means 'bucket'); *upasangamya* > approaching; *raja* > the king; *vachanam* > words; *abravit* > spoke.

**Sanjaya said:**
**Indeed, O king,**
**after seeing the army of the Pandavas arrayed in battle formation,**
**King Duryodhana approached his military teacher, Drona,**
**and spoke the following words:**

**3**
*pashyaitam pandu-putranam / acharya mahatim chamum*
*vyudham drupada-putrena / tava shishyena dhimata*

*pashya* > behold; *etam* > this; *pandu-putranam* > of the sons of Pandu; *acharya* > O master; *mahatim* > great; *chamum* > military forces; *vyudham* > arrayed; *drupada-putrena* > by the son of King Drupada (Drishtadyumna,

'one of outstanding splendor,' brother of the Pandavas' wife
Draupadi and commander-in-chief of the Pandava army);
*tava* > your; *shishyena* > student; *dhimata* > wise.

**O master, behold [those who oppose us —]**
**This great army of the sons of Pandu**
**Arranged by your wise student Dhrishtadyumna,**
**the son of Drupada.**

**4**
*atra shura maheshvasa / bhimarjuna-sama yudhi*
*yuyudhano viratash cha / drupadash cha maharathah*

*atra* > here; *shurah* > heroes; *maha-ishu-asah* > mighty arrow hurlers;
*bhima-arjuna* > to Bhima ('the terrible one') and Arjuna ('one who
radiates a silver aura'); *samah* > equal; *yudhi* > in fighting skill;
*yuyudhanah* > Yuyudhana ('he who is eager for battle'); *viratah* > Virata
('one of broad rulership,' the king with whom the Pandavas took refuge
during their final year of exile from their kingdom); *cha* > also;
*drupadah* > Drupada (king of Panchala, father-in-law of the Pandavas,
'the swift-footed one'); *cha* > also; *maha-rathah* > great warriors.

**Here are heroic, mighty archers**
**equal in battle to Bhima and Arjuna —**
**Great warriors such as Yuyudhana,**
**King Virata, and King Drupada.**

Yuyudhana was one of Krishna's own charioteers. He was also known as
Satyaki, and is referred to as such in upcoming verse 17.

**5**
*dhrishtaketush chekitanah / kashirajash cha viryavan*
*purujit kuntibhojash cha / shaibyash cha nara-pungavah*

*dhrishtaketuh* > Dhrishtaketu (the king of Chedi, 'one who is bold in
leadership'); *chekitanah* > Prince Chekitana ('one of lofty intelligence');
*kashirajah* > the king of Kashi (that territory which encompasses modern
Benares); *cha* > also; *viryavan* > very heroic; *purujit* > Prince Purujit ('one of
broad conquests'); *kuntibhojah* > Prince Kuntibhoja (the brother of Prince
Purujit who adopted the Pandavas' mother Pritha, and thus she
became known as Kunti); *cha* > and; *shaibyah* > the king of the
Shibi tribe; *cha* > and; *nara-pungavah* > a bull among men.

Here also is King Dhrishtaketu, Prince Chekitana,
the princes Purujit and Kuntibhoja,
The valorous king of the Kashis,
and King Shaibya, who is like a bull among men.

6

*yudhamanyush cha vikranta / uttamaujash cha viryavan*
*saubhadro draupadeyash cha / sarva eva maharathah*

*yudhamanyuh* > Yudhamanyu ('one of great fighting spirit'); *cha* > and;
*vikrantah* > bold, courageous; *uttamaujah* > Uttamauja ('one who possesses
limitless capability'); *cha* > and; *viryavan* > heroic; *saubhadrah* > the son
of Arjuna's wife Subhadra (Abhimanyu, 'he who dives into anger' against
his enemies); *draupadeyah* > the five sons of the Pandavas' wife Draupadi
(Yudhisthira's son Prativindhya, Bhima's son Sutasoma, Arjuna's son
Shrutakirti, Nakula's son Shatanika, and Sahadeva's son Shrutakarma);
*cha* > and; *sarve* > all; *eva* > indeed; *maha-rathah* > great chariot-warriors.

And there are the courageous Yudhamanyu,
the incomparable Uttamauja,
Subhadra's son Abhimanyu,
And the sons of Draupadi,
all of whom are indeed great chariot-warriors.

7

*asmakam tu vishistha ye / tan nibodha dvijottama*
*nayaka mama sainyasya / samjnartham tan bravimi te*

*asmakam* > our own; *tu* > but; *vishishtah* > prominent;
*ye* > who; *tan* > them; *nibodha* > give attention to; *dvija-uttama* > O best
of the twice-born (the brahmin class of priests and teachers);
*nayakah* > leaders, heroes; *mama* > of mine; *sainyasya* > of the troops;
*samjna-artham* > for the purpose of agreement; *tan* > them;
*bravimi* > I shall mention by name, I shall announce; *te* > to you.

But now, O best of the brahmins,
Please carefully hear [who I have selected to be]
our own most prominent commanders.
I shall tell you the names of those leading my military forces
in order to confirm that you are in agreement [with my choices].

**8**

*bhavan bhishmash cha karnash cha / kripash cha samitim-jayah*
*ashvatthama vikarnash cha / saumadattis tathaiva cha*

*bhavan* > your good self; *bhishmah* > Bhishma ('the awe-inspiring one,'
brother of Vyasa and Vichitravirya, granduncle and seniormost teacher of
both the Pandavas and the Kauravas); *cha* > also; *karnah* > Karna ('by the ear');
*cha* > and; *kripah* > Kripa ('the compassionate one,' brother-in-law
of Drona); *cha* > and; *samitim-jayah* > always victorious in battle;
*ashvatthama* > Ashvatthama (the son of Drona, 'one endowed with the
strength of a horse'); *vikarnah* > Vikarna ('one with great ears,' connoting
one with a keen sense of hearing, the chief among Duryodhana's
ninety-nine brothers); *cha* > also; *saumadattih* > the son of Somadatta
(Bhurishravas, king of the Bahlika tribe 'whose praises are
abundantly sung'); *tatha* > as well as; *eva* > indeed; *cha* > also.

**Besides your lordship,**
**there is Bhishma, Karna,**
**Kripa, Ashvatthama, Vikarna,**
**and Bhurishravas, the son of Somadatta,**
**All of whom are always victorious in battle.**

There are of course different opinions as to whether the Mahabharata epic
and its section with Bhagavad-Gita is: (a) an authentic historical document
of actual events, (b) a purely mythological and allegorical presentation,
(c) partly factual and partly symbolic, or (d) both: historical with additional
profound underlying symbolic meaning. According to the much-beloved
spiritual teacher Paramahansa Yogananda and many other raja-yoga masters
who have commented on the Bhagavad-Gita from perspective (d) above, the
battlefield of Kurukshetra described here also symbolically represents the
human body, and the various soldiers also represent the different qualities
which either assist or hinder spiritual seekers in their endeavors to recognize
the truth of their own primal nature as the one undivided Reality.

The members of the Pandavas' army symbolize the characteristics which
conduce to Self-realization: Satyaki represents devotion and beneficence,
Virata is the focus of intention, Drupada is dispassion, and Dhrishtadyumna
represents encouragement derived from the perception of light and other
sensory phenomena in meditation. Chekitana symbolizes memory, the King
of Kashi represents discernment, Uttamauja is vigor, Draupadi is the
*kundalini-shakti* concentrated at the base of the spinal column, and her five
sons represent the sound and light frequencies perceived in the *chakras*

(energy vortexes) upon the *kundalini* energy's rising and moving through them on its way to the region at the top of the head known as the *sahasrara*. Shikhandi, mentioned in upcoming verse 17, represents knowledge.

In relation to the eight limbs of Patanjali's yoga system, Dhrishtaketu is said to represent *yama* (abstentions or external disciplines), Shaibya represents *niyama* (observances or internal disciplines), Kuntibhoja is *asana* (physical postures and exercises), Yudhamanyu is *pranayama* (regulation of the breath and energy flow), Purujit is *pratyahara* (withdrawal of the mind and senses from their corresponding objects), and Abhimanyu represents *samyama*, the sustained union of *dharana*, *dhyana*, and *samadhi* (concentration, meditation, and realization).

The Kauravas' army is said to symbolize qualities which perpetuate unconsciousness in regard to one's own unborn essence. King Dhritarashtra is said to represent a mind darkened by delusion (although his minister Sanjaya represents the divine insight of an illumined mind), Duryodhana represents malefic ambition, Dronacharya represents *samskaras* (mental impressions or recollections of previous experiences), Ashvatthama is desire, and Bhurishravas is combativeness.

In relation to the five *kleshas* (disturbing afflictions), Bhishma symbolizes *asmita* (the sense of individuated selfhood or distinction as an entity), Kripa represents *avidya* (the ignoring tendency), Vikarna is *dvesha* (hatred), and Jayadratha, mentioned in verse 11.34, represents *abhinivesha* (stubbornness) or recklessness. Karna is said to represent *raga* (longing) as well as the nobler attributes of faith and loyal commitment to duty. Karna was actually the sixth Pandava, the eldest, although he was unknown as such by either himself or his five brothers. Due to his being conceived prior to his mother's marriage, he was orphaned immediately after his birth. Then later as an adult he was befriended and crowned the king of Anga by Duryodhana, and thus he unintentionally became a prominent general in the army of his brothers' enemies.

### 9

*anye cha bahavah shura / madarthe tyakta-jivitah*
*nanashastra-praharanah / sarve yuddha-visharadah*

*anye* > others; *cha* > also; *bahavah* > a great many; *shurah* > heroes; *mat-arthe* > for my purpose; *tyakta-jivitah* > those who are prepared to give up their lives; *nana* > various; *shastra-praharanah* > equipped with weapons for striking and for hurling; *sarve* > all of them; *yuddha-visharadah* > skilled in the art of combat.

And there are a great many other heroes
who are also prepared to risk their lives in support of my cause.
All of them are well-equipped with various kinds of weapons
both for striking and for hurling,
and they are highly skilled in the art of combat.

**10**

*aparyaptam tad asmakam / balam bhishma-'bhiraksheetam*
*paryaptam tvidam etesham / balam bhima-'bhiraksheetam*

*aparyaptam* > immeasurable, insufficient; *tat* > that; *asmakam* > of ours;
*balam* > strength; *bhishma* > by Bhishma; *abhiraksheetam* > protected;
*paryaptam* > sufficient; *tu* > but; *idam* > this; *etesham* > of them (the Pandavas);
*balam* > strength; *bhima* > by Bhima; *abhiraksheetam* > guarded.

**Our forces protected by Bhishma are innumerable,
yet nonetheless insufficient;
Whereas the [lesser] forces of the Pandavas guarded by Bhima
are indeed quite sufficient.**

**11**

*ayaneshu cha sarveshu / yatha-bhagam avasthitah*
*bhishmam eva-bhirakshantu / bhavantah sarva eva hi*

*ayaneshu* > circulating in this manner; *cha* > also; *sarveshu* > everywhere;
*yatha-bhagam* > each within his respective position; *avasthitah* > stationed;
*bhishmam* > unto Bhishma; *eva* > indeed; *abhirakshantu* > give full
protection; *bhavantah* > your lordships (referring to the
assembled warriors); *sarve* > all; *eva hi* > certainly.

**Therefore, stationed at your respective strategic positions
all throughout the phalanx of our army,
All of you venerable kshatriyas
must be especially attentive in giving full protection to Bhishma.**

The *kshatriyas* are the royal order of administrators and protectors. In this
and the previous verse, Duryodhana is subtly chiding Bhishma. Although
Duryodhana's soldiers vastly outnumber those on the Pandavas' side, he feels
that Bhishma's great affection for the Pandavas relegates the Kauravas' army
to a weakened position, thus rendering them 'insufficient,' whereas Bhima's
unalloyed fury toward the Kauravas lends added strength to the Pandava
forces, thereby making them 'quite sufficient.'

**12**

*tasya sanjanayan harsham / kuru-vriddhah pitamahah*
*singhanadam vinadyochchaih / shankham dadhmau pratapavan*

*tasya* > to him (Duryodhana); *sanjanayan* > producing; *harsham* > delight;
*kuru-vriddhah* > seniormost of the Kuru dynasty; *pitamahah* > the grandsire
(Bhishma); *singha-nadam* > the sound of a lion; *vinadya* > roaring; *uchchaih* >
loudly; *shankham* > conchshell; *dadhmau* > he blew; *pratapavan* > full of valor.

**[Sanjaya continued:]**
**[In response to that remark,] Bhishma —**
**the grandsire, seniormost of the Kuru dynasty —**
**Delighted Duryodhana by loudly blowing his conchshell with great valor,**
**producing a sound like that of a lion's roar.**

**13**

*tatah shankhash cha bheryash cha / panavanaka-gomukhah*
*sahasaiva 'bhyahanyanta / sa shabdas tumulo 'bhavat*

*tatah* > then; *shankhah* > conchshells; *cha* > also; *bheryah* > large kettledrums;
*cha* > and; *panava-anaka* > small drums and cymbals; *gomukhah* > horns;
*sahasa* > all of a sudden; *eva* > indeed; *abhyahanyanta* > were sounded;
*sah* > this; *shabdah* > sound; *tumulah* > tumultuous; *abhavat* > became.

**Then other conchshells,**
**along with large and small drums, cymbals, and horns,**
**All suddenly sounded,**
**creating a tumultuous sound.**

The word *gomukhah* literally means 'cow-faced,' giving the impression that
the soldiers' bugles were made from the horns of deceased cows and bulls.

**14**

*tatah shvetair hayair yukte / mahati syandane sthitau*
*madhavah pandavas chaiva / divyau shankhau pradadhmatuh*

*tatah* > thereupon; *shvetaih hayaih* > with white horses; *yukte* > yoked;
*mahati* > in the very great; *syandane* > in 'that which runs' (the chariot);
*sthitau* > both situated; *madhavah* > the descendant of Madhu
(Krishna), likened to the spring season; *pandavah* > the son
of Pandu (Arjuna); *cha* > and; *eva* > just so; *divyau* > both divine;
*shankhau* > conchshells; *pradadhmatuh* > they both blew.

**At which time Madhava (Krishna)
and the son of Pandu (Arjuna),
Both situated together on a magnificent chariot drawn by white horses,
also blew their divine conchshells.**

### 15

*panchajanyam hrishikesho / devadattam dhananjayah
paundram dadhmau maha-shankham / bhima-karma vrikodarah*

*panchajanyam* > Panchajana's conchshell (taken from that demon after he was slain by Krishna); *hrishika-ishah* > Krishna, the 'master of the senses'; *devadattam* > the conchshell which was a 'gift of the gods'; *dhananjayah* > Arjuna, the 'winner of wealth'; *paundram* > King Paundra's conch (gifted to Bhima); *dadhmau* > he blew; *maha-shankham* > the mighty conchshell; *bhima-karma* > one who performs terrific deeds; *vrika-udarah* > the 'wolf-bellied' one (a name attributed to Bhima due to his voracious appetite).

**Krishna blew his conchshell taken from the demon Panchajana;
Arjuna blew his, which was a gift of the gods;
And Bhima, the performer of terrific deeds,
blew the mighty conchshell gifted to him by King Paundra.**

### 16

*ananta-vijayam raja / kunti-putro yudhisthirah
nakulah sahadevas cha / sughosha-manipushpakau*

*ananta-vijayam* > the conchshell proclaiming 'everlasting victory'; *raja* > the king; *kunti-putrah* > the son of Kunti; *yudhisthirah* > King Yudhisthira ('ever-steadfast in battle'); *nakulah* > Nakula (so named because at the time of his birth his skin was 'the color of a mongoose'); *sahadevah* > Sahadeva ('accompanied by the gods'); *cha* > and; *sughosha* > the 'sweet-sounding' conch; *manipushpakau* > the 'gem-bedecked' conch.

**Kunti's son King Yudhisthira
blew his conchshell which proclaims everlasting victory;
Nakula blew his sweet-sounding conch;
and Sahadeva blew his gem-bedecked conch.**

According to Paramahansa Yogananda and several other revered commentators from the raja-yoga traditions, the conchshell sounds mentioned in verses 15 and 16 symbolize the astral sounds emanating from the *chakras* (energy vortexes) of the subtle body which are heard by the meditating yogi. Sri Krishna represents the omnipresent Spirit-Self, the 'inner guru' or guiding universal intuitive Intelligence, and *kutastha*, Its pure reflection in the 'third-eye,' the *ajna chakra*. His conch's vibration is said to represent the combined sound of the five *chakras* from the base of the spine up to the throat which manifests at the point between the eyebrows.

Regarding the Pandava brothers, Yudhisthira is said to represent steadfast righteousness, serenity, and the ethereal element of the *vishuddha chakra* in the throat region, and the blowing of his conch represents the sound of the rumbling cloud from that energy-center. Bhima symbolizes the *prana* (life-force), dauntless vitality, and the air element within the *anahata chakra* at the heart-center, and his conch's vibration symbolizes the sound of the bell from that region. Arjuna represents the *jiva* principle—the living or functioning of Spirit through a body/mind system, as well as the power of self-control and the fire element in the stomach region's *manipura chakra*. The blowing of his conch is said to represent the sound of the stringed instrument known as the *vina* from that point aligned with the navel.

Nakula represents attentiveness, the power to follow the internal disciplines or observances, and the water element of the *svadhishthana chakra* in the genital region, and his conch vibration represents the sound of the flute from that energy-center. And Sahadeva symbolizes restraint of the senses, the power to obey the external disciplines or abstentions, and the earth element of the *muladhara chakra* at the base of the spine, his conch vibration symbolizing the sound of bees from that region.

### 17-18
*kashyas cha parameshvasah / shikhandi cha maharathah*
*dhrishtadyumno viratas cha / satyakis chaparajitah*

*drupado draupadeyash cha / sarvashah prithivipate*
*saubhadrash cha mahabahuh / shankhan dadhmuh prithak prithak*

*kashyah* > the King of Kashi; *cha* > and; *parama-ishvasah* > the greatest of archers; *shikhandi* > Shikhandi ('one who wears a *shikha*,' a wound-around ponytail in the hair); *cha* > also; *maha-rathah* > great warrior; *dhrishtadyumnah* > Dhrishtadyumna; *viratah* > Virata; *cha* > also; *satyakih* > Satyaki ('one who is truthful by nature,' also known as Yuyudhana); *cha* > and; *aparajitah* > the undefeatable;

*drupadah* > Drupada; *draupadeyah* > the sons of Draupadi; *cha* > and; *sarvashah* > collectively; *prithivi-pate* > O king of the Earth; *saubhadrah* > Abhimanyu, the son of Subhadra; *cha* > also; *maha-bahuh* > mighty-armed; *shankhan* > conchshells; *dadhmuh* > blew; *prithak prithak* > each in turn.

**The king of Kashi, who is the greatest of archers,**
**the great warrior Shikhandi,**
**Dhrishtadyumna, Virata, the undefeatable Satyaki,**
**Drupada, the sons of Draupadi,**
**and the mighty-armed Abhimanyu, son of Subhadra —**
**Each blew his conchshell in turn, O king of the Earth.**

### 19

*sa ghosho dhartarashtranam / hridayani vyadarayat*
*nabhash cha prithivim chaiva / tumulo vyanunadayan*

*sah ghoshah* > this sound; *dhartarashtranam* > of the sons of
Dhritarashtra; *hridayani* > hearts; *vyadarayat* > shattered; *nabhah* > the sky;
*cha* > and; *prithivim* > the Earth; *cha* > also; *eva* > indeed;
*tumulah* > tumultuous; *vyanunadayan* > resounding, filling with noise.

**These uproarious sounds**
**shattered the hearts of your sons, my lord,**
**As they resounded both in the sky**
**and on the surface of the Earth.**

### 20

*atha vyavasthitan drishtva / dhartarashtran kapidhvajah*
*pravritte shastra-sampate / dhanur udyamya pandavah*

*atha* > thereupon; *vyavasthitan* > arrayed; *drishtva* > seeing;
*dhartarashtran* > the sons of Dhritarashtra; *kapi-dhvajah* > 'one with
a banner displaying a monkey' (a name attributed to Arjuna because
he had an image of Hanuman, the celebrated servant of King
Ramachandra, on his chariot's flag); *pravritte* > started to engage;
*shastra-sampate* > in the confrontation of weapons; *dhanuh* > bow;
*udyamya* > raising up; *pandavah* > the son of Pandu (Arjuna).

**Upon seeing your sons arrayed in battle formation,**
**Arjuna, whose chariot bears a banner displaying a monkey,**
**Took up his bow in preparation**
**for the upcoming confrontation of weapons.**

### 21-22

*hrishikesham tada vakyam / idam aha mahipate*
*senayor ubhayor madhye / ratham sthapaya me 'chyuta*

*yavad etan nirikshe 'ham / yoddhu-kaman avasthitan*
*kair maya saha yoddhavyam / asmin rana-samudyame*

*hrishikesham* > to Sri Krishna, master of the senses; *tada* > at that time; *vakyam* > words; *idam* > this; *aha* > [Arjuna] said; *mahi-pate* > O king; *senayoh* > of the armies; *ubhayoh* > both; *madhye* > inbetween; *ratham* > the chariot; *sthapaya* > place it, situate it; *me* > my; *achyuta* > O infallible one;

*yavat* > while; *etan* > these; *nirikshe* > look upon; *aham* > I; *yoddhu-kaman* > desiring to fight; *avasthitan* > arrayed, situated; *kaih* > with whom; *maya* > by me; *saha yoddhavyam* > to be fought with; *asmin* > in this; *rana* > conflict; *samudyame* > in undertaking.

**At that time, O king,
Arjuna said these words to Sri Krishna:**

**Please keep my chariot stationed between the two armies, O infallible one,
While I see who is arrayed here anxious to fight,
And with whom I must contend
in undertaking this conflict.**

**23**
*yotsyamanan avekshe 'ham / ya ete 'tra samagatah
dhartarashtrasya durbuddher / yuddhe priya-chikirshavah*

*yotsyamanan* > those who are eager to fight; *avekshe aham* > I see; *ye* > who; *ete* > these; *atra* > here; *samagatah* > assembled; *dhartarashtrasya* > for the son of Dhritarashtra (Duryodhana); *durbuddheh* > evil-minded; *yuddhe* > in warfare; *priya* > kindness, favor; *chikirshavah* > wishing to do.

**I must see who has assembled here
eager to fight for the cause of the evil-minded Duryodhana,
Wishing to do him a kind favor
by engaging in warfare.**

As with Duryodhana's earlier chiding remarks, Arjuna's touch of sarcasm here is a refreshing glimpse into another facet of his personality before he becomes overwhelmed by what he sees in upcoming verses 26 and 27.

**24**
*sanjaya uvacha:
evam ukto hrishikesho / gudakeshena bharata
senayor ubhayor madhye / sthapayitva rathottamam*

*sanjaya uvacha* > Sanjaya said; *evam* > thus; *uktah* > addressed; *hrishika-ishah* > the one who has mastery over the senses (Krishna);

*gudaka-ishena* > by the one who has mastery over the power of sloth, by the conqueror of sleep (Arjuna); *bharata* > O descendant of King Bharata (*bharata* refers to India and to one who speaks with eloquence); *senayoh* > of the armies; *ubhayoh* > both; *madhye* > in the middle; *sthapayitva* > placing, situating; *ratha-uttamam* > the finest chariot.

**Sanjaya said:**
**O noble descendant of King Bharata,**
**Having thus been addressed by the conqueror of sleep,**
**The master of his senses brought that finest of chariots**
**inbetween the two armies.**

King Bharata was a descendant of the sage Vishvamitra who ruled all of India prior to the time of the confrontation at Kurukshetra. Sanjaya here deliberately addresses Dhritarashtra as the descendant of King Bharata, an address used for Arjuna throughout the Gita as well, in order to remind the king of his familial relationship with the Pandavas. By this and other remarks, such as saying that the sound of the Pandavas' conchshells shattered the hearts of Dhritarashtra's sons (*hridayani vyadarayat* in verse 19), it seems as if Sanjaya is trying to persuade the king to intervene and make another attempt at stopping the war before any further bloodshed takes place.

**25**
*bhishma-drona-pramukhatah / sarvesham cha mahiksheetam*
*uvacha partha pashyaitan / samavetan kurun iti*

*bhishma* > Bhishma; *drona* > Drona; *pramukhatah* > facing, in front of; *sarvesham* > all of these; *cha* > also; *mahiksheetam* > rulers of the world; *uvacha* > (Krishna) said; *partha* > O son of Pritha; *pashya* > behold; *etan* > these; *samavetan* > gathered together; *kurun* > members of the Kuru dynasty (which includes both the Pandavas and the Kauravas); *iti* > thus.

**Facing Bhishma, Drona, and all the rulers of the world,**
**Krishna said:**
**"O son of Pritha,**
**behold these members of the Kuru family gathered together here."**

**26**
*tatra-'pashyat sthitan parthah / pitrin atha pitamahan*
*acharyan matulan bhratrin / putran pautran sakhims tatha*

*tatra* > there; *apashyat* > he saw; *sthitan* > stationed; *parthah* > Arjuna, the son of Pritha; *pitrin* > fathers; *atha* > also; *pitamahan* > grandfathers;

*acharyan* > teachers; *matulan* > maternal uncles; *bhratrin* > brothers;
*putran* > sons; *pautran* > grandsons; *sakhin* > friends; *tatha* > as well.

**There Arjuna saw,**
**stationed within the ranks of both armies,**
**Fathers and grandfathers,**
**teachers, maternal uncles,**
**brothers, sons, grandsons,**
**And cherished friends as well.**

**27**
*svashuran suhridash chaiva / senayor ubhayor api*
*tan samikshya sa kaunteyah / sarvan bandhun avasthitan*

*svashuran* > fathers-in-law; *suhridah* > affectionate or simply sincere
well-wishers; *cha* > and; *eva* > indeed; *senayoh* > in the armies;
*ubhayoh* > of both; *api* > also; *tan* > them; *samikshya* > thoroughly inspecting,
becoming acutely aware of; *sah* > he; *kaunteyah* > the son of Kunti
(Arjuna); *sarvan* > all; *bandhun* > relatives; *avasthitan* > positioned.

**The son of Kunti saw fathers-in-law**
**and other affectionate well-wishers also within both armies.**
**Upon thoroughly surveying [the battlefield],**
**he became acutely aware of all the relatives positioned there.**

**28-29**
*kripaya parayavishto / visihdann idam abravit*
*drishtvemam svajanam krishna / yuyutsum samupasthitam*

*sidanti mama gatrani / mukham cha parisushyati*
*vepathush cha sharire me / romaharshash cha jayate*

*kripaya* > with compassion; *paraya* > by exceeding; *avishtah* > overwhelmed
by; *vishidan* > feeling despair; *idam* > this; *abravit* > he (Arjuna) spoke;
*drishtva* > seeing; *imam* > all these; *sva-janam* > own kinsmen;
*krishna* > O Krishna ('the dazzling dark one');
*yuyutsum* > eager to fight; *samupasthitam* > standing nearby;

*sidanti* > they weaken; *mama* > my; *gatrani* > limbs of the body;
*mukham* > mouth; *cha* > also; *parisushyati* > it becomes dry;
*vepathuh* > trembling; *cha* > and; *sharire* > in the body; *me* > my;
*roma-harshah* > hair standing on end; *cha* > also; *jayate* > produced.

**Overwhelmed by despair and deep compassion, Arjuna said:**
**O Krishna, seeing all of my own kinsmen**
**standing nearby eager to fight,**
**My limbs suddenly feel weak**
**and my mouth is parched.**
**My body is also trembling, its hairs standing on end.**

**30**

*gandivam sramsate hastat / tvak chaiva paridahyate*
*na cha shaknomyavasthatum / bhramativa cha me manah*

*gandivam* > the 'rhinoceros-like' bow of Arjuna; *sramsate* > it drops; *hastat* > from the hand; *tvach* > skin; *cha* > and; *eva* > indeed; *paridahyate* > it burns; *na* > not; *cha* > and; *shaknomi* > I am able; *avasthatum* > to remain standing; *bhramati* > it reels; *iva* > so to speak; *cha* > and; *me* > my; *manah* > mind.

**My Gandiva bow slips down from my hand,**
**and a burning sensation flows throughout my skin.**
**My mind is reeling,**
**and I am unable to remain standing.**

**31**

*nimittani cha pashyami / viparitani keshava*
*na cha shreyo 'nupashyami / hatva svajanam ahave*

*nimittani* > omens; *cha* > also; *pashyami* > I see; *viparitani* > inauspicious; *keshava* > Krishna, who possesses luxurious hair; *na* > not; *cha* > and; *shreyah* > good fortune; *anupashyami* > I foresee; *hatva* > slaying; *sva-janam* > own kinsmen; *ahave* > in the battle.

**I see inauspicious omens,**
**O Keshava,**
**And I do not foresee any good fortune resulting**
**from slaying my own kinsmen in battle.**

The syllable *ka* represents Lord Brahma, the letter *a* represents Lord Vishnu (which is also mentioned in verse 10.33), *isha* is a name of Lord Shiva, and one of the definitions of *va* is 'like.' In this way, another meaning of the name Keshava is 'One who is like an embodiment of the combined characteristics of Brahma, Vishnu, and Shiva,' a depiction also attributed to the great sage Dattatreya since ancient times. Interestingly, Krishna's discourse known as the *Uddhava Gita* in Book Eleven of the Bhagavata Purana begins with his describing the twenty-four gurus of Dattatreya as having simply been different elements and creatures found in nature. In this way he beautifully conveyed that whatever is being referred to as enlightenment is openly and equally accessible to everyone, both male and female alike, at all times.

### 32
*na kankshe vijayam krishna / na cha rajyam sukhani cha*
*kim no rajyena govinda / kim bhogair jivitena va*

*na* > nor; *kankshe* > I wish; *vijayam* > victory; *krishna* > Krishna; *na* > not; *cha* > and; *rajyam* > kingship; *sukhani* > pleasures; *cha* > and; *kim* > what; *nah* > to us; *rajyena* > with a kingdom; *govinda* > Krishna, 'who tends cows'; *kim* > what; *bhogaih* > enjoyment; *jivitena* > by living; *va* > or.

**I have no wish for any victory, O Krishna,**
**nor for any kingship or pleasures obtained thereby.**
**What use have we for a kingdom, Govinda?**
**Of what use is enjoyment,**
**or even life itself?**

### 33
*yesham arthe kanksheetam no / rajyam bhogah sukhani cha*
*ta ime 'vasthita yuddhe / pranans tyaktva dhanani cha*

*yesham* > of whom; *arthe* > for the sake of; *kanksheetam* > wanted, wished for; *nah* > by us; *rajyam* > sovereignty; *bhogah* > pleasures; *sukhani* > happiness; *cha* > and; *te* > they; *ime* > these; *avasthitah* > standing; *yuddhe* > in battle; *pranan* > lives; *tyaktva* > casting away; *dhanani* > riches; *cha* > and.

**All those for the sake of whom**
**we had wanted sovereignty, pleasures, and happiness**
**Are standing here poised for battle,**
**throwing away their lives and wealth.**

### 34
*acharyah pitarah putras / tathaiva cha pitamahah*
*matulah shvashurah pautrah / shyalah sambandhinas tatha*

*acharyah* > teachers; *pitarah* > fathers; *putrah* > sons; *tatha* > as well; *eva* > indeed, even; *cha* > also; *pitamahah* > grandfathers; *matulah* > maternal uncles; *shvashurah* > fathers-in-law; *pautrah* > grandsons; *shyalah* > brothers-in-law; *sambandhinah* > relatives; *tatha* > as well.

**Teachers...fathers...sons...
indeed, even grandfathers...
As well as maternal uncles, fathers-in-law, grandsons...
brothers-in-law and other relatives....**

### 35

*etan na hantum ichchami / ghnato 'pi madhusudana
api trailokya-rajyasya / hetoh kim nu mahi-krite*

*etan* > these; *na* > not; *hantum* > to kill; *ichchami* > I wish; *ghnatah* > those who are killing; *api* > although; *madhusudana* > O vanquisher of the demon Madhu (different from Krishna's ancestor Madhu who was a patriarch of the Yadu dynasty); *api* > even; *trai-lokya* > of the three worlds; *rajyasya* > for the sovereignty; *hetoh* > because; *kim nu* > what then; *mahi-krite* > for the sake of the Earth.

**Though they may kill me, O Madhusudana,
I do not wish to kill them
even for gaining sovereignty over the three worlds,
let alone this Earth.**

The three worlds mentioned here refer to *bhur bhuvah svah* — the earthly sphere, the intermediate astral region, and the subtle domain of the celestials.

### 36

*nihatya dhartarashtran nah / ka pritih syaj janardana
papam evashrayed asman / hatvaitan atatayinah*

*nihatya* > by killing; *dhartarashtran* > the sons of Dhritarashtra; *nah* > to us; *ka* > what; *pritih* > satisfaction, pleasure; *syat* > it would be; *janardana* > Krishna, 'one who excites people'; *papam* > evil; *eva* > indeed; *ashrayet* > it will adhere, it will dwell; *asman* > with us; *hatva* > by slaying; *etan* > these; *atatayinah* > they whose bows are drawn to take others' lives.

**O Janardana, what satisfaction will we derive
by killing the sons of Dhritarashtra?
Rather, if we slay them,
the same evil moving these men to take others' lives
will take up dwelling within us as well.**

## 37

*tasman narha vayam hantum / dhartarashtran svabandhavan*
*svajanam hi katham hatva / sukhinah syama madhava*

*tasmat* > therefore; *na* > not; *arhah* > obligated, allowed, justified;
*vayam* > we; *hantum* > to kill; *dhartarashtran* > the sons of Dhritarashtra;
*svabandhavan* > one's own friends; *svajanam* > one's own family;
*hi* > indeed; *katham* > how; *hatva* > by killing; *sukhinah* > happy;
*syama* > we will become; *madhava* > O descendant of Madhu.

**Therefore we are not obligated**
**to slay the sons of Dhritarashtra**
**[and thus poison ourselves].**
**O Madhava, how could we possibly become happy**
**by killing our own friends and family members?**

## 38-39

*yadyapyete na pashyanti / lobhopahata-chetasah*
*kulakshaya-kritam dosham / mitradrohe cha patakam*

*katham na jneyam asmabhih / papad asman nivartitum*
*kulakshaya-kritam dosham / prapashyadbhir janardana*

*yadi* > if; *api* > even; *ete* > these (men); *na* > not; *pashyanti* > they see;
*lobha* > greed; *upahata* > overpowered; *chetasah* > thoughts,
minds; *kula-kshaya* > in destroying the family; *kritam* > done;
*dosham* > fault; *mitra-drohe* > in injuring friends; *cha* > and;
*patakam* > that which causes one to fall down, crime;

*katham* > how; *na* > not; *jneyam* > to be understood; *asmabhih* > by us;
*papat* > from sins; *asmat* > from this; *nivartitum* > to turn away;
*kula-kshaya* > the destruction of a dynasty; *kritam* > done;
*dosham* > evil; *prapashyadbhih* > by discernment;
*janardana* > O one who excites people.

**Even if these men whose minds are overpowered by greed**
**see no fault in slaying one's family**
**and no crime in injuring friends,**
**How is it that we, O Janardana,**
**cannot understand by discernment that destroying a dynasty is evil,**
**and thus turn away from such sins?**

**40**

*kula-kshaye pranashyanti / kula-dharmah sanatanah*
*dharme nashte kulam kritsnam / adharmo 'bhibhavatyuta*

*kula-kshaye* > in destroying the family; *pranashyanti* > they vanish;
*kula-dharmah* > the family traditions; *sanatanah* > ancient;
*dharme* > religion; *nashte* > in the loss; *kulam* > family; *kritsnam* > all;
*adharmah* > irreligion; *abhibhavati* > it overtakes; *uta* > as well.

**With the destruction of a family,
its ancient religious traditions vanish;
And upon that loss,
all [the surviving members of] the family
are overtaken by irreligion as well.**

**41**

*adharma-'bhibhavat krishna / pradushyanti kula-striyah*
*strishu dushtasu varshneya / jayate varna-sankarah*

*adharma* > irreligion; *abhibhavat* > due to predominance; *krishna* > O Krishna;
*pradushyanti* > they become defiled, they become polluted; *kula-striyah* > the
women of the family; *strishu* > women; *dushtasu* > corrupted, contaminated;
*varshneya* > O descendant of Vrishni (*vrishni* means 'potent' or 'virile');
*jayate* > it is produced; *varna-sankarah* > a mixture of the castes.

**When irreligion becomes predominant, O Krishna,
the women of the family become defiled;
And from such corrupted women, O descendant of Vrishni,
comes the intermingling of castes.**

Vrishni was a descendent of Yadu who had a son named Devamidhusha
by his wife Madri. The grandson of Devamidhusha was Krishna's father
Vasudeva (pronounced '*Vuhh*sudev').

There are some interesting further glimpses into Arjuna's psychological
makeup here. First, in verse 36 he launches headlong into forcefully
defending his right to decline participation in the battle before even
encountering any objections to his decision — Krishna doesn't begin asking
him to reconsider the matter until verse 2.2. Then there is his concern that the
women will become defiled, but not the men. One reading of that is that only
something which is considered pure can be spoken of as being in danger
of becoming defiled, whereas in the case of the men in Arjuna's family,

from Arjuna's perspective there couldn't be any such consideration because if they weren't *already* corrupt, they wouldn't be standing there on the battlefield in Duryodhana's army.

And lastly there is his assumption underlying the connotation of *jayate varnasankarah*, which is that if there were to be intermingling or inter-marriage between different castes—this in itself being considered synonymous with adultery at the time—that the result would automatically be 'adulterated' progeny born with innate inclinations toward lawlessness. The cultural conditioning that Arjuna received which spawned these types of ideas will become even more evident in the verses that follow, yet such ideas, along with numerous other illustrations of the prevailing belief-system of the time, will be summarily dismissed by Krishna in verses 42 through 46 of the next chapter. Therein Krishna speaks reprovingly of those who embrace a superficial interpretation of the Vedas, which were the primary source of Arjuna's beliefs.

**42**

*sankaro narakayaiva / kula-ghnanam kulasya cha*
*patanti pitaro hyesham / lupta-pindodaka-kriyah*

*sankarah* > intermingling (of the castes); *narakaya* > to hell; *eva* > surely;
*kula-ghnanam* > the destroyers of the family; *kulasya* > of the family;
*cha* > and; *patanti* > they go down, they fall; *pitarah* > the ancestors;
*hi* > certainly; *esham* > of these; *lupta* > deprived; *pinda* > the
compressed ball of rice; *udaka* > water; *kriyah* > ritual offerings.

**Such intermingling of the castes surely leads
both the destroyers of the family and the family itself to the netherworld
By depriving their deceased ancestors
of the ritual offerings of rice and water,
thus causing them to fall [to that region].**

**43**

*doshair etaih kula-ghnanam / varna-sankara-karakaih*
*utsadyante jati-dharmah / kula-dharmash cha shashvatah*

*doshaih* > by the evils; *etaih* > by these; *kula-ghnanam* > of the family
destroyers; *varna-sankara* > intermingling of castes; *karakaih* > by producing;
*utsadyante* > they decay, they disappear; *jati-dharmah* > laws and
duties of the caste; *kula-dharmah* > laws and duties of the
family; *cha* > and; *shashvatah* > timeless, ageless.

As a result of the evil deeds of those who destroy the family
by introducing the intermingling of castes,
Laws and duties of both the family and the caste
which had been observed for countless generations
Gradually decay and disappear altogether
[due to being neglected by descendants tainted with immorality].

### 44
*utsanna-kula-dharmanam / manushyanam janardana*
*narake 'niyatam vaso / bhavati 'tyanushushruma*

*utsanna* > decayed, disappeared; *kula-dharmanam* > of the
family laws and duties; *manushyanam* > of humankind;
*janardana* > O one who agitates people; *narake* > in hell;
*aniyatam* > indeterminately; *vasah* > residing; *bhavati* > it is;
*iti* > thus; *anushushruma* > we have heard repeatedly.

We have heard repeatedly, O agitator of people,
That those among humankind
whose family laws and duties have disappeared
Reside in the netherworld for an indeterminate period of time.

This is the third time so far that Arjuna, in his agitated condition, has
addressed Krishna as Janardana, 'an agitator of people,' as Krishna remains
calmly and silently standing in Arjuna's chariot listening to him speaking.
He will do so again in verse 3.1.

### 45
*aho bata mahat papam / kartum vyavasita vayam*
*yad rajyasukha-lobhena / hantum svajanam udyatah*

*aho* > O! *bata* > alas; *mahat* > great, large; *papam* > evil;
*kartum* > to perpetrate; *vyavasitah* > resolved; *vayam* > we;
*yat* > which; *rajya-sukha-lobhena* > due to greed for royal pleasures;
*hantum* > to kill; *svajanam* > our own kinsmen; *udyatah* > intent on.

O! Alas, we have resolved to perpetrate immensely evil deeds!
Due to our greed for royal pleasures,
We are intent
on killing our own kinsmen!

**46**

*yadi mam apratikaram / ashastram shastra-panayah*
*dhartarashtra rane hanyus / tan me kshemataram bhavet*

*yadi* > if; *mam* > me; *apratikaram* > unresisting; *ashastram* > unarmed;
*shastra-panayah* > those with weapons in hand; *dhartarashtrah* > the sons
of Dhritarashtra; *rane* > in the battle; *hanyuh* > they may kill; *tat* > that;
*me* > for me; *kshemataram* > greater happiness; *bhavet* > it would be.

**I would derive far greater happiness**
**if the sons of Dhritarashtra,**
**weapons in hand,**
**Were to kill me unarmed and unresisting on the battlefield.**

**47**

*sanjaya uvacha:*
*evam uktvarjuna sankhye / rathopastha upavishat*
*visrijya sasharam chapam / shoka-samvigna-manasah*

*sanjayah uvacha* > Sanjaya said; *evam* > thus; *uktva* > having spoken;
*arjunah* > Arjuna; *sankhye* > on the battlefield; *ratha* > chariot;
*upasthe* > on the seat; *upavishat* > he sat down; *visrijya* > throwing down;
*sa-sharam* > along with arrows; *chapam* > the bow; *shoka* > sorrow;
*samvigna* > overwhelmed; *manasah* > with the mind, with the heart.

**Sanjaya said:**
**Having thus spoken on the battlefield,**
**Arjuna sat down on the seat of his chariot**
**and threw down his bow and arrows,**
**his heart overwhelmed by sorrow.**

*om tat saditi srimad bhagavad-gita / supanishatsu brahma-vidyayam*
*yoga-shastre srikrishnarjuna samvade / arjuna-vishada-yogo*
*nama prathamo 'dhyayah*

From the Ambrosial Song of God —
A conversation between Krishna and Arjuna
which is a Upanishad (confidential sharing)
of wisdom-teachings regarding the Absolute
And a scripture concerning Self-realization —
Thus ends the First Chapter entitled Arjuna-vishada-yoga,
Arjuna's Approach To the Recognition of Divine Unicity By Way of Despair.

# Chapter Two

# Sankhya-yoga
## (Recognizing Divine Unicity By Way of Empirical Knowledge)

"Formed for the sake of fulfilling the purpose of the Spirit-Self (Purusha), the subtle body appears in different roles like a dramatic performer, owing to the connection of causes and effects and through conjunction with the universal power of Nature (Prakriti)."

"Verily, the Spirit-Self is neither bound nor emancipated, nor does It transmigrate; it is Nature alone, abiding in myriad forms, that is bound, released, and transmigrates."

"Through the attentive observation of Nature's principles arises the ultimate, undistracted, direct knowing that: 'Neither I am, nor is anything mine, nor am I embodied.' Possessed of this Self-knowing, the proliferation of Nature ceases, and pure Spirit stands apart and abides at ease, like a spectator."

"When separation from the body takes place and Nature ceases to act, Its purpose having been fulfilled, the Spirit-Self recognizes Its absolute freedom."                    — *Sankhya Karika*, verses 42, 62, 64-65, and 68

"Desire has to do with the present, imagination is a process of the future, and memory comes from the past. In this way, all three — present, past, and future — are in a dream. The world is also created in the same way. There is one physical object, but that object is seen according to our desires, we imagine how it relates to us, and we keep a memory of it. ...As long as the mind is projecting its desires and attachment onto objects, we are dreaming the world as if it is real. As soon as the mind stops this projection, we wake up in the world and we see the Reality."    — Baba Hari Dass

### 1
*sanjaya uvacha:*
*tam tatha kripaya-'vishtam / ashrupurna-'kulekshanam*
*vishidantam idam vakyam / uvacha madhusudanah*

*sanjayah uvacha* > Sanjaya said; *tam* > to him (Arjuna); *tatha* > in this way; *kripaya* > by pity; *avishtam* > overwhelmed; *ashru-purna* > full of tears; *akula-ikshanam* > downcast agitated eyes; *vishidantam* > despondent, in despair; *idam vakyam* > these words; *uvacha* > he said; *madhu-sudanah* > the slayer of Madhu.

Sanjaya said:
**Seeing Arjuna overwhelmed in this way by pity and despair,**
**his agitated eyes downcast and full of tears,**
**Krishna, the slayer of the demon Madhu,**
**spoke the following words.**

**2**

*sri bhagavan uvacha:*
*kutas tva kashmalam idam / vishame samupasthitam*
*anarya-jushtam asvargyam / akirti-karam arjuna*

*sri bhagavan uvacha* > the illustrious one (Krishna) said; *kutah* > how;
*tva* > to you; *kashmalam* > timidity; *idam* > this; *vishame* > in this difficult time;
*samupasthitam* > come to; *anarya-jushtam* > not honorable or befitting;
*asvargyam* > not leading to heaven; *akirti* > disgrace, loss of
good reputation; *karam* > causing; *arjuna* > O Arjuna.

**The illustrious Krishna said:**
**Arjuna, how has such timidity come upon you**
**in this difficult situation?**
**This is most unbecoming for you and will not lead to heaven,**
**but rather to the loss of your fine reputation.**

**3**

*klaibyam ma sma gamah partha / naitat tvayyupapadyate*
*kshudram hridaya-daurbalyam / tyaktvottishtha parantapa*

*klaibyam* > weakness, timidity; *ma* > never; *sma* > certainly;
*gamah* > you should fall into, you should consent to;
*partha* > O son of Pritha (*pritha* means 'delighted,' 'joyful');
*na* > neither; *etat* > this; *tvayi-upapadyate* > it is befitting for you;
*kshudram* > tiny, insignificant; *hridaya* > of the heart;
*daurbalyam* > weakness; *tyaktva* > abandoning;
*uttishtha* > arise!; *parantapa* > O scourge of foes.

**You have certainly never embraced timidity before;**
**neither does it befit one who was born from joy (Pritha).**
**So arise, O scourge of foes! —**
**as abandoning any weak-heartedness**
**is a very small, insignificant affair for you.**

**4**
*arjuna uvacha:*
*katham bhishmam aham sankhye / dronam cha madhusudana*
*ishubhih pratiyotsyami / pujarhav arisudana*

*arjunah uvacha* > Arjuna said; *katham* > how; *bhishmam* > Bhishma; *aham* > I;
*sankhye* > in battle; *dronam* > Drona; *cha* > also; *madhusudana* > O slayer
of Madhu; *ishubhih* > with arrows; *pratiyotsyami* > I shall attack;
*puja-arhau* > deserving of worship; *arisudana* > O slayer of enemies.

**Arjuna said:**
**O slayer of Madhu and other enemies,**
**How can I attack Bhishma and Drona with arrows in battle**
**when they deserve to be worshipped by me?**

**5**
*gurun ahatva hi maha-'nubhavan / shreyo bhoktum bhaikshyam apiha loke*
*hatvartha-kamans tu gurun ihaiva / bhunjiya bhogan rudhira-pradigdhan*

*gurun* > teachers; *ahatva* > instead of killing; *hi* > certainly; *maha-anubhavan* >
high-minded, magnanimous souls; *shreyah* > better; *bhoktum* > to experience,
to endure; *bhaikshyam* > by begging; *api* > even; *iha* > here; *loke* > in the world;
*hatva* > killing; *artha* > gains; *kaman* > desiring; *tu* > but; *gurun* > superiors,
elders; *iha* > here in the world; *eva* > indeed; *bhunjiya* > I would enjoy;
*bhogan* > pleasures; *rudhira* > blood; *pradigdhan* > besmeared.

**I prefer to live in this world by begging than to kill my teachers,**
**who are all great souls.**
**Even though they may desire worldly gain,**
**they are nonetheless my superiors,**
**And any pleasures I enjoyed at the cost of their lives**
**would be smeared with their blood.**

**6**
*na chaitad vidmah kataran no gariyo / yad va jayema yadi va no jayeyuh*
*yan eva hatva na jijivishamas / te 'vasthitah pramukhe dhartarashtrah*

*na* > nor; *cha* > and; *etat* > this; *vidmah* > we know; *katarat* > which of the two;
*nah* > for us; *gariyah* > preferable; *yat va* > whether; *jayema* > we should
conquer; *yadi* > if; *va* > or; *nah* > us; *jayeyuh* > they should conquer;
*yan* > whom; *eva* > indeed; *hatva* > killing; *na* > not; *jijivishamah* >
we desire to live; *te* > they; *avasthitah* > standing in position;
*pramukhe* > in front of us; *dhartarashtrah* > the sons of Dhritarashtra.

**Nor do we even know which is preferable for us —
conquering them or being conquered by them.
Those whom, having killed, we would no longer desire to live —
the sons of Dhritarashtra —
Stand positioned before us.**

7

*karpanya-doshopahata-svabhavah / prichchami tvam dharma-sammudha-chetah
yachchreyah syan nishchitam bruhi tan me /
shishyas te 'ham shadhi mam tvam prapannam*

*karpanya* > pity, compassion; *dosha* > defect; *upahata* > afflicted;
*sva-bhavah* > own nature; *prichchami* > I ask; *tvam* > to you; *dharma* > duty;
*sammudha* > confused; *chetah* > mind; *yat* > what; *shreyah* > better, best;
*syat* > it should be; *nishchitam* > for certain; *bruhi* > tell; *tat* > that; *me* > to me;
*shishyah* > student, disciple; *te* > of you; *aham* > I; *shadhi* > instruct, direct;
*mam* > me; *tvam* > to you; *prapannam* > having approached for refuge.

**My nature [as a warrior] is afflicted by the blemish of compassion,
and thus my mind is confused as to my duty.
Therefore I seek refuge in you as your disciple,
Asking that you please guide me
and tell me for certain what is best for me.**

This is a distinct turning point in the story of Arjuna. He had four times
previously expressed a disinterest in continuing to live — in verses 1.32, 1.35,
1.46, and 2.6 — which here leads to his courageous admission of failure in
attempting to sustain his assumed ego-persona and his humble request for
enlightened guidance. What follows is his penetrating inquiry into the nature
of truth throughout the entire remainder of the Gita's eighteen chapters. This
demonstrates in a very practical way how despair can be potentially useful in
precipitating an awakening to one's true nature, and hence the title of the
Gita's first chapter.

8

*na hi prapashyami mama-'panudyad / yach chokam uchchoshanam indriyanam
avapya bhumav asapatnam riddham / rajyam suranam api chadhipatyam*

*na* > not; *hi* > truly; *prapashyami* > I see; *mama* > of me; *apanudyat* > it should
dispel; *yat* > which; *shokam* > grief; *uchchoshanam* > shriveling, desiccating;
*indriyanam* > of the body's power, of the sensing faculties; *avapya* > obtaining;
*bhumau* > on the Earth; *asapatnam* > unrivaled; *riddham* > prosperous;

*rajyam* > royal power; *suranam* > of the denizens of heaven; *api* > even; *cha* > and; *adhipatyam* > sovereignty.

**Truly, I can find no means to dispel this grief**
**which is sapping all the strength from my mind and body,**
**Even at the prospect**
**of obtaining unrivaled royal power and prosperity on Earth**
**Or sovereignty over the denizens of heaven.**

**9**
*sanjaya uvacha:*
*evam uktva hrishikesham / gudakeshah parantapah*
*na yotsya iti govindam / uktva tushnim babhuva ha*

*sanjayah uvacha* > Sanjaya said; *evam* > thus; *uktva* > having spoken; *hrishikesham* > to Krishna, who is master over his sense-faculties; *gudakeshah* > Arjuna, who is master over the influence of sleep; *parantapah* > the scourge of foes; *na yotsye* > I shall not fight; *iti* > thus; *govindam* > to Krishna, chief of the cowherd men; *uktva* > having spoken; *tushnim* > silent; *babhuva* > he became; *ha* > indeed.

**Sanjaya said:**
**Having spoken in this way**
**to Krishna, the master of his senses,**
**Arjuna, the master over the influence of sleep**
**and the scourge of his foes, said:**
**"O chief of the cowherd men, I shall not fight,"**
**and thus became silent.**

Arjuna was actually Krishna's cousin. Accounts of Krishna's life state that he was born of *kshatriya* parents but was raised in a foster family of *vaishya* cowherders in Vrindaban near Delhi. He became reunited with his *kshatriya* family in Mathura at the age of 16 when he overthrew his uncle, the murderous tyrant King Kamsa. He freed all those whom Kamsa had imprisoned during his reign, including both Krishna's and Kamsa's own parents. Krishna was actually a powerful king himself — of Dwaraka on the coast of Gujarat — when he offered to become Arjuna's charioteer, which itself is quite a testament to his humility and to his love for his cousin/friend.

**10**
*tam uvacha hrishikeshah / prahasann iva bharata*
*senayor ubhayor madhye / vishidantam idam vachah*

*tam* > to him; *uvacha* > he spoke; *hrishikeshah* > Krishna; *prahasan* > smiling;
*iva* > a little bit; *bharata* > O descendant of Bharata (King Dhritarashtra);
*senayoh* > of the armies; *ubhayoh* > of both; *madhye* > inbetween;
*vishidantam* > despondent; *idam* > this; *vachah* > speech.

**O descendant of Bharata, then,
inbetween both the armies,
Krishna smiled slightly and spoke to the despondent Arjuna
these words:**

### 11

*sri bhagavan uvacha:*
*ashochyan anvashochas tvam / prajna-vadams cha bhashase*
*gatasun agatasuns cha / nanushochanti panditah*

*sri bhagavan uvacha* > the venerable one (Krishna) said; *ashochyan* > not to be
lamented; *anvashochah* > you are lamenting; *tvam* > you; *prajna* > wisdom;
*vadan* > words; *cha* > and; *bhashase* > you speak; *gatasun* > bodies from which
the breath has gone; *agata asun* > bodies from which the breath has not gone;
*cha* > and; *na* > not; *anushochanti* > they lament; *panditah* > those who are wise.

**The venerable Krishna said:
Arjuna, this lamentation of yours is unwarranted.
You speak words which [you were taught to believe] represent wisdom,
But those who are truly wise
do not agonize over the fate of bodies from which the breath has gone
or bodies within which the breath yet remains.**

### 12

*na tvevaham jatu nasam / na tvam neme janadhipah*
*na chaiva na bhavishyamah / sarve vayam atah param*

*na* > not; *tu* > but; *eva* > truly; *aham* > I; *jatu* > ever; *na* > not; *asam* > I existed;
*na* > nor; *tvam* > you; *na* > nor; *ime* > these; *jana-adhipah* > commanders
of men; *na* > nor; *cha* > and; *eva* > just so; *na* > not; *bhavishyamah* >
we shall exist; *sarve vayam* > all of us; *atah param* > hereafter.

**Truly there was never a time when I did not exist,
nor you,
nor all these commanders of men;
Nor shall any of us ever cease to exist
at any time hereafter.**

Krishna's statement here applies not only to the singular Omnipresence pervading all the figures on the battlefield, but also to the figures themselves potentially enduring as *samskaras*, creative memory-impressions preserved within the same one infinite Consciousness.

### 13
*dehino 'smin yatha dehe / kaumaram yauvanam jara*
*tatha dehantara-praptir / dhiras tatra na muhyati*

*dehinah* > of the embodied (Spirit-Presence or Awareness); *asmin* > in this; *yatha* > just as; *dehe* > in the body; *kaumaram* > childhood; *yauvanam* > youth; *jara* > old age; *tatha* > so also; *deha-antara* > within another body; *praptih* > acquiring, discovering, entering; *dhirah* > one with steady composure; *tatra* > in regard to this matter; *na* > not; *muhyati* > one is confused.

**Just as indwelling Awareness**
**discovers [the wonders of] childhood, youth, and old age**
**in this body,**
**So does It [discover Itself] within other bodies as well.**
**One with steady composure is not confused about this.**

The Spirit-Self or pure Awareness is 'within the body' by virtue of Its being all-pervasive, as will be confirmed in upcoming verses 17 (*tatam*), 18 (*aprameyasya*), and 24 (*sarvagatah*). It is not confined within the body, just as the all-pervasive sky is not confined within any container. When, however, there is an unquestioned, firmly-held conviction within Consciousness that "I am exclusively this one particular container," then the feeling of confinement naturally arises.

### 14
*matra-sparshas tu kaunteya / sheetoshna-sukha-duhkhadah*
*agamapayino 'nityas / tans titikshasva bharata*

*matra* > the physical elements; *sparshah* > sensations; *tu* > indeed; *kaunteya* > O son of Kunti; *sheeta* > cold; *ushna* > heat; *sukha* > happiness; *duhkha* > distress; *dah* > giving, causing; *agama* > coming; *apayinah* > going; *anityah* > temporary; *tan* > them; *titikshasva* > patiently endure; *bharata* > O descendant of the Bharata dynasty.

**O son of Kunti, contact with the physical elements**
**causes sensations such as heat, cold, happiness, and distress,**
**which are temporary and simply come and go.**
**Please do patiently endure them, O descendant of Bharata.**

In regard to happiness being on the list of sensations which are temporary, the heightened sense of exhilaration experienced when the senses encounter their objects is what one is aware of, whereas the *ananda* aspect of one's true nature is the unqualified contentment which one simply *is*.

### 15

*yam hi na vyathayantyete / purusham purusharshabha*
*sama-duhkha-sukham dhiram / so 'mritatvaya kalpate*

*yam* > whom; *hi* > because; *na* > not; *vyathayanti* > they disturb; *ete* > these; *purusham* > a person; *purusha-rishabha* > O chief among men; *sama* > the same; *duhkha* > distress; *sukham* > happiness; *dhiram* > steadily composed; *sah* > that one; *amritatvaya* > for immortality; *kalpate* > is fit.

**Because a person who remains undisturbed by these conditions,**
**O chief among men —**
**Equally composed in both happiness and distress —**
**is fit for [embodying the realization of one's] immortality.**

There is no becoming immortal for that which is mortal, as will be confirmed in upcoming verse 27 ("For anything that is born, death is assured"). However, the mortal vehicle for expression known as a person can be utilized as an instrument with which pure Consciousness can embody the truth of Its eternally unborn and deathless nature.

### 16

*nasato vidyate bhavo / nabhavo vidyate satah*
*ubhayor api drishto'ntas / tvanayos tattvadarshibhih*

*na* > not; *asatah* > of the unreal, of that which is not true; *vidyate* > it is found; *bhavah* > being, existence; *na* > not; *abhavah* > non-being, non-existence; *vidyate* > it is found; *satah* > of the real, of that which is true; *ubhayoh* > of both; *api* > certainly; *drishtah* > directly perceived; *antah* > conclusion; *tu* > indeed; *anayoh* > of these two; *tattva* > truth; *darshibhih* > by the seers.

**It is found that the unreal never comes into being**
**and the Real never ceases to be —**
**The certainty of both these conclusions**
**has been directly perceived by seers of the truth.**

According to Krishna's statement here, the world cannot be defined as entirely unreal if something has come into being within which there is a conversation occurring about what is unreal and what is not. At the same time, the world also cannot be considered as real because it certainly ceases to be at different times. The brilliant quantum physicist David Bohm described the characteristics of the universe as most closely resembling those of a holographic image, which is strikingly similar to the ancient sage Dattatreya's description of it as *mrigatoya*, 'the water in a mirage,' in his *Avadhuta Gita*. The commonality in both illustrations is the depiction of the world as essentially nothing more than an optical illusion, which would make its apparent substantiality and continuity nothing short of astounding.

### 17
*avinashi tu tad viddhi / yena sarvam idam tatam*
*vinasham avyayasyasya / na kashchit kartum arhati*

*avinashi* > indestructible; *tu* > indeed; *tat* > That (the *dehinah* of verse 13 and the *satah* of verse 16); *viddhi* > know for certain; *yena* > by which; *sarvam idam* > all of this (the world); *tatam* > extended, spread throughout; *vinasham* > destruction; *avyayasya asya* > of this which is imperishable; *na* > not; *kashchit* > anyone; *kartum* > to accomplish; *arhati* > is able.

**Be assured:**
**That [Reality] which extends throughout all of this world**
**is indestructible.**
**There is no one who is able to accomplish**
**the destruction of this imperishable [Presence].**

### 18
*antavanta ime deha / nityasyoktah sharirinah*
*anashino prameyasya / tasmad yudhyasva bharata*

*anta-vantah* > having an end; *ime* > these; *dehah* > bodies; *nityasya* > of the eternal; *uktah* > declared, taught; *sharirinah* > of the animating Presence within all bodies; *anashinah* > of the indestructible; *aprameyasya* > of the immeasurable; *tasmat* > therefore; *yudhyasva* > do fight; *bharata* > Arjuna, the descendant of Bharata.

**It is declared that [although] these bodies come to an end,**
**The eternal animating Presence within all bodies**
**is indestructible and immeasurable.**
**Therefore, do participate in the conflict, Arjuna.**

**19**

*ya enam vetti hantaram / yash chainam manyate hatam*
*ubhau tau na vijanito / nayam hanti na hanyate*

*yah* > who; *enam* > This (the indwelling Presence introduced in verse 13);
*vetti* > views, regards; *hantaram* > slayer; *yah* > who; *cha* > and;
*enam* > This (Presence); *manyate* > considers; *hatam* > slain; *ubhau* > both;
*tau* > they two; *na* > not; *vijanitah* > they understand; *na* > not;
*ayam* > This (Presence); *hanti* > it slays; *na* > nor; *hanyate* > it is slain.

**One who regards this Presence as a slayer**
**and one who considers It to be slain —**
**Neither of them understand**
**that pure Presence neither slays nor is slain.**

**20**

*na jayate mriyate va kadachin / nayam bhutva bhavita va na bhuyah*
*ajo nityah shashvato 'yam purano / na hanyate hanyamane sharire*

*na* > not; *jayate* > It takes birth; *mriyate* > It dies; *va* > either;
*kadachit* > sometimes, anytime; *na* > not; *ayam* > This (Presence);
*bhutva* > having previously been; *bhavita* > It is caused to be, It is
transformed into, It is made to become; *va* > or; *na* > not; *bhuyah* > again;
*ajah* > unborn; *nityah* > eternal; *shashvatah* > continuous, permanent;
*ayam* > This (Presence); *puranah* > primeval; *na* > not; *hanyate* > It is
slain; *hanyamane* > in being slain; *sharire* > of the body.

**This Presence does not take birth or die at any time,**
**Nor had It previously been [something]**
**which was made to become [something else] again.**
**It is primeval, unborn, and eternal,**
**and Its nature as such is permanent.**
**Thus It is not slain when the body is slain.**

This is one of the most important verses for contemplation in the entire
Gita. Physical bodies undergo a dramatic transformation of their elements,
thus certainly giving the convincing appearance of a birth and a death.
So between verses 12 and 30, Krishna states that there is never any birth or
transformation of the Spirit-Presence animating the bodies at any time, and
that Its nature of being birthless is permanent and unchanging. Remarkably,
although there can't be any question of rebirth for That which is never born at
all, in this particular verse Krishna even addresses the idea of reincarnation

by saying *nayam bhutva bhavita va na bhuyah*, that Spirit had not previously been [such-and-such] which was later made to become [fill-in-the-blank]. What is sometimes experienced, however, are memory-impressions of previous dreamlike forms appearing *within* absolute Consciousness, as indicated in verse 12.

### 21

*veda-'vinashinam nityam / ya enam ajam avyayam*
*katham sa purushah partha / kam ghatayati hanti kam*

*veda* > one who knows; *avinashinam* > indestructible; *nityam* > everlasting; *yah* > which; *enam* > This (Presence); *ajam* > unborn; *avyayam* > not subject to change; *katham* > how; *sah purushah* > that person; *partha* > O son of Pritha; *kam* > whom; *ghatayati* > causes to slay; *hanti* > slays; *kam* > whom.

**One who knows this Presence to be indestructible,**
**everlasting, unborn, and not subject to change —**
**How would such a person view himself as slaying someone, O Partha?**
**And exactly whom would he be slaying?**

### 22

*vasamsi jirnani yatha vihaya / navani grihnati naro 'parani*
*tatha sharirani vihaya jirnany / anyani samyati navani dehi*

*vasamsi* > garments; *jirnani* > old, worn out, ruined; *yatha* > just as; *vihaya* > leaves aside, disregards; *navani* > new; *grihnati* > takes; *narah* > a person; *aparani* > others; *tatha* > in this way; *sharirani* > bodies; *vihaya* > leaves aside, disregards; *jirnani* > old, worn out, ruined; *anyani* > others; *samyati* > one encounters, one comes together with; *navani* > new; *dehi* > the Indweller within bodies.

**Just as a person leaves aside old, worn-out garments**
**and takes on new ones,**
**So also does the one Indweller within all forms**
**disassociate from old, worn-out bodies**
**and encounter new ones.**

In the recitation of the second line of this verse, the words *jirnanyanyani* are actually conjoined as a unit, with the slight pause occurring between *jirnan* and *yanyani* to keep the meter intact.

**23**

*nainam chindanti shastrani / nainam dahati pavakah*
*na chainam kledayantyapo / na shoshayati marutah*

*na* > not; *enam* > This (Presence); *chindanti* > they pierce; *shastrani* > weapons;
*na* > nor; *enam* > This (Presence); *dahati* > it burns; *pavakah* > fire; *na* > nor;
*cha* > and; *enam* > This (Presence); *kledayanti* > they moisten; *apah* > the
waters; *na* > nor; *shoshayati* > it causes to dry up; *marutah* > the wind.

**This Presence can never be pierced by any weapon,**
**Nor burned by fire,**
**Nor moistened by water,**
**Nor dried up by the wind.**

**24**

*achchedyo 'yam adahyo 'yam / akledyo 'shoshya eva cha*
*nityah sarvagatah sthanur / achalo 'yam sanatanah*

*achchedyah* > indivisible, impenetrable; *ayam* > This (Presence);
*adahyah* > incapable of being burned; *ayam* > This (Presence); *akledyah* >
insoluble; *ashoshyah* > incapable of being dried up; *eva* > indeed; *cha* > and;
*nityah* > everlasting; *sarvagatah* > all-pervading; *sthanuh* > firmly immovable;
*achalah* > unmoving; *ayam* > This (Presence); *sanatanah* > primordial.

**This Presence is indivisible and insoluble,**
**and can never be burned or withered.**
**It is primordial, everlasting, and all-pervading,**
**firmly immovable and unmoving.**

Because the Self is omnipresent Consciousness, pure Subjectivity and not an
object, Krishna informs Arjuna that It is indivisible, not able to be divided up
and moved apart into separated independent 'selves.' And he uses two words
here — *sthanuh*, 'firmly immovable,' and *achalah*, 'unmoving' — to convey the
relief-giving message to Arjuna that That which is unmoving subsequently
does not 'fall from grace' or 'enter the netherworld' as Arjuna was expressing
apprehension about back in verses 42 through 44 of Chapter One. What can
happen, however, is that temporary, dreamlike experiences can coalesce and
dissipate *within* Consciousness. In the discourse known as the *Uddhava Gita*
within the Bhagavata Purana, verse 11.22.55, Krishna says to another one of
his dear friends, Uddhava: "O descendant of Dasharha, just as the fantasies of
one's imagination are insubstantial, so also are all experiences from birth to
death simply like those seen in a dream."

**25**

*avyakto 'yam achintyo 'yam / avikaryo 'yam uchyate*
*tasmad evam viditvainam / nanushochitum arhasi*

*avyaktah* > unmanifest, imperceptible; *ayam* > This (Presence);
*achintyah* > inconceivable; *ayam* > This (Presence); *avikaryah* > unchangeable,
immutable; *ayam* > This (Presence); *uchyate* > it is said; *tasmat* > therefore;
*evam* > thus; *viditva* > knowing; *enam* > This (Presence); *na* > not;
*anushochitum* > to lament; *arhasi* > proper, fitting.

**It is said that this Presence is unmanifest,**
**unimaginable, and unchangeable.**
**Knowing It to be thus,**
**it is therefore not fitting for you to lament.**

Krishna distinctly uses two words — *avyayam*, 'not subject to change,' in verse
21, and *avikaryah*, 'unchangeable,' here — to further emphasize the fact that the
living Spirit animating all bodies expresses Itself as all forms in a creative,
imaginary way without losing Its formless (and hence unimaginable) nature;
that It expresses as the born without losing Its unborn nature.

**26**

*atha chainam nitya-jatam / nityam va manyase mritam*
*tathapi tvam mahabaho / nainam shochitum arhasi*

*atha* > but; *cha* > and; *enam* > This (Presence); *nitya* > perpetually;
*jatam* > born; *nityam* > continually; *va* > or; *manyase* > you imagine,
you believe; *mritam* > dying; *tatha api* > even then; *tvam* > you;
*maha-baho* > O mighty-armed one; *na* > not; *enam* > this;
*shochitum* > to grieve; *arhasi* > you are obliged, you are required.

**But even if you believe that this Omnipresence**
**is perpetually taking birth and dying,**
**It is still not necessary for you to grieve,**
**O mighty-armed one.**

**27**

*jatasya hi dhruvo mrityur / dhruvam janma mritasya cha*
*tasmad apariharye'rthe / na tvam shochitum arhasi*

*jatasya* > of the born; *hi* > because; *dhruvah* > assured; *mrityuh* > death;
*dhruvam* > stable, unchanging constant; *janma* > birth; *mritasya* > of the dead;

*cha* > and; *tasmat* > therefore; *apariharye* > of the inevitable; *arthe* > on this account; *na* > not; *tvam* > you; *shochitum* > to mourn; *arhasi* > you are obliged.

**Because for anything that is born, death is assured;**
**and for anything which has died, new birth is certain.**
**As this is an inevitable constant [within Life],**
**there is therefore nothing in such affairs which warrants your mourning.**

Death is not an inevitability for Life; only for that which is born. What is referred to as death is the point at which an object, a body/mind vessel, completes its duration of functioning. By contrast, in previous verses the pure energetic Life-Presence has been described as being unborn and undying because It is not an object. Even in regard to objects, however, it is demonstrated by the laws of physics that neither matter nor energy is ever actually created or destroyed. Matter is simply transformed, and hence 'new birth is certain' for those material elements.

### 28
*avyakta-'dini bhutani / vyakta-madhyani bharata*
*avyakta-nidhananyeva / tatra ka paridevana*

*avyakta* > unmanifest; *adini* > in the beginning; *bhutani* > living beings; *vyakta* > manifest; *madhyani* > in the middle; *bharata* > Arjuna, the descendant of Bharata; *avyakta* > unmanifest; *nidhanani* > in the end; *eva* > indeed; *tatra* > about this; *ka* > what; *paridevana* > concern, complaint.

**All living beings (the expressions of pure Being)**
**Proceed from being unmanifest in the beginning**
**to being unmanifest at the end,**
**With only their intermediate stage being manifest, O Arjuna.**
**What is your concern about this [natural process]?**

### 29
*ashcharyavat pashyati kashchid enam / ashcharyavad vadati tathaiva chanyah*
*ashcharyavach chainam anyah shrinoti / shrutvapyenam veda na chaiva kashchit*

*ashcharyavat* > wondrously; *pashyati* > perceives; *kashchid* > someone; *enam* > this (the process of unmanifest Being becoming manifest described in the previous verse); *ashcharyavat* > wondrously; *vadati* > speaks of; *tatha* > thus; *eva* > indeed; *cha* > and; *anyah* > another; *ashcharyavat* > wondrously; *cha* > and; *enam* > this (mysterious process); *anyah* > another; *shrinoti* > hears of; *shrutva* > having heard; *api* > even; *enam* > this (mystery); *veda* > knows; *na* > not; *cha* > and; *eva* > surely; *kashchit* > anyone.

**Some view this [process of unmanifest Being becoming manifest]
as a source of great wonder;
Others speak of it as such,
while still others hear of it as such.
Yet regardless of how much is heard about this [mystery],
there is of course no one who can *know* anything about it.**

It bears noting here that there is no mind or intellect which can ever know
how or why Life presents Itself in the manner which It does. This not
knowing is an entirely natural characteristic of the finite mind in regard to
the infinite Potential, in the same way as a person's reflection in a mirror
cannot know the person standing in front of the mirror.

### 30

*dehi nityam avadhyo 'yam / dehe sarvasya bharata
tasmat sarvani bhutani / na tvam shochitum arhasi*

*dehi* > the Indweller in bodies; *nityam* > eternally; *avadhyah* > not capable
of being harmed; *ayam* > this; *dehe* > within the body; *sarvasya* > of all;
*bharata* > O descendant of Bharata; *tasmat* > therefore; *sarvani bhutani* >
all living beings; *na* > not; *tvam* > you; *shochitum* > to mourn,
to worry; *arhasi* > you are required, you are obliged.

**The indwelling Aliveness within all bodies
is eternally safe from harm, O descendant of Bharata.
Therefore it is not necessary for you to worry about the fate
of any [of Its expressions as] living beings.**

The teaching here is not intended to encourage apathy or insensitivity in
one's interactions with other living beings, as will be confirmed several times
throughout Krishna's discourse. In verse 18.25, for example, he states that
any action which is performed with a disregard for the well-being of oneself
or others is born of darkness. What is being highlighted in the present verse
is the importance of recognizing the unchanging truth of life in the midst of
life's ever-changing appearances — especially when one is called upon to
fulfill natural responsibilities in very challenging situations, as was Arjuna.

### 31

*svadharmam api chavekshya / na vikampitum arhasi
dharmyad dhi yuddhach-'chreyo 'nyat / kshatriyasya na vidyate*

*svadharmam* > one's own occupational duty (based on the natural characteristics of one's body/mind system); *api cha* > only; *avekshya* > focusing; *na* > not; *vikampitum* > to hesitate; *arhasi* > you should; *dharmyat* > just, rightful; *hi* > truly; *yuddhat* > than fighting; *shreyah* > better, more beneficial, preferable; *anyat* > other; *kshatriyasya* > of the royal administrators and protectors; *na* > not; *vidyate* > it is found.

**You should not hesitate
to focus solely on your own specific duty,
Because it is found that for the royal administrators and protectors,
there is truly nothing better than fighting for a just cause.**

### 32

*yadrichchaya chopapannam / svarga-dvaram apavritam
sukhinah kshatriyah partha / labhante yuddham idrisham*

*yadrichchaya* > by chance, spontaneously; *cha* > and; *upapannam* > that which comes, that which has been provided; *svarga* > heaven; *dvaram* > gate; *apavritam* > open; *sukhinah* > happy; *kshatriyah* > members of the royal order; *partha* > O son of Pritha; *labhante* > they encounter; *yuddham* > battle; *idrisham* > of such type.

**Happy are the members of the royal order
who encounter a battle such as this, O son of Pritha,
Which spontaneously comes
and opens for them the gates of heaven.**

### 33

*atha chet tvam imam dharmyam / sangramam na karishyasi
tatah svadharmam kirtim cha / hitva papam avapsyasi*

*atha* > now; *chet* > if; *tvam* > you; *imam* > this; *dharmyam* > rightful, righteous; *sangramam* > engagement in conflict; *na* > not; *karishyasi* > you will do; *tatah* > then; *svadharmam* > one's own natural duty; *kirtim* > good reputation, fame; *cha* > and; *hitva* > having deserted, having disregarded; *papam* > trouble, misfortune; *avapsyasi* > you will obtain, you will suffer.

**But if at this time you do not accept
rightful engagement in the conflict,
Then, having disregarded your natural duty and noble reputation,
you will invite trouble upon yourself.**

**34**

*akirtim chapi bhutani / kathayishyanti te 'vyayam*
*sambhavitasya chakirtir / maranad atirichyate*

*akirtim* > dishonor; *cha* > and; *api* > also; *bhutani* > people;
*kathayishyanti* > they will speak to each other; *te* > about you; *avyayam* >
undecaying, not liable to change; *sambhavitasya* > for the honored; *cha* > and;
*akirtih* > infamy, disgrace; *maranat* > than dying; *atirichyate* > it exceeds.

**For all time to come**
**people will dishonor you when speaking about you,**
**And for one who has been honored,**
**dishonor is worse than death.**

**35**

*bhayad ranad uparatam / mansyante tvam maharathah*
*yesham cha tvam bahumato / bhutva yasyasi laghavam*

*bhayat* > out of fear; *ranat* > from the conflict; *uparatam* > having
withdrawn from; *mansyante* > they will think; *tvam* > you;
*maha-rathah* > the great warriors; *yesham* > for whom; *cha* > and;
*tvam* > you; *bahu-matah* > highly regarded; *bhutva* > having been;
*yasyasi* > you will come; *laghavam* > insignificance.

**The truly great warriors**
**will think that you have withdrawn from the conflict out of fear,**
**And you will thus come to be regarded as insignificant**
**by those who had previously held you in high esteem.**

**36**

*avachya-vadansh cha bahun / vadishyanti tavahitah*
*nindantas tava samarthyam / tato duhkha-taram nu kim*

*avachya* > not to be spoken; *vadan* > words; *cha* > and; *bahun* > many;
*vadishyanti* > they will say; *tava* > of you; *ahitah* > hostile; *nindantah* >
deriding; *tava* > your; *samarthyam* > abilities; *tatah* > from that;
*duhkha-taram* > greater misery; *nu kim* > what indeed.

**And the more hostile warriors**
**will use many words which should not be spoken**
**in deriding your abilities.**
**What could cause you greater misery than that?**

## 37

*hato va prapsyasi svargam / jitva va bhokshyase mahim*
*tasmad uttishtha kaunteya / yuddhaya krita-nishchayah*

*hatah* > having been slain; *va* > either; *prapsyasi* > you will attain;
*svargam* > the heavenly strata within infinite Consciousness; *jitva* > having
conquered; *va* > or; *bhokshyase* > you will enjoy; *mahim* > the Earth;
*tasmat* > therefore; *uttishtha* > arise; *kaunteya* > O son of Kunti;
*yuddhaya* > to fighting; *krita* > made; *nishchayah* > determination.

**Either your body will be slain and you will attain heaven,**
**Or you will conquer [the aggressors] and enjoy the Earth.**
**Therefore arise, O son of Kunti,**
**determined to fight.**

## 38

*sukha-duhkhe same kritva / labha-'labhau jayajayau*
*tato yuddhaya yujyasva / naivam papam avapsyasi*

*sukha* > happiness; *duhkhe* > distress; *same* > alike; *kritva* > having done;
*labha-alabhau* > gain and loss; *jaya-ajayau* > victory and defeat; *tatah* > then;
*yuddhaya* > to battle; *yujyasva* > join with; *na* > not; *evam* > thus;
*papam* > trouble, misfortune; *avapsyasi* > you will obtain, you will suffer.

**Considering happiness and distress to be the same —**
**As well as gain and loss, victory and defeat —**
**engage in the battle.**
**By doing so you will not inherit any misfortune.**

## 39

*esha te 'bhihita sankhye / buddhir yoge tvimam shrinu*
*buddhya yukto yaya partha / karma-bandham prahasyasi*

*esha* > this (the wisdom shared throughout the course of verses 13 to 30);
*te* > to you; *abhihita* > spoken, declared; *sankhye* > the system of acquiring
knowledge by analyzing, enumerating, and classifying the different
elemental components experienced in the world (Prakriti) and discerning
them from their Experiencer (Purusha); *buddhih yoge* > recognizing the
spontaneous functioning of universal intuitive Intelligence (Mahat-buddhi)
throughout all life; *tu* > but; *imam* > this; *shrinu* > now hear; *buddhya yuktah* >
the subtle inner body (sukshma sharira) aligned with universal intuitive
Intelligence as a clear conduit; *yaya* > by which; *partha* > O son of Pritha;

*karma-bandham* > being bound up by the cycle of action and reaction (which Arjuna expressed concern about in Chapter One, verses 31, 36, and 40-44); *prahasyasi* > you will laugh, you will make jokes about.

> **The wisdom imparted to you thus far is based on Sankhya,**
> **the system of acquiring knowledge empirically.**
> **But now hear, O Partha,**
> **About recognizing the spontaneous functioning**
> **of universal intuitive Intelligence throughout all life,**
> **For when your subtle inner body is a clear conduit for That,**
> **You will come to laugh about [your worries in regard to] being bound up**
> **by the cycle of action and reaction.**

The *sukshma sharira* or 'subtle body' is also known as the *linga sharira*, the 'body which is a signifier' of the Purusha (Spirit-Presence), and yet another name for it is the *antahkarana*, the 'internal instrument' comprising the fourfold network of *manas* (mind), *buddhi* (intellect), *ahamkara* (the egoic sense of self), and *chitta*. *Chitta* is the faculty of thinking, feeling, and willing based on information gathered by the mind, defined and evaluated by the intellect, and self-referenced by the ego. This Nature-born subtle inner body is always predominated by one or another of the three *gunas* (components of Nature), either *sattva* (clarity, luminosity, lightness, and balance), *rajas* (creation, activation, coloration, and intensification), or *tamas* (darkness, heaviness, inertia, and dissolution). So Mahat-buddhi, classified in Sankhya as the very first manifestation of Prakriti (Nature) and as the source of the self-preservational ego-sense, is the universal instinctive/intuitive Intelligence guiding all of life. As such, there is no form of life in existence which is not endowed with It. Even so, within the context of this oneness, the fullest connotation of *buddhi-yoga* is the realization of *being* It, and *buddhi yukta* connotes the body/mind system's functioning as a clear channel for living in accordance with that realization. Such functioning fully invites a flow of wisdom and love which is only possible when the entire structure of self-centeredness has fallen away. Yet this is not in any way synonymous with the instinct for physical self-preservation falling away, as one aspect of Self-realization is realizing the body/mind instrument to be of great value in serving the oneness which is being directly perceived.

To use a simple example for illustrating the principle of *buddhi yukta*, when the light of the sun (pure Awareness) shines through a window (the subtle inner body) which has completely clean, clear glass (*sattva-guna*), the rays coming forth into the room are the most accurate representations possible of the pure sunlight, and all things in the room can easily be seen as they actually are. When the same unchanged sun shines through a stained-glass window (*rajas-guna*), the rays entering the room are red, blue, green, etc., which are distorted representations of the same pure sunlight; so although things in the room are still seen, they are not seen as they actually are. And when the same unchanged sun shines through a window which is covered with dust and dirt (*tamas-guna*), the same pure sunlight is significantly obstructed and thus very little of it shines through, making it difficult to see the things in the room at all, what to speak of seeing them as they actually are. In this way, although all of the windows are equally channels for the same one sunlight, the degree of the window's clarity determines how fully and accurately the sunlight will be represented after passing through the windows.

In regard to the presentation of the Sankhya philosophy, there can be a dualistic *perception* of a Subject and objects — Purusha and Prakriti, the Experiencer and the experienced, yet it is also possible for the same to be perceived as a singularity of Experiencing. This is akin to looking at pictures where there appears to be two silhouettes of human faces facing each other, and the space between the silhouettes appears to be a vase. Focusing on the silhouetted faces one would perceive two things there, whereas focusing on the vase one would perceive only one thing in the exact same picture without changing anything whatsoever in the picture. If we again use the example of the sun, which is just one particular object — in conceiving of the sun as being sentient and experiencing its own nature/energy of heat and light, it would not be experiencing something other than itself.

**40**

*nehabhikrama-nasho 'sti / pratyavayo na vidyate*
*svalpam apyasya dharmasya / trayate mahato bhayat*

*na* > not; *iha* > here; *abhikrama* > endeavor, approach; *nashah* > loss; *asti* > there is; *pratyavayah* > reversal, contrary effect; *na* > not; *vidyate* > it is found; *svalpam* > very little; *api* > even; *asya* > of this; *dharmasya* > of religious practice; *trayate* > it protects; *mahatah* > very great; *bhayat* > from fear, from danger.

**In this endeavor [to recognize such functioning],
no loss or contrary effect is to be found,
And even a very small amount of this type of religious practice
protects one from the greatest fears and dangers.**

The statements which Arjuna made in Chapter One and in verses 4 through 9 of this chapter indicated that his fear, anxiety, and despondency had their roots in the religious beliefs he had accumulated from past sources. So in response to his concern about being overtaken by irreligion in verses 1.40-41, Krishna offers a 'religious' means of defense to protect him from that, which simply entails Arjuna's perceiving things as they actually are rather than the way he had been taught to believe they are. Moreover, another meaning of the word *dharma* connotes appropriately utilizing the natural characteristics of one's body/mind system in the performance of one's occupational duty. Krishna will begin focusing on this principle with specific emphasis on such duties being performed without attachment to particular results (karma-yoga) in upcoming verse 48.

### 41
*vyavasayatmika buddhir / ekeha kuru-nandana*
*bahu-shakha hyanantash cha / buddhayo 'vyavasayinam*

*vyavasaya-atmika* > active, full of resolve or energy;
*buddhih* > universal Intelligence; *eka* > one; *iha* > here,
in this world; *kuru-nandana* > O delight of the Kuru dynasty;
*bahu-shakhah* > many branches; *hi* > indeed; *anantah* > eternal,
endless, boundless; *cha* > and; *buddhayah* > awakenings,
enlightenments; *avyavasayinam* > of the inactive
(those who are 'asleep' to their true nature).

**There is one Intelligence active here in the world,**
**O delight of the Kuru dynasty;**
**And that One eternally branches out endlessly**
**for awakening the 'sleeping' [manifestations of Itself].**

### 42
*yam imam pushpitam vacham / pravadantya-'vipashchitah*
*vedavada-ratah partha / nanyad astiti vadinah*

*yam* > which; *imam* > this; *pushpitam* > flowery; *vacham* > language;
*pravadanti* > they proclaim; *avipashchitah* > the unwise; *veda-vada* >
presentations within the Vedas (referring to those sections which describe
heavenly pleasures and the means to attain them, as confirmed in the
next verse); *ratah* > delighting in; *partha* > O son of Pritha; *na* > not;
*anyat* > anything else; *asti* > there is; *iti* > thus; *vadinah* > asserting.

**O son of Pritha,**
**Delighting in [certain] proclamations**
**presented in flowery language within the Vedas,**
**The unwise assert that "There is nothing beyond this."**

**43**

*kamatmanah svarga-para / janma-karmaphala-pradam*
*kriya-vishesha-bahulam / bhogaishvarya-gatim prati*

*kama-atmanah* > those who are driven by desire; *svarga-parah* > intent upon
attaining heaven; *janma* > birth; *karma-phala* > the resultant fruit (reward)
of action; *pradam* > bestowing; *kriya-vishesha-bahulam* > an extensive
variety of religious rituals; *bhoga* > sensory pleasure; *aishvarya* > wealth,
power; *gatim* > going, moving; *prati* > in the opposite direction.

**Those who are driven by the desire**
**for wealth, power, and sensory pleasure**
**Are intent upon attaining birth in heaven**
**as the reward bestowed upon them**
**for having performed a wide variety of religious rituals.**
**Yet they are moving in the opposite direction**
**[of the heaven already present within themselves].**

In this chapter Krishna refers to 'heaven' with two very different
connotations. In this verse and the previous one Krishna describes those
who have heaven as their goal as being 'unwise' and 'desire-driven,' and in
upcoming verse 49 he further refers to them as 'pitiable.' Yet only moments
ago in verses 32 and 37, he was encouraging Arjuna to 'fight and attain the
kingdom of heaven.' This apparent contradiction is later resolved in verses
71-72, wherein Krishna says that upon the abandonment of all conditioned
patterns of longings, there is an ineffable peace to be discovered within
oneself which is the unchanging constant of one's natural 'state' as Brahman
or pure Awareness. Strictly speaking, Awareness is not a state; It is That
which is aware of all states, as most fittingly conveyed by the term *kshetrajna*
used in Chapter Thirteen. In any case, this same principle is also found in the
words attributed to Jesus in Luke 17:21: "...Behold, the kingdom of God is
within you." So this is one heaven, and the other is a temporary dreamlike
manifestation which comes and goes *within* Awareness. Another distinction
is that one heaven is spoken of as a goal in the hereafter for those who are
driven by desires, while the other is described as being a recognition in the
here-and-now by those who are free from desires.

**44**
*bhogaishvarya-prasaktanam / tayapahrita-chetasam*
*vyavasayatmika buddhih / samadhau na vidhiyate*

*bhoga* > enjoyment; *aishvarya* > wealth, power; *prasaktanam* > those who are attached or fixed in purpose; *taya* > by this; *apahrita-chetasam* > whose minds have been stolen away; *vyavasaya-atmika* > having firm resolve or intention within oneself; *buddhih* > incisive discernment; *samadhau* > in applying, in arranging, in settling; *na* > not; *vidhiyate* > it is established, it is manifest.

**Within those whose minds have been stolen away
by such attachment to wealth, power, and sense-enjoyment,
The firm resolve to apply incisive discernment
[in perceiving things as they truly are]
does not become established.**

**45**
*traigunya-vishaya veda / nistraigunyo bhavarjuna*
*nirdvandvo nitya-sattvastho / niryogakshema atmavan*

*traigunya* > the three components of Nature (described in the notes to verse 39); *vishayah* > scope, subject matter; *vedah* > the Vedas (four collections of ancient religious lore); *nistrai-gunyah* > exempt from adulteration by the three components of Nature; *bhava* > being; *arjuna* > O Arjuna; *nirdvandvah* > indifferent to the pairs of opposites (such as heat and cold, pain and pleasure, victory and defeat, etc.); *nitya* > always; *sattva-sthah* > abiding in the truth; *niryogakshema* > without concern about acquisition or maintenance; *atmavan* > self-composed.

**[The majority of] the Vedas' subject matter
pertains to the three components of Nature;
Yet being exempt from adulteration by those three components, O Arjuna,
You [as pure Spirit] are indifferent
to the pairs of opposites [found in Nature].
Ever abiding in this truth,
without concern about acquisition or maintenance,
be thou self-composed.**

The four Vedas—the Rig, Sama, Yajur, and Atharva—are divided into a total of 1,180 sections, about two-thirds of which are presentations of eulogies, prayers, incantations, mystical formulae, and their explanations, along with guidelines for conducting ritual ceremonies intended to cultivate a reciprocal relationship between humankind and the celestials representing the various aspects of Nature. Krishna will speak about this relationship in verses 10 through 16 of Chapter Three, declaring that one who does not participate in this process of reciprocation is to be regarded as a thief. Therefore the question arises as to whether the ambition to pursue wealth, power, and sense-enjoyment as mentioned in verses 43 and 44 is actually mandated in the Vedas themselves, or if it is based on an interpretation of the Vedas by those who are driven by the desire for those things. In any case, the larger portion of the Vedas described above is what Krishna is referring to in this verse, and the remaining portion comprises the Upanishads, which present conversations regarding the nature of the Absolute just as the Bhagavad-Gita does. Hence, down through the ages Krishna's teaching has come to be known as the *Gitopanishad*.

### 46

*yavan artha udapane / sarvatah samplutodake*
*tavan sarveshu vedeshu / brahmanasya vijanatah*

*yavan* > as much; *arthah* > purpose, value; *uda-pane* > in a well of water; *sarvatah* > everywhere; *sampluta* > overflowing; *udake* > with water; *tavan* > so much; *sarveshu* > in all; *vedeshu* > in the Vedas; *brahmanasya* > of the brahmin, one within whom there is realization of being Brahman; *vijanatah* > wise.

**As much value as there is in a well**
**when water is abundantly flowing in all directions —**
**So also is the value of all the Vedas for the wise one**
**within whom there is the realization of being Brahman**
**(the purely contented presence of Awareness [Sat-Chid-Ananda]).**

### 47

*karmanyeva-'dhikaras te / ma phaleshu kadachana*
*ma karmaphala-hetur bhur / ma te sango 'stvakarmani*

*karmani* > in regard to actions; *eva* > alone; *adhikarah* > jurisdiction; *te* > your; *ma* > never; *phaleshu* > in the fruits (results); *kadachana* > at any time; *ma* > never; *karma-phala* > fruits of actions (results of work); *hetuh bhuh* > being the cause; *ma* > never; *te* > your; *sangah* > attachment; *astu* > it can be so; *akarmani* > to inactivity.

Your jurisdiction is strictly in regard to actions alone,
and never with the resulting fruits of action at any time.
You can never cause the results of your actions,
nor can you ever remain inactive.

**48**

*yogasthah kuru karmani / sangam tyaktva dhananjaya*
*siddhyasiddhyoh samo bhutva / samatvam yoga uchyate*

*yoga-sthah* > steadfast in the performance of selfless action (karma-yoga);
*kuru* > you do; *karmani* > activities, work; *sangam* > attachment; *tyaktva* >
abandoning; *dhananjaya* > O winner of wealth; *siddhi-asiddhyoh* > in success
and failure; *samah* > equipoised; *bhutva* > being; *samatvam* > equanimity;
*yogah* > Self-realization; *uchyate* > it is said to be, it is known as.

Steadfast in the performance of selfless action,
simply perform your work, O winner of wealth,
Abandoning all attachment to its results
and remaining equipoised in success or failure.
Such equanimity is said to be [a sign of] Self-realization.

**49**

*durena hyavaram karma / buddhi-yogad dhananjaya*
*buddhau sharanam anvichcha / kripanah phala-hetavah*

*durena* > by far; *hi* > certainly; *avaram* > inferior; *karma* > actions
(referring to those which are desire-driven, as mentioned in verse 43);
*buddhi-yogat* > recognizing one universal instinctive/intuitive Intelligence
functioning throughout all Life; *dhananjaya* > O winner of wealth;
*buddhau* > in illumined wisdom; *sharanam* > refuge; *anvichcha* > look for,
wish for; *kripanah* > wretched, pitiable; *phala-hetavah* > they
whose motives are to obtain the fruits of their actions.

Actions impelled by self-centered desire are certainly inferior by far
To [those actions inspired by] the recognition of a single universal
Intelligence functioning throughout all of life.
Take refuge in that illumined wisdom
[which is your own heart's treasure], O winner of wealth,
For pitiable are they
whose only motives are to obtain the fruits of their labor.

## 50

*buddhi-yukto jahatiha / ubhe sukrita-dushkrite*
*tasmad yogaya yujyasva / yogah karmasu kaushalam*

*buddhi-yuktah* > functioning as a clear conduit for universal
Intelligence; *jahati* > one abandons, one relinquishes; *iha* > in this world;
*ubhe* > both; *sukrita-dushkrite* > good and evil actions; *tasmat* > therefore;
*yogaya* > to Self-recognition; *yujyasva* > homogeneous integration;
*yogah* > recognition of the unitary wholeness of Life; *karmasu* > in
actions; *kaushalam* > skillfulness, good fortune, well-being.

**One who is functioning as a clear conduit for universal Intelligence**
**Relinquishes all [sense of being the independent doer of]**
**good and evil actions in this world.**
**Therefore, recognize yourself to be homogeneously integrated**
**into the unitary wholeness of Life,**
**For such recognition endows one with a natural skillfulness in actions.**

The interpretation of the first half of this verse is based on Krishna's
having said *ma karmaphala-hetur bhur* ("You can never cause the results of
your actions") in verse 47, in conjunction with his upcoming statements
emphasizing non-doership in verses 2.71, 3.27, and 4.20. Yet another
possible reading of it could be: "One who is functioning as a clear channel
for universal Intelligence relinquishes all [conditioned beliefs about what are]
good and evil actions in this world," because it was such beliefs that brought
Arjuna to his condition of inner turbulence and subsequent unwillingness to
perform his necessary duty at Kurukshetra. And in regard to the unitary
wholeness of Life, it includes both changeless Being or formless Awareness
and Its dreamlike expression as changeful Becoming, the infinite variety of
forms for infinite Awareness to be aware of.

## 51

*karmajam buddhi-yukta hi / phalam tyaktva manishinah*
*janma-bandha-vinirmuktah / padam gachchantya-'namayam*

*karma-jam* > produced by actions; *buddhi-yuktah* > living 'connectedly'
as a clear channel for universal Intelligence; *hi* > truly; *phalam* > fruits
(results); *tyaktva* > having cast aside; *manishinah* > those endowed
with wisdom, those who are contemplative; *janma* > birth;
*bandha* > bondage; *vinirmuktah* > exempt, liberated; *padam* > standpoint;
*gachchanti* > they go; *anamayam* > healthy, free from disease.

**For those endowed with the wisdom received**
**through authentically living as a clear channel for universal Intelligence,**
**All concerns about the results of actions are cast aside.**
**They are liberated from [beliefs about] birth and bondage**
**And function from a standpoint**
**reflecting a natural, healthy condition of life.**

The phrase *janma-bandha-vinirmuktah* cannot be taken literally to mean 'released from the bondage of birth' because Krishna had previously stated in verses 20 and 21 that for the Omnipresence animating all body/mind vessels there is no birth at any time to be released from. Yet it can plausibly be taken to mean that for the body/mind system there is liberation from the bondage of fears and anxieties created by beliefs — beliefs imbibed about the *concepts* of birth and rebirth, as indicated in the very next verse.

### 52

*yada te moha-kalilam / buddhir vyatitarishyati*
*tada gantasi nirvedam / shrotavyasya shrutasya cha*

*yada* > when; *te* > of you; *moha* > bewilderment, delusion, error; *kalilam* > thicket; *buddhih* > the intellect, the faculty of forming and retaining concepts and notions; *vyatitarishyati* > it will pass through; *tada* > then; *ganta asi* > you will go; *nirvedam* > disgust, complete indifference; *shrotavyasya* > of that which is yet to be heard; *shrutasya* > of that which has been heard and orally passed down; *cha* > and.

**When your shining intellect**
**has passed through the dark thicket of misbelief,**
**You will come to feel some disgust for much of what you heard**
**which was orally passed down [from generation to generation],**
**As well as for what is yet to be heard in the future.**

### 53

*shruti-vipratipanna te / yada sthasyati nishchala*
*samadhav-achala buddhis / tada yogam avapsyasi*

*shruti* > doctrinal ideas which have been heard and passed down through the ages; *vipratipanna* > disregarding, dissenting from; *te* > of you; *yada* > when; *sthasyati* > it will remain; *nishchala* > firmly settled; *samadhau* > in being restored to clarity; *achala* > unmoving; *buddhih* > mind, intellect, faculty of discernment; *tada* > then; *yogam* > recognition of one's true nature; *avapsyasi* > you will attain, you will reach.

When your mind disregards the doctrinal ideas
which have been heard and [reflexively] passed down through the ages,
And instead remains firmly settled
[in its direct experience of the living present] —
Then, once unmoving,
it will have been restored to [its original] clarity,
and you will recognize your true nature.

As previously mentioned in regard to the Vedas in the notes to verse 45, Krishna's statement here as well is not a sweeping generalization of *all* the doctrines traditionally passed down throughout the course of time. Some practical examples of ancient doctrines that may justifiably merit disregard are those that propagate sectarianism, casteism, racism, sexism, male supremacy, misogyny, bigotry, homophobia, oppression, repression, or any other type of ordained unconscious, dysfunctional, fear-based behavior. It may then be perceived even more vividly that because the truth of oneself is the unchanging constant which is always available at every moment, the opportunity to awaken to that truth is also available at every moment. Yet as it's also typical for one to experience a spiritual awakening and then 'go back to sleep,' Arjuna's next question is particularly poignant. He's essentially asking: "How can I recognize one who has awakened to the truth and *stayed* awake?"

### 54
*arjuna uvacha:*
*sthita-prajnasya ka bhasha / samadhi-sthasya keshava*
*sthitadhih kim prabhasheta / kim asita vrajeta kim*

*arjunah uvacha* > Arjuna said; *sthita-prajnasya* > firmly established
in the insight-wisdom born of universal Intelligence; *ka* > what;
*bhasha* > definition, description; *samadhi-sthasya* > stabilized in original
clarity or 'emptiness' of mind; *keshava* > O handsome-haired one;
*sthitadhih* > imperturbable, steady-minded; *kim* > how;
*prabhasheta* > one would speak; *kim* > from where; *asita* > one
would sit, one would dwell; *vrajeta* > one would move; *kim* > how.

**Arjuna inquired:**
**O Keshava, what are the characteristics of one**
**who is stabilized in original clarity of mind,**
**Who is imperturbable,**
**And is firmly established in the insight-wisdom**
**born of universal Intelligence?**

**Where would such a one be dwelling,
And in what manner would that person speak
and move about [in the world]?**

As mentioned in regard to the word *Brahman* used in the notes to verse 43, the term *samadhi* is also synonymous with one's true nature and is not a state. It is spoken of as a state in relation to particular types of experiences registered in a body/mind system for a particular period of time, yet in fact refers to That which entirely forgets Its imagined affiliation with both the body/mind system and time altogether.

### 55

*sri bhagavan uvacha:*
*prajahati yada kaman / sarvan partha manogatan*
*atmanyevatmana tooshtah / sthita-prajnas tadochyate*

*sri bhagavan uvacha* > the radiant one (Krishna) said; *prajahati* > leaves, departs; *yada* > when; *kaman* > desires; *sarvan* > all; *partha* > O son of Pritha; *manah-gatan* > arising in the mind; *atmani* > in oneself; *eva* > only; *atmana* > by oneself; *tooshtah* > contented; *sthita-prajnah* > firmly established in insight-wisdom; *tada* > then; *uchyate* > it is said.

**The radiant Krishna replied:
When all wanting departs from the mind, O Partha,
and one finds contentment simply in oneself alone —
One is then said to be firmly established in the wisdom of the heart.**

Because contentment (*ananda*) is an aspect of pure Spirit along with presence (*sat*) and awareness (*chid*), it is unconditioned and unconditional in regard to all that is.

### 56

*duhkheshva-'nudvigna-manah / sukheshu vigata-sprihah*
*vita-raga-bhaya-krodhah / sthitadhir munir uchyate*

*duhkheshu* > in adversity, in misery; *anudvigna-manah* > one whose mind is not shaken; *sukheshu* > in pleasures; *vigata-sprihah* > whose cravings have disappeared; *vita* > vanished; *raga* > impassionment; *bhaya* > fear; *krodhah* > anger; *sthita-dhih* > one who is steady-minded; *munih* > a sage, a seer, one who is moved by inner inspiration or ecstasy; *uchyate* > one is said to be.

One whose mind is not shaken in times of adversity,
Whose cravings for sense-pleasures have disappeared,
And whose impassionment, fear, and anger have vanished —
Such a one is said to be a steady-minded sage or sagess
moved by inner inspiration.

**57**

*yah sarvatra-'nabhisnehas / tat tat prapya shubhashubham
nabhinandati na dveshti / tasya prajna pratishthita*

*yah* > who; *sarvatra* > at all times, in all cases; *anabhisnehah* > unimpassioned;
*tat tat* > this or that; *prapya* > encountering; *shubha* > agreeable;
*ashubham* > disagreeable; *na* > not; *abhinandati* > rejoicing; *na* > not;
*dveshti* > hating; *tasya* > of this one; *prajna* > heart-wisdom,
insight-wisdom; *pratishthita* > firmly established.

One who always remains unimpassioned, whatever is encountered —
whether agreeable or disagreeable —
Who neither rejoices nor despises —
Such a one displays signs of being firmly established
in the heart's wisdom.

**58**

*yada samharate chayam / kurmonganiva sarvashah
indriyan'-indriyarthebhyas / tasya prajna pratishthita*

*yada* > when; *samharate* > one withdraws; *cha* > and; *ayam* > this one;
*kurmah* > tortoise; *angani* > limbs; *iva* > like; *sarvashah* > altogether;
*indriyani* > senses; *indriya-arthebhyah* > from the objects of the senses;
*tasya* > that one; *prajna* > insight-wisdom; *pratishthita* > firmly established.

And when one altogether withdraws the senses
from [attachment to specific] objects
Just as a tortoise retracts its limbs into its shell,
[This, too, indicates that] insight-wisdom within one
has been firmly established.

Another possible reading of this verse is that it could be referring to one
whose senses are altogether withdrawn from their objects temporarily during
the practice of meditation. It can't, however, be taken to mean that one's
senses are altogether withdrawn from all objects at all times, because in such
a situation life could not be maintained within the body, as Krishna will later
confirm in verse 3.8.

### 59

*vishaya vinivartante / niraharasya dehinah*
*rasavarjam raso 'pyasya / param drishtva nivartate*

*vishayah* > the energetic influence of objects which are pleasing to the senses; *vinivartante* > cessation, turning back; *niraharasya* > from the fasting; *dehinah* > of one with attention localized to one particular body; *rasa varjam* > except the taste (meaning that the memory of the taste for the objects yet remains); *rasah* > taste; *api* > although; *asya* > of this one; *param* > beyond, the highest; *drishtva* > viewing, perceiving; *nivartate* > it ceases, it retreats.

**Objects pleasing to the senses**
**cease to energetically influence one who is 'fasting' from them**
**(whose interest is withdrawn from them),**
**Yet the memory of the taste for those objects still lingers.**
**That [conditioned residual] taste also retreats, however,**
**When one begins perceiving beyond [the appearance of] localization**
**in one particular body.**

### 60

*yatato hyapi kaunteya / purushasya vipashchitah*
*indriyani pramathini / haranti prasabham manah*

*yatatah* > of the one who exerts effort; *hi* > truly; *api* > even; *kaunteya* > O son of Kunti; *purushasya* > of a person; *vipashchitah* > of great learning; *indriyani* > the senses; *pramathini* > tormenting; *haranti* > they carry away; *prasabham* > forcibly; *manah* > the mind.

**The senses can be so tormenting**
**as to forcibly carry away the mind**
**Even of a very learned person**
**who is exerting great effort [to control them], O Kaunteya.**

### 61

*tani sarvani samyamya / yukta asita matparah*
*vashe hi yasyendriyani / tasya prajna pratishthita*

*tani* > these (senses); *sarvani* > all; *samyamya* > restraining, subduing; *yuktah* > endowed with; *asita* > sitting; *mat-parah* > focused upon Me, considering Me to be supreme; *vashe* > under control; *hi* > certainly; *yasya* > of whom;

*indriyani* > the senses; *tasya* > of that one; *prajna* > insight-wisdom, the heart's wisdom; *pratishthita* > firmly established.

**But one is endowed with natural restraint of all the senses**
**by simply sitting focused upon Me (pure Awareness Itself).**
**One whose senses are under control in this way**
**is certainly firmly established in insight-wisdom.**

Krishna here speaks from the standpoint of being the one omnipresent Spirit-Self of all life, which He will later confirm in verse 10.20: *aham atma gudakesha / sarva-bhutashaya-sthitah, aham adishcha madhyam cha / bhutanam anta eva cha* — "I am the Self, O conqueror of sloth, abiding within the heart of every living being. I am the beginning, the middle, and indeed, the end of all beings in existence." And in verse 10.22 He states: *bhutanam asmi chetana* — "I am Consciousness in all beings." At the same time, it has been demonstrated by many devotee-saints throughout recorded history such as Tukaram, Mirabai, Namadeva, and Raghunath Das Goswami that the same effortless sense-restraint was available when the focus of attention was on the humanlike form of Krishna.

**62**
*dhyayato vishayan pumsah / sangas teshupajayate*
*sangat sanjayate kamah / kamat krodho 'bhijayate*

*dhyayatah* > of dwelling upon; *vishayan* > objects of the senses;
*pumsah* > of a person; *sangah* > attachment; *teshu* > to them;
*upajayate* > it arises; *sangat* > from attachment; *sanjayate* > it is produced;
*kamah* > desire; *kamat* > from desire; *krodhah* > anger; *abhijayate* > it is born.

**When a person dwells upon objects of the senses,**
**attachment arises;**
**From attachment, desire is produced;**
**and desire gives birth to anger.**

Anger can certainly be birthed by mentally ruminating upon potential obstructions to the fulfillment of a desire, or by becoming frustrated in the attempt to acquire a desired object. Yet the more immediate and often overlooked cause of anger may be the subconscious feeling that having any desire at all signifies some kind of lack, weakness, or incompleteness in oneself. The very condition of wanting may be subtly sensed to be contrary to our true nature as *ananda* or causeless contentment Itself.

## 63

*krodhad bhavati sammohah / sammohat smriti-vibhramah*
*smriti-bhramshad buddhi-nasho / buddhi-nashat pranashyati*

*krodhat* > from anger; *bhavati* > it comes about, it happens;
*sammohah* > delusion; *sammohat* > from delusion; *smriti* > memory;
*vibhramah* > wavering unsteadily, vacillating to and fro;
*smriti-bhramshat* > from memory declining or slipping down;
*buddhi-nashah* > deterioration of the power of discernment;
*buddhi-nashat* > from destruction of the power of
discernment; *pranashyati* > one is lost.

**From anger, delusion comes about,**
**and from delusion comes wavering of memory.**
**When memory declines, the power of discernment deteriorates,**
**And when the power of discernment is ruined,**
**one is lost [in the dream of misidentified selfhood].**

The Absolute never loses Its true nature; It can only temporarily lose the
*perceiving* of Its true nature when It is functioning through a body/mind
system which is out of alignment as a clear conduit for It (*ayukta*, verse 5.12).
This is confirmed by Krishna in verse 20 — *ajo nityah shashvato 'yam* (this
Presence is unborn and Its nature as such is permanent), and verse 21 —
*enam ajam avyayam* (this Presence is unborn and is not subject to change).

## 64

*ragadvesha-viyuktais tu / vishayan indriyaish charan*
*atma-vashyair vidheyatma / prasadam adhigachchati*

*raga* > inflamed longings; *dvesha* > aversions; *viyuktaih* > detached;
*tu* > but; *vishayan* > sense-objects; *indriyaih* > by the senses; *charan* > engaging;
*atma-vashyaih* > by self-restraint; *vidheya-atma* > to be utilized or ruled by
the Spirit-Self (refers to the mind, as confirmed in the next verse);
*prasadam* > clarity, serenity; *adhigachchati* > one attains.

**But there is a [natural] detaching from inflamed longings and aversions**
**And [effortless] self-restraint in the senses' interactions with their objects**
**When the mind utilized by the Spirit-Self attains clarity**
**(Thus allowing for Awareness to shine through it**
**without obstruction or distortion).**

The specific elements of the clarity mentioned here will be delineated by Krishna in upcoming verse 71. Like a mirror, the mind cannot see the radiant Presence reflected within it, but if the mirror is clear, that Radiance can intuitively know Itself, although not as an object. Because It is not a thing composed of material elements, the supreme fullness known as Brahman has sometimes been likened to the Emptiness (*shunyata*) spoken of in the teachings of Buddhism.

## 65

*prasade sarva-duhkhanam / hanir asyopajayate*
*prasanna-chetaso hyashu / buddhih paryavatishthate*

*prasade* > in clarity and serenity; *sarva* > all;
*duhkhanam* > of suffering; *hanih* > cessation; *asya* > of this;
*upajayate* > it arises; *prasanna-chetasah* > of one whose mind is clear;
*hi* > indeed; *ashu* > quickly, immediately; *buddhih* > incisive
discernment; *paryavatishthate* > it becomes steady.

**In that pristine clarity and serenity**
**arises the cessation of all suffering.**
**Indeed, for one whose mind is clear,**
**the power of incisive discernment quickly becomes steady.**

## 66

*nasti buddhir ayuktasya / na chayuktasya bhavana*
*na chabhavayatah shantir / ashantasya kutah sukham*

*na asti* > there is not; *buddhih* > incisive discernment; *ayuktasya* > of one
who is unrestrained; *na* > not; *cha* > and; *ayuktasya* > of the unrestrained one;
*bhavana* > conceiving, contemplating, directing of attention; *na* > not;
*cha* > and; *abhavayatah* > of one lacking the power to conceive, contemplate,
or direct one's attention; *shantih* > peace; *ashantasya* > of one
without peace; *kutah* > from where; *sukham* > happiness.

**The power of incisive discernment does not manifest**
**within one whose senses are completely unrestrained;**
**nor does the power to direct one's attention.**
**Without the power to direct one's attention, there can be no peace;**
**and without peace, where will one find happiness?**

As with the clarity mentioned previously, the peace mentioned here is also an aspect of one's true nature. This will be confirmed in upcoming verse 72.

### 67

*indriyanam hi charatam / yan mano 'nuvidhiyate*
*tadasya harati prajnam / vayur navam ivambhasi*

*indriyanam* > of the senses; *hi* > indeed; *charatam* > in wandering;
*yat* > when; *manah* > the mind; *anuvidhiyate* > it is guided; *tat* > that;
*asya* > of one; *harati* > it carries away; *prajnam* > intuitive wisdom;
*vayuh* > wind; *navam* > boat; *iva* > like; *ambhasi* > on the water.

**As a boat on a body of water is swept off course**
**by turbulent winds,**
**So is one's intuitive wisdom carried away by the turbulent mind**
**when it is guided by the wandering senses.**

### 68

*tasmad yasya maha-baho / nigrihitani sarvashah*
*indriyanindriy'-arthebhyas / tasya prajna pratishthita*

*tasmat* > therefore; *yasya* > of whom; *maha-baho* > O mighty-armed one;
*nigrihitani* > restrained, withdrawn; *sarvashah* > altogether, collectively;
*indriyani* > the senses; *indriya-arthebhyah* > from the objects of the senses;
*tasya* > of one; *prajna* > insight-wisdom; *pratishthita* > firmly established.

**Therefore, O mighty-armed one,**
**Whenever one's collective senses are withdrawn from their objects,**
**This allows insight-wisdom [an opportunity]**
**to become firmly established.**

### 69

*ya nisha sarva-bhutanam / tasyam jagarti samyami*
*yasyam jagrati bhutani / sa nisha pashyato muneh*

*ya* > what; *nisha* > night; *sarva-bhutanam* > of all sentient beings;
*tasyam* > in this (insight-wisdom); *jagarti* > one is awake;
*samyami* > the self-restrained one; *yasyam* > in that (the doctrine
which had been heard, believed, and passed down through
the ages, as described in verses 42, 46, 52, and 53);
*jagrati* > they are awake; *bhutani* > sentient beings;
*sa* > that; *nisha* > night; *pashyatah* > of those who perceive;
*muneh* > of the male and female sages.

The self-restrained ones are awake
to [the guiding illumination of] the heart's wisdom,
which is like nighttime for all sentient beings [who are asleep to it];
And the ['guiding light' of] inherited doctrine and dogma
which all sentient beings are awake to
Is like the darkness of night for the sages and sagesses
who perceive [things as they truly are].

### 70

*apuryamanam achala-pratishtham / samudram apah pravishanti yadvat*
*tadvat kama yam pravishanti sarve / sa shantim apnoti na kama-kami*

*apuryamanam* > becoming filled; *achala* > unmoved; *pratishtham* > remaining
steadfast; *samudram* > ocean; *apah* > the waters (such as rivers and rains);
*pravishanti* > they enter; *yadvat* > as; *tadvat* > in this way; *kamah* > desires;
*yam* > whom; *pravishanti* > they enter; *sarve* > all; *sah* > this one;
*shantim* > peace, stillness; *apnoti* > one reaches; *na* > not;
*kama-kami* > desiring that which is desirable.

As the ocean remains steadfast
and unmoved by all the waters which enter into it,
So do those who reach [the recognition of being] Stillness Itself
remain unmoved by all the desires which enter into them.
Yet this is not so for those
within whom there is seeking for the fulfillment of desires.

Upon the recognition of being dynamically aware stillness, there is the
perceiving and living of life from that realization rather than from
identification with the thoughts and emotions which arise and subside
within the stillness. In the words of Ramana Maharshi: "Let what comes
come, let what goes go, and simply notice what never comes or goes."

### 71

*vihaya kaman yah sarvan / pumansh charati nihsprihah*
*nirmamo nirahamkarah / sa shantim adhigachchati*

*vihaya* > having abandoned; *kaman* > desires, longings; *yah* > who;
*sarvan* > all; *puman* > the person; *charati* > lives; *nihsprihah* > free from
wanting anything; *nirmamah* > free from the sense of being the possessor
of anything; *nirahamkarah* > free from the egoic sense of being the
independently-functioning doer of any actions; *sah* > this one;
*shantim* > peace; *adhigachchati* > discovers.

**Having abandoned all conditioned patterns of longings,**
**Living free from wanting [or seeking] anything,**
**Free from the sense of being the possessor of anything,**
**And free from the sense of being the doer of any actions —**
**Such a one discovers profound peace.**

*Nirmamah*, freedom from the sense that 'this is mine,' does not refer only to objects, but also to thoughts, emotions, beliefs, opinions, attitudes, complaints, experiences, relationships, and identities — in short, to any stories about oneself.

### 72

*esha brahmi sthitih partha / nainam prapya vimuhyati*
*sthitvasyam antakale 'pi / brahma-nirvanam richchati*

*esha* > this (profound peace); *brahmi* > of one's true nature as Brahman; *sthitih* > continuance in being, constancy; *partha* > O son of Pritha; *na* > not; *enam* > this; *prapya* > having attained; *vimuhyati* > one is confused, one is infatuated; *sthitva* > firmly situated, settled; *asyam* > in this; *anta-kale* > at the end of the body's lifespan; *api* > even; *brahma* > in Brahman, absolute Consciousness; *nirvanam* > cessation, 'extinguishing the flame'; *richchati* > one meets with (referring to the assumed egoic self).

**This ineffable peace is the unchanging constant of one's natural state**
**as Brahman (pure Consciousness), O Partha.**
**Having attained [recognition of] that,**
**one does not again fall prey to confusion or infatuation.**
**Settled thus even at the time**
**when the functioning of the physical body altogether ceases,**
**The assumed self meets with cessation in absolute Consciousness,**
**Just as a candle's flame is extinguished.**

Eventually, all attempts to describe Brahman with words also meet with cessation at a certain point. Until that time, however, the word 'Consciousness' appearing throughout the Gita is not ever intended as a synonym for thought or thinking, but is only used to indicate That which is conscious *of* all thought and thinking.

*om tat saditi srimad bhagavad-gita / supanishatsu brahma-vidyayam*
*yoga-shastre srikrishnarjuna samvade / sankhya-yogo nama dvitiyo 'dhyayah*

From the Ambrosial Song of God—
A conversation between Krishna and Arjuna
which is a Upanishad (confidential sharing)
of wisdom-teachings regarding the Absolute
And a scripture concerning Self-realization—
Thus ends the Second Chapter entitled Sankhya-yoga,
Recognizing Divine Unicity By Way of Empirical Knowledge.

# Chapter Three

---

# Karma-yoga
## (Recognizing Divine Unicity By Way of Selfless Action)

"No thing exists, there are only actions. We live in a world of verbs, and nouns are only shorthand for those verbs whose actions are sufficiently stationary to show some thing-like behavior. These statements may seem like philosophy or poetry, but in fact they are an accurate description of the material world, when we take into account the quantum nature of reality.... In the words of [David Mermin]: 'Correlations have physical reality; that which they correlate does not.' In other words, matter acts, but there are no actors behind the actions; the verbs are verbing all by themselves without a need to introduce nouns. Actions act upon other actions. The ontology of the world thus becomes remarkably simple, with no duality between the existence of a thing and its properties: properties are all there is. Indeed, there are no things." — Piet Hut

"Having decided to do whatever you choose to do, thereafter what is your own personal experience? Have all your decisions turned into actual actions? Supposing some of your decisions have indeed turned into actions; have all those actions always produced the results that you have anticipated, and for which you have held yourself responsible? The answer is obvious: some of your decisions have turned into actions, some have not; some of your actions have produced the anticipated results, some have not. Indeed, quite a few of 'your' actions have produced results quite contrary to your expectations. Therefore, it is your own experience that your 'free will' extends merely to making a decision. What happens thereafter is, from your own experience, not in your control because various other factors come into play over which you have no control.

"Now, let us investigate the supposed free will you have to make a decision. What is 'your' decision based on? If you investigate this point you will find out that you always base your decision on your 'programming,' i.e. your genes or DNA, and your conditioning which includes your education and practical experience, over which you truly have had no control.

"...So consider for yourself: how genuine is my 'free will'?.... There must be an honest and thorough investigation into what you think are 'your' actions from day to day." — Ramesh S. Balsekar

**1**
*arjuna uvacha:*
*jyayasi chet karmanas te / mata buddhir janardana*
*tat kim karmani ghore mam / niyojayasi keshava*

*arjunah uvacha* > Arjuna said; *jyayasi* > superior; *chet* > if;
*karmanah* > than the performance of actions; *te* > by you; *mata* > thought,
considered; *buddhih* > incisive discernment; *janardana* > O agitator
of people; *tat* > then; *kim* > why; *karmani* > to the performance of actions;
*ghore* > terrible; *mam* > me; *niyojayasi* > you are urging
to engage; *keshava* > O handsome-haired one.

**Arjuna said:**
**O agitator of people,**
**If you consider [the application of] incisive discernment**
**to be superior to [engaging the senses in] performing actions,**
**Then why, O handsome one,**
**do you urge me to engage in the terrible actions of warfare?**

**2**
*vyamishreneva vakyena / buddhim mohayasiva me*
*tad ekam vada nishchitya / yena shreyo 'ham apnuyam*

*vyamishrena* > by contradictory; *iva* > as if, seemingly; *vakyena* > by
words; *buddhim* > power of discernment, intellect; *mohayasi* > you
are confusing; *iva* > somewhat; *me* > my; *tat* > that; *ekam* > one;
*vada* > tell; *nishchitya* > having ascertained; *yena* > by which;
*shreyah* > the greater benefit; *aham* > I; *apnuyam* > would obtain.

**Your seemingly contradictory words**
**are somewhat confusing to my discerning ability.**
**Please tell me what you ascertain to be the one thing**
**which would be most beneficial for me.**

In verses 65 and 66 of Chapter Two, Krishna told Arjuna that for one whose
mind is clear, the power of incisive discernment quickly becomes steady, but
that this power does not manifest within one whose senses are unrestrained.
And in verse 68 he said that when one's collective senses are withdrawn
from their objects, this allows insight-wisdom to become firmly established.
So Arjuna's gentle protest here is entirely justifiable, as he has been doing
nothing else *but* expressing his keen interest in withdrawing his senses from
the battlefield since the middle of Chapter One.

**3**
*sri bhagavan uvacha:*
*loke 'smin dvividha nishtha / pura prokta mayanagha*
*jnana-yogena sankhyanam / karma-yogena yoginam*

*sri bhagavan uvacha* > the adorable one said; *loke asmin* > in this world;
*dvi-vidha* > of two types; *nishtha* > steadfast devotion, applied conviction;
*pura* > formerly, in ancient times; *prokta* > taught; *maya* > by me; *anagha* >
O faultless one; *jnana-yogena* > by the cultivation of direct knowing through
direct experience; *sankhyanam* > for those engaged in empirical analysis of the
material elements which constitute the world and discerning them from the
Spirit-Self; *karma-yogena* > by the performance of selfless work; *yoginam* >
for those engaged in disciplining and purifying the body/mind system.

**The adorable one (Krishna) said:**
**Two types of devotion have formerly been taught by me**
**in this world, O faultless one:**
**The cultivation of direct knowing through direct experience**
**for those engaged in empirically analyzing the body/mind system**
**and discerning it from the Spirit-Self,**
**And the performance of selfless work**
**for those engaged in disciplining and purifying the body/mind system**
**[in preparation for the cultivation of direct knowing].**

**4**
*na karmanam anarambhan / naishkarmyam purusho 'shnute*
*na cha sannyasanad eva / siddhim samadhi-gachchati*

*na* > not; *karmanam* > from activity; *anarambhat* > by abstention;
*naishkarmyam* > freedom from the cycle of action and reaction;
*purushah* > a person; *ashnute* > one attains; *na* > not; *cha* > and;
*sannyasanat* > by renunciation; *eva* > alone; *siddhim* > perfection;
*samadhigachchati* > one goes toward, one comes near to.

**Not by abstaining from activity does a person obtain freedom**
**from the cycle of action and reaction,**
**Nor by renunciation alone**
**does one approach perfection.**

**5**
*na hi kashchit kshanamapi / jatu tishthatya-'karmakrit*
*karyate hyavashah karma / sarvah prakriti-jair gunaih*

*na* > not; *hi* > indeed; *kashchit* > anyone; *kshanam* > a moment; *api* > even; *jatu* > at any time; *tishthati* > one remains; *akarma-krit* > not performing action; *karyate* > one is compelled to perform; *hi* > surely; *avashah* > unwillingly, helplessly; *karma* > action; *sarvah* > everyone; *prakriti-jaih* > originating in Nature; *gunaih* > by the qualities, by the components.

**Indeed, no one can remain without performing some type of action**
**at any time, even for a moment.**
**Everyone is helplessly compelled to perform activity**
**in accordance with the qualities originating in Nature.**

**6**
*karmendriyani samyamya / ya aste manasa smaran*
*indriyarthan vimudhatma / mithya-'charah sa uchyate*

*karma-indriyani* > the active sense-organs; *samyamya* > restraining;
*yah* > who; *aste* > one sits; *manasa* > by the mind; *smaran* > thinking of;
*indriya-arthan* > objects of the senses; *vimudhatma* > self-deluded;
*mithya-acharah* > behaving hypocritically; *sah* > this;
*uchyate* > one is said to be.

**One who restrains the active sense-organs**
**yet dwells on the objects of the senses within the mind**
**Is said to be behaving**
**in a self-deluded, hypocritical way.**

**7**
*yas tvindriyani manasa / niyamya 'rabhate'rjuna*
*karmendriyaih karma-yogam / asaktah sa vishishyate*

*yah* > who; *tu* > but; *indriyani* > the senses; *manasa* > by way of the mind;
*niyamya* > directing, defining; *arabhate* > one attempts; *arjuna* > O Arjuna;
*karma-indriyaih* > by the active sense-organs; *karma-yogam* > the performance
of action without any motive for personal gain; *asaktah* > without
attachment; *sah* > that one; *vishishyate* > is superior.

**But one who attempts to direct the senses**
**by way of the mind, O Arjuna,**
**Engaging the active sense-organs in performing actions**
**without any attachment or motives for personal gain**
**is superior.**

The more there is the clarity of mind mentioned in verse 2.65 (*prasanna-chetasah*), the greater is the influence of one's unborn nature (pure Spirit or infinite Consciousness) on one's born nature (the dreamlike expression of Spirit as the physical body and internal network). Thereby the directing of the senses encouraged by Krishna here and elsewhere throughout the Gita becomes possible through the focusing of intention and the directing of attention, two capabilities naturally inherent within Consciousness.

**8**

*niyatam kuru karma tvam / karma jyayo hyakarmanah*
*sharira-yatrapi cha te / na prasiddhyed akarmanah*

*niyatam* > established, prescribed, customary; *kuru* > do perform;
*karma* > duty; *tvam* > you; *karma* > activity; *jyayah* > better;
*hi* > truly; *akarmanah* > than inactivity; *sharira* > the physical body;
*yatra* > maintenance; *api* > even; *cha* > and; *te* > your; *na* > not;
*prasiddhyet* > it can be accomplished; *akarmanah* > without activity.

**Therefore do perform your appropriately established duty,**
**because activity is truly better than inactivity,**
**And even the maintenance of your physical body**
**could not be accomplished without activity...!**

**9**

*yajnarthat karmano 'nyatra / loko 'yam karma-bandhanah*
*tadartham karma kaunteya / mukta-sangah samachara*

*yajna-arthat* > for the purpose of giving or offering something
of oneself; *karmanah* > proceeding from action; *anyatra* > aside from;
*lokah* > world; *ayam* > this; *karma-bandhanah* > bound by action;
*tat* > that; *artham* > purpose; *karma* > duty; *kaunteya* > O son of Kunti;
*mukta-sangah* > freed from attachment; *samachara* > do perform.

**Aside from those actions which are performed**
**for the purpose of giving or offering something of oneself,**
**Actions tend to have a binding effect within this world.**
**Therefore, do perform your duties with that purpose, O son of Kunti,**
**free from attachment.**

The principle which Krishna mentions here about the binding effect of egocentric action is so comprehensively applicable that sometimes, when spiritual students become obsessive *even* about achieving enlightenment on the basis of personal exertion, teachers have been known to advise them to "Just stop now. *Tat tvam asi* — you are already That (pure Spirit). There's nothing which you need to accomplish." And indeed, Krishna himself will state that "There's nothing I need to accomplish" in upcoming verse 22. Yet when spiritual students are observed to adopt this as an *attitude* without the genuine realization of their true nature, teachers have also been known to say: "My friend, it would be best for you not to court laziness and self-indulgence. I would strongly recommend continuing your spiritual practices with renewed determination." This is why it has so often been said that it's far better to receive direct individual guidance from a living Self-realized spiritual teacher if one is available than to rely solely on the books of teachers who are no longer physically present in the world. Such living teachers may also be able to draw out fuller perspectives on the words and writings of teachers from the past, and present them in a way which is most immediately relevant to each student in his or her own particular situation.

**10**
*saha-yajnah prajah srishtva / purovacha prajapatih*
*anena prasavishyadhvam / esha vo'stvishta-kamadhuk*

*saha* > along with; *yajnah* > the principle of sacrifice, the dedicating principle, the energetic inclination of giving; *prajah* > humankind; *srishtva* > having created, having emitted or produced; *pura* > in the beginning; *uvacha* > said; *praja-patih* > the 'Lord of all creatures'; *anena* > by this (referring to the giving or dedicating spirit); *prasavishyadhvam* > may you bring forth (referring to progeny and prosperity); *eshah* > this; *vah* > your; *astu* > be it so; *ishta-kama-dhuk* > fulfilling all desires like a Cow of Plenty.

**In the beginning, the Lord of all beings**
**created humankind along with the principle of sacrifice**
**and said: "May you happily flourish and prosper.**
**May the performance of sacrifices be for you**
**a wish-fulfilling Cow of Plenty.**

*Prajapati* traditionally refers to Brahma ('growth,' 'expansion,' 'evolution,' 'development'), represented as the personified creative aspect of infinite Consciousness which performs the function of spontaneously manifesting the dreamlike universes. An alternate expanded interpretation of this verse might read: "At the very moment that infinite Consciousness became aware that It exists ('I am'), Its innate creative power produced of Itself a conceptual space within which to exist — a space filled with an infinitude of variegated life-forms within which It could continue expressing Its creativity ad infinitum. This represents a movement from *asamprajnata samadhi*, seedless

Awareness without any contents, to *samprajnata samadhi*, Awareness containing the seed-ideation of time, space, and forms. Those forms were imbued with the innate inclination of giving, along with the sense that by living according to that natural predilection, all of life's necessities would be provided as naturally as milk is provided by a cow."

Also, when the word 'sacrifice' here is understood in its fullest and most immediate context, it is not limited to only meaning an extravagant ritual ceremony or painful act of self-denial. Rather, it connotes a simple availability and willingness to contribute to the wholeness of life by meeting the necessity of each moment with an earnest inquiry of: "What is really called for in this situation?" Thereby the word 'sacrifice' would more holistically represent a unifying spirit of sharing, caring, and serving, in contrast to its energetically separating opposite of hoarding, ignoring, and exploiting.

### 11

*devan bhavayatanena / te deva bhavayantu vah*
*parasparam bhavayantah / shreyah param avapsyatha*

*devan* > the celestials (expressions of Being in more subtle
dimensions of Consciousness); *bhavayata* > may you nurture;
*anena* > by this (the energetic vibration of giving); *te* > they;
*devah* > the celestials; *bhavayantu* > may they nurture; *vah* > you;
*parasparam* > mutually; *bhavayantah* > attending to the
well-being of one another; *shreyah* > benefit;
*param* > highest; *avapsyatha* > you will obtain.

**"May you nurture the celestials by these sacrifices,**
**and may they nurture you as well.**
**By attending to the mutual well-being of one another,**
**you will both obtain the highest benefit.**

Another meaning of *devan* is 'the gods, the shining ones.' So from the standpoint of the biblical statement "I say that ye are all gods, all children of the Most High" in Psalms 82:6, *devan* here would be inclusive of other human beings as well rather than exclusively refer to subtler life-forms in other strata of Consciousness. And as the celestials represent the various elements, energies, and aspects of Nature, this verse would also be advocating reciprocal tending and caregiving of humankind with the Earth, its oceans, its skies, and all of life.

**12**

*ishtan bhogan hi vo deva / dasyante yajna-bhavitah*
*tair dattan apradayaibhyo / yo bhunkte stena eva sah*

*ishtan* > wished-for, loved; *bhogan* > experiences, feelings, perceptions, enjoyments; *hi* > certainly; *vah* > unto you; *devah* > the celestials; *dasyante* > they will provide; *yajna-bhavitah* > nurtured by sacrifice; *taih* > by these; *dattan* > gifts; *apradaya* > not offering; *ebhyah* > to them; *yah* > who; *bhunkte* > one enjoys; *stenah* > thief; *eva* > surely; *sah* > that one.

**"Being nurtured by sacrifice,**
**the celestials will certainly provide you**
**with all wished-for experiences."**
**Thus, one who enjoys the [miraculous] gifts of the celestials**
**without making some offering to them in return**
**must surely be considered a thief.**

The word 'miraculous' has been included here because if there is even a momentary pause for reflection on the phenomenon of the one undivided Love conceiving of Itself in an infinite variety of forms for experiencing the infinite variety of feelings, sensations, sounds, sights, tastes, textures, and fragrances, it immediately inspires a profound sense of wonder, humility, and gratitude.

**13**

*yajna-shishtashinah santo / muchyante sarva-kilbishaih*
*bhunjate te tvagham papa / ye pachantyatma-karanat*

*yajna-shishta* > the food remaining after portions have been offered (either to one's ishtadeva [preferred deity or representative of Life's inherent divinity], to the celestials, to one's teachers or priests, or to others); *ashinah* > eating; *santah* > virtuous, kindly, openhearted; *muchyante* > they are released; *sarva-kilbishaih* > from all kinds of fault, guilt, or affliction; *bhunjate* > eat; *te* > they; *tu* > but; *agham* > impurity, misery; *papah* > the wretched or selfish ones; *ye* > who; *pachanti* > they prepare food; *atma-karanat* > only for themselves.

**The openhearted ones,**
**who eat after offering their food to the celestials and others,**
**are relieved from all kinds of afflictions.**
**But the closed-hearted,**
**who prepare food only for themselves,**
**verily consume the misery [of their own mindset].**

**14**

*annad bhavanti bhutani / parjanyad anna-sambhavah*
*yajnad bhavati parjanyo / yajnah karma-samudbhavah*

*annat* > from food; *bhavanti* > they exist; *bhutani* > the living beings;
*parjanyat* > from rain; *anna* > food; *sambhavah* > source; *yajnat* > from giving,
from sacrificing; *bhavati* > comes to be; *parjanyah* > rain; *yajnah* > offering,
sacrificing; *karma* > action; *samudbhavah* > cause, origin.

**Living beings are sustained by food,**
**Food is produced as a result of rainfall,**
**Rainfall is an offering, a sacrifice on the part of Nature,**
**And that sacrifice is brought about by action.**

**15**

*karma brahmodbhavam viddhi / brahmakshara-samudbhavam*
*tasmat sarva-gatam brahma / nityam yajne pratishthitam*

*karma* > action; *brahma* > Brahma (the Creator aspect of pure Spirit);
*udbhavam* > springing from; *viddhi* > please know; *brahma* > Brahman
(pure Spirit, infinite Consciousness); *akshara* > the imperishable;
*samudbhavam* > originating from, being the source of; *tasmat* > therefore;
*sarva-gatam* > all-pervading; *brahma* > Brahman, the Supreme Truth;
*nityam* > eternally; *yajne* > in sacrifice; *pratishthitam* > abiding in, situated in.

**Know that all action —**
**which springs from Brahma, the initial creative impulse —**
**Has its origin in the imperishable Brahman, infinite Consciousness.**
**Therefore the omnipresent Truth eternally dwells**
**in expressions of sacrifice [such as giving and nurturing].**

Some translations of the Gita present that sacrificial action comes from
the Vedas, most likely owing to sacrificial action being so emphatically
inculcated in the Vedas. In any case, the *Mundaka Upanishad* 1.1.9 states:
"That imperishable Brahman which is the Knower of all that can ever be
known or experienced — *whose austerity consists of knowing* — from That is born
the Creator Brahma, names, forms, and food." This *tapas* (austerity) accepted
by the Absolute has also been described as 'purposeful intensity.'

**16**

*evam pravartitam chakram / nanuvartayatiha yah*
*aghayur indriyaramo / mogham partha sa jivati*

*evam* > thus; *pravartitam* > caused to roll forward, set in motion; *chakram* >
the wheel (referring to the ongoing reciprocation mentioned in verse 11);
*na* > not; *anuvartayati* > one rolls forward, one follows up; *iha* > in this world;
*yah* > who; *aghayuh* > malicious; *indriya-aramah* > delighting the senses;
*mogham* > uselessly; *partha* > O son of Pritha; *sah* > that one; *jivati* > lives.

> **Thus, one who in this world does not take part**
> **in turning the wheel which has been set in motion**
> **[Of reciprocal tending and caregiving**
> **between humankind and the rest of nature]**
> **is malicious, O Partha.**
> **Indeed, one who lives only for delighting the senses**
> **lives in vain.**

The turning of the wheel mentioned herein again connotes the *dharma* of
living consciously with a heartfelt spirit of service and support for the whole
of Life. And the *aghayuh*, the maliciousness mentioned in this verse, refers
to living unconsciously in pursuit of one's own interests regardless of the
impact one's actions may have on the Whole.

> **17**
> *yas tvatma-ratir eva syad / atma-triptash cha manavah*
> *atmanyeva cha santooshtas / tasya karyam na vidyate*

*yah* > who; *tu* > but; *atma-ratih* > whose joy is in the Spirit-Self; *eva* > only;
*syat* > one will be; *atma-triptah* > whose sense of fullness or completeness
is in the Spirit-Self; *cha* > and; *manavah* > a human being; *atmani* > in the
Spirit-Self; *eva* > only; *cha* > and; *santooshtah* > fully content; *tasya* > of that
one; *karyam* > obligatory duty or religious practice to be performed,
purpose to be achieved; *na* > not; *vidyate* > it is found.

> **But for one among humankind**
> **whose entire joy is in the Spirit-Self alone,**
> **Whose entire sense of completeness is in the Self alone,**
> **And whose entire contentment is in the Self alone —**
> **Such a one finds no activity which absolutely must be performed.**

Although the one mentioned here is no longer driven by desires to
accomplish personal goals, her or his body/mind system quite often still
continues to be engaged in some kind of benevolent activity as a natural
outflow of the love and compassion inherent in the true Self. This is a
spontaneous functioning which occurs with no sense of personal doership

(*nirahamkara*) or proprietorship (*nirmama*), and no attachment to either
the activity or its results.

### 18

*naiva tasya kritenartho / nakriteneha kashchana*
*na chasya sarva-bhuteshu / kashchid artha-vyapashrayah*

*na* > not; *eva* > indeed; *tasya* > of that one; *kritena* > by activity;
*arthah* > purpose; *na* > nor; *akritena* > by inactivity;
*iha* > in this world; *kashchana* > anything whatsoever; *na* > not;
*cha* > and; *asya* > of that one; *sarva-bhuteshu* > from among
all living beings; *kashchit* > any whatsoever;
*artha* > object or objective, advantage;
*vyapashrayah* > needing to rely or depend upon.

**Indeed, such a one has no purpose whatsoever to fulfill**
**by either performing or not performing any activity in this world,**
**Nor has that one any need to rely upon any living being**
**to provide any specific object [or facilitate any specific objective],**
**whatever it may be.**

### 19

*tasmad asaktah satatam / karyam karma samachara*
*asakto hyacharan karma / param apnoti purushah*

*tasmat* > therefore; *asaktah* > unattached [to receiving rewards or producing
expected results]; *satatam* > constantly; *karyam* > duty; *karma* > activities;
*samachara* > do perform; *asaktah* > without attachment; *hi* > indeed;
*acharan* > performing; *karma* > activities; *param* > the highest;
*apnoti* > one reaches; *purushah* > a person.

**Therefore, remaining ever unattached to receiving rewards**
**or producing expected results,**
**simply perform those activities which are your duty,**
**For in the performing of all activities without attachment,**
**a person reaches his or her highest [potential].**

### 20

*karmanaiva hi samsiddhim / asthita janakadayah*
*loka-sangraham evapi / sampashyan kartum arhasi*

*karmana* > by actions; *eva* > only; *hi* > indeed; *samsiddhim* > perfection; *asthitah* > attained; *janaka-adayah* > of kings beginning with Janaka ('progenitor,' king of Videha and father of Sita, the wife of King Ramachandra); *loka-sangraham* > maintenance and protection of the people; *eva* > only; *api* > even; *sampashyan* > seeing to, looking after; *kartum* > to perform actions; *arhasi* > you are obliged.

**Indeed, kings such as Janaka attained perfection
solely on the basis of his actions.
Thus, even if only for the sake of seeing to the maintenance and protection
of the general populace,
you are obliged to perform actions.**

In regard to King Janaka's 'attaining perfection,' it bears remembering that the body/mind apparatus known as King Janaka was not an independently-functioning entity. It is established in the Gita that all that exists is omnipresent Spirit (*vasudevah sarvam iti*, verse 7.19), and that each body/mind vessel is simply an instrument for the One to function through ("Just become a mere instrument in My hands, O ambidextrous archer" — *nimitta-matram bhava savyasachin*, verse 11.33). So when a body/mind system functions in a way which fully embodies the realization of oneness in all of life's day-to-day situations, it can then be said to have reached its highest potential or attained perfection. This is entirely different from the setting of goals in accordance with conditioned or contrived concepts about what perfection is.

### 21
*yadyad acharati shreshthas / tattad evetaro janah
sa yat pramanam kurute / lokas tad anuvartate*

*yad yad* > whatever; *acharati* > one exemplifies by his or her manner of behavior; *shreshthah* > most excellent, seniormost; *tat tad* > this and that, various; *eva* > indeed; *itarah* > other; *janah* > people; *sah* > that one; *yat* > which; *pramanam* > standard; *kurute* > one establishes; *lokah* > the world; *tat* > that; *anuvartate* > it follows, it attends to.

**Whatever manner of behavior is displayed by an outstanding person,
Other people will indeed [try to emulate] those various characteristics;
And whatever standards are established by the exemplary one,
the world will follow.**

## 22

*na me parthasti kartavyam / trishu lokeshu kinchana*
*nanavaptam avaptavyam / varta eva cha karmani*

*na* > not; *me* > of me; *partha* > O son of Pritha; *asti* > there is;
*kartavyam* > to be accomplished; *trishu lokeshu* > in the three worlds;
*kinchana* > anything whatsoever; *na* > nor; *anavaptam* > not obtained;
*avaptavyam* > yet to be obtained; *varte* > I engage;
*eva cha* > nonetheless; *karmani* > in actions.

**O Partha, within all the three worlds,**
**there is nothing whatsoever which I must accomplish,**
**Nor is there anything not yet obtained which I must obtain;**
**Yet nonetheless I engage in activity.**

## 23

*yadi hyaham na varteyam / jatu karmanyatandritah*
*mama vartma-'nuvartante / manushyah partha sarvashah*

*yadi* > if; *hi* > because; *aham* > I; *na* > not; *varteyam* > should
engage; *jatu* > ever; *karmani* > in activity; *atandritah* > full of vigor;
*mama* > my; *vartma* > path, way (as in by way of example);
*anuvartante* > they would follow; *manushyah* > humankind;
*partha* > O son of Pritha; *sarvashah* > collectively, everywhere.

**Because if I were [observed to be] to be full of vigor**
**yet never engaged in any activity,**
**Humankind everywhere would follow my path,**
**O son of Pritha.**

## 24

*utsideyur ime loka / na kuryam karma ched aham*
*sankarasya cha karta syam / upahanyam imah prajah*

*utsideyuh* > they would fall into ruin or decay, they would disappear, they
would be withdrawn; *ime* > these; *lokah* > worlds; *na* > not; *kuryam karma* >
I should perform activity; *chet* > if; *aham* > I; *sankarasya* > of mixing together,
of confusion; *cha* > and; *karta* > creator; *syam* > I would be; *upahanyam* >
I would harm, I would destroy; *imah* > these; *prajah* > offspring, living beings.

**If I did not perform activity,**
**the worlds would fall into ruination,**
**And I would be the creator of confusion and destruction**
**among living beings.**

From the viewpoint of Krishna representing absolute Consciousness, the meaning of the word *utsideyuh* really comes alive, as it is directly experienced that when all activity in Consciousness ceases and It is completely at rest — as in deep dreamless sleep or *asamprajnata samadhi* — all objects do indeed disappear, withdrawn from being perceived in any way. The difference between those two 'states' is that in deep dreamless sleep, although Awareness is fully present, the mind — the instrument through which perception of the environment takes place — is veiled by the quality of darkness (*tamas-guna*), so one can only recollect that nothing had been perceived when one awakens the following morning. In *asamprajnata samadhi*, however, which is beyond all states, the mind is completely clear, and so at that time when time is actually absent, self-illuminating Awareness is fully conscious of Its unlimited vastness and 'emptiness.'

### 25
*saktah karmanya-'vidvamso / yatha kurvanti bharata*
*kuryad vidvams tathasaktash / chikirshur loka-sangraham*

*saktah* > with attachment; *karmani* > in activities; *avidvamsah* > the unwise ones; *yatha* > as; *kurvanti* > they act; *bharata* > Arjuna, the descendant of Bharata; *kuryat* > one should do; *vidvan* > the wise ones; *tatha* > thus; *asaktah* > without attachment; *chikirshuh* > intending to do; *loka-sangraham* > maintenance of the world.

**As those who are unwise perform their activities with attachment,**
**O descendant of Bharata,**
**So should the wise act without attachment**
**with the intention of maintaining the world.**

As we'll continue to see in Krishna's discourse, his criteria for distinguishing between the wise and the unwise is not based on ability — intellectual acumen or skill in memorizing information — but on availability, the openness and willingness to discern what is actually true from what is only believed to be true. When one's genuine interest in such courageous Self-inquiry expands one's openness into the perspective of unitary wholeness, actions can then truly be performed selflessly, without desires and attachments that are inevitable when there is a sense of separation.

### 26
*na buddhi-bhedam janayed / ajnanam karma-sanginam*
*joshayet sarva-karmani / vidvan yuktah samacharan*

*na* > not; *buddhi* > mind, resolve, point of view; *bhedam* > difference, change, breaking; *janayet* > one ought to cause or generate; *ajnanam* > of the unwise; *karma-sanginam* > of those who perform activities with attachment; *joshayet* > one ought to approve of or give delight to; *sarva* > all; *karmani* > activities; *vidvan* > the wise one; *yuktah* > connected (as a channel for universal Intelligence, as discussed in Chapter Two, verses 39 through 53); *samacharan* > observing.

**Those who are wise**
**Ought not try to change the mindset or break the resolve**
**of the unwise who work with attachment;**
**They ought to encourage and enthuse them in all of their activities,**
**Observing that they, too, are functioning**
**precisely in accordance with the one universal Intelligence.**

Life functions as a unitary whole, with nothing whatsoever unconnected, including the unwise ones and all others in all forms. This principle is later reiterated in verse 5.18.

**27**
*prakriteh kriyamanani / gunaih karmani sarvashah*
*ahamkara-vimudhatma / kartaham iti manyate*

*prakriteh* > of Nature; *kriya-manani* > being done, movements or processes (*kriya*) being honored (*manani*); *gunaih* > by the components; *karmani* > activities; *sarvashah* > everywhere; *aham-kara* > the making (*kara*) of a 'me' (*aham*), the creation of an identity; *vimudha-atma* > a confused sense of self; *karta* > doer; *aham* > I; *iti* > thus; *manyate* > one believes, one imagines, one concludes.

**All activities everywhere**
**Are movements [within infinite Consciousness]**
**being honored and effectuated by the components of [Its own] Nature.**
**[When pure Consciousness perceives**
**through a dreamlike form appearing within It],**
**A confused sense of self-identity is created**
**[by innocent identification with that form].**
**Thus a belief ensues that "I [as the dreamform]**
**am the doer of my actions."**

Being is dreaming of doing. It is said in the *Sankhya-Karika*, verses 19-20: "...The Purusha (Spirit-Self) is the solitary, neutral, witnessing non-agent.

By association with the Self, the insentient Pradhana—the as-yet unevolved potential of the universe which has no independent sentience apart from Purusha—seems to possess its own sentience. And although the agency really belongs to the *gunas* (components) of Nature, the neutral Purusha appears as if It were active." This is likened to a magnet causing the illusion that moving pieces of metal have a life of their own.

**28**
*tattvavit tu mahabaho / gunakarma-vibhagayoh*
*guna guneshu vartanta / iti matva na sajjate*

*tattva-vit* > the knower of truth; *tu* > but; *maha-baho* > O mighty-armed one; *guna-karma* > the interactions of the components of Nature (sattva, rajas, and tamas, described in the notes to verse 2.39); *vibhagayoh* > in the dual role, in the dual dispensation; *gunah* > the components (as the senses); *guneshu* > within the components (as the sense-objects); *vartante* > they turn, they stir, they move; *iti* > thus; *matva* > considering, perceiving; *na* > not; *sajjate* > one is attached.

**But one who knows the truth, O mighty-armed Arjuna,**
**Perceives that actions happen**
**due to the components of Nature rousing and moving each other**
**in the dual role of the senses and the sense-objects,**
**And thus such a one lives without attachment.**

**29**
*prakriter guna-sammudhah / sajjante guna-karmasu*
*tan akritsnavido mandan / kritsnavin na vichalayet*

*prakriteh* > of Nature; *guna* > by the components; *sammudhah* > those who are confused; *sajjante* > they are attached; *guna-karmasu* > to interactions of the components; *tan* > them; *akritsna-vidah* > knowing or perception which is contracted, which is not whole or complete; *mandan* > foolish; *kritsna-vit* > one whose knowing or perception is expansive or whole; *na* > not; *vichalayet* > one would divert, one would redirect.

**Those who are confused regarding the components of Nature**
**become attached to specific interactions of those components.**
**Incomplete perception causes them to behave foolishly at times,**
**[Yet nonetheless,] one whose perception is whole**
**would not [willfully] try to change them.**

This verse presents a very similar idea to the statement in verse 26. The word 'willfully' has been included here because those who perceive the unicity of Life don't view a different type of perception from their own as a problem to be solved. Still, if they are approached by one who is confused and suffering, they may be spontaneously moved by compassion to serve as an instrument through which some potential relief work may take place. This type of willingness (not willfulness) reaches its zenith in the *bodhisattva* principle found in Mahayana Buddhism, whereby one is prepared to postpone one's own 'liberation' indefinitely for the sake of relieving the sufferings of all sentient beings.

### 30
*mayi sarvani karmani / sannyasyadhyatma-chetasa*
*nirashir nirmamo bhutva / yudhyasva vigatajvarah*

*mayi* > to Me; *sarvani* > all; *karmani* > actions; *sannyasya* > renouncing, entrusting; *adhyatma* > the one omnipresent Spirit-Self; *chetasa* > conscious of; *nirashih* > without conditioned wants or wishes; *nirmamah* > indifferent to the idea of what is 'mine' (such as friends and family members for Arjuna); *bhutva* > being, becoming; *yudhyasva* > engage in the fight; *vigata-jvarah* > cured of fever or mental anguish (produced by what Arjuna was taught to believe which he expressed in Chapter One).

**Therefore, being conscious of the omnipresence of the Spirit-Self,**
**simply entrust all of your actions to Me —**
**Letting go of what you learned to want,**
**and becoming indifferent to ideas about what belongs to you.**
**Engage in the confrontation here free of the feverish condition**
**[produced by what you've been taught to believe].**

Here, as previously in verse 2.61, Krishna speaks from the standpoint of representing the Oversoul or dynamic Spirit-Presence animating all life, as conveyed by the term *adhyatma*. In the next verse, he speaks as a vital personification of that same undivided Presence. There will be further discussion about the principle of personification beginning in Chapter Eight.

### 31
*ye me matam idam nityam / anutishthanti manavah*
*shraddha-vanto 'nasuyanto / muchyante te 'pi karmabhih*

*ye* > who; *me* > my; *matam* > advice, opinion, guidance, teaching; *idam* > this; *nityam* > always; *anutishthanti* > they follow, they practice;

*manavah* > humans, persons; *shraddha-vantah* > full
of faith; *anasuyantah* > without bitterness or resentment;
*muchyante* > they are released; *te* > they; *api* > even, also;
*karmabhih* > from actions and their resultant consequences.

**Even those persons who are simply full of faith,
always attending to my teaching without bitterness or resentment —
They are also released from [the affective quality of] actions
and their resultant consequences.**

Throughout Chapter Three Krishna has been indicating the types of
individually unique expressions of the One which in their functioning
display a certain freedom from the engrossing, adhesive quality of actions
and their reactions. He mentioned the one who derives all contentment
from the Spirit-Self alone (*atmanyeva cha santooshtas*, verse 17), the one who
performs work without attachment to its results (*asakto hyacharan karma*,
verse 19), the one who knows the truth about the dual role of Nature
(*tattvavit gunakarma-vibhagayoh*, verse 28), and the one who consciously
entrusts all actions to the omnipresent Self (*sannyasyadhyatma-chetasa*,
verse 30). Yet the current verse indicates that even if none of these particular
characteristics are present, the same freedom is possible if there is simply
heartfelt resonance with the teachings about one's true nature accompanied
by the openness to embrace whatever pointers have been offered in regard to
its recognition. The inimitable Nisargadatta Maharaj is a superb example of
one who simply had faith in the words of his guru and experienced divine
awakenment within a very short time.

**32**
*ye tvetad abhyasuyanto / nanutishthanti me matam
sarvajnana-vimudhans tan / viddhi nashtan achetasah*

*ye* > who; *tu* > but; *etat* > this (the wisdom which Krishna is sharing
with Arjuna); *abhyasuyantah* > indignant, envious, antagonistic; *na* > not;
*anutishthanti* > they follow, they attend to; *me* > my; *matam* > advice,
guidance; *sarva-jnana* > all that is known, all accumulated knowledge;
*vimudhan* > confused; *tan* > them; *viddhi* > please know; *nashtan* > lost;
*achetasah* > those who are unconscious (living unconsciously).

**But those who are antagonistic toward this wisdom I am sharing with you
and do not heed my advice —
Understand that all of their accumulated knowledge is confused;
They are lost [in the trance of egocentrism]
and are thus living unconsciously.**

The totality of the Absolute includes the infinitude of the unknown, which cannot be known by the extremely useful yet finite instrument known as the human mind. Hence, a vast proportion of the *ahamkara* or egoic sense of separate self constitutes what the human mind *assumes* to know yet does not actually know at all. For example, out of the innumerable fascinating and inspiring stories presented in any religious literature, most of them are not actually known to be true, but are simply believed to be true. In the same way, honest introspection may reveal that this same principle is applicable to any information that we've ever gathered about anything from any source which we've not directly experienced to be true. It is this confusing of the not-known with the known which creates a very fertile breeding ground for unconscious behavior leading to extensive hostility, conflict, violence, and suffering on both an individual and a global level.

When there is instead conscious acknowledgment and complete acceptance of everything that is not known, a newly-liberating space of openness is created within oneself which permits freedom from an enormous amount of anxiety, fear, anger, hatred, and obsessive-compulsive behavior. This is later confirmed by Krishna in verse 4.10: "Many, purified by the austerity of true knowing (*jnana-tapasa*), and whose impassionment, fear, and anger have therefore disappeared, have reached the actualization of experiencing My state of being." Because Krishna's state of being also cannot be known by the mind, some of India's time-honored devotional schools emphasize *jnana-shunya prema-bhakti*, loving devotion which is not only entirely devoid of all that is unconsciously assumed to be known, but is likewise devoid of all ego-driven attempts to be an 'all-knower.' That said, verses 31 and 32 sound very much like another attempt on the part of Sanjaya to persuade King Dhritarashtra to try putting an end to the war.

### 33
*sadrisham cheshtate svasyah / prakriter jnanavan api*
*prakritim yanti bhutani / nigrahah kim karishyati*

*sadrisham* > accordingly, suitably, comfortably; *cheshtate* > one moves, one works, one exerts effort; *svasyah* > by one's own; *prakriteh* > nature (referring to the acquired form or condition of the body/mind system derived from the primordial creative energy); *jnana-van* > one with direct knowing of divine truth; *api* > even; *prakritim* > nature; *yanti* > they proceed, they behave; *bhutani* > all living beings; *nigrahah* > suppression; *kim* > what; *karishyati* > it will accomplish.

**All living beings move in accordance with their own nature;**
**Even one with direct knowing of divine truth**
**behaves according to the acquired nature [of his or her body/mind system].**
**What will suppression [of your kshatriya disposition] accomplish?**

In regard to the body/mind vessels within which pure Consciousness has awakened to Itself, the fact that they also function according to their acquired natures does not mean that the way in which they function does not change after realization occurs. More often than not, it does change, and sometimes quite dramatically. Yet as Krishna later states in verse 18.40: "There is not a single living being—either here on Earth, or even among the celestials—who is entirely free of characteristics derived from the three components of Nature."

### 34

*indriyasyendriyasyarthe / raga-dveshau vyavasthitau*
*tayor na vasham agachchet / tau hyasya paripanthinau*

*indriyasya* > of the senses; *indriyasya arthe* > in relation to the objects of the senses; *raga* > attraction, interest; *dveshau* > aversion; *vyavasthitau* > residing within; *tayoh* > of these two; *na* > not; *vasham* > domination, control; *agachchet* > let one come under; *tau* > these two; *hi* > indeed; *asya* > of one; *paripanthinau* > two impediments, two hindrances.

**Attraction and aversion are both residing within the senses**
**in relation to their respective objects.**
**Let one not come under the control of these two,**
**for they are indeed impediments [to Self-recognition].**

### 35

*shreyan svadharmo vigunah / para-dharmat svanusthitat*
*svadharme nidhanam shreyah / para-dharmo bhayavahah*

*shreyan* > better; *sva-dharmah* > one's own occupational duty based on the natural characteristics of one's body/mind system; *vigunah* > defective, imperfect; *para-dharmat* > than duties prescribed for others; *su-anusthitat* > performed well; *sva-dharme* > in one's own natural duties; *nidhanam* > death; *shreyah* > better; *para-dharmah* > duties prescribed for others; *bhaya-avahah* > inviting fear or danger.

**Better to imperfectly perform work which is suited to your own nature**
**than to excellently perform work intended for others**
**[who have an altogether different nature];**

And better to meet with death [sooner]
in the course of performing your own natural duty
Than to live [a longer] life fraught with fear and danger
by taking up work prescribed for others.

### 36
*arjuna uvacha:*
*atha kena prayukto 'yam / papam charati purushah*
*anichchannapi varshneya / balad iva niyojitah*

*arjunah uvacha* > Arjuna said; *atha* > then; *kena* > by what;
*prayuktah* > stirred, pushed, seized; *ayam* > this; *papam* > trouble,
harm (referring to taking up work prescribed for others,
as mentioned in the previous verse); *charati* > one moves,
one engages in; *purushah* > a person; *anichchan* > not desiring,
unwilling; *api* > even; *varshneya* > O descendant of Vrishni;
*balat* > by force; *iva* > as if; *niyojitah* > impelled, urged.

**Arjuna inquired:**
**Then what seizes a person to undertake this kind of trouble**
**[in adopting the ways prescribed for others]**
**Even against one's will as if impelled by force,**
**O descendant of Vrishni?**

### 37
*sri bhagavan uvacha:*
*kama esha krodha esha / rajoguna-samudbhavah*
*mahashano maha-papma / viddhyenam iha vairinam*

*sri bhagavan uvacha* > the blessed one said; *kamah* > desire;
*eshah* > this (referring to the energetic force which Arjuna inquired about);
*krodhah* > anger; *eshah* > this (force); *rajah-guna* > the activating component
of Nature; *samudbhavah* > arisen or produced from; *maha-ashanah* > greatly
eating, greatly consuming; *maha-papma* > greatly troublesome, great producer
of unhappiness or misfortune; *viddhi* > please know; *enam* > this;
*iha* > here in this world; *vairinam* > the adversary, the opponent
(as in the energetic force of opposing and separating).

**The blessed Krishna replied:**
**That force is desire and anger,**
**which is produced from the activating component of Nature (rajas-guna).**
**Know that energetic force of opposing and separating**
**to be the all-consuming producer of misery in this world.**

We may observe that most of our desires reflexively arise in response to our immediate experience of a given moment, and quite often, as in cases such as Arjuna's at Kurukshetra, they present themselves as an expression of caring about the survival or well-being of someone or something. Yet because the fabric of the veiling ego-self which obstructs the perception of one's true nature is literally composed of desire alone — the desire to either obtain something or avoid something, Krishna therefore devotes the remaining verses of this chapter to speaking about the nature of desire.

There are differing opinions among scholars in regard to the original number of verses comprising the Bhagavad-Gita. Some say that the Gita contained as many as 45 additional verses which were lost in its passage down through the ages, while others refer to Krishna's explanation of the phrase *Om Tat Sat* at the end of Chapter Seventeen as an example of even some of the standard 700 verses that were added in by the brahmin community at a later date. In any case, there are fifteen additional verses in the Kashmiri Shaivite recension of the Gita known as the *Gitartha Samgraha* presented by the great mystical philosopher Sri Abhinavagupta. Of those fifteen verses occurring within five chapters of the Gita, ten of them are slightly rephrased variations of standard verses which serve to either more emphatically highlight a certain point, or intensify a particular expression of feeling, such as when Arjuna offers prayers as he beholds Krishna's universal form in Chapter Eleven. The five remaining additional verses, however, which occur between the current verse and the next, express something other than what is already given in the standard presentation of the text, and may be of interest to more serious, long-time students and lovers of the Gita.

## '37-A'
*arjuna uvacha:*
*bhavatyesha katham krishna / katham chaiva vivardhate*
*kim atmakah kim acharas / tanmam achakshva prichchatah*

*arjuna uvacha* > Arjuna said; *bhavati* > arising, producing, happening; *eshah* > this (the force of desire and anger); *katham* > how; *krishna* > O Krishna; *katham* > from where; *cha* > and; *eva* > exactly; *vivardhate* > it grows, it increases; *kim* > what; *atmakah* > consisting of, having the nature of; *kim* > what; *acharah* > pattern of behavior or activity; *tat* > that; *mam* > to me; *achakshva* > please tell; *prichchatah* > which I am asking about.

Arjuna said:
O Krishna, I ask that you please tell me:
How is that force of desire and anger produced,
and from where exactly does it grow?
What is its actual nature and pattern of behavior?

'37-B'
*sri bhagavan uvacha:*
*esha sukshmah parah shatrur / dehinam indriyaih saha*
*sukha-tantra iv'asino / mohayan partha tishthati*

*sri bhagavan uvacha* > the divine one (Krishna) said; *eshah* > this (the force of desire and anger); *sukshmah* > subtle; *parah shatruh* > the greatest enemy; *dehinam* > of 'the embodied one' (pure Consciousness functioning through a body/mind system); *indriyaih* > with the senses; *saha* > together (by way of utilization and identification); *sukha* > happiness; *tantra* > a theoretical framework or premise; *iva* > as if, like; *asinah* > sitting, situated; *mohayan* > deluding, deceiving, infatuating; *partha* > O son of Pritha; *tishthati* > it remains.

The divine one replied:
[Although] this force is subtle, it is the greatest enemy
for pure Consciousness affiliated with the senses [of a body/mind vessel].
By sitting and posing as a promise of happiness,
it remains a deluding influence, O Partha.

'37-C'
*kama-krodhamayo ghorah / stambha-harsha samudbhavah*
*ahamkaro bhiman'-atma / dushtarah papa-karmabhih*

*kama-krodha-mayah* > composed of desire and anger; *ghorah* > forcefulness, poison; *stambha-harsha* > the inflating of excitement; *samudbhavah* > arisen from, produced from; *ahamkarah* > from the egoic sense of personal doership; *abhimana* > pride, arrogance; *atmah* > in its essence, itself; *dushtarah* > irresistible, unconquerable, difficult to overcome; *papa-karmabhih* > by those who perform wicked or harmful actions.

The force composed of desire and anger
arises from the inflation of excitement (rajas),
Which itself comes from a sense of pride
in the assumption of personal doership.
It is very difficult to overcome
by those who perform wicked deeds.

**'37-D'**
*harsham asya nivartyaisha / shokam asya dadati cha*
*bhayam chasya karotyesha / mohayams tu muhur-muhuh*

*harsham* > excitement; *asya* > of this; *nivarta* > the returning;
*eshah* > this; *shokam* > affliction, anguish, sorrow; *asya* > of this;
*dadati* > it gives one; *cha* > and; *bhayam* > fear; *cha* > and; *ahsya* >
in relation to the mouth or organ of speech; *karoti esha* > it does this
(the reappearing); *mohayams* > by the speaking of things which are
erroneous; *tu* > indeed; *muhur-muhuh* > again and again, repeatedly.

**The continual return of this excitement
brings one much sorrow and fear,
And indeed, its reappearances
are [often] in relation to the organ of speech,
through repeatedly speaking things which are untrue.**

**'37-E'**
*sa esha kalushah kshudrash / chidra-prakshi dhananjaya*
*rajah parvritto mohatma / manushyanam upadravah*

*sa esha* > this one (the twin force of desire and anger); *kalushah* > foul,
unclean; *kshudrash* > cruel, avaricious; *chidra-prakshi* > looking for an opening;
*dhananjaya* > O winner of wealth; *rajah* > by the activating and distorting
component of Nature (rajas-guna); *parvrittah* > it is set into motion,
it is commenced; *mohatma* > one who is prone to infatuation or confusion;
*manushyanam* > among humankind; *upadravah* > bringing misfortune.

**Being foul and avaricious,
This twin force of desire and anger
is always seeking an opportunity [to manifest into expression],
O winner of wealth.
Being set into motion by the activating and distorting component of Nature,
Among humankind it brings misfortune
to those who are prone to infatuation or confusion.**

**38**
*dhumena-'vriyate vahnir / yathadarsho malena cha*
*yatholbena-'vrito garbhas / tatha tenedam avritam*

*dhumena* > by smoke; *avriyate* > it is obscured, it is covered;
*vahnih* > fire; *yatha* > just as; *adarshah* > mirror; *malena* > by dust;

*cha* > and; *yatha* > just as; *ulbena* > by the membrane; *avritah* > enveloped; *garbhah* > foetus; *tatha* > so; *tena* > in that manner; *idam* > this (the world or universe); *avritam* > veiled, shrouded.

**Just as fire is obscured by smoke,**
**as a mirror is covered by dust,**
**and as a foetus is enveloped in an embryonic sac,**
**So also in the same manner does this universe have its shroud.**

*Vahni* refers to the bearer of offerings made to the celestials, a service said to be rendered by the fire-god Agni because at ritual ceremonies, the offerings of grains and ghee, etc. are placed into the fire with the exclamation *Svaha* ("Hail to thee!").

**39**
*avritam jnanam etena / jnanino nitya-vairina*
*kama-rupena kaunteya / dushpurena 'nalena cha*

*avritam* > concealed; *jnanam* > direct, innate knowing; *etena* > by this; *jnaninah* > the wise ones; *nitya-vairina* > by the perpetual adversary; *kama-rupena* > in the form of desire; *kaunteya* > O son of Kunti; *dushpurena* > insatiable; *analena* > by fire; *cha* > and.

**O son of Kunti,**
**[Recognition of] direct, innate knowing is concealed**
**by this perpetual adversary of the wise,**
**Whose form composed of desire**
**burns like an insatiable fire.**

It will be revealed in upcoming verse 41 that one's true nature is actually 'concealed' in plain view, usually the last place one would think to look for it, and that it is simply a matter of *vijnana*, of recognizing that.

**40**
*indriyani mano buddhir / asya-'dhishthanam uchyate*
*etair vimohayatyesha / jnanam avritya dehinam*

*indriyani* > the senses; *manah* > the mind; *buddhih* > the intellect; *asya* > of this (desire, as mentioned in the previous verse); *adhishthanam* > dwelling place, abode; *uchyate* > it is said; *etaih* > by these; *vimohayati* > it confuses; *eshah* > this; *jnanam* > clear, direct, innate knowing; *avritya* > obscuring; *dehinam* > 'the embodied one' (pure Spirit-Presence).

The senses, mind, and intellect
are said to be the dwelling places of desire,
Which causes confusion and obscures the [recognition of] direct knowing
when Life, pure Beingness, functions as a living being.

**41**

*tasmat tvam indriyanyadau / niyamya bharatarshabha*
*papmanam prajahi hyenam / jnana-vijnana-nashanam*

*tasmat* > therefore; *tvam* > you; *indriyani* > the senses; *adau* > initially,
beginning with; *niyamya* > by disciplining, by regulating;
*bharata-rishabha* > O chief amongst the descendants of Bharata
who possesses the strength of a bull; *papmanam* > misfortune, trouble;
*prajahi* > abandon; *hi* > indeed; *enam* > this (desire); *jnana* > clear, direct,
innate knowing; *vijnana* > recognizing; *nashanam* > losing, removing.

**Therefore, by initially regulating the senses,
O powerful chief of the Bharatas,
Abandon desire,
which spawns the trouble of losing the recognition
of one's clear, direct, innate knowing.**

The abandoning of a desire usually happens when careful attention is given
to identifying the core beliefs fueling the desire, and to investigating whether
or not what is being believed is actually known to be true.

**42**

*indriyani paranyahur / indriyebhyah param manah*
*manasas tu para buddhir / yo buddheh paratas tu sah*

*indriyani* > the senses; *parani* > high in power and importance;
*ahuh* > they (the learned ones) say; *indriyebhyah* > than the senses;
*param* > superior; *manah* > the mind; *manasah* > than the mind; *tu* > but;
*para* > higher; *buddhih* > intellect; *yah* > who; *buddheh* > than the
intellect; *paratah* > the highest; *tu* > but; *sah* > This (the *dehinam*
or pure Spirit-Presence mentioned in verse 40).

**The learned ones say
that the senses have their particular power and importance,
But that the mind is superior to the senses,
the intellect is higher than the mind,
And still higher than the intellect, supreme over all,
is the pure Spirit-Presence.**

**43**

*evam buddheh param buddhva / samstabhyatmanam atmana*
*jahi shatrum mahabaho / kama-rupam durasadam*

*evam* > thus; *buddheh* > than the intellect; *param* > superior;
*buddhva* > having learned; *samstabhya* > having been supported or
strengthened, having received courage; *atmanam* > the expressed self;
*atmana* > by the Spirit-Self; *jahi* > slay; *shatrum* > the adversary;
*maha-baho* > O mighty-armed one; *kama-rupam* > in the form of desire;
*durasadam* > difficult to encounter, difficult to approach.

**Having thus now also learned what is superior to the intellect,
Receive courage and strength from the Spirit-Self [which you are]
for Its expression as the [Arjuna-] self,
And slay that adversary which assumes the form of desire
though it be difficult to face, O mighty-armed one.**

This 'slaying' of desires—if such be taken to mean permanently for the
duration of one's lifetime—does not usually occur by way of combative
struggle. Human experience has vividly demonstrated that desires which
were thought to be slain by forceful efforts unexpectedly 'resurrected' at a
later time, because one who focuses attention on a particular object with the
intent to resist it creates the same sturdy link of attachment with that object as
one who has a wish to acquire it. Fortunately, however, what has also been
experienced is a considerably greater potential for change to occur by slaying
the misbelief that the continuous fulfillment of desires will in some way make
one feel more whole or complete. By consciously observing what is actually
being experienced within one's body/mind system during the pursuit of
desired objects or objectives, upon their acquisition, and during the period
which follows thereafter, a great many things can be noticed. For example,
when a particular object is acquired, one is provided with temporary relief
*from desiring*, and it is actually this freedom from wanting that creates the
temporary sense of happiness, not the object itself. When such things are
recognized, in due course attention simply ceases fixating on objects or
objectives which were previously being interpreted as desirable, and a great
many desires just spontaneously and nonviolently drop away on their own
without struggle.

*om tat saditi srimad bhagavad-gita / supanishatsu brahma-vidyayam*
*yoga-shastre srikrishnarjuna samvade / karma-yogo nama tritiyo 'dhyayah*

From the Ambrosial Song of God—
A conversation between Krishna and Arjuna
which is a Upanishad (confidential sharing)
of wisdom-teachings regarding the Absolute
And a scripture concerning Self-realization—
Thus ends the Third Chapter entitled Karma-yoga,
Recognizing Divine Unicity By Way of Selfless Action.

# Chapter Four

---

# Jnana-yoga
## (Recognizing Divine Unicity By Way of Direct Knowing)

"By means of scriptural study, self-control, traditional instruction by a teacher, logical inference, and direct experience, genuine discernment between the Real and the unreal dawns within one. This leads to the realization that whatever exists at the beginning and the end of this universe — which causes and reveals it — indeed alone exists during its middle period of manifestation as well.

"Just as raw gold which has not been shaped into fine ornaments is alone present before and after its modification into ornaments, and the same gold present in its intermediate stage is merely *named* 'a ring,' 'a bracelet,' etc. — so also am I alone the only existing Reality before the creation of the universe, after its dissolution, and during its interim manifest phase as well.

"Dear friend Uddhava, recognize what is here which distinctly remains the fourth principle beyond all the threes — the three conditions of waking, dreaming, and deep sleep; the three constituents of Nature; and the threefold division of interrelated causes, effects, and agents — for only That alone is the Real.

"It is My conclusive opinion that whatever is composed of or brought into being by another substance can only be that original substance and nothing else; that anything which did not exist prior to its appearance and which ceases to exist after its disappearance has no factual existence in its intermediate stage either, except as a mere name only."
— Sri Krishna, Srimad Bhagavata Purana, Book Eleven, verses 28.18-21

### 1
*sri bhagavan uvacha:*
*imam vivasvate yogam / proktavan aham avyayam*
*vivasvan manave praha / manur ikshvakave 'bravit*

*sri bhagavan uvacha* > the beautiful lord (Krishna) said; *imam* > this; *vivasvate* > unto Vivasvan ('the brilliant one,' 'shining forth'), the sun-god; *yogam* > the science of recognizing the unicity of all Life; *proktavan* > taught, told to; *aham* > I; *avyayam* > imperishable; *vivasvan* > Vivasvan; *manave* > unto Vivasvan's son Vaivasvata Manu ('the great thinker coming from the sun,'

one of the ancient progenitors and lawgivers of humankind);
*praha* > he instructed; *manuh* > Manu; *ikshvakave* > unto Vaivasvata
Manu's son King Ikshvaku ('sugarcane'); *abravit* > he related.

**The beautiful Lord Krishna said:**
**I taught this imperishable science of recognizing the unicity of all life**
**to the sun-god Vivasvan;**
**Vivasvan taught it to his son Vaivasvata Manu,**
**and Manu imparted it to his son King Ikshvaku.**

It is said that an entire dynasty of saintly kings descended from King
Ikshvaku, including the families of Lord Ramachandra and King Janaka
portrayed in the epic Ramayana.

**2**
*evam parampara-praptam / imam rajarshayo viduh*
*sa kaleneha mahata / yogo nashtah parantapa*

*evam* > thus; *parampara* > in succession from one to another;
*praptam* > received; *imam* > this; *raja-rishayah* > the sages who were kings;
*viduh* > they knew; *sah* > this; *kalena* > over the course of time;
*iha* > here in this world; *mahata* > of great length; *yogah* > the science
of recognizing oneself to be pure Awareness; *nashtah* > disappeared,
perished; *parantapa* > O conqueror of foes (Arjuna).

**Thus received in succession from one to another,**
**This science of recognizing oneself to be pure Awareness**
**was known by the sages who served as kings.**
**But over the course of a long period of time in this world,**
**the teaching disappeared, O conqueror of foes.**

**3**
*sa evayam maya te 'dya / yogah proktah puratanah*
*bhakto 'si me sakha cheti / rahasyam hyetad uttamam*

*sah* > it; *eva* > truly; *ayam* > this; *maya* > by me; *te* > unto you;
*adya* > now, today; *yogah* > the science of Self-recognition;
*proktah* > taught, declared; *puratanah* > existing from ancient times;
*bhaktah* > devotee; *asi* > you are; *me* > my; *sakha* > friend; *cha* > and;
*iti* > thus; *rahasyam* > mysterious teaching; *hi* > indeed;
*etat* > this; *uttamam* > best, highest.

**Because you are my devoted friend,**
**Today I am imparting to you this science of Self-recognition**
**which has existed from ancient times.**
**This secret teaching is indeed the highest.**

The fact that what was a secret teaching a few thousand years ago is currently no longer a secret is itself a divine dispensation of incalculable value. In previous times people would leave their homes and families and go traveling and searching extensively, undergoing many hardships in order to receive the opportunity to hear the type of transmission found in the Bhagavad-Gita.

**4**
*arjuna uvacha:*
*aparam bhavato janma / param janma vivasvatah*
*katham etad vijaniyam / tvam adau proktavan iti*

*arjunah uvacha* > Arjuna said; *aparam* > later; *bhavatah* > of you; *janma* > birth; *param* > prior; *janma* > birth; *vivasvatah* > of Vivasvan; *katham* > how; *etat* > this (teaching); *vijaniyam* > I should understand; *tvam* > you; *adau* > in the beginning; *proktavan* > taught; *iti* > thus.

**Arjuna said:**
**Your birth was later,**
**And Vivasvan's birth was prior to yours.**
**How am I to understand**
**that in the beginning you imparted this teaching to him?**

**5**
*sri bhagavan uvacha:*
*bahuni me vyatitani / janmani tava charjuna*
*tanyaham veda sarvani / na tvam vettha parantapa*

*sri bhagavan uvacha* > the glorious one (Krishna) said; *bahuni* > many; *me* > my; *vyatitani* > have passed away; *janmani* > births; *tava* > your; *cha* > and; *arjuna* > Arjuna; *tani* > them; *aham veda* > I know; *sarvani* > all; *na* > not; *tvam vettha* > you know; *parantapa* > O subduer of the enemy.

**The glorious one, Krishna, said:**
**Many 'births' have passed away for both you and I, Arjuna.**
**I know all of them,**
**but you cannot, O subduer of the enemy.**

Back in verse 2.20 Krishna stated that there is actually no birth or death for the Spirit-Self at any time, and in the upcoming verse He mentions that the apparent births of the one Self (infinite Consciousness) are simply manifestations effectuated by the power of Its own Nature. The capacity for knowing or remembering such manifest forms is of course only available to Consciousness (Krishna); it is not available to one of the thought-forms appearing within Consciousness (Arjuna). Hence Krishna's statement here that "I can know and you cannot."

**6**

*ajo 'pi sann avyayatma / bhutanam ishvaro 'pi san*
*prakritim svam adhishthaya / sambhavamyatma-mayaya*

*ajah* > unborn; *api* > although; *san* > being; *avyaya* > immutable, imperishable; *atma* > Self; *bhutanam* > of all beings; *ishvarah* > Lord; *api* > although; *san* > being; *prakritim* > Nature; *svam* > My own; *adhishthaya* > by utilizing, by governing; *sambhavami* > I arise, I appear, I come into being; *atma-mayaya* > by My own energetic potency, by My own ability to produce perceivable phenomena.

**Although I am the unborn, immutable Self
and Lord of all beings,
By utilizing My own Nature,
I appear in a perceivable form by My own energetic Potency.**

**7**

*yada yada hi dharmasya / glanir bhavati bharata*
*abhyutthanam adharmasya / tadatmanam srijamyaham*

*yada yada* > whenever; *hi* > indeed; *dharmasya* > of living consciously in accordance with Life-centered values; *glanih* > decrease, debilitation; *bhavati* > it becomes; *bharata* > O descendant of Bharata; *abhyutthanam* > uprising, increasing; *adharmasya* > of living unconsciously in accordance with self-centered values; *tada* > then; *atmanam* > Myself; *srijami* > I show, I reveal, I manifest; *aham* > I.

**Whenever there is a withering
of conscious living and Life-centered values,
And a flourishing of unconscious living and self-centered values,
At that time I manifest Myself,
O descendant of Bharata.**

**8**

*paritranaya sadhunam / vinashaya cha dushkritam*
*dharma-samsthapanarthaya / sambhavami yuge yuge*

*paritranaya* > for the protection, for the support;
*sadhunam* > of the virtuous, of the honest; *vinashaya* > for the
annihilation, for the removal; *cha* > and; *dushkritam* > of that which is false
and produces suffering; *dharma* > the principles of conscious living
in relationship to all of Life; *samsthapana* > to establish;
*arthaya* > for the purpose; *sambhavami* > I appear, I come into being;
*yuge yuge* > in every age of the universal time-cycle.

**For supporting what is true and authentic;**
**For removing what is false and produces suffering;**
**And for reestablishing the principles of conscious living**
**in relationship to all of Life —**
**For these purposes I appear in every age of the universal time-cycle.**

Verses 7 and 8 may be viewed as alluding to a spontaneous process of
catharsis which occurs within Consciousness when there is an imbalance
of energetic influences.

**9**

*janma karma cha me divyam / evam yo vetti tattvatah*
*tyaktva deham punar-janma / naiti mam eti so'rjuna*

*janma* > birth; *karma* > actions; *cha* > and; *me* > My; *divyam* > divine;
*evam* > in this manner; *yah* > who; *vetti* > one knows; *tattvatah* > in truth;
*tyaktva* > upon expulsion from, upon withdrawing from; *deham* > the body;
*punah* > again; *janma* > birth; *na* > not; *eti* > one goes to; *mam* > to Me;
*eti* > one comes; *sah* > that one; *arjuna* > O Arjuna.

**One who knows the truth**
**regarding My divine appearances and workings in this manner**
**Is not born again upon dissociation from the present body,**
**But comes to Me, O Arjuna.**

Pure omnipresent Consciousness, described in verse 2.21 as eternally unborn,
has the natural power (*sambhavamyatma-mayaya*, verse 4.6) to playfully
conceive of Itself as an apparently localized entity possessing a particular
pattern of *samskaras*, a repository of mental impressions and recollections.

And although back in verse 2.12 Krishna stated that neither he, nor Arjuna, nor all the commanders present at Kurukshetra would ever cease to exist in the future, later in verse 15.15 Krishna states that *mattah smritir jnanam apohanam cha* — "From Me (pure Consciousness) comes memory of that which is known (*smritir jnanam*), and the removal of that memory as well (*apohanam cha*)." So it is the forgetting of a particular pattern of *samskaras* within infinite Consciousness that is indicated in the present verse, and as previously stated in verse 2.72, it is the sense of being a fictitious independent self which is not reborn.

### 10

*vita-ragabhaya-krodha / manmaya mam upashritah*
*bahavo jnana-tapasa / puta madbhavam agatah*

*vita* > departed, disappeared; *raga* > impassionment; *bhaya* > fear; *krodhah* > anger; *manmaya* > absorbed in Me; *mam* > Me; *upashritah* > taking complete refuge; *bahavah* > many; *jnana* > direct knowing; *tapasa* > by the austerity; *putah* > purified; *mat-bhavam* > My state of being; *agatah* > reached (refers to the actualization of experiencing).

**Ever absorbed in Me and taking complete refuge in Me,**
**Many — purified by the austerity which direct knowing entails,**
**and whose impassionment, fear, and anger have therefore disappeared —**
**Have reached the actualization of experiencing My state of being.**

As previously discussed in relation to verse 3.32, a very promising beginning to awakening to the truth of oneself can simply be the clear discernment between what is genuinely known and what is genuinely not known. This is facilitated by perceiving everything exactly as it is, without modification of any kind by beliefs, judgments, ideas, or opinions *about* what is perceived. Our true nature — Krishna's state of being, the Unmanifest conceiving of Itself as the totality of manifest phenomena — is not knowable to the phenomenal objects called the mind and senses, and therefore three helpful suggestions have been offered in this verse. They are *manmaya*, immersing one's attention in what is actually known to be real and true; *mam upashritah*, taking complete refuge in what is real and true; and *jnana-tapasa*, embracing the austerity of staying alert to and aligned with what is real and true. All three of these are made possible by simply not filtering direct experience through acquired patterns of uninvestigated beliefs. Refraining from identification with self-referencing thoughts is only an austerity as long as there is not sustained attention or complete refuge in what is real and true; yet when total surrender happens, it becomes spontaneous, effortless, and joyous.

In Merriam-Webster's Dictionary, one of the definitions of the word 'austere' is 'markedly simple or unadorned.' This is also part of the austerity suggested here by Krishna: childlike simplicity unadorned by any sense of expertise in relation to one's spiritual studies, practices, or abilities. Genuine innocence delights in exploring the mystery of oneself without aggressively trying to solve the mystery. Wherever sincere Self-inquiry is occurring and there is this type of humble curiosity without a demand that the curiosity be satisfied, it's quite typical for impassionment, fear, and anger to naturally diminish by themselves. This happens without one's living in a continual state of resistance or trying to or get rid of those things through strenuous effort. Perhaps it also bears mentioning that the actualization of experiencing Krishna's state of being does not imply somehow becoming the person known as Krishna. Each expression of the Absolute is entirely unique unto itself, although Krishna states that one can 'arrive at a nature similar to my own' (*mama sadharmyam agatah*, verse 14.2).

**11**

*ye yatha mam prapadyante / tams tathaiva bhajamyaham*
*mama vartma 'nuvartante / manushyah partha sarvashah*

*ye* > who; *yatha* > in whatever manner; *mam* > Me;
*prapadyante* > they take refuge in; *tan* > them; *tatha* > thus;
*eva* > indeed; *bhajami* > bestow; *aham* > I; *mama* > My;
*vartma* > path; *anuvartante* > they follow; *manushyah* > humankind;
*partha* > O son of Pritha; *sarvashah* > collectively, altogether.

**All of humankind follows a path established by Me,**
**O son of Pritha.**
**And in whatever manner one takes refuge in Me,**
**I bestow what they seek accordingly.**

The path referred to in this verse is generally thought to be one of the ones Krishna mentioned in verse 3.3—the Sankhya student's path of cultivating Self-knowing or the karma-yogi's path of performing selfless action. Yet it actually refers to all paths followed within humankind, as will be confirmed in upcoming verse 13. And *yatha*, 'in whatever manner,' could be read in a number of different ways. It could mean 'by whatever method,' twelve of which will be mentioned in upcoming verses 25 through 30. It could mean with either a longing for Self-realization or with a desire for heavenly pleasures; or it could mean "by approaching Me as either Krishna, or as Vishnu, or as Shiva, Devi, Ganesha, Karttikeya, or Surya...," etcetera.

**12**

*kankshantah karmanam siddhim / yajanta iha devatah*
*kshipram hi manushe loke / siddhir bhavati karmaja*

*kankshantah* > wishing for; *karmanam* > results derived from actions;
*siddhim* > success; *yajante* > they make sacrifices for, they offer to; *iha* > here
in this world; *devatah* > the celestials (those dwelling within the subtler
strata of Consciousness representing the multifarious elements,
energies, and aspects of Nature); *kshipram* > very quickly; *hi* > indeed;
*manushe* > in human society; *loke* > in the world; *siddhih* > success;
*bhavati* > it manifests, it occurs; *karmaja* > produced by such action.

**Those wishing to derive successful results from their actions in this world
make offerings to the celestials.
Quickly indeed does such offertory action
manifest success here in human society.**

This verse is associated with verses 11 and 12 of Chapter Three which
describe a reciprocal relationship between humankind and the celestials/
elementals.

**13**

*chatur-varnyam maya srishtam / gunakarma-vibhagashah*
*tasya kartaram api mam / viddhya-'kartaram avyayam*

*chatur-varnyam* > the system of social unity based on the four types
of human proclivities; *maya* > by Me; *srishtam* > emitted, emanated,
let loose; *guna* > quality; *karma* > activity; *vibhaga* > sharing in,
participation; *shah* > according to; *tasya* > of this; *kartaram* > creator;
*api* > although; *mam* > Me; *viddhi* > you should know; *akartaram* >
a non-doer, one who performs no actions; *avyayam* > eternal.

**I emanated the system for establishing harmonious cooperation
between the four branches of human society,
Which is based upon each person's participation
according to their particular qualities and activities.
Yet you should know that although I am the creator of this system,
I am eternally a non-doer of action.**

Although the sun emanates the light and warmth which creates all the flora
on the Earth, it is not engaged in any action in such creation, nor does it have
a vested interest in radiating its light and warmth. By the sun simply being

what it is, its nature is to cause vegetation to grow. In the same manner, it is Prakriti, the Nature of the Absolute, which causes all of life to evolve as it does. So as Krishna represents the one undivided Omnipresence throughout all forms, His statement here that He is such a non-doer is extremely noteworthy. The myth that the eternally Unborn reincarnates had been addressed in verse 2.20, and here, the myth that an eternal Non-performer of action accrues *karma* — the alleged cause of such reincarnation — is revealed as yet another misbelief which Arjuna is given the opportunity to let go of at this time. The affirmation that pure Spirit is not subject to karma is continued in the next verse.

The four branches of society mentioned here are the brahmins (teachers and priests), *kshatriyas* (royal administrators and warriors), *vaishyas* (farmers and merchants), and *shudras* (craftspeople, skilled laborers, and life-assistants).

**14**

*na mam karmani limpanti / na me karma-phale spriha*
*iti mam yo 'bhijanati / karmabhir na sa badhyate*

*na* > not; *mam* > Me; *karmani* > actions; *limpanti* > they pollute, they taint, they defile; *na* > nor; *me* > My; *karma-phale* > in the fruits of action; *spriha* > aspiration, longing, eagerness; *iti* > thus; *mam* > Me; *yah* > who; *abhijanati* > one accepts, one perceives, one understands; *karmabhih* > by the actions; *na* > not; *sah* > that one; *badhyate* > one is bound, one is oppressed, one is harassed.

**There are no actions which contaminate Me,
Nor do I ever aspire for the fruits of any action.
One who resonates with this truth about Me
[who am the Self in all forms of Life]
Does not feel bound up or oppressed
by the actions [of one's body/mind system].**

All of Life is one unified Totality. Even a small amount of contemplation on this verse could evoke a tangible feeling of relief from whatever resistance there may be to meeting the rest of Life as It presents Itself in Its own way. One may also experience profound calmness upon realizing that Life is not a problem to be solved. It feels like a problem when there is an aggressive attempt to control It, to try to manipulate It to suit the conditioned mind's ideas about what will bring happiness to the imagined separate self. But when this sense of separation is replaced by an authentic sense of all-inclusiveness, a wondrous depth of fulfillment is discovered to be readily available.

**15**

*evam jnatva kritam karma / purvair api mumukshubhih*
*kuru karmaiva tasmat tvam / purvaih purva-taram kritam*

*evam* > thus; *jnatva* > knowing; *kritam* > performed; *karma* > actions;
*purvaih* > by those in ancient times; *api* > even; *mumukshubhih* > by
those seeking liberation; *kuru* > you should perform; *karma* > actions;
*eva* > certainly; *tasmat* > therefore; *tvam* > you; *purvaih* > by those in ancient
times; *purva-taram* > previously, formerly; *kritam* > performed, had done.

**Knowing this principle,**
**Even those seeking liberation in ancient times performed actions;**
**Therefore, you should certainly perform actions**
**[which are called for in the moment],**
**Just as the ancient ones had done in previous times.**

**16**

*kim karma kim akarmeti / kavayo 'pyatra mohitah*
*tat te karma pravakshyami / yaj jnatva mokshyase 'shubhat*

*kim* > what is; *karma* > action; *kim* > what is; *akarma* > inaction, non-action;
*iti* > thus; *kavayah* > the poet-sages; *api* > even; *atra* > in this matter;
*mohitah* > confused; *tat* > that; *te* > unto you; *karma* > action;
*pravakshyami* > I shall explain; *yat* > which; *jnatva* > knowing;
*mokshyase* > you will be liberated; *ashubhat* > from misfortune.

**"What is considered to be action? What is non-action?" —**
**Even the poet-sages are confused in this matter.**
**I shall explain to you what action is,**
**knowing which you will be freed from all misfortune.**

**17**

*karmano hyapi boddhavyam / boddhavyam cha vikarmanah*
*akarmanash cha boddhavyam / gahana karmano gatih*

*karmanah* > of action; *hi* > indeed; *api* > also; *boddhavyam* > to be known,
to be understood; *boddhavyam* > to be aware of, to be acquainted with;
*cha* > also; *vikarmanah* > of 'mis-action'; *akarmanah* > of non-action;
*cha* > also; *boddhavyam* > to be informed of, to be taught about;
*gahana* > very deep, difficult to comprehend; *karmanah* > of action;
*gatih* > way of proceeding, manner of operation.

**And along with knowing what action is,
it is also of value to be conscious of 'mis-action,'
as well as to know what non-action is.
The way in which action operates
is a deeply profound subject matter indeed.**

Interestingly, the word *vikarma* does not appear a second time throughout the entirety of the Bhagavad-Gita, which points to the truth that from the perspective of the one Absolute Intelligence, there are no wrong, evil, or mistaken actions. From the relative standpoint, however, there are undeniably actions which produce suffering conditions within the world in contrast to those actions which produce conditions of well-being. Therefore, a 'mis-action' may perhaps be serviceably defined as one which is unconscious, harmful, or self-centered, contrary to the *dharma* principles which are whole-life-centered for the well-being of all.

### 18
*karmanya-'karma yah pashyed / akarmani cha karma yah
sa buddhiman manushyeshu / sa yuktah kritsna-karmakrit*

*karmani* > in action; *akarma* > non-action; *yah* > who; *pashyet* > one
perceives; *akarmani* > in non-action; *cha* > and; *karma* > action;
*yah* > who; *sah* > that one; *buddhiman* > full of intelligence;
*manushyeshu* > among humankind; *sah* > that one;
*yuktah* > connected, aligned (functioning as a clear channel
for universal Intelligence, as discussed in Chapter Two);
*kritsna-karma-krit* > in the performance of all actions.

**One who perceives non-action in action
and action in non-action
is most intelligent among humankind,
Functioning as a clear channel for the one universal Intelligence
in the performance of all actions.**

Non-action in action refers to actions performed with no desires, no attachment to results, and no sense of personal doership, as stated in the next two verses. Action in non-action refers to abstaining from actions with a desire to obtain very specific results by such abstinence.

### 19
*yasya sarve samarambhah / kama-sankalpa-varjitah
jnanagni-dagdha-karmanam / tam ahuh panditam budhah*

*yasya* > of whom; *sarve* > all; *samarambhah* > endeavors; *kama* > desire; *sankalpa* > self-serving motivation, expectation of advantage; *varjitah* > excluded; *jnana* > direct knowing; *agni* > fire; *dagdha* > burned; *karmanam* > relating to actions (specifically relating to the binding effects of considering oneself to be the doer of actions), reactions proceeding from actions; *tam* > this one; *ahuh* > they declare; *panditam* > one who is wise; *budhah* > those who are awake.

**One who excludes desire and self-serving motives from all endeavors,**
**Burning up the binding effects**
**of considering oneself to be the doer of actions**
**in the fire of direct knowing —**
**Such a one is declared to be truly wise**
**by those who are awake [to their true nature].**

This verse is a reminder of *gunakarma-vibhagayoh / guna guneshu vartanta* from verse 3.28, that actions simply happen due to the components of Nature rousing and moving each other in the dual role of the senses and the sense-objects. In the notes to verse 13 it was mentioned that the sun is not engaged in any action in causing flora to grow, yet the flora is also not engaged in any action to cause its growth. By its simply being what it is, growth happens. In the same way, neither pure Spirit nor the illusory ego-self are doers of actions, and this can be directly known just as one knows that one is not doing anything to cause one's heart to beat or one's blood to circulate throughout the body.

**20**
*tyaktva karmaphala-sangam / nityatripto nirashrayah*
*karmanyabhipravritto 'pi / naiva kinchit karoti sah*

*tyaktva* > lacking, abandoning; *karmaphala-sangam* > attachment to the fruits of action; *nitya* > always; *triptah* > content; *nirashrayah* > without shelter or support (completely vulnerable); *karmani* > in action; *abhipravrittah* > engaging in, proceeding with; *api* > even; *na* > not; *eva* > truly; *kinchit* > anything whatsoever; *karoti* > one does; *sah* > that one.

**Devoid of any attachment to the results of actions,**
**Completely vulnerable yet ever content —**
**Even when [the body/mind system is] engaging in actions,**
**one is truly not the doer of anything whatsoever.**

### 21

*nirashir yata-chittatma / tyakta-sarva-parigrahah
shariram kevalam karma / kurvan napnoti kilbisham*

*nirashih* > without hoping that a wish will be fulfilled; *yata* > held,
governed; *chitta* > that which is noticed, attention, observation;
*atma* > oneself; *tyakta* > discarded, abandoned; *sarva* > all;
*parigrahah* > seizing, possessing; *shariram* > with the body;
*kevalam* > only, alone; *karma* > action; *kurvan* > doing;
*na* > not; *apnoti* > one incurs, one meets with;
*kilbisham* > fault, guilt, offense.

**Holding this observation of oneself [as a non-doer]
without hoping that a particular wish will be fulfilled;
Relinquishing all sense of possessiveness
and thus performing actions solely with the body alone —
Such a one incurs no fault.**

Some translations of the Gita have Krishna here instructing Arjuna to
completely relinquish all possessions. Yet that would seem to provide Arjuna
with a golden opportunity to respond in the next verse with something like:
"Yes, Krishna, I totally agree to relinquish all of my possessions right at this
very moment. I already threw down my bow and arrows (in verse 1.47), so
now here's my shield, and my helmet too. I also relinquish my armor, and
of course the chariot and all the horses.... This is exactly what I wanted to
do from the very beginning, but—Krishna, you jokester—you really had me
going there for a while, asking me to fight with my relatives!" Therefore
*tyakta-sarva-parigrahah* is instead synonymous with *nirmamah*, previously
mentioned in verse 2.71 as being without a sense of possessiveness. Again,
this includes physical objects, but does not refer as much to physical objects
as to the accumulated stories we believe about ourselves based on memories
of acquired information and experiences. These ego-reinforcing stories have a
much more binding and affective quality by far than, for example, the items
in one's wardrobe.

### 22

*yadrichcha-labha-santooshto / dvandvatito vimatsarah
samah siddhav asiddhau cha / kritvapi na nibadhyate*

*yadrichcha* > spontaneously, of its own accord; *labha* > meeting with,
acquiring; *santooshtah* > deeply contented; *dvandva* > dualities,
contrasting pairs of opposites; *atitah* > passed through, gone beyond;

*vimatsarah* > free from envy or jealousy; *samah* > even-minded,
the same, balanced; *siddhau* > in success; *asiddhau* > in failure;
*cha* > and; *kritva* > having acted; *api* > even though; *na* > not;
*nibadhyate* > one is confined, one is bound up.

**Deeply content with whatever comes of its own accord,**
**Unperturbed by the contrasting pairs of opposites,**
**Free from envy,**
**Of the same balanced mind in both success and failure —**
**Even though performing actions,**
**Such a one is never bound up by them.**

*Dvandvatito* ('transcending the pairs of opposites') is generally interpreted
to mean that one who awakens to the truth of pure Being will no longer
feel heat or cold, pain or pleasure, etc. Yet the direct experiences of Sri
Ramakrishna, Ramana Maharshi, Anandamayi Ma, Nisargadatta Maharaj,
and countless others are that those sensations are still felt, yet one passes
through and beyond the sensations without attaching a story to them or
supporting an identity in relation to them.

**23**
*gata-sangasya muktasya / jnana-'vasthita-chetasah*
*yajnaya-'charatah karma / samagram praviliyate*

*gata-sangasya* > of one who is free from attachment; *muktasya* > of one
who is loosened, relaxed, or opened; *jnana* > that which is truly known,
that which is known to be true; *avasthita* > contained within, remaining
settled in; *chetasah* > of conscious attention; *yajnaya* > as a sacrifice,
as an act of giving or offering; *acharatah* > undertaking; *karma* > the
continuum of action and reaction; *samagram* > altogether,
completely; *praviliyate* > it becomes dissolved.

**One who is free from attachment,**
**Relaxed and open,**
**Whose attention is settled in what is known to be true,**
**And whose every endeavor is undertaken**
**as an offering or an opportunity for giving —**
**For such a one the [dreamlike] continuum of action and reaction**
**becomes completely dissolved.**

**24**
*brahmarpanam brahma havir / brahmagnau brahmana hutam*
*brahmaiva tena gantavyam / brahmakarma-samadhina*

*brahma* > Brahman ('swelling of the soul,' 'outpouring of the heart,' the one self-existent Absolute); *arpanam* > the process of making an offering; *brahma* > Brahman; *havih* > the item which is offered (such as grains or clarified butter); *brahma* > Brahman; *agnau* > in the fire; *brahmana* > by Brahman; *hutam* > poured out; *brahma* > Brahman; *eva* > indeed; *tena* > by that one; *gantavyam* > to be approached, to be reached; *brahma-karma* > the actions of Brahman; *samadhina* > by settling, by reconciling, by adjusting.

**Brahman, the one self-existent Absolute,
is the process of making an offering,
and Brahman is the item offered;
Brahman is the one pouring out the offering,
and Brahman is the fire receiving the offering.
Indeed, one approaches [the realization of being] Brahman
by reconciling [one's perspective of] Brahman-in-action.**

Krishna's dynamic invitation here is to internally accept and adjust to the two main paradoxes mentioned earlier: that the One expresses as the All, and that the eternally unmoving Non-actor functions in action. The awakened perspective is that it is the nature of the Absolute to function with the simplicity of affectionate intelligence just as it is simply the nature of a flowing river to carry things along on its currents without exerting any effort or having any agenda to carry out.

**25**
*daivam evapare yajnam / yoginah paryupasate
brahmagnav-apare yajnam / yajnenaivo 'pajuhvati*

*daivam* > to the celestials; *eva* > alone; *apare* > some (refers to those seeking Self-realization through the performance of prescribed rituals and selfless work); *yajnam* > sacrificial offering; *yoginah* > yogis; *paryupasate* > they worship; *brahma-agnau* > in the fire of Brahman; *apare* > others (refers to those seeking realization by way of either empirical knowledge or direct knowing); *yajnam* > sacrificial offering; *yajnena* > of the one offering the sacrifice (the illusory 'me' or pseudo-doer); *eva* > alone; *upajuhvati* > they offer (a *juhva* is a ladle used to pour ghee into a ritual sacrificial fire).

**Some yogis [devoted to karma-yoga]
offer worship solely to the celestials
(expressions of Brahman in different divine forms),
Whereas others [devoted to jnana]
offer the sacrificer itself (the assumed ego-self)
into the sacrificial fire of [formless] Brahman alone.**

Verse 6.2.1 of the *Chandogya Upanishad* states *ekam evadvitiyam*, that the Absolute is One only, with nothing second existing anywhere. Yet as long as within the One there is a sense of being something other than the only-existing One, there will accordingly be many different ways of offering *yajna* (sacrifice) for attaining realization of that oneness. Verses 25 through 30 of the Gita describe some of the more prominent traditional ways that such offerings have been made throughout the course of human history beginning with the karma-yogi's use of ritual items such as ghee-wick lamps, scented oils, incense, flowers, natural fans, and other articles of worship. These are generally offered to one's preferred manifestations of Spirit represented in pictures (*alekhya*), in statues (*murtis*), in sacred symbols (*lingams*), and in sacred diagrams (*yantras*). Others, however—the students of *jnana* or Sankhya—internally offer their sense of separate selfhood or sense of personal doership into formless Spirit alone rather than making external offerings to any of Its expressions or representations in forms.

Offerings need not be made with the intention of trying to solve a problem (the appearance of separation in the One), but can simply be made in a spirit of loving reciprocation with the rest of life—with the rest of one's true Self— as encouraged in verses 9 through 16 of Chapter Three. Yet if one's motive *is* to 'unite with Brahman,' then in due course the realization dawns that one *is* that pure Substance ("*aham brahmasmi*") which was thought to be something else.

### 26
*shrotra 'dinindriyanyanye / samyamagnishu juhvati*
*shabdadin vishayan anya / indriyagnishu juhvati*

*shrotra-adini* > beginning with the ears; *indriyani* > the senses; *anye* > others (refers to *brahmacharis* and *sannyasis*, those practicing celibacy and renunciation); *samyama* > of restraint with great effort; *agnishu* > in the fires; *juhvati* > they offer; *shabda-adin* > beginning with sounds; *vishayan* > objects of sense-pleasure; *anye* > others (refers to *grihasthas*, those with families, property, etc.); *indriya* > of the sense-organs; *agnishu* > in the fires; *juhvati* > they offer.

**Others [practicing celibacy and renunciation]**
**Offer their senses beginning with the ears**
**into the fire of arduous self-restraint;**
**While still others [with families, property, and the like]**
**Offer the objects of sense-pleasure beginning with sounds**
**into the fires of the sense-organs.**

The ten senses 'beginning with the ears' are the ears, eyes, nose, tongue, skin, hands, legs, anus, genital, and power of speech. The first five are called *jnanendriyas*, knowledge-acquiring senses, and the remaining five are known as *karmendriyas* or working senses.

There are at least three potential considerations of motive in regard to offering the objects of sense-pleasure into the fires of the sense-organs. One of them may be an interest in pleasing a preferred deity, celestial, or departed spiritual teacher by providing their favorite items to be enjoyed through the devotee making the offering. Another intention may be to completely burn up any still-yet-to-be-enjoyed fruits of karma left from past virtuous works if one feels apprehensive that otherwise, some karma may remain to cause another birth after dissociation from the present body. And a third possibility may be the perspective that the one absolute Reality dwelling within the body is the only recipient and enjoyer of all pleasurable objects offered, vide verse 5.29: "Knowing Me to be the enjoyer of all sacrifices and austerities...one attains everlasting peace."

**27**

*sarvanindriya-karmani / prana-karmani chapare*
*atma-samyama-yogagnau / juhvati jnana-dipite*

> *sarvani indriya-karmani* > the functions of all ten sense-organs;
> *prana-karmani* > functions of the five vital life-airs; *cha* > and;
> *apare* > others; *atma-samyama* > self-discipline with great effort;
> *yoga-agnau* > in the fire of the practice; *juhvati* > they offer;
> *jnana-dipite* > kindled by wisdom, illumined by knowledge.

**And others, with minds illumined by knowledge,**
**Apply great effort in offering the functions**
**of all ten sense-organs and five vital life-airs**
**into the fire of practiced self-discipline.**

The five vital life-airs are *prana*, *apana*, *vyana*, *samana*, and *udana*. There appears to be some difference of opinion among prominent authorities on the *ashtanga-yoga* system as to whether *prana* and *apana* refer to exhalation and inhalation respectively, or the reverse. With all due respect, the first perspective has been supported herein on the basis that verse 1.3.3 of the *Chandogya Upanishad* states: "That which one breathes out is the *prana*, and that which one breathes in is the *apana*." Additionally, *apana* is defined as 'the downward-moving air,' and it is when we inhale that the air enters the nostrils and moves downward into the lungs. So *prana* and *apana* are involved in respiration, with *apana* also governing excretion; *vyana* is the force propelling blood circulation; *samana* enables digestion; and *udana* ('the upward-moving air') is said to have the functions of moving the body/mind system from the state of waking into sleep, and moving perception out of the physical body altogether at the time of the body's death.

**28**

*dravya-yajnas tapoyajna / yoga-yajnas tathapare*
*svadhyaya-jnana-yajnashcha / yatayah samsheeta-vratah*

*dravya-yajnah* > those for whom the principle of sacrifice is exemplified by relinquishing the objects in one's possession; *tapah-yajnah* > those for whom the principle of sacrifice is epitomized by performing austerities; *yoga-yajnah* > those for whom the principle of sacrifice is expressed by practicing dhyana-yoga (meditation) or the raja-yoga system (which has meditation as its nucleus); *tatha* > so also; *apare* > others; *svadhyaya-jnana-yajnah* > those for whom the principle of sacrifice is embodied by studying and reciting the wisdom-teachings of the scriptures; *cha* > and; *yatayah* > those who are self-disciplined; *samsheeta-vratah* > firm vows, strict rules, commitments which are painful to uphold.

**For some, the principle of sacrifice**
**is exemplified by relinquishing one's possessions,**
**Whereas others feel that sacrifice is best expressed**
**by performing austerities.**
**Still others offer sacrifice by practicing meditation**
**in accordance with the raja-yoga system,**
**While there are also those**
**for whom sacrifice entails adhering to strict vows**
**in regard to studying and reciting the wisdom-teachings of the scriptures.**

The austerities mentioned here may or may not involve the concept of penance or of wishing to atone for what were considered to be misdeeds. *Dravya-yajna* may also refer to distributing one's wealth or gifts to others in charity. Raja-yoga has come to be identified with Patanjali's 'eight-limbed' system of ashtanga-yoga. And memorization of a scripture's original language along with its meticulously accurate pronunciation are also often part of the sacrifice mentioned here in conjunction with the study and recitation of ancient texts.

**29**

*apane juhvati pranam / prane 'panam tathapare*
*pranapana-gati ruddhva / pranayama-parayanah*

*apane* > the incoming breath; *juhvati* > they (the raja-yogis and hatha-yogis) offer; *pranam* > the outgoing breath; *prane* > the exhaled breath; *apanam* > the inhaled breath; *tatha* > so also; *apare* > some others (among the raja-yogis and hatha-yogis); *prana-apana-gati* > the pathways of outgoing and incoming breath; *ruddhva* > obstructing, suppressing, stopping; *pranayama* > control of the vital life-force for achieving the state of breathlessness; *parayanah* > intent upon, wholly devoted to.

**Some raja-yogis and hatha-yogis offer their incoming breath
into their outgoing breath (which is known as rechaka, emptying out);
Whereas others offer their exhaled breath
into their inhaled breath (which is known as puraka, filling in);
[Yet both of them are] wholly devoted to controlling the vital life-force,
stopping the circulation of air through the respiratory system,
and attaining the state of breathlessness.**

The practice of *pranayama* is generally commenced by inhaling through one nostril and exhaling through the other, followed by then inhaling through the second nostril and exhaling through the first. This continues in an alternating rhythmic sequence for a little while before the yoga practitioner moves on to more advanced breathing techniques.

### 30
*apare niyata-harah / pranan praneshu juhvati
sarve 'pyete yajnavido / yajna-kshapita-kalmashah*

*apare* > others; *niyata-aharah* > those who regulate their food intake (either by reducing the quantity, restricting the types taken, or both); *pranan* > the vital life-airs; *praneshu* > into the vital life-airs; *juhvati* > they offer; *sarve api ete* > all of these (described in verses 25 through 30); *yajna-vidah* > those who are learned in regard to sacrifice; *yajna-kshapita* > destroyed by acts of sacrifice, diminished by the offerings; *kalmashah* > darkness, stains, impurities.

**Still others reduce or restrict their intake of food,
thereby offering their vital life-airs into themselves.
All these who are learned in the art of sacrifice
have their darkness removed by their respective offerings.**

The darkness mentioned here refers to the sense of separation from the only-existing One. It may also refer to a number of other things which are corollaries of that, such as fear, greed, hatred, uninvestigated beliefs, confusion, attachment, or the sense of personal doership (*ahamkara*), all of which undoubtedly serve to perpetuate the illusion of independent selfhood and obscure the recognition of one's true nature. Therefore the removal of this darkness may very likely take a considerably shorter period of time if one is devoid of a sense of having become highly adept in the performance of whatever type of sacrifice the body/mind system has been engaged in.

### 31
*yajna-shishtamrita-bhujo / yanti brahma sanatanam*
*nayam loko 'styayajnasya / kuto 'nyah kuru-sattama*

*yajna-shishta* > the remnants of sacrifice (reciprocation for the different offerings described in verses 25 through 30); *amrita-bhujah* > those who enjoy the nectar which confers healing or immortality; *yanti* > they arrive; *brahma sanatanam* > primeval, everlasting Spirit; *na* > not; *ayam* > this; *lokah* > world; *asti* > it belongs to, it is enough for; *ayajnasya* > for one who performs no sacrifice or offering of oneself; *kutah* > how; *anyah* > other; *kuru-sattama* > O best of the Kurus.

**Those who partake of the nectar-remnants of such sacrifices
[in due course] arrive at [the recognition of being] timeless Brahman.
O best of the Kurus,
If even this world is not for one who has no giving spirit,
How could the other [heavenly] domain be so?**

*Yajna-shishta* traditionally refers specifically to the foods, liquids, flowers, perfumed oils, etc. remaining at a ceremonial site after the divine expressions of the Absolute in unseen subtler forms have first been offered their ritual share. Yet again, we are reminded of the broader perspective discussed in relation to verses 3.11-12 wherein all provisions are made available to those who are themselves available for offering what is needed when it is needed in the ordinary course of interactive daily life.

### 32
*evam bahu-vidha yajna / vitata brahmano mukhe*
*karmajan viddhi tan sarvan / evam jnatva vimokshyase*

*evam* > thus; *bahu-vidhah* > of many types; *yajnah* > offerings, sacrifices; *vitatah* > spread out, extended; *brahmanah mukhe* > in the Vedas (referred to therein as 'the mouth of Brahman,' or as 'the breath of Brahman' in the *Brihad-aranyaka Upanishad* 2.4.10); *karma-jan* > born of action; *viddhi* > you should know; *tan* > them; *sarvan* > all; *evam* > thus; *jnatva* > knowing; *vimokshyase* > you will be liberated, you will be freed (from the darkness of illusion mentioned in verse 30 and the 'dark thicket of misbelief' mentioned in verse 2.52).

Thus sacrifices of many different types
have been disseminated in the Vedas.
You should know all such sacrifices to be born of action,
For by knowing them as such, you will be freed
from the darkness of illusion.

**33**

*shreyan dravya-mayad yajnaj / jnana-yajnah parantapa*
*sarvam karma-'khilam partha / jnane parisamapyate*

*shreyan* > better; *dravya-mayat* > the use of material objects; *yajnat* > than the sacrifice; *jnana-yajnah* > sacrifice made for the sake of discovering innate wisdom; *parantapa* > one who eliminates enemies, one who gives much trouble to enemies; *sarvam* > all; *karma* > actions; *akhilam* > without exception; *partha* > O son of Pritha; *jnane* > in knowing, in wisdom; *parisamapyate* > it arrives at completion, it is fully completed.

**Better than sacrifices involving the use of [external] objects**
**Are [internal] sacrifices made for the sake of discovering**
**one's own innate wisdom, O eliminator of enemies.**
**O Partha, all actions without exception**
**culminate in some measure of wisdom.**

Sacrifices involving the use of physical objects include relinquishing one's possessions and dispensing gifts in charity, as well as utilizing material paraphernalia for the performance of ritual ceremonies. Ironically, the presentation of the phrase *jnana-yajnah* as 'the sacrifice of knowledge' in many Gita translations has an extra poignancy — presumably unintended — in that it connotes letting go of all ego-reinforcing, self-referenced 'knowledge' comprised of unexplored beliefs. This premise actually is essential to discovering the truth of one's original unborn nature.

**34**

*tad viddhi pranipatena / pariprashnena sevaya*
*upadekshyanti te jnanam / jnaninas tattva-darshinah*

*tat* > that; *viddhi* > please know; *pranipatena* > by bowing respectfully; *pariprashnena* > by inquiring sincerely; *sevaya* > by humbly rendering service; *upadekshyanti* > they will advise, they will point to; *te* > you; *jnanam* > clear perception of what is true; *jnaninah* > those who perceive via the immediacy of direct experience; *tattva* > the true, the real, the essence or substance; *darshinah* > those who see.

**Know that by respectfully bowing,**
**sincerely inquiring,**
**and humbly offering service**
**To those with clear, undistorted perception**
**of what is truly known and what is truly unknown,**
**Those seers of the truth will offer pointers to you**
**in regard to perceiving via the immediacy of direct experience**
**[rather than perceiving through conditioned patterns of thought].**

Direct knowing is direct experience completely unaltered by self-referenced memory. This is different from understanding. One can fully understand what an Indian chikoo fruit is, yet it's not even remotely possible to know what it tastes like by hearing even the most detailed description about it.

### 35

*yaj jnatva na punar moham / evam yasyasi pandava*
*yena bhutanyasheshena / drakshyasyatmanyatho mayi*

*yad* > which; *jnatva* > directly knowing, directly perceiving what is true; *na* > not; *punah* > again; *moham* > confusion; *evam* > thus; *yasyasi* > you will fall into, you will be harassed by; *pandava* > O son of Pandu; *yena* > by means of which; *bhutani* > living beings; *asheshena* > entirely, without remainder; *drakshyasi* > you will see; *atmani* > within yourself, within the Spirit-Self; *atho* > likewise, therefore; *mayi* > within Me.

**Upon directly perceiving what is true,**
**you will not fall into confusion again, O son of Pandu,**
**For by such perception you will see that the entirety of living beings**
**are within you, the Spirit-Self,**
**And therefore also within Me (the same one Self).**

We may recall Krishna's statement in verse 2.24 that all-pervasive Spirit is not subject to the excruciating dilemma of being divided up into parts (*achchedyo 'yam*, "This Presence is indivisible"). Thus one's true nature only need be remembered, not 're-membered' (as in having Its severed pieces put back together).

### 36

*api ched asi papebhyah / sarvebhyah papa-krittamah*
*sarvam jnana-plavenaiva / vrijinam santarishyasi*

*api* > even; *ched* > if; *asi* > you are; *papebhyah* > of the wicked,
of those who are instrumental in bringing or increasing misfortune;
*sarvebhyah* > of all; *papa-krit-tamah* > performers of the most
harmful deeds; *sarvam* > all; *jnana* > clear, direct knowing;
*plavena* > by the boat; *eva* > certainly; *vrijinam* > wickedness,
deceit, affliction; *santarishyasi* > you will completely cross over.

**Even if you were the most wicked**
**among all perpetrators of harmful deeds,**
**You would certainly cross over all such wickedness**
**in the boat of clear, direct knowing.**

### 37

*yathaidhamsi samiddho'gnir / bhasmasat kurute'rjuna*
*jnanagnih sarva-karmani / bhasmasat kurute tatha*

*yatha* > as; *edhamsi* > kindling sticks, firewood; *samiddhah* > inflamed,
blazing; *agnih* > fire; *bhasmasat* > to ashes; *kurute* > it reduces,
it diminishes; *arjuna* > O Arjuna; *jnana-agnih* > the fire of direct knowing;
*sarva* > all; *karmani* > reactions proceeding from performed actions;
*bhasmasat* > to ashes; *kurute* > it reduces, it diminishes; *tatha* > in that way.

**As a blazing fire reduces firewood to ashes, O Arjuna,**
**So in the same way**
**does the fire of direct knowing reduce to ashes**
**[the potential for experiencing] reactions to performed actions.**

There are three types of reactions to actions which could potentially be
experienced in a dreamlike way within infinite Consciousness. Those three,
which are burnt up by directly knowing that one is never a doer of action
at any time (vide verse 20) are: (1) *sanchita*, the accumulated repository of
reactions which have not yet manifest in response to actions which occurred
in the past; (2) *prarabdha*, reactions which *have* already manifest in response
to actions which occurred in the past; and (3) *agami*, future reactions to
actions occurring at the present time. The way in which the second type is
burned up is by being significantly lessened in intensity and duration, but
anything which is already present cannot realistically be said to have been
obliterated prior to its presence.

### 38

*na hi jnanena sadrisham / pavitram iha vidyate*
*tat svayam yoga-samsiddhah / kalenatmani vindati*

*na* > not; *hi* > certainly; *jnanena* > to direct knowing; *sadrisham* > equal;
*pavitram* > purifier; *iha* > here in this world; *vidyate* > it is found; *tat* > that
(knowing); *svayam* > one's own; *yoga* > perception of the unitary wholeness of
Spirit and Its expression as all of Life; *samsiddhah* > healed, cured, restored;
*kalena* > in due course of time; *atmani* > in oneself; *vindati* > one finds.

**Certainly no purifier equal to direct knowing is to be found in this world.**
**By that knowing,**
**In due course of time one discovers within oneself**
**restored perception of the unitary wholeness of Life.**

### 39

*shraddhavan labhate jnanam / tatparah samyatendriyah*
*nanam labdhva param shantim / achirena 'dhigachchati*

*shraddhavan* > possessing faith; *labhate* > one discovers, one perceives;
*jnanam* > direct knowing, innate wisdom; *tat-parah* > devoted to that;
*samyata* > held in check, self-contained; *indriyah* > the senses;
*jnanam* > direct knowing; *labdhva* > having met with, having
gained; *param shantim* > the supreme peace; *achirena* > soon,
quickly; *adhigachchati* > one finds, one notices.

**Possessing faith in [the value and availability of] innate wisdom,**
**One discovers it [within oneself];**
**Being devoted to that [wisdom which is discovered],**
**the senses become naturally calm and self-contained;**
**And having gained [consistency in the body/mind system's**
**functioning in alignment with] that innate wisdom,**
**One soon finds supreme Peace (one's true nature).**

### 40

*ajnash chashradda-dhanash cha / samshayatma vinashyati*
*nayam loko sti na paro / na sukham samshayatmanah*

*ajnah* > without knowing; *cha* > and; *ashradda-dhanah* > having no faith;
*cha* > and; *samshaya-atma* > the doubting ego-self, the irresolute one;
*vinashyati* > one is destroyed, one perishes; *na* > not; *ayam* > this;
*lokah* > world; *asti* > there is; *na* > not; *parah* > beyond; *na* > nor;
*sukham* > happiness; *samshaya-atmanah* > of the doubting
ego-self, of the irresolute assumed self.

But without knowing [about such wisdom]
and having no faith [in its value or accessibility],
One is verily ruined by one's own doubts,
Because one with a sense of self habituated to doubting
finds no happiness either in this world or beyond it.

### 41

*yoga sannyasta karmanam / jnana sanchinna samshayam*
*atmavantam na karmani / nibadhnanti dhananjaya*

*yoga* > engagement in the selfless work of karma-yoga;
*sannyasta* > renounced; *karmanam* > of actions; *jnana* > direct
knowing; *sanchinna* > cut off, cut to pieces; *samshayam* > doubts;
*atma-vantam* > self-contained; *na* > not; *karmani* > actions;
*nibadhnanti* > they confine, they hold down;
*dhananjaya* > O winner of wealth.

O winner of wealth,
Whatever actions are renounced
by those engaged in the selfless work of karma-yoga —
Their doubts having been cut to pieces
by direct, experiential knowing —
For such self-contained ones, actions impose no bondage.

It would seem that the basis for Krishna's reassurance here is that renouncing
an action is also an action. At the same time, another possible reading of this
verse is that for those self-disciplined, Self-realized ones who have renounced
all of their previously self-centered activities, whatever actions they still
perform for self-preservation impose no bondage upon them. This
perspective would be based on Krishna's statement in verse 3.8 that the
physical body cannot be maintained without engaging in some actions.

### 42

*tasmad ajnana-sambhutam / hritstham jnana-'sinatmanah*
*chittvainam samshayam yogam / atishthottishtha bharata*

*tasmat* > therefore; *ajnana-sambhutam* > produced by non-cognizance;
*hrit-stham* > dwelling in the heart; *jnana-asina* > by the sword of direct
knowing; *atmanah* > of your own; *chittva* > cutting apart; *enam* > this;
*samshayam* > doubting, irresolution; *yogam* > engagement in selfless
work (karma-yoga); *atishtha* > resort to, act upon, carry out;
*uttishtha* > arise; *bharata* > O descendant of Bharata.

**Therefore, utilize your very own sword of experiential knowing**
**For cutting apart the doubts dwelling in your heart**
**which were produced by non-perception [of Life's unitary wholeness].**
**Arise and selflessly carry out your prescribed engagement [in the battle],**
**O descendant of Bharata!**

*om tat saditi srimad bhagavad-gita / supanishatsu brahma-vidyayam*
*yoga-shastre srikrishnarjuna samvade / jnana-yogo nama chaturtho 'dhyayah*

From the Ambrosial Song of God —
A conversation between Krishna and Arjuna
which is a Upanishad (confidential sharing)
of wisdom-teachings regarding the Absolute
And a scripture concerning Self-realization —
Thus ends the Fourth Chapter entitled Jnana-yoga,
Recognizing Divine Unicity By Way of Direct Knowing.

# Chapter Five

## Karma-sannyasa-yoga
### (Recognizing Divine Unicity By Way of Renouncing Self-Centered Action)

"As a bee gathers nectar from a flower without harming its color or fragrance and then moves on, so does the sage-renunciate pass through a village.... We who possess nothing indeed live happily, feasting on joy as do the luminous celestials." — The Dhammapada 4.49 and 15.200

"When mental fluctuations cease, the remaining delusion can be the sense of I-ness. When this is renounced, pure Awareness perceives no individual self and no independent universe. The universe is God's manifesting energy. When the contents of the mind are renounced, their forces flow into the unmanifest field of primordial forces." — Roy Eugene Davis

"In sense-enjoyment there is the fear of disease; in social position, the fear of downfall; in wealth, the fear of thieves; in being honored, the fear of humiliation; in power, the fear of enemies; in beauty, the fear of old age; in scriptural scholarship, the fear of opponents; in virtue, the fear of seducers; and in affiliation with the body, the fear of death. All the things of this mortal world are attended by fear, and renunciation alone bestows fearlessness."
— Sri Bhartrihari, *Vairagya-shatakam*, verse 31

"By all means do renounce the world in every way, and also renounce the poisonous idea that you ever owned anything which could be renounced. By Its very nature the Self is taintless, ageless, and changeless."
— *The Avadhuta Gita of Dattatreya*, verse 3.46

**1**
*arjuna uvacha:*
*sannyasam karmanam krishna / punar yogam cha shamsasi*
*yach chreya etayor ekam / tan me bruhi sunishchitam*

*arjunah uvacha* > Arjuna said; *sannyasam* > renunciation; *karmanam* > of actions; *krishna* > O Krishna; *punah* > again; *yogam* > karma-yoga, the performance of action without attachment to either the action itself or its results; *cha* > and; *shamsasi* > you praise; *yat* > which; *shreyah* > better; *etayoh* > of these two; *ekam* > one; *tat* > that; *me* > to me; *bruhi* > tell; *sunishchitam* > definitely.

**Arjuna said:**
**O Krishna, you praise renunciation of action,**
**And then again you praise the performance of selfless action.**
**Which one of these two is better?**
**Please tell me definitively.**

Arjuna heard Krishna say in verse 3.17 that for one whose entire joy, sense of completeness, and contentment are in the Self alone, there is no activity which must be performed, and this statement seems to be completely contradictory to Krishna's ongoing exhortation to perform all activities without personal motives.

**2**
*sri bhagavan uvacha:*
*sannyasah karma-yogash cha / nihshreyasa-karav ubhau*
*tayos tu karma-sannyasat / karma-yogo vishishyate*

*sri bhagavan uvacha* > the illustrious master said; *sannyasah* > renunciation; *karma-yogah* > action performed without attachment; *cha* > and; *nihshreyasa* > incomparable bliss, ultimate beatitude; *karau* > leading to; *ubhau* > both; *tayoh* > of the two; *tu* > but; *karma-sannyasat* > than renunciation of action; *karma-yogah* > action performed without attachment; *vishishyate* > it is superior.

**The illustrious master said:**
**Both renunciation of action**
**and the performance of action without attachment**
**lead to ultimate beatitude;**
**But of the two,**
**the performance of selfless activity**
**is superior to the renunciation of all activity.**

**3**
*jneyah sa nitya-sannyasi / yo na dveshti na kankshati*
*nirdvandvo hi mahabaho / sukham bandhat pramuchyate*

*jneyah* > to be known; *sah* > that one; *nitya* > perpetual; *sannyasi* > renunciate; *yah* > who; *na* > not; *dveshti* > one hates; *na* > nor; *kankshati* > one desires; *nirdvandvah* > indifferent to the pairs of opposites; *hi* > truly; *maha-baho* > O mighty-armed one; *sukham* > easily; *bandhat* > from bondage; *pramuchyate* > one is liberated.

Those who are free from hatred and desire
are to be known as the perpetual renunciates,
O mighty-armed one.
Because they are indifferent to the pairs of opposites,
They are easily liberated from [that] bondage
[which is inherent in the attempt to control
how the opposites are experienced].

**4**

*sankhya-yogau prithag balah / pravadanti na panditah*
*ekam apyasthitah samyag / ubhayor vindate phalam*

*sankhya* > the cultivation of empirical knowledge; *yogau* > the performance of karma-yoga or selfless work; *prithak* > different; *balah* > childish; *pravadanti* > they declare; *na* > not; *panditah* > those who are wise; *ekam* > one; *api* > even; *asthitah* > undertaken, practiced; *samyanch* > wholly, one-pointedly, correctly; *ubhayoh* > of both; *vindate* > finds; *phalam* > the fruit, the results.

"The cultivation of empirical knowledge
is different from the performance of selfless work" —
The childish declare this; not the wise.
Even one of these practiced wholeheartedly
yields the fruit of both.

During the time period attributed to the Gita's recitation, it was typical for the more serious students of the Sankhya cosmology to renounce all pursuits deemed worldly and embrace monasticism as part of their spiritual quest for *atmajnana* or Self-realization. So Krishna is not moving on to a different subject here, but is continuing his reply to Arjuna's question about renunciation in verse 1. The Purusha and Prakriti spoken of in Sankhya is essentially the same Brahman and Maya spoken of in Vedanta ('the culmination of all Vedic knowledge'), which is also essentially the same Tao and Te of the Tao Te Ching — the ineffable Absolute and Its inherent Power.

**5**

*yat sankhyaih prapyate sthanam / tad yogair api gamyate*
*ekam sankhyam cha yogam cha / yah pashyati sa pashyati*

*yat* > which; *sankhyaih* > by the followers of the Sankhya process; *prapyate* > it is attained; *sthanam* > state, status; *tat* > that; *yogaih* > by the karma-yogis; *api* > also; *gamyate* > it is reached; *ekam* > one; *sankhyam* > the cultivation of empirical knowledge; *cha* > and; *yogam* > the performance of selfless work; *cha* > and; *yah* > who; *pashyati* > one sees; *sah pashyati* > one truly sees.

That state [of Self-recognition]
which is attained by the followers of the Sankhya process
is also arrived at by the karma-yogis.
The way of cultivating empirical knowledge
and the way of performing selfless work are one,
And one who sees this truly sees.

6

*sannyasas tu maha-baho / duhkham aptum ayogatah*
*yoga-yukto munir brahma / na chirena 'dhigachchati*

*sannyasah* > renunciation; *tu* > indeed, yet; *maha-baho* > O mighty-armed one;
*duhkham* > difficult, distressful; *aptum* > to endure, to undergo;
*ayogatah* > without engagement in selfless work; *yoga-yuktah* > engaged in
karma-yoga; *munih* > one who is moved by inner inspiration or ecstasy,
one who deeply values silence or has taken a vow of silence;
*brahma* > Brahman, pure Spirit, the infinite beatific Presence;
*na chirena* > not a long time, soon; *adhigachchati* > one reaches (realizes).

Renunciation of activity is indeed difficult to endure
without [having first undergone a period of] engagement in selfless work,
O mighty-armed one;
Yet those who are moved by inner inspiration to engage in karma-yoga
Before long come to realize
that they are Brahman, the infinite beatific Presence.

It has been observed that many who attempt to take up a life of renunciation
coming directly from a life of predominantly self-centered pursuits remain
predominantly self-centered, and sometimes become even more so after
abandoning their familial and societal responsibilities. For this reason it has
been strongly recommended that one first engage in some years of selfless
work in order to shift the orientation of one's internal system from being
ego-centered to being whole-life-centered.

7

*yoga-yukto vishuddhatma / vijitatma jitendriyah*
*sarva-bhutatma-bhutatma / kurvann api na lipyate*

*yoga-yuktah* > engaged in selfless action; *vishuddha-atma* > one whose
internal network of mind, intellect, ego, and feelings is a clear, transparent
medium for the light of the true Self; *vijita-atma* > one who is self-disciplined;

*jita-indriyah* > one whose senses have been calmed;
*sarva-bhuta-atma-bhuta-atma* > one's Self being the same Self within
all living creatures; *kurvan* > performing activities;
*api* > even though; *na* > not; *lipyate* > one is contaminated.

**A self-disciplined one engaged in selfless action —
Whose senses have been calmed,
Whose internal network is a clear, transparent medium
for the light of the true Self,
And who perceives that Self
as the same one Self within all living beings —
is not contaminated even though performing actions.**

Arjuna was deeply troubled that he would become tainted by sin if he
engaged in battle against his relatives, so Krishna is letting him know that
he would not become contaminated by that activity as he had been taught
to believe he would.

**8-9**
*naiva kinchit karomiti / yukto manyeta tattvavit
pashyan shrinvan sprishan jighrann / ashnan gachchan svapan shvasan*

*pralapan visrijan grihnann / unmishan nimishann api
indriyan'-indriya'rtheshu / vartanta iti dharayan*

*na* > not; *eva* > really; *kinchit* > anything whatsoever;
*karomi* > I do; *iti* > thus; *yuktah* > aligned; *manyeta* > one considers,
one perceives; *tattva-vit* > one who knows the truth; *pashyan* > seeing;
*shrinvan* > hearing; *sprishan* > touching; *jighran* > smelling; *ashnan* > eating;
*gachchan* > walking; *svapan* > sleeping; *shvasan* > breathing;

*pralapan* > talking; *visrijan* > letting go of objects, expelling bodily waste
materials; *grihnan* > taking hold of objects; *unmishan* > opening the eyes;
*nimishan* > closing the eyes; *api* > even; *indriyani* > the senses;
*indriya-artheshu* > in the sense-objects; *vartante* > they move,
they interact; *iti* > thus; *dharayan* > holding, maintaining
(referring to the perception of being a non-doer of action).

**One who knows the truth of the Self
and whose body/mind system functions in alignment with that truth
perceives: "I (pure Awareness)
am actually not doing anything whatsoever."**

Thus, whether [the body is] engaged in seeing, hearing, touching,
smelling, eating, walking, sleeping, breathing,
Speaking, taking hold of or letting go of objects, excreting,
or even simply opening and closing the eyelids,
Such a one maintains the perception
that the senses are merely interacting with their respective sense-objects.

### 10

*brahmanyadhaya karmani / sangam tyaktva karoti yah*
*lipyate na sa papena / padma-pattram ivambhasa*

*brahmani* > to Brahman, infinite Spirit; *adhaya* > giving, offering;
*karmani* > actions; *sangam* > attachment; *tyaktva* > abandoning;
*karoti* > one does; *yah* > who; *lipyate* > one is contaminated;
*na* > not; *sah* > that one; *papena* > by sin, by blameworthiness;
*padma-pattram* > a lotus petal; *iva* > like; *ambhasa* > by water.

As a lotus petal remains ever unmoistened by water,
So does one who abandons attachment
and offers all actions [of the body/mind system]
to Brahman (the totality of Life)
Remain ever untainted by sin or blameworthiness.

The phrase 'to Brahman' further denotes 'in Brahman, with Brahman,
as Brahman,' as portrayed in verse 4.24.

### 11

*kayena manasa buddhya / kevalair indriyair api*
*yoginah karma kurvanti/ sangam tyaktvatma-shuddhaye*

*kayena* > with the body; *manasa* > with the mind; *buddhya* > with the intellect;
*kevalaih* > merely; *indriyaih* > with the senses; *api* > even; *yoginah* > the yogis;
*karma* > actions; *kurvanti* > they perform; *sangam* > attachment, emotional
investment; *tyaktva* > abandoning; *atma-shuddhaye* > for self-purification.

Abandoning any emotional investment,
The yogis perform actions with the body,
with the mind,
with the intellect,
or even merely with the senses,
For the purpose of self-purification.

There is undeniably great practical value in any work, worship, study, or meditation practice which resonantly points one in the direction of unconditioned truth. This truth has been indicated in an infinite number of ways, such as in the *Katha Upanishad*, verse 6.1: "Brahman is eternally pure, unchanging, free, and deathless"; or in verse 8 of the *Isha Upanishad*: "Brahman is radiant, incorporeal, inviolable, without parts, pure, and untouched by evil." So the self-purification mentioned here ultimately refers to a shift in the way one perceives oneself, as encouraged via karma-yoga in verse 6. In the words of Ramesh S. Balsekar: "Consciousness is all there is as pure Subjectivity. So all that can happen is that the seeker 'becomes' Consciousness or That Which Always Is when there *is* no seeker. It's either the seeker or that Consciousness; the seeker cannot *know* that Consciousness. But usually what the seeker does is that he or she spends years wanting to know what Consciousness is, and so long as there is a seeker wanting to know Consciousness, then what the seeker has done is usurped the subjectivity of the pure Subject. And worse, the seeker has converted pure Subjectivity into an object which the *pseudo*-Subject wants to understand! This is really my interpretation of 'the original sin,' if there can be anything like a sin at all. Yet nothing can happen unless it is the will of God, so even this 'original sin' could not have happened unless it is the will of God."

**12**
*yuktah karma-phalam tyaktva / shantim apnoti naisthikim
ayuktah kama-karena / phale sakto nibadhyate*

*yuktah* > functioning in alignment with the truth of pure Being; *karma-phalam* > the fruits (rewards) of action; *tyaktva* > having abandoned; *shantim* > peace; *apnoti* > one reaches (realizes); *naisthikim* > perfect, complete, final; *ayuktah* > not functioning in alignment with the truth of pure Being; *kama-karena* > actions motivated by desire; *phale* > in the fruits (rewards); *saktah* > attached; *nibadhyate* > one is bound up.

**Having abandoned [all interest in] rewards
resulting from the performance of actions,
Those who function in alignment with the truth of pure Being
realize themselves to be that perfect Peace Itself;
Whereas those who are not thus aligned,
whose actions are motivated by desires,
are bound up by attachment to the fruits of their labors.**

**13**
*sarva-karmani manasa / sannyasyaste sukham vashi
nava-dvare pure dehi / naiva kurvan na karayan*

*sarva* > all; *karmani* > actions; *manasa* > by the mind (referring to the recognition that "I am actually not doing anything whatsoever," as stated in verse 9); *sannyasya* > renouncing, casting aside, letting go of; *aste* > one sits; *sukham* > at ease, comfortably, happily; *vashi* > having autocratic sovereignty; *nava-dvare* > having nine gates; *pure* > in the city; *dehi* > the indwelling presence of Awareness within the body (here specifically referring to that particular body mentioned in the previous verse within which there is the realization of being perfect Peace); *na* > neither; *eva* > at all, exactly so; *kurvan* > performing actions; *na* > nor; *karayan* > causing actions.

**Having internally let go of [the sense of independent doership
in regard to] all actions within a particular body,
Pure Awareness abides perfectly at ease
as the sovereign in that city of nine gates,
Neither performing nor causing actions at any time**.

As mentioned earlier, the abidance of pure Consciousness is not a state, and this verse also does not refer exclusively to a final state of functioning *within* Consciousness. It speaks of an opportunity that is available at every moment, the outgrowth of which may last for any length of time up until the point when awakened perception stabilizes in a particular body/mind system. The nine gates of the physical body are the two eyes, two ears, two nostrils, the navel, genital, and anus.

**14**
*na kartritvam na karmani / lokasya srijati prabhuh
na karmaphala-samyogam / svabhavas tu pravartate*

*na* > not; *kartritvam* > the agency or means of action; *na* > nor;
*karmani* > factors associated with actions; *lokasya* > of people;
*srijati* > It creates; *prabhuh* > the master (referring to the sovereign
of the physical body described in the previous verse) *na* > nor;
*karma-phala-samyogam* > the union of an action with its fruits (results);
*svabhavah* > the spontaneity of Nature; *tu* > but; *pravartate* > it proceeds.

**That Sovereign does not infuse anyone
with [the compulsion to perform] actions;
Nor does It arrange the various factors associated with actions;
Nor does It dispense all the sweet and bitter fruits of actions.
Rather, Nature proceeds spontaneously [in all of this momentum].**

**15**

*nadatte kasyachit papam / na chaiva sukritam vibhuh*
*ajnanena-'vritam jnanam / tena muhyanti jantavah*

*na* > neither; *adatte* > it takes; *kasyachit* > of anyone whatsoever;
*papam* > malefic; *na* > nor; *cha* > and; *eva* > even; *sukritam* > beneficent
deeds; *vibhuh* > Omnipresence; *ajnanena* > by ignoring, by overlooking,
by not acknowledging; *avritam* > enveloped; *jnanam* > pure innate knowing;
*tena* > by this; *muhyanti* > there is confusion; *jantavah* > people, human beings.

**Omnipresence does not take account
of the malefic nor even the beneficent deeds of anyone whatsoever.
Confusion naturally arises within [Its expressions in] humanlike forms
when pure knowing is enveloped by ignoring [what is actually known
and not acknowledging what is actually unknown].**

The reading of *na adatte* ('It does not take') as 'It does not take account of'
supports the statement in the previous verse that the Sovereign in all bodies
does not dispense the sweet and bitter fruits of actions. This essentially
means that infinite Consciousness does not judge and accordingly reward or
punish the dreamlike images temporarily appearing within It. Or it may be
read in the sense that pure Consciousness does not take on any karmic burden
as a result of events occurring within Its dreams. From either perspective,
however, the reactions to all helpful or harmful actions still proceed
spontaneously by the kinetic functioning of Nature, as stated in several
previous verses. And when there is *yoga-yukta*, functioning in alignment with
the recognition of unicity in a particular body/mind vessel, there is then
typically a natural inclination to offer more toward relieving suffering in the
world rather than creating suffering. This is a completely uncontrived
expression of *dharma*.

**16**

*jnanena tu tad ajnanam / yesham nasheetam atmanah*
*tesham adityavaj jnanam / prakashayati tat param*

*jnanena* > by direct knowing; *tu* > but; *tat* > that;
*ajnanam* > the condition of ignoring or overlooking, incognizance;
*yesham* > whose; *nasheetam* > destroyed, removed; *atmanah* > of the true Self;
*tesham* > of them; *aditya-vat* > like the sun; *jnanam* > experiential knowing;
*prakashayati* > it illumines, it reveals; *tat param* > that supreme Reality.

**But for those within whom the condition of overlooking the true Self
is removed by experiential knowing,
That knowing, like the sun,
reveals the supreme Reality [to Itself].**

Just as both the brilliance of daylight and the darkness of nighttime are
combinedly aspects of a single twenty-four-hour day, both all-knowingness
(*sarvajna*) and unknowingness (*mugdha*) are conjointly eternal aspects of
the singular absolute Consciousness. So there can't be a cessation of
unknowingness in the Absolute, but there *can* be a cessation of inadvertently
ignoring the eternal nature of oneself when the One is functioning through a
body/mind vehicle. Poetically speaking, the One's 'missing Itself' happens
when It bypasses Its own immediacy due to being captivated by the
compelling story of the fictitious ego-self. Who doesn't love great fiction?

### 17

*tad-buddhayas tad-atmanas / tan-nishthas tat-parayanah
gachchantya-'punar-avrittim / jnana-nirdhuta-kalmashah*

*tat-buddhayah* > those whose mind and intellect are absorbed in That
(the supreme Reality mentioned in the previous verse); *tat-atmanah* > those
whose sense of self is as That; *tat-nishthah* > those who are conclusively
resolved in regard to being That, those who have firm devotion to realizing
that they are That; *tat-parayanah* > those for whom realization of being That
is their primary objective, those who consider That to be their ultimate
refuge; *gachchanti* > they arrive at, they fall into; *apunah* > not again;
*avrittim* > repetition of rebirth; *jnana* > direct knowing; *nirdhuta* > shaken off;
*kalmashah* > dust, dirt (refers to the misconception that one is something other
than the only abiding Reality, as indicated in the first half of this verse).

**Those whose mind and intellect are absorbed in that supreme Reality —
Whose sense of self is as That —
Who have firm devotion to realizing that they are That —
Or who consider That to be their ultimate refuge —
All of them arrive at the cessation of [the dream of] repeated births,
Having shaken off the dust of misconception
through directly knowing the truth.**

### 18

*vidya-vinaya-sampanne / brahmane gavi hastini
shuni chaiva shvapake cha / panditah sama-darshinah*

*vidya* > learning, scholarship; *vinaya* > having good upbringing, possessing fine character; *sampanne* > endowed; *brahmane* > in the brahmin priest; *gavi* > upon a cow; *hastini* > upon an elephant; *shuni* > upon a dog; *cha* > and; *eva* > even; *shva-pake* > upon one who cooks and eats dogs; *cha* > and; *panditah* > those who are wise; *sama-darshinah* > seeing equally.

**Those who are truly wise view [all living beings] equally —**
**A brahmin priest endowed with learning and fine character,**
**A cow,**
**An elephant,**
**A dog,**
**And even one who eats dogs.**

Krishna is specifically addressing the social tendencies of his time, which were to give all honor to cultured and scholarly persons from the brahmin caste while deriding illiterate or simple tribal people. It was also common for men to protect and worship cows while using other animals for religious sacrifices.

**19**
*ihaiva tairjitah sargo / yesham samye sthitam manah*
*nirdosham hi samam brahma / tasmad brahmani te sthitah*

*iha* > here in this world; *eva* > even; *taih* > by them; *jitah* > overcome; *sargah* > gushing forth into manifestation, emission or outflow of created matter; *yesham* > whose; *samye* > in equability and impartiality; *sthitam* > established; *manah* > mind; *nirdosham* > flawless; *hi* > truly; *samam* > equilibrium; *brahma* > Brahman; *tasmat* > therefore; *brahmani* > in Brahman; *te* > they; *sthitah* > situated, abiding.

**Even here in this world,**
**All that gushes forth into manifestation**
**is overcome by those whose minds are established**
**in equability and impartiality.**
**Flawless is the equilibrium of pure Spirit;**
**Thus they abide as [clear reflections of] That.**

What is meant by the 'overcoming' of phenomena flowing from the limitless wellspring of creativity within Consciousness is explained in the next verse.

**20**
*na prahrishyet priyam prapya / nodvijet prapya chapriyam*
*sthira-buddhir asammudho / brahmavid brahmani sthitah*

*na* > not; *prahrishyet* > one should rejoice; *priyam* > dear, favored;
*prapya* > obtaining; *na* > not; *udvijet* > one should feel agitated or afflicted;
*prapya* > meeting with; *cha* > also; *apriyam* > disagreeable, disliked;
*sthira-buddhih* > steadfast or unwavering intelligence; *asammudhah* >
unconfused; *brahma-vit* > one who 'knows Brahman' (as an 'other'),
one who has had some direct experience of being perfect Peace as
mentioned in verse 12; *brahmani* > in Brahman; *sthitah* > situated, abiding.

**Neither becoming exhilarated upon obtaining what is favored
nor becoming disturbed upon encountering what is disliked,
Possessing steadfast intelligence, unconfused —
One who has had direct experience of being unalloyed Serenity
abides as That.**

### 21
*bahya-sparsheshvasaktatma / vindatyatmani yat sukham
sa brahmayoga-yuktatma / sukham akshayam ashnute*

*bahya* > external, that which is outside; *sparsheshu* > in experiencing
through sensory contact; *asakta* > unattached, having no emotional
investment; *atma* > oneself; *vindati* > one finds; *atmani* > in oneself,
in the Spirit-Self; *yat* > who; *sukham* > happiness; *sah* > this one;
*brahma-yoga-yukta-atma* > whose expressed self — the entire
psychophysiological network — is stabilized in alignment with
the realization that only Spirit exists expressing Itself as all of Life;
*sukham* > happiness; *akshayam* > imperishable; *ashnute* > one arrives at.

**One who has no emotional investment
in one's contact with the objects of the senses
Finds happiness naturally inherent within oneself;
And upon the entirety of the expressed self
becoming stabilized in alignment with the realization of being pure Spirit,
Such a one arrives at imperishable (ever-new) happiness.**

### 22
*ye hi samsparshaja bhoga / duhkha-yonaya eva te
adyanta-vantah kaunteya / na teshu ramate budhah*

*ye* > who; *hi* > indeed; *samsparsha-jah* > born of sensory contact;
*bhogah* > pleasures; *duhkha* > trouble; *yonayah* > sources of; *eva* > just,
merely; *te* > they; *adi* > beginning; *anta* > end; *vantah* > having;
*kaunteya* > O son of Kunti; *na* > not; *teshu* > in them; *ramate* > one is
delighted, one is contented; *budhah* > the intelligent one.

**Pleasures derived through sensory contact**
**are just sources of trouble, O son of Kunti.**
**As they have a beginning and an end,**
**One who is intelligent notices**
**that they are not actually sources of contentment.**

As mentioned in the notes to verse 3.43, by attentive observation it can be perceived that the happiness felt when a desired object is acquired is not actually caused by the object itself, but by the cessation of desiring it.

### 23

*shaknotihaiva yah sodhum / prak sharira-vimokshanat*
*kamakrodhod-bhavam vegam / sa yuktah sa sukhi narah*

*shaknoti* > one is able; *iha* > here in this world; *eva* > even; *yah* > who; *sodhum* > to tolerate; *prak* > before; *sharira* > the body; *vimokshanat* > release from, giving up; *kama* > desire; *krodha* > anger; *udbhavam* > produced from, arising from; *vegam* > agitation, impulses; *sah* > that one; *yuktah* > aligned with truth; *sah* > that one; *sukhi* > happy; *narah* > a human being, a person.

**Even while still in this world**
**and before giving up [utilization of] the body,**
**One who is able to tolerate the impulses produced by desire and anger**
**Lives happily aligned with truth**
**during the experience of being human.**

### 24

*yo'ntah-sukho'ntara-'ramas / tathantar-jyotir eva yah*
*sa yogi brahma-nirvanam / brahma-bhuto 'dhigachchhati*

*yah* > who; *antah-sukhah* > happiness within; *antah-aramah* > contentment within; *tatha* > in like manner, as well; *antah-jyotih* > illumination within; *eva* > only; *yah* > who; *sah yogi* > that yogi; *brahma-nirvanam* > complete extinguishing of the imagined self in Brahman; *brahma-bhutah* > being Brahman; *adhigachchhati* > one attains, one finds.

**One whose happiness is obtained from within,**
**whose contentment is found within,**
**And whose illumination [in ascertaining what is true]**
**comes only from within as well—**
**That yogi [fully embodying the realization of] being Brahman**
**attains complete extinguishing of the imagined self in Brahman.**

*Brahma-bhuta* can also be translated as 'becoming Brahman,' which would be meant in the same sense as *brahmayoga-yuktatma* in verse 21 or *tad-atmanas* in verse 17. But in truth nothing other than Brahman exists to become Brahman, vide *Chandogya Upanishad* 3.14.1: *sarvam khalvidam brahma* ("All this is Brahman") and Bhagavad-Gita 7.19: *vasudevah sarvam iti* ("All is divine Omnipresence").

**25**

*labhante brahma-nirvanam / rishayah kshina-kalmashah*
*chinna-dvaidha yatatmanah / sarvabhuta-hite ratah*

*labhante* > they attain; *brahma-nirvanam* > cessation of self-conceptualization in the Absolute; *rishayah* > the seer-poets; *kshina* > diminished, waned, worn away; *kalmashah* > taints of darkness in the internal subtle body; *chinna* > cut away, removed; *dvaidhah* > sense of dualism, doubts; *yata-atmanah* > self-restrained; *sarva-bhuta* > all living beings; *hite* > for the benefit or well-being of others; *ratah* > delighting in, devoted to.

**Those seers of truth whose taints of internal darkness have worn away,**
**Whose dualistic perspective has been removed,**
**Who are self-controlled**
**and delight in the welfare of all beings —**
**They attain complete cessation of self-conceptualization in the Absolute.**

The internal darkness mentioned here refers to the *aghayur indriyaramo* mentioned in verse 3.16, the inclination to live unconsciously in a self-centered way for one's own pleasure rather than living consciously in a Life-centered way for the good of the whole. This is further affirmed by the phrase *sarvabhuta-hite ratah* herein, 'delighting in the welfare of all beings.' And self-control does not refer to exerted willfulness, but rather to the earnest willingness to simply be free from unnecessary sense-indulgence.

**26**

*kamakrodha-viyuktanam / yatinam yata-chetasam*
*abhito brahma-nirvanam / vartate viditatmanam*

*kama-krodha-viyuktanam* > of those who have disconnected themselves from indulgence in desires and anger; *yatinam* > of the ascetics; *yata* > restrained, subdued; *chetasam* > mind; *abhitah* > on both sides, before and after; *brahma-nirvanam* > the complete cessation of the pseudo-doer in the Absolute; *vartate* > it stays; *vidita-atmanam* > of those who know the truth of being the pure Spirit-Self, of those who know the truth of the imagined self being purely imaginary.

For those whose asceticism is displayed
by abstaining from indulgence in desires and anger,
Whose mind is subdued,
And who know the truth regarding the actual Self and the imagined self,
There is complete cessation of the assumed self in the Absolute
both while still with the body, and thereafter.

Subduing the mind means subduing the habitual impulse to filter direct experience through self-referencing thought-patterns or memories. This shift in the orientation of the internal mechanism becomes possible by consciously taking notice of one's 'default settings' when they are actively engaged — at the moments when this type of reflexive action is happening within. *Brahma-nirvana* refers to the effacement of all *vasanas* or subconscious mental impressions based on remembrances of the past, imaginings about the future, and interpretations of one's experiences in the moment-to-moment present.

### 27-28
*sparshan kritva bahir bahyamsh / chakshush chaivantare bhruvoh*
*pranapanau samau kritva / nasabhyantara-charinau*

*yatendriya-manobuddhir / munir moksha-parayanah*
*vigatechcha-bhaya-krodho / yah sada mukta eva sah*

*sparshan* > sensory contact; *kritva* > having done;
*bahih* > external; *bahyan* > eliminated; *chakshuh* > gaze; *cha* > and;
*eva* > indeed; *antare* > between; *bhruvoh* > of the two eyebrows;
*prana* > exhalation of the breath; *apanau* > inhalation of
the breath; *samau* > equal; *kritva* > having made;
*nasa-abhyantara* > within the nose; *charinau* > moving;

*yata* > subdued, restricted; *indriya* > senses; *manah* > mind; *buddhih* > intellect;
*munih* > the sage or sagess; *moksha-parayanah* > whose highest aim is
emancipation, who is wholly devoted to release; *vigata* > disappeared;
*ichcha* > desire; *bhaya* > fear; *krodhah* > anger; *yah* > who; *sada* > always,
forever; *muktah* > liberated; *eva* > certainly; *sah* > that one.

For one who has [in any given moment]
eliminated sensory contact with the external environment,
Fixed the [inward] gaze between the two eyebrows,
And equalized the flow of the incoming and outgoing breath
moving through the nostrils —

> Whose senses, mind, and intellect are calm,
> Who is wholly devoted to release
> [from the trance of identification with a pseudo-self],
> And from whom desire, fear, and anger have disappeared —
> That sage or sagess is certainly liberated forever.

This again refers to the potential within infinite Consciousness to forget one of Its infinitely many expressions in form, as mentioned in regard to verse 4.9.

### 29

*bhoktaram yajna-tapasam / sarvaloka-maheshvaram*
*suhridam sarva-bhutanam / jnatva mam shantim richchati*

*bhoktaram* > the enjoyer; *yajna-tapasam* > of sacrifices and austerities (as enumerated in verses 4.25-30); *sarva-loka* > of all worlds, of all regions throughout space; *maha-ishvaram* > great Lord; *suhridam* > affectionate friend, kind-hearted ally; *sarva-bhutanam* > of all living beings; *jnatva* > knowing; *mam* > Me (pure Spirit); *shantim* > peace; *richchati* > one reaches, one attains.

> Knowing Me to be the enjoyer of all sacrifices and austerities,
> the great Lord of all regions throughout space,
> and the affectionate friend of all living beings,
> one attains everlasting peace.

Krishna here once again expresses from the standpoint of being the one omnipresent Reality within all life-forms first mentioned in verse 2.24.

*om tat saditi srimad bhagavad-gita / supanishatsu brahma-vidyayam / yoga-shastre*
*srikrishnarjuna samvade / karma-sannyasa-yogo nama panchamo 'dhyayah*

> From the Ambrosial Song of God —
> A conversation between Krishna and Arjuna
> which is a Upanishad (confidential sharing)
> of wisdom-teachings regarding the Absolute
> And a scripture concerning Self-realization —
> Thus ends the Fifth Chapter entitled Karma-sannyasa-yoga,
> Recognizing Divine Unicity By Way of Renouncing Self-Centered Action.

# Chapter Six

---

# Dhyana-yoga
## (Recognizing Divine Unicity By Way of Meditation)

"Perceiving the distinction between the true Self and that which is born of Nature (the mind), the continuance of self-conceptualization ceases. From that point onward, the internal faculty of thinking, feeling, and willing has a natural tendency to function in accordance with the recognition of this distinction, and thus Consciousness gravitates toward realizing Its perfect oneness (*kaivalya*)."

"For one who is completely disinterested even in the most exalted states of meditative perception due to *viveka-khyati* (perceiving the distinction between the Real and the dreamlike), there is *dharma-megha samadhi*, a flooding downpour of divine recognition of one's true nature by the raincloud of integrative absorption [within Consciousness]."

"Subsequently, there is cessation of the sequential transformations of the components of Nature, their purpose having been completely fulfilled."

"[What is known as] perfect oneness is when the three components of Nature (Prakriti) become utterly devoid of any purpose to fulfill for pure Spirit (Purusha), and so return to their original [latent, unmanifest] condition. Thus the energetic power inherent in Consciousness (*chiti-shakti*) is re-situated in Its own [unborn] essence."
—Patanjali's *Yoga-Sutras*, verses 4.25-26, 4.29, 4.32, and 4.34

## 1

*sri bhagavan uvacha:*
*anashritah karma-phalam / karyam karma karoti yah*
*sa sannyasi cha yogi cha / na niragnir na chakriyah*

*sri bhagavan uvacha* > the opulent one (Krishna) said;
*anashritah* > not depending upon; *karma-phalam* > the resulting fruits of action; *karyam* > to be done; *karma* > actions; *karoti* > one performs; *yah* > who; *sah* > that one; *sannyasi* > the renunciate; *cha* > and; *yogi* > the practitioner of selfless work or meditation; *cha* > and; *na* > not; *nih* > without; *agnih* > fire; *na* > nor; *cha* > and; *akriyah* > without sacred rites.

**The opulent one, Krishna, said:**
**Those who perform actions which need to be done [in any given moment]**
**without depending upon the resulting fruits of actions —**
**They are the true renunciates and the true yogis as well;**
**not those who are merely without a consecrated fire and sacred rites.**

'Without a consecrated fire and sacred rites' refers to those who attempt to embrace inactivity as a spiritual practice, as reproved by Krishna in verses 4 through 8 of Chapter Three. Additionally, in previous times in India, some men would put on saffron-colored robes and declare themselves renunciates when they simply no longer wished to have the responsibility of attending to the maintenance of their families, which often included the conducting of *yajnas* (ceremonial offerings) if they were members of the brahmin caste. So here Krishna is saying that anyone who is open and available to be utilized as an instrument for whatever needs to be done when it needs to be done is actually the authentic *sannyasi* (renunciate).

**2**
*yam sannyasam iti prahur / yogam tam viddhi pandava*
*na hyasannyasta-sankalpo / yogi bhavati kashchana*

*yam* > which; *sannyasam* > renunciation; *iti* > thus; *prahuh* > they (the sages) say; *yogam* > engagement in selfless work (karma-yoga) or meditation (dhyana-yoga); *tam* > this; *viddhi* > know that; *pandava* > O son of Pandu; *na* > not; *hi* > indeed; *asannyasta* > without renouncing; *sankalpah* > motives, wishes, expectations; *yogi* > the practitioner of selfless work or meditation; *bhavati* > one becomes; *kashchana* > anyone.

**What the sages call renunciation —**
**Know that to be engagement in selfless work or meditation,**
**O son of Pandu;**
**For indeed, no one can become a karma-yogi or a dhyana-yogi**
**without renouncing expectations.**

The word *yogam* here refers to both selfless work and meditation, as Krishna reintroduced the practice of raja-yoga into his dialogue with Arjuna at the end of the last chapter in verses 27-28, and he resumes speaking about it again in greater detail in upcoming verses 10-14.

**3**
*arurukshor muner yogam / karma karanam uchyate*
*yoga-rudhasya tasyaiva / shamah karanam uchyate*

*arurukshoh* > of one who desires to ascend, advance, or progress;
*muneh* > of the sage or sagess; *yogam* > to realization of unicity;
*karma* > activity; *karanam* > the means, the way; *uchyate* > it is said;
*yoga-arudhasya* > of one who has ascended to the recognition of divine
unicity; *tasya* > of that one; *eva* > indeed; *shamah* > tranquility,
rest; *karanam* > the means, the way; *uchyate* > it is said.

**For the sage or sagess who wishes to progress
toward the realization of divine unicity,
Activity [such as inquiring into one's true nature]
is said to be the way;
For one who has already realized oneness,
Tranquility (simply abiding in one's true nature)
is said to be the way.**

The activity indicated here encompasses all the various *sadhanas* (spiritual
practices) enumerated in verses 25-30 of Chapter Four, as well as all those
offered on all the various paths in all schools of spiritual ideology. In
accordance with one's acquired nature one may feel inclined to experiment
with some particular practice in the hope that such *sadhana* may lead to
Self-realization. This may take the form of studying books, attending
*satsangs*, meditating, performing ashtanga-yoga, engaging in charitable
work, chanting mantras, singing *bhajans* (devotional songs), worshipping
images, or going on pilgrimage to holy places. Whatever the *sadhana*, by
paying careful attention to one's direct experience in relation to it, one may
notice which practices are creating a greater sense of clarity, receptivity,
serenity, and contentment, and which ones are creating more confusion,
resistance, anxiety, and frustration. By engaging in the activity, is one feeling
more relaxed, flowing, expansive, and connected with others, or more tense,
blocked, contracted, and separate from others? Over time, certain practices
may become intensified while others are discontinued, and potentially, in
due course the realization dawns that the body/mind system had simply
been functioning spontaneously in accordance with Nature, while the actual
Self had all along been the non-participating witnessing of all the *sadhanas* as
the pure presence of Awareness.

As previously mentioned in verses 5.8-9, this Witnessing which one is abides
as pure Stillness during all of the body's activities. Thus the tranquility of the
realized one mentioned herein is not synonymous with inactivity of the
physical body. In most cases, after realization the physical body continues

to be as active as it ever was, functioning in completely natural selfless service to the Whole once the compelling egoic trance has collapsed. Moreover, one comes to later appreciate all the spiritual practices one had engaged in along the way to Self-recognition because "all actions without exception culminate in wisdom" (verse 4.33).

**4**

*yada hi nendriyartheshu / na karmasva-'nusajjate*
*sarva-sankalpa-sannyasi / yogarudhas tadochyate*

*yada* > when; *hi* > truly; *na* > not; *indriya-artheshu* > in the objects of the senses; *na* > nor; *karmasu* > in actions; *anusajjate* > one is attached, one has an emotional investment; *sarva-sankalpa* > all imagined ideas, all expectations of advantages; *sannyasi* > renouncing; *yoga-arudhah* > ascended to the perception of unitary wholeness; *tada* > then; *uchyate* > one is said to be.

**When one truly has no emotional investment**
**In regard to either objects of the senses**
**or the performance of actions,**
**Having renounced all expectations of advantages,**
**One is then said to have ascended**
**to the perception of unitary wholeness.**

The sense conveyed here is that if, for example, a particular food item is not available, then another one will do just as well; if a certain course of action cannot be arranged, then a different one will also be fine. And again we find the word *uchyate* used here: one is said to have 'ascended' because that one has a perspective which is all-inclusive rather than localized by self-interest.

**5**

*uddhared atmanatmanam / natmanam avasadayet*
*atmaiva hyatmano bandhur / atmaiva ripur atmanah*

*uddharet* > let one extricate, let one draw out; *atmana* > by oneself; *atmanam* > the assumed self comprised of the physical body and the fourfold internal network; *na* > not; *atmanam* > the assumed self; *avasadayet* > one causes to sink down into, one contracts; *atma* > oneself; *eva* > only, alone; *hi* > truly; *atmanah* > oneself; *bandhuh* > friend; *atma* > oneself; *eva* > really; *ripuh* > enemy; *atmanah* > of oneself.

**Let one extricate oneself
from [misidentification with] the imagined self
And not sink down
into the [contracted perspective of that] contrived self.
For one is really the only true friend to oneself,
And one is verily one's only enemy as well.**

Fortunately, even the dreamlike experience of being like an enemy to oneself
is only temporary, having a beginning at around the age of two-and-a-half
years and ending either upon spiritual awakening or upon the death of
the physical body. The extrication mentioned here happens when there is
ongoing discernment between pure Awareness and that which Awareness
is aware of; between 'the story of me' and That which is observing the story.

### 6

*bandhur atmatmanas tasya / yenatmaivatmana jitah
anatmanas tu shatrutve / vartetatmaiva shatruvat*

*bandhuh* > friend; *atma* > the assumed self; *atmanah* > of oneself;
*tasya* > of that one; *yena* > by whom; *atma* > the assumed self;
*eva* > really, truly; *atmana* > by oneself; *jitah* > conquered;
*anatmanah* > of that which is not the true Self; *tu* > but;
*shatrutve* > in resistance, in opposition; *varteta* > it will abide,
it will move; *atma* > the assumed self; *eva* > truly;
*shatruvat* > like an adversary.

**For one whose [misidentification as the] assumed self has been conquered,
the assumed self is truly a friend to oneself;
But the assumed self which functions in resistance and opposition
[to the experience of any given moment]
verily moves in a manner resembling an adversary.**

### 7

*jitatmanah prashantasya / paramatma samahitah
sheetoshna-sukha-duhkheshu / tatha mana-'pamanayoh*

*jita-atmanah* > of one whose habit of self-conceptualization or
self-referencing has been conquered; *prashantasya* > of one who is serene
and unaffected; *parama-atma* > the Supreme Self or Oversoul of the universe;
*samahitah* > recognized; *sheeta* > cold; *ushna* > heat; *sukha* > happiness;
*duhkheshu* > distress; *tatha* > likewise; *mana* > honor; *apamanayoh* > dishonor.

**That one whose habit of self-referencing has been conquered
is recognized as the Supreme Self, the Oversoul of the universe —
Serene and unaffected in both heat and cold,
happiness and distress,
honor and dishonor.**

What is presented by Krishna here appears to be a slight variation of a 'spiritual mathematical formula' given by the great Swami Rama Tirtha at around the beginning of the twentieth century. He expressed that "God + mind = man; man minus mind = God." Poetically speaking, this verse expresses that "God + ego = human being; human being minus ego = God."

**8**

*jnana-vijnana-triptatma / kutastho vijitendriyah
yukta ityuchyate yogi / sama-loshtashma-kanchanah*

*jnana* > pure innate knowing; *vijnana* > effortless discernment;
*tripta-atma* > one whose expressed self glows with satisfaction;
*kutasthah* > 'standing at the top' (firmly established in an all-inclusive
perspective), immovable, unchanging; *vijita-indriyah* > one whose
senses are calmed; *yuktah* > aligned with the truth of pure Being;
*iti* > thus; *uchyate* > one is said to be; *yogi* > one who has realized
the unicity of Life; *sama* > equal; *loshta* > a lump of earth
or clay; *ashma* > iron; *kanchanah* > gold.

**One whose expressed self glows with satisfaction
Engendered by pure innate knowing of what is
and effortless discernment of what is not —
Whose senses have been calmed —
Who is firmly established in an all-inclusive perspective of all that is,
and thus views as equal a lump of clay, iron, or gold —
Such a realized one is said to be aligned with the truth of pure Being.**

From a raja-yoga perspective, the definition of *kuthastha* connotes the awakening of inner spiritual vision by the opening of the 'third eye' *chakra* situated between the eyebrows ('standing at the top' of the nose). This will be confirmed by Krishna's instruction to direct attention to that point in upcoming verse 13. It also poetically depicts those who are standing at the top of a mountain peak with an overarching view, likening them to those who have 'ascended to the perception of unitary wholeness' mentioned in verse 4. Such perception naturally allows them to observe considerably more than what is seen from a limiting egoic perspective.

**9**

*suhrin-mitraryudasina / madhyastha-dveshya-bandhushu*
*sadhushvapi cha papeshu / sama-buddhir vishishyate*

*suhrid* > kindhearted, ally; *mitra* > friend, companion;
*ari* > hostile, foe; *udasina* > 'sitting apart' impartially without
a vested interest; *madhyastha* > neutrally situated in the middle;
*dveshya* > hateful, repugnant; *bandhushu* > among relatives
and associates; *sadhushu* > among the righteous; *api* > even;
*cha* > and; *papeshu* > among the vile, among the vicious;
*sama-buddhih* > equality in mental perception;
*vishishyate* > one is most excellent, one is distinguished.

**One whose impulses are completely impartial**
**whether toward a kindhearted ally,**
**a cherished friend, or a hostile adversary;**
**Who abides neutrally among both affectionate relatives**
**and hateful persons alike;**
**And who maintains equality in mental perception**
**when viewing the virtuous and even the vicious —**
**Such a one is outstanding among humankind.**

*Sama-buddhih* means that information received through the senses is
'processed' equally, without triggering feelings of preference or prejudice
based on acquired mental impressions.

**10**

*yogi yunjita satatam / atmanam rahasi sthitah*
*ekaki yata-chittatma / nirashir aparigrahah*

*yogi* > the dhyana practitioner, one aspiring for enlightenment
by way of meditation; *yunjita* > let one direct attention to, let one
adhere to; *satatam* > continuously, uninterruptedly; *atmanam* > the Spirit-Self,
pure Awareness; *rahasi* > in solitude, in a private place; *sthitah* > remaining,
settled; *ekaki* > alone; *yata* > held, sustained; *chitta* > that which is noticed,
observing; *atma* > oneself; *nirashih* > without wishing or hoping for anything;
*aparigrahah* > without taking possession, without claiming proprietorship.

**Let one practicing meditation**
**keep attention directed toward Awareness Itself,**
**Remaining alone in a private place**
**and observing oneself in a sustained manner —**

**Without hoping for anything [specific to happen],**
**And without taking possession of anything**
**[which does or does not happen].**

*Rahasi sthitah ekaki*, 'remaining alone in a private place,' does not necessarily imply isolating oneself from the rest of society for one's entire lifetime. Some persons may certainly do that, but the suggestion also refers to retreats which may last for one year, one month, one week, one day, or even one hour, because even within the span of one hour, every moment within that hour offers the opportunity to welcome a greater conductivity and connectivity with all that is. Awakening to truth is not about *escaping from* the world, or from anything whatsoever, but exactly the opposite—it means becoming completely *intimate with* the world based on directly perceiving oneself, the true Self, appearing in, through, and as all things. This type of intimacy has nothing to do with sensory indulgence; it is a corollary of the unconditional Love that pure Spirit is.

It has already been established by Krishna in previous chapters that pure Spirit, the absolute Reality, is all that exists (verse 2.16) as a singular, all-encompassing Omnipresence (verse 2.24) which is not a doer of actions (4.13), and has nothing whatsoever to accomplish (3.22). It is the Awareness in all living beings (*bhutanam asmi chetana*, verse 10.22) animating the otherwise lifeless body/mind system of the meditator, and that body/mind system also has been established as a non-doer of actions (in verse 3.27). Therefore, it is fittingly consistent that Krishna is here suggesting that both Awareness and Its expression as the body/mind system simply be noticed as what they always already are without requiring them to be what they aren't, such as a doer, controller, preventer, achiever, etc. There's no doing involved in merely being aware of being Awareness, nor in simply noticing whatever is naturally occurring within the scope of direct experience in any given moment.

*Yata-chittatma* is also consonant with Krishna's advice in verse 3.30 to "Entrust all of your actions to Me" in its invitation to observe how pure Awareness (oneself) is the unchanging Constant which notices the arising and subsiding of all else. Awareness notices all passing thoughts, feelings, perceptions, and sensations without reacting to them in any judgmental or adversarial way; rather, It sympathetically accommodates them. 'Accommodating' is not, however, synonymous with holding on to or owning, as indicated by the term *aparigrahah* used here, 'not taking possession.' This principle also encompasses not attributing success in personal doership to an assumed self for certain states experienced in meditation, and not attributing failure to an assumed self for certain states *not* experienced in meditation. In short, it means not creating *any* stories around whatever states are experienced in meditation which would serve to support or prolong the illusion of separate selfhood. As indicated in verse 2.71, the relinquishing of all tendencies to seize and stake claims for personal glory or infamy precedes the discovery of that profound peace which is one's true nature. In the words of Saint Francis of Assisi, "That which you are seeking is what is doing the seeking."

When complete surrender occurs, the particular perception which had been contracted into the limited boundaries of the meditator ego-self expands into the vast spaciousness of whole Awareness, as presented in verse 7. Such surrender happens not through the successful efforts of an ego/'surrenderer,' but rather through the realization that enlightenment can never be achieved by an ego/doer because what is called 'enlightenment' is the complete absence of an ego/doer. Until pure Being relinquishes the idea of being a diligently striving meditator, however, the endeavor for purification from such misidentification continues, and therefore instruction is offered toward that end in the verses which follow.

### 11-12
*shuchau deshe pratishthapya / sthiram asanam atmanah*
*natyuchchritam natinicham / chailajina-kushottaram*

*tatraikagram manah kritva / yata-chittendriya-kriyah*
*upavishyasane yunjyad / yogam atma-vishuddhaye*

*shuchau-deshe* > in a pure (clean or wholesome) place;
*pratishthapya* > establishing; *sthiram* > steady, unmoving;
*asanam* > seat; *atmanah* > for oneself; *na* > not; *ati-uchchritam* > raised too high;
*na* > nor; *ati-nicham* > excessively low; *chaila-ajina* > a cloth-covered
animal skin either from an antelope, a goat, a tiger, or a deer;
*kusha* > the grass Poa Cynosuroides which has long
pointed stalks; *uttaram* > surface, covering;

*tatra* > there; *eka-agram* > with singularly focused attention;
*manah* > the mind; *kritva* > making; *yata-chitta* > steadfast in observing;
*indriya-kriyah* > the activities of the senses; *upavishya* > sitting; *asane* > on the
seat; *yunjyat* > let one adhere to; *yogam* > the practice of meditation
(dhyana-yoga); *atma-vishuddhaye* > for self-purification.

**Establishing a steady seat for oneself in a clean place,**
**neither too high nor too low —**
**The seat being a cloth-covered animal skin placed upon kusha grass —**

**There, steadfast in observing the activities of the mind and senses
with singularly focused attention,
Let one sit on that seat adhering to this practice of meditation
as a means of purification [from the idea of being an entity].**

Animal skins were utilized by yogis for their sitting places in previous times
because snakes would not crawl onto them and thus disturb the yogi's
meditation in a forest or mountain cave. However, as Patanjali Rishi has
asserted in his *Yoga Sutras* that the principle of *ahimsa*—nonviolence, even
within one's mind—is essential in this practice of meditation, it is assumed
that the skins were not procured at the cost of the animal's life. A suitable
skin could be removed from any animal whose body had already stopped
functioning as a result of natural causes, and if one type of skin was not
available, the prospective yogi could instead use a different type as was
readily available by nature's arrangement. *Ajina* could refer to the skin of
either a goat, an antelope, a deer, or a tiger.

The clear, *sattvic* mind is a priceless tool with which all arising thoughts,
feelings, and sensory stimuli can be perceived exactly for what they
are without distortion or obscuration, and without their evoking a
confrontational reaction. Thus there can be complete equipoise during
their passage through Awareness. In due course the opportunity presents
itself to notice that the Awareness which one is is not a 'thing,' not an object,
as mentioned in the notes to verse 2.64.

### 13-14
*samam kaya-shirogrivam / dharayann achalam sthirah
samprekshya nasikagram svam / dishash chanavalokayan*

*prashantatma vigatabhir / brahmachari-vrate sthitah
manah samyamya machchitto / yukta asita matparah*

*samam* > straight; *kaya* > body; *shirah* > head; *grivam* > neck;
*dharayan* > holding; *achalam* > unmoving; *sthirah* > steady; *samprekshya* >
observe carefully, focus upon; *nasika-agram* > the top of the nose;
*svam* > own; *dishah* > directions; *cha* > and; *anavalokayan* > not looking at;

*prashanta-atma* > self-composed; *vigata-bhih* > dispelling fear;
*brahmachari-vrate* > with a vow of celibacy, with a vow of continence;
*sthitah* > established; *manah* > mind; *samyamya* > subduing;
*mat-chittah* > noticing Me; *yuktah* > attentive to;
*asita* > let one sit; *mat-parah* > devoted to Me.

> Holding the body, neck, and head steady and motionless
> in a straight, upright position;
> Focusing one's gaze [either internally or externally]
> toward the area above the nose and not looking anywhere else;
> Remaining self-composed with fear dispelled and mind subdued,
> and observing a vow of continence —
> Let one sit noticing Me [as pure Awareness aware of Itself]
> with a devoted heart and rapt attention.

*Nasikagram* is usually translated as 'the tip of the nose' because two of the many definitions of *agra* are 'tip' and 'front'; yet for the sake of consistency, some other definitions of *agra* such as 'top,' 'summit,' and 'uppermost part' have been favored here. In verse 5.27 Krishna said *chakshush chaivantare bhruvoh*, 'focusing the gaze between the eyebrows,' and later in verse 8.10 he says *bhruvor madhye pranam aveshya samyak,* 'causing the vital life-airs to enter directly between the eyebrows.'

In regard to pure Awareness aware of Itself (known as *apperceiving*) in the present verse, or 'beholding one's true Self reflected in the expressed self' in upcoming verse 20, this does not imply a subject-object relationship as when one sees one's reflection in a mirror. It is more akin to the example of an eye which, although unable to see itself, can know itself by virtue of its ability to see. And the fear that is dispelled or the mind which is subdued in the one who sits in meditation are not accomplishments on the part of the body/mind instrument, just as when a musician sits down and plays magnificent music on a piano, that music is not the result of efforts made by the piano. The conditions which exist in a particular body/mind system are the result of innumerable factors which cannot be known or controlled by that system; however, the available resources of intention and attention are present within pure Consciousness, which is the source of human and all other expression. The illumined contemporary spiritual teacher Adyashanti offers the following in regard to viewing the practice of meditation as an invitation to relax attention in its source:

"True meditation is pure wordless surrender, pure silent prayer with no direction or goal, because all methods aiming at achieving a certain state of mind are limited, impermanent, and conditioned. It is simply abidance as primordial Awareness, as fascination with states leads only to bondage and dependency. True meditation is what spontaneously appears in Awareness when no attempt is made to manipulate or control Awareness. When you first start to meditate, you notice that attention is often being held captive by focus on some object — on thoughts, bodily sensations, emotions, memories, sounds, etcetera. This is because the mind is conditioned to focus and contract upon objects. Then the mind compulsively interprets and tries to control what it is aware of—the object—in a mechanical and distorted way. It begins to draw conclusions and make assumptions according to past conditioning. Yet in true meditation, all objects—thoughts, feelings, emotions, memories, etc.—are left to their natural functioning. This means that no effort is made to focus on, manipulate, control, or suppress any object of Awareness. The emphasis is on being Awareness itself; not on being aware of objects, but on resting as the primordial source in which all objects arise and subside.

"So when we sit down to meditate, the first and most simple thing is to just let go of any seeking, any struggle, any sense that one is supposed to get somewhere. Therefore, check and see if you've let go of all the goals the mind might hold—anything that might disrupt you from being present in just a simple and relaxed way. If you find any idea of striving, any thought that would cause you to psychologically contract, just notice it, and in the noticing, you can stop giving it energy. Feel in your body for anywhere that may be exhibiting signs of struggle—any area that's tight, that's holding, anywhere there may be tension; and in the noticing of that, the tension can let itself go.

"In the most basic sense, meditation is really allowing attention to move from the mind to Awareness. And the quickest way for attention to move out of the mind space—the space of seeking, or figuring out, or trying to control—is to simply come into a state of listening. Listening not just with the ears, but with your entire being, with all of your senses open and relaxed so that you're in touch with the entirety of experience—from whatever sounds there are, to your feelings, to your feet on the floor, to sitting in a chair, to your breathing rising and falling. As you relax into this state of listening, where you're simply aware with no struggle and no attempt to be *more* aware, you notice that all of your experiences occur within the field of Awareness— every sound, every feeling, every beat of your heart, every breath—and we're still not giving the dutiful meditator anything to do. We're not trying to change anything, and whether there's any understanding of Awareness or not doesn't matter. Awareness is self-luminous, which means that it has the capacity to recognize itself.

"As you rest in this natural state of listening and ease, you'll find that Awareness has a certain openness to it, that it's not a constricted or narrow thing. Awareness is quite naturally open. There's really no saying where it begins or ends, and it's not for or against anything. You'll also notice that Awareness itself is not trying to be more aware, or have more experiences, or have less experiences. It's just like a mirror taking everything in and reflecting everything without any distortion. And you begin to sense and feel that this open and unconditioned Awareness is ever-present, that you don't have to manufacture it or create it. You *can't* manufacture or create it; it simply *is*, and registers throughout your body/mind as a subtle sense of presence or energy of aliveness. There's no anticipation in that energy, however; Awareness is not trying to get to a future. It has no concern for the next moment, no concern for attaining or pushing anything away. So the movement from the dimension of mind into the dimension of Awareness is a movement into a dimension that is outside of time.

"You may notice that this dimension can be very, very still, almost motionless, and that without your trying to make anything still, this stillness is already present before you seek it. Let that stillness be felt—not just noticed, but felt. And in the same way, notice that silence is also already present before you try to make anything silent. Even if there are thoughts, notice that they are occurring within silence. All the sounds that are heard are also occurring within silence. If noise arises outside, or thoughts arise in your mind, Awareness itself is entirely quiet and undisturbed. Nothing disturbs it because it never goes into opposition with what is. If attention gets lost for a moment in thought, notice that Awareness doesn't mind; it just has a way of coming back to itself. And in a deeper way, notice the absence of a someone who is aware. Actually there is just Awareness, and the someone is just an idea. Direct experience reveals that Awareness is aware, Consciousness is conscious, and there's not someone there who owns Awareness or possesses it. It stands on its own.

"Resting in this dimension of Awareness, your whole being just goes into a natural rhythm: breath breathes naturally, the heart beats naturally, the body naturally finds a comfortable position—all of you returns to a very natural, very fluid way of being. There's no controller in this dimension of freedom; there's simply being what you *are*. As you're sitting literally being what you are, just notice the quality of your true nature as unconditioned awakeness, letting go of thought. Again, in this meditation there's nothing to think about, nothing to understand, and no attempt to become more aware. We're just allowing everything to be as it is and exploring the nature of Awareness through simple observation without any images or words about it. Through this exploration, we can come to a more clear recognition of what we truly are. If your mind starts to wander, simply come back to the state of listening with your senses open and alert—to your body breathing, to the abdomen filling up and exhaling—once again noticing the openness of yourself as the space within which everything is experienced.

"From Awareness, it can be seen quite naturally that what we are cannot be found in thought. A thought is just a thought. In and of itself it's empty of any meaning, empty of a self. Thought just produces images and ideas, but always there is something before thought which is more intimate and closer than the thought. So notice that when you look for your 'self' in thought, that it's actually not there. Thoughts occur within you and to you, but they're not you. In the same way, each sensation in the body is something that is occurring to you, to what you are, but what you are is prior to them. Although Awareness stands prior to these experiences, notice that Awareness is in no way distant or disassociated from them; it's actually entirely intimate with all of experience. Resting as Awareness, you become extraordinarily connected and extraordinarily sensitive to everything that's happening. At the level of the heart, you experience your being as a subtle radiance or brightness which is completely undefended. In the seat of your belly you may notice a different feeling to it — something like a velvety, dark silence, an infinite mystery.

"As you gently continue relaxing into listening, the mind's compulsive contraction around objects will fade. The silence of *being* will come more clearly into Consciousness as a welcoming to rest and abide. An attitude of open receptivity, free of any goal or anticipation, will facilitate the presence of silence and stillness to be revealed as your natural condition. By resting in this stillness even more profoundly, your attention becomes free of the mind's contractions, identifications, and compulsive attempts at control, and naturally returns to its source in the non-state of absolute unmanifest potential, the silent abyss beyond all knowing."

In regard to one's allowing everything to be as it is, Adyashanti emphasizes a very clear distinction between *allowing* and *indulging* what arises within Awareness. For example, if one were sitting in a room, and something either very appealing or very disturbing were to enter the room, simply allowing that thing to pass through the room is quite different from investing one's attention and energy in engaging interactively with it. The latter is exactly the opposite of allowing. So similarly is the case with thoughts that enter the mind or feelings that enter the body either during meditation or at any other time. Allowing things to be as they are also does not imply neglecting human responsibility; it means allowing responsibilities to be fulfilled in accordance with the need of the moment for supporting the well-being of the Whole, just as Krishna is requesting of Arjuna throughout the entirety of the Bhagavad-Gita.

**15**

*yunjann evam sadatmanam / yogi niyata-manasah*
*shantim nirvana-paramam / mat-samstham adhigachchati*

*yunjan* > conjoining with, aligning with; *evam* > thus; *sada* > continuously;
*atmanam* > the Spirit-Self; *yogi* > the dhyana-yogi, the meditator;
*niyata-manasah* > with a subdued (completely relaxed) mind; *shantim* > peace;
*nirvana-paramam* > supreme (total) cessation (refers to the pseudo-self in
relation to Krishna's statements in verses 5 and 6); *mat-samstham* > is finished
in Me, comes to an end in Me; *adhigachchati* > one finds, one meets with.

**Thus remaining continuously aligned with the truth of the Spirit-Self**
**(purely being without doing),**
**The dhyana-yogi of completely relaxed mind finds peace**
**upon the total cessation of the pseudo-doer/meditator,**
**which comes to an end in Me (pure Awareness).**

**16**

*natyashnatas tu yogo 'sti / na chaikantam anashnatah*
*na chati-svapna-shilasya / jagrato naiva charjuna*

*na* > not; *ati-ashnatah* > of excessive eating; *tu* > but; *yogah* > in the
practice of raja-yoga or meditation; *asti* > there is; *na* > nor; *cha* > also;
*ekantam* > absolutely; *anashnatah* > of not eating at all; *na* > nor; *cha* > also;
*ati-svapna* > excessive sleeping; *shilasya* > habituated to, addicted to; *jagratah* >
of remaining awake; *na* > nor; *eva* > indeed; *cha* > and; *arjuna* > O Arjuna.

**Neither eating excessively nor abstaining from eating altogether**
**is conducive to this practice of meditation, O Arjuna;**
**Neither is addiction to sleeping excessively**
**nor remaining continually awake without any sleep at all.**

**17**

*yuktahara-viharasya / yukta-cheshtasya karmasu*
*yukta-svapnava-'bodhasya / yogo bhavati duhkhaha*

*yukta* > moderate, skillful, attentive; *ahara* > food; *viharasya* > of recreation,
of amusement, of engaging in sports; *yukta* > moderate; *cheshtasya* > of
behavior, of the mode of living, of endeavors; *karmasu* > in the performance
of actions, in working; *yukta* > moderate; *svapna-avabodhasya* > in sleeping
and wakefulness; *yogah* > the practice of meditation; *bhavati* > it becomes;
*duhkha-ha* > the destroyer of sorrows, the remover of troubles.

For one who is moderate in eating and in sleeping,
in work and in recreation —
In one's entire mode of living —
This practice of meditation
becomes the destroyer of all of one's sorrows.

**18**

*yada viniyatam chittam / atmanyeva-'vatishthate*
*nihsprihah sarva-kamebhyo / yukta ityuchyate tada*

*yada* > when; *viniyatam* > regulated (as outlined in the previous verse);
*chittam* > the inner faculty of thinking, feeling, and willing; *atmani* > in
oneself, in the Spirit-Self; *eva* > only; *avatishthate* > one penetrates deeply into,
one is absorbed or immersed in; *nihsprihah* > free from wanting, free
from longing; *sarva* > all; *kamebhyah* > from wishes, from desires;
*yuktah* > aligned; *iti* > thus; *uchyate* > one is said to be; *tada* > then.

When the inner faculty of thinking, feeling, and willing is thus regulated,
Absorbed only in the truth of the Self
without longing for any desire at all to be fulfilled,
One is then said to be truly aligned [with Reality].

Krishna's use of the word *uchyate* ('one is said to be' or 'it is known as') a great
many times throughout the course of his Gita is deeply significant. By this
he conveys the understanding that there are certain uses of language which
become established in routine communication between people which do not
actually present truth with complete accuracy, but come as close to doing so
as the limitations of language will allow. It has already been established that
Reality is a singular Omnipresence appearing as all life-forms, and thus there
are not two individual things to be 'aligned.' Yet as discussed hereinbefore,
when the light of pure truth shines through a body/mind system without
distortion or obscuration, they are said to be in alignment.

**19**

*yatha dipo nivatastho / nengate sopama smrita*
*yogino yata-chittasya / yunjato yogam atmanah*

*yatha* > as; *dipah* > a light (as from a candle, ghee-lamp, or lantern);
*nivata-sthah* > in a windless place; *na* > not; *ingate* > it flickers;
*sa-upama* > containing a simile or comparison; *smrita* > remembered;
*yoginah* > of the dhyana-yogi; *yata-chittasya* > whose attention
is unwavering; *yunjatah* > of that which is steadfast;
*yogam atmanah* > recognizing the oneness of oneself with all that is.

This comparison is remembered:
As a candle in a windless place does not flicker,
So does the yogi's attention remain unwaveringly steady
in the recognition of his or her oneness with all that is.

**20-21**
*yatroparamate chittam / niruddham yogasevaya*
*yatra chaivatman'-atmanam / pashyann atmani tooshyati*

*sukham atyantikam yat tad / buddhi-grahyam atindriyam*
*vetti yatra na chaivayam / sthitash chalati tattvatah*

*yatra* > where; *uparamate* > it becomes motionless, it comes
to rest; *chittam* > imaginings born of thought; *niruddham* > stopped;
*yoga-sevaya* > by serving the truth of unicity, by the practice of meditation;
*yatra* > where; *cha* > and; *eva* > truly; *atmana* > by way of the expressed self or
subtle inner body; *atmanam* > Oneself, the Spirit-Self; *pashyan* > observing,
beholding; *atmani* > within oneself; *tooshyati* > one is contented;

*sukham* > happiness; *atyantikam* > uninterrupted, infinite;
*yat* > which; *tat* > that; *buddhi* > the faculty of understanding,
the power of forming and retaining concepts or notions;
*grahyam* > taken, captured; *atindriyam* > beyond the senses,
unattainable by the senses (including the subtle inner senses
such as mind and intellect); *vetti* > one feels, one experiences;
*yatra* > where; *na* > not; *cha* > and; *eva* > indeed; *ayam* > this one;
*sthitah* > established; *chalati* > one moves, one turns from,
one deviates; *tattvatah* > from the truth of Reality.

In that place where all fabrications born of thoughts come to rest,
having been stopped by serving the truth of unicity —
And where there is deep contentment within oneself
upon beholding one's true Self reflected in the expressed self —
One feels perpetual happiness owing to the faculty of understanding
having been stolen away by That which is beyond all the senses.
Once [perception is] established there,
one does not veer from [perceiving] the truth of Reality.

**22**
*yam labdhva chaparam labham / manyate nadhikam tatah*
*yasmin sthito na duhkhena / gurunapi vichalyate*

*yam* > which; *labdhva* > having found, having attained; *cha* > and; *aparam* > other; *labham* > perception, attainment; *manyate* > one imagines; *na* > not; *adhikam* > greater, superior; *tatah* > than that, after that; *yasmin* > in which; *sthitah* > abiding in, situated in; *na* > not; *duhkhena* > by misfortunes, by difficulties; *guruna* > severe, extensive; *api* > even; *vichalyate* > one is shaken, one is disturbed.

**And having found that perception,**
**one can imagine no other which could be greater than that.**
**Abiding thus,**
**one is not shaken even by extreme misfortunes.**

**23**
*tam vidyad duhkha-samyoga / viyogam yoga-samjnitam*
*sa nishchayena yoktavyo / yogo 'nirvinna-chetasa*

*tam* > this; *vidyat* > let it be known; *duhkha-samyoga* > connection with suffering, contact with miseries; *viyogam* > separation, disjunction; *yoga-samjnitam* > known as Yoga, called Yoga; *sah* > this; *nishchayena* > with inquiry; *yoktavyah* > to be joined, to be practiced; *yogah* > meditation; *anirvinna* > not discouraged; *chetasa* > with heart, with mind.

**Let it be known that this severing of one's connection with suffering**
**is what can authentically be called Yoga.**
**This awareness meditation, along with Self-inquiry,**
**is to be practiced with an undiscouraged heart.**

**24-25**
*sankalpa-prabhavan kamans / tyaktva sarvan asheshatah*
*manasaivendriya-gramam / viniyamya samantatah*

*shanaih shanair uparamed / buddhya dhriti-grihitaya*
*atma-samstham manah kritva / na kinchid api chintayet*

*sankalpa* > motives, expectations; *prabhavan* > born of, sprung from; *kaman* > desires; *tyaktva* > abandoning; *sarvan* > all; *asheshatah* > without exception; *manasa* > conceived in the mind, present in the mind; *eva* > even; *indriya-gramam* > the collective senses, the multitude of senses; *viniyamya* > restricting, limiting; *samantatah* > completely;

*shanaih shanaih* > gradually, little by little; *uparamet* > let one stop, let one desist; *buddhya* > with the faculty of intellectual understanding;

*dhriti* > contentment, joy; *grihitaya* > seized, taken; *atma-samstham* > perished
in the Spirit-Self, ended within oneself; *manah kritva* > that which is
mind-made, having been done by the mind; *na* > not; *kinchit* > anything
whatsoever; *api* > truly; *chintayet* > one should care about,
one should feel anxious about, one should sorrow about.

**Abandoning without exception all motives and expectations
born of desires —
Even [the motive] to completely restrict the collective senses
and what arises in the mind —
Gradually, little by little, let one simply stop,
Content to have the faculty of intellectual understanding stolen away
[by the Ineffable which surpasses it].
There is truly nothing whatsoever to feel anxious about
as everything fabricated by the mind comes to an end within oneself.**

Within the charmingly poetic words of spiritual teacher Swami B.R. Sridhar
Maharaj, a connection can be found between the *yoga-sevaya* in verse 20 —
'serving the truth of Unicity' — and the expiration of the sense of pseudo-
selfhood which began in verse 15. This theme continues through verse 21
with the faculty of understanding being stolen away by That which is beyond
all the senses, and is reiterated in the present verse concluding with all things
mind-made coming to an end within oneself. It develops further and extends
into the realm of love in upcoming verse 31, as well as at the conclusion of
this chapter in verse 47.

According to Sridhar Maharaj, real inner fulfillment attends unconditional
service to 'the absolute center,' as such a life exemplifies the greatest degree
of integrity to the truth of oneness-in-diversity which one has realized. He
states that for such service to be authentic, one must 'die to live,' meaning
that one's egocentric tendency to exploit or even conceive of oneself as a
renouncer of anything must die so that one may live with a new perspective
wherein the Absolute is at the center instead, *that* center being everywhere
with circumference nowhere. The *Mundaka Upanishad* 2.2.9 states that "There
is a knot in the heart which must be cut asunder" — very similar to Krishna's
words in Gita verse 4.42 — so therefore one's search for Reality the beautiful is
best conducted in the realm of the heart guided by one's inner taste. And it is
directly experienced that when one's *atma-vichara* or Self-inquiry is conducted
at *satsang* gatherings in the association of those who have dynamic, awakened
perception, one's 'tasting ability' is considerably sharpened.

What is soon discovered thereby is that "Reality is by Itself and for Itself." It is not only beautiful, but It is also an autocrat—not subordinate to anything within the plane of relativity, yet able to accommodate *everything*. This Absolute Good beyond all relative conceptions of good and bad generates a dynamic power which functions beyond all calculative brainwork as an innate principle found everywhere in nature, even within the birds and beasts. The mother bird has some intuitive affection for the fledglings when they are growing, so she comes to feed and nurture them before finally leaving them on their own. In this way the intuitive energy of love is functioning, conducting the world's affairs. It is unaccountable in that we don't know where it comes from, yet it comes to serve nonetheless and may then apparently disappear according to its own sweet will. Therefore, aligning with that wave of mercy and affection wherever it is found to be available may assist those who feel themselves to be wandering throughout the mind-created world in a helpless condition. In conclusion, Swami Sridhar Maharaj mentions that because genuine love is based on 'self-forgetfulness,' sincere selfless service is not only the most constructive expression of truth in action, but the most powerful catalyst for inner transformation as well, because one completely forgets to be concerned about whether or not one is making personal spiritual progress.

## 26

*yato yato nishcharati / manas chanchalam asthiram*
*tatas tato niyamyaitad / atmanyeva vasham nayet*

*yatah yatah* > from wherever; *nishcharati* > it travels, it wanders away;
*manah* > the mind; *chanchalam* > restless; *asthiram* > unsteady;
*tatah tatah* > from there; *niyamya* > governing, settling, fixing upon;
*etat* > this; *atmani* > in the Spirit-Self; *eva* > still, only;
*vasham* > willing, submissive; *nayet* > let one direct.

**Regardless of wherever the restless and unsteady mind**
**may wander away to,**
**Let one be willing to redirect it back from there**
**to be settled only in the Self (the pure presence of Awareness).**

## 27

*prashanta-manasam hyenam / yoginam sukham uttamam*
*upaiti shanta-rajasam / brahma-bhutam akalmasham*

*prashanta-manasam* > one whose mind is tranquil; *hi* > indeed;
*enam* > this one; *yoginam* > the dhyana-yogi; *sukham* > happiness;

*uttamam* > the highest; *upaiti* > one encounters; *shanta-rajasam* > whose infatuations have calmed; *brahma-bhutam* > fully embodying the realization of being Brahman; *akalmasham* > stainless.

**The yogi whose mind is tranquil,**
**Who is unstained [by self-objectification],**
**Whose infatuations have calmed**
**and who fully embodies the realization of being Brahman—**
**Such a one indeed encounters the highest happiness.**

### 28
*yunjann evam sadatmanam / yogi vigata-kalmashah*
*sukhena brahma-samsparsham / atyantam sukham ashnute*

*yunjan* > adhering, clinging to; *evam* > thus; *sada* > always, ever; *atmanam* > oneself; *yogi* > the dhyana-yogi; *vigata-kalmashah* > who is free of stains, whose darkness has disappeared; *sukhena* > effortlessly, naturally; *brahma-samsparsham* > 'making contact with' Brahman (realizing oneself to be Brahman); *atyantam* > very intense, thorough, without end; *sukham* > joy, comfort; *ashnute* > one arrives at, one is overcome by.

**Thus ever adhering to [the divine truth of] oneself,**
**The yogi whose darkness [of misidentification] has disappeared**
**Is naturally overcome by intense joy**
**upon the realization of being pure Spirit.**

### 29
*sarvabhuta-stham atmanam / sarva-bhutani chatmani*
*ikshate yoga-yuktatma / sarvatra sama-darshanah*

*sarva-bhuta-stham* > present in all beings; *atmanam* > the Spirit-Self; *sarva-bhutani* > all living beings; *cha* > and; *atmani* > in the Self; *ikshate* > one sees; *yoga-yukta-atma* > one who lives fully in alignment with his or her realization of divine unicity; *sarvatra* > everywhere, at all times; *sama-darshanah* > seeing the same.

**One who lives fully in alignment**
**with his or her realization of divine unicity**
**Sees the same one Spirit-Self present in all forms of life everywhere,**
**And all forms of life present within the one [all-pervasive] Self.**

## 30

*yo mam pashyati sarvatra / sarvam cha mayi pashyati*
*tasyaham na pranashyami / sa cha me na pranashyati*

*yah* > who; *mam* > Me; *pashyati* > one sees; *sarvatra* > everywhere; *sarvam* > all
things; *cha* > and; *mayi* > in Me; *pashyati* > one sees; *tasya* > to that one;
*aham* > I; *na* > not; *pranashyami* > I am lost, I have disappeared; *sah* > that one;
*cha* > and; *me* > to Me; *na* > nor; *pranashyati* > one is lost, one has disappeared.

**One who sees Me everywhere and sees all things in Me**
**Never loses the perceiving of Me (the unitary wholeness of Life),**
**Nor does that one ever disappear to Me**
**(to the Awareness within all body/mind instruments of perception).**

## 31

*sarvabhuta-sthitam yo mam / bhajatyekatvam asthitah*
*sarvatha vartamano 'pi / sa yogi mayi vartate*

*sarva-bhuta-sthitam* > abiding within all beings; *yah* > who; *mam* > Me;
*bhajati* > one worships, one loves, one reveres; *ekatvam* > oneness;
*asthitah* > entered or fallen into, abiding in; *sarvatha* > in all ways,
in whatever way; *vartamanah* > moving, living; *api* > even; *sah* > that one;
*yogi* > the Self-realized one; *mayi* > in Me; *vartate* > one abides, one lives.

**Loving and revering Me**
**as the One abiding in all beings,**
**In whatever way the Self-realized one lives and moves,**
**She or he abides within Me.**

Again, this is analogous to a dream-figure abiding within the consciousness
of a dreamer while that consciousness abides as the substratum of all the
dream-figures.

## 32

*atmaupamyena sarvatra / samam pashyati yo'rjuna*
*sukham va yadi va duhkham / sa yogi paramo matah*

*atma* > oneself; *aupamyena* > by resemblance, by comparison;
*sarvatra* > in all cases, everywhere; *samam* > the same;
*pashyati* > one ascertains, one surveys; *yah* > who; *arjuna* > O Arjuna;
*sukham* > happiness; *va yadi va* > whether, or if; *duhkham* > distress;
*sah* > this one; *yogi* > the yogi; *paramah* > highest; *matah* > is considered to be.

Those who determine the happiness and distress of all others
By utilizing the same standard of assessment
as they would in regard to their own direct experience
Are considered to be the highest type of yogis, O Arjuna.

### 33

*arjuna uvacha:*
*yo 'yam yogas tvaya proktah / samyena madhusudana*
*etasyaham na pashyami / chanchalatvat sthitim sthiram*

*arjunah uvacha* > Arjuna said; *yah* > which; *ayam* > this; *yogah* > the method
of meditation; *tvaya* > by You; *proktah* > taught, explained; *samyena* > with
equilibrium, with equability; *madhusudana* > O vanquisher of the demon
Madhu; *etasya* > of this (refers to the mind, as confirmed in the next verse);
*aham* > I; *na* > not; *pashyami* > I can see; *chanchalatvat* > because
of unsteadiness, due to instability; *sthitim* > maintenance,
continuance; *sthiram* > constant, unfluctuating, motionless.

Arjuna said:
O vanquisher of the demon Madhu,
Due to the mind's instability,
I cannot see how it can be kept motionless —
How the equilibrium can be constantly maintained
in the method of meditation taught by you.

One of the meanings of *madhu* is a sweet intoxicating liquor, which in Eastern
spiritual literature is often poetically said to have been imbibed by those who
are 'under the influence' of *maya*, the illusion-producing power inherent in
Consciousness. So Arjuna's addressing Krishna as *madhusudana* here carries
the connotation that he is confident that Krishna will be able to vanquish the
confusion or disorientation he feels overcome by.

### 34

*chanchalam hi manah krishna / pramathi balavad dridham*
*tasyaham nigraham manye / vayor iva sudushkaram*

*chanchalam* > restless; *hi* > truly; *manah* > the mind; *krishna* > O Krishna;
*pramathi* > troubling, harassing; *balavat* > strong, dense, intense;
*dridham* > obstinate; *tasya* > of it; *aham* > I; *nigraham* > restraining,
subduing; *manye* > I think; *vayoh* > of the wind; *iva* > like;
*sudushkaram* > extremely difficult to accomplish.

The mind is truly restless, troubling, obstinate,
and very strong, O Krishna;
I think that restraining the mind is as difficult to accomplish
as restraining the wind.

**35**
*sri bhagavan uvacha:*
*asamshayam mahabaho / mano durnigraham chalam*
*abhyasena tu kaunteya / vairagyena cha grihyate*

*sri bhagavan uvacha* > the resplendent one (Krishna) said;
*asamshayam* > undoubtedly; *maha-baho* > O mighty-armed one;
*manah* > the mind; *durnigraham* > difficult to subdue or restrain;
*chalam* > restless; *abhyasena* > by repetition, by the practice
(described in verses 10 through 14); *tu* > but; *kaunteya* > O son of Kunti;
*vairagyena* > by indifference, by disinterest; *cha* > and; *grihyate* > it is calmed.

The resplendent Krishna said:
O mighty-armed one,
It is undoubtedly difficult to subdue the restless mind;
But by practice and by disinterest [in sensory stimuli]
the mind is calmed, O son of Kunti.

Throughout the routine course of daily life, thoughts arise as they do, even
uninvited, and it can indeed be challenging to subdue the tendency of
thoughts to mesmerize and hold one's attention captive for various periods of
time. But by practice of observational meditation and disinterest in whatever
is observed to come and go within the scope of Awareness, there is profound
settling of the internal terrain (the fourfold subtle body).

**36**
*asamyatatmana yogo / dushprapa iti me matih*
*vashyatmana tu yatata / shakyo 'vaptum upayatah*

*asamyata-atmana* > by one whose mode of living is unregulated;
*yogah* > recognition of one's true nature; *dushprapah* > difficult to attain;
*iti* > thus; *me* > my; *matih* > opinion; *vashya-atmana* > by one who is willing,
by one who is submissive; *tu* > but; *yatata* > by being devoted or
intent upon, by conforming or complying with; *shakyah* > possible;
*avaptum* > to attain; *upayatah* > by the means (mentioned in verse 17).

**Recognition of one's true nature is admittedly difficult to attain
for one whose mode of living is unregulated;
But it is my opinion that it is possible
for one who is willing to comply
with the means [which I have recommended].**

Krishna here reminds Arjuna about what was communicated in verses 16
and 17—that meditation cannot be practiced if one's habits in regard to
eating, sleeping, work, or recreation are at either extreme, but that the same
practice can usher in the end to all of one's sorrows if one is moderate in one's
entire mode of living.

37

*arjuna uvacha:*
*ayatih shraddhayopeto / yogach chalita-manasah*
*aprapya yoga-samsiddhim / kam gatim krishna gachchati*

*arjunah uvacha* > Arjuna said; *ayatih* > the one lacking diligence;
*shraddhaya* > with faith; *upetah* > one who has approached or arrived;
*yogat* > from the practice of meditation; *chalita* > disturbed, caused to deviate;
*manasah* > whose mind; *aprapya* > not attaining; *yoga-samsiddhim* > perfection
in Self-realization; *kam* > what; *gatim* > situation, fate, path;
*krishna* > O Krishna; *gachchati* > one goes toward, one comes upon.

**Arjuna inquired:**
**O Krishna, what is the fate of the ones lacking diligence
who approach the practice of meditation with genuine faith,
But who are deviated by the mind's disturbance,
thus causing them to not attain perfection in Self-realization?
What becomes of them?**

38

*kachchin nobhaya-vibhrashtash / chinna-'bhram iva nashyati*
*apratishtho maha-baho / vimudho brahmanah pathi*

*kachchit na* > is one not; *ubhaya* > in both (the ways of activity [karma-yoga]
and tranquility [jnana] mentioned by Krishna in verse 3); *vibhrashtah* > failed,
separated; *chinna* > vanished, divided apart; *abhram* > raincloud; *iva* > like;
*nashyati* > one is lost, one is destroyed; *apratishthah* > having no solid
foundation, having no safety or stability; *maha-baho* > O mighty-armed one;
*vimudhah* > confused, confounded; *brahmanah* > to Brahman,
to pure Spirit; *pathi* > on the road, on the journey.

**O mighty-armed Krishna,**
**One who is baffled on the journey to Brahman**
**By having lost both [the eligibility to attain heaven**
**through engagement in selfless work**
**and the possibility of attaining liberation via Self-recognition] —**
**Is not such a one destroyed like a scattered cloud**
**[and left] without any support anywhere?**

Arjuna's use of the words *vimudho brahmanah pathi,* 'confounded on the road to pure Spirit,' is noteworthy. Krishna had been informing Arjuna that he *is* pure Spirit since the beginning of Chapter Two, yet here we find Arjuna inquiring about the fate of those who are unsuccessful in their efforts to bridge the distance between themselves and Spirit. Additionally, throughout all of verse 37 and into the beginning of 38, we find Arjuna already anticipating failure before making any attempt whatsoever to simply notice the presence of awareness as earlier suggested to him. Upon seeing that Arjuna's questions are still being asked from a condition predominated by fear and confusion, Krishna responds with sensitivity and compassion, speaking words which are exactly what Arjuna needs to hear at this particular point in their dialogue.

### 39
*etan me samshayam krishna / chettum arhasyasheshatah*
*tvadanyah samshayasyasya / chetta na hyupapadyate*

*etat* > this; *me* > my; *samshayam* > doubt, dilemma, uncertainty;
*krishna* > O Krishna; *chettum* > to cut through, to remove;
*arhasi* > you are able; *asheshatah* > completely; *tvad-anyah* > other than
you; *samshayasya* > of this doubt, dilemma, or uncertainty; *asya* > of this;
*chetta* > one who cuts through or removes; *na* > not; *hi* > truly;
*upapadyate* > one is present, one is accessible.

**This is my dilemma, O Krishna,**
**which I know you are able to cut through completely.**
**Other than you, there is truly no one**
**who can eradicate this uncertainty of mine.**

### 40
*sri bhagavan uvacha:*
*partha naiveha namutra / vinashas tasya vidyate*
*na hi kalyana-krit kashchid / durgatim tata gachchati*

*sri bhagavan uvacha* > the majestic one (Krishna) said; *partha* > O son
of Pritha; *na* > neither; *eva* > indeed; *iha* > here in this world;
*na* > nor; *amutra* > there in the other world; *vinashah* > destruction,
loss; *tasya* > of that one; *vidyate* > it is found; *na* > not; *hi* > truly;
*kalyana* > that which is virtuous, beneficial, or auspicious;
*krit* > engaging in; *kashchit* > anyone; *dur-gatim* > to misfortune,
to an unfortunate end; *tata* > dear one, beloved one;
*gachchati* > one goes to, one falls to, one arrives at.

**The majestic Krishna replied:**
**O son of Pritha,**
**That one [about whom you are inquiring]**
**is ruined neither in this world nor in any other.**
**Truly, beloved one,**
**It is found that one who engages in that which is beneficial**
**does not fall to misfortune.**

Arjuna's most recent inquiry pertained to one whom he viewed as having
apparently dismantled his or her present life-situation yet was also
unsuccessful at 'earning' any better life-situation hereafter as a result of
that dismantling. *Kalyana-krit* (engaging in that which is beneficial) connotes
the performance of any right actions with right intentions as later outlined
in the Buddha's Noble Eightfold Path. The other six principles of that Path
are right perspective, right speech, right livelihood, right endeavor, right
focus of attention, and right 'concentration,' meaning right abidance and
absorption in the right focus of attention.

**41**
*prapya punya-kritam lokan / usheetva shashvatih samah*
*shucinam shrimatam gehe / yoga-bhrashto 'bhijayate*

*prapya* > to be attained; *punya-kritam* > of the performers of virtuous
or auspicious deeds; *lokan* > place, region; *usheetva* > after dwelling;
*shashvatih* > countless; *samah* > years; *shuchinam* > of the pure, of the innocent;
*shrimatam* > of the splendid, of the prosperous; *gehe* > in the house;
*yoga-bhrashtah* > separation from the unfolding process of
Self-awakening; *abhijayate* > another one is born.

**After attaining to a place among the performers of auspicious deeds**
**and dwelling there for countless years,**
**If with one particular body there has been an interruption**
**in the unfolding process of Self-awakening,**

**Then another body is born
in the home of those who are very pure-hearted and prosperous.**

The presentation in verses 41 through 45 describe dreamlike experiencing which occurs within absolute Consciousness, yet as stated by Krishna in verses 2.21 and 2.25, the unborn nature of the Absolute remains changeless. Bodies come and go (verses 2.22 and 2.28); Spirit is unmoving (verse 2.24). This perspective that bodies are born within the true Self is exactly the opposite of what is generally believed and conveyed in the majority of the world's spiritual teachings, which portray the Spirit-Self as a segregated entity that transmigrates from one body to another. The process of the One awakening to the truth of Itself in a particular dreamsheath is one in which pure Spirit recognizes that *It does not know Itself as an entity at all.* There is direct knowing (*jnana*) that one does not know Oneself as any illusory physical object or mental image created within Oneself (pure Awareness). There is cessation of identifying with any of the twenty-four material elements enumerated in the Sankhya cosmology. This journey of Self-awakening is known as *lila,* a playful sport or divine pastime.

### 42

*athava yoginam eva / kule bhavati dhimatam
etad dhi durlabha-taram / loke janma yad idrisham*

*athava* > otherwise, or perhaps; *yoginam* > of yoga-practitioners,
of those who are awake to their true nature; *eva* > indeed; *kule* > in the family;
*bhavati* > one comes into being; *dhimatam* > of the wise; *etat* > this;
*hi* > indeed; *durlabha-taram* > very difficult to find, very rare;
*loke* > in the world; *janma* > birth; *yat* > which;
*idrisham* > endowed with such qualities, of such type.

**Or perhaps a new body may come into being
in a family of wise yogis
who are awake to their true nature.
This type of birth is indeed very rare in the world.**

There is the potential for what is described here to likewise be perceived within eternally undivided Awareness.

### 43

*tatra tam buddhi-samyogam / labhate paurva-dehikam
yatate cha tato bhuyah / samsiddhau kuru-nandana*

*tatra* > there, in that; *tam* > this one; *buddhi-samyogam* > connecting with the experiential sense of knowing what is true; *labhate* > one receives, one recovers; *paurva-dehikam* > from a previous body; *yatate* > one is devoted to, one is intent upon; *cha* > and; *tatah* > from there; *bhuyah* > once again; *samsiddhau* > toward full restoration, toward complete healing; *kuru-nandana* > O descendant of Kuru.

**There, in that [dreamlike situation],**
**One connects with an experiential sense of knowing what is true**
**recovered from [the utilization of] a previous body,**
**And from there once again becomes intent**
**upon the full restoration [of perception to wholeness],**
**O descendent of Kuru.**

The word *buddhi* used here also carries with it the connotation of a particular unique type of disposition or *bhava* which accompanies the unfolding of perception and the recovering of insights within a body/mind expression of the One.

**44**
*purva-'bhyasena tenaiva / hriyate hyavasho 'pi sah*
*jijnasur api yogasya / shabda-brahma-'tivartate*

*purva-abhyasena* > by prior practice; *tena* > on that account, for that reason; *eva* > indeed; *hriyate* > one is carried onward; *hi* > indeed; *avashah* > unwillingly; *api* > even; *sah* > that one; *jijnasuh* > inquiring into, examining, wishing to know; *api* > even; *yogasya* > of recognizing the divine unicity of life; *shabda-brahma* > 'the sound of Brahman' (refers to the ritual prescriptions and proscriptions enjoined in the Vedas and other scriptures); *ativartate* > one surpasses.

**As a result of that prior practice,**
**One is carried onward —**
**indeed, even unwillingly.**
**Those who even inquire into the recognition of divine unicity**
**Surpass [the necessity of attending to] the ritual injunctions**
**enjoined in the Vedas and other scriptures.**

The prior practice mentioned here refers not only to *dhyana* or meditation but to any sincerely performed spiritual practice. *Hriyate hyavasho 'pi*, 'one is carried onward even unwillingly,' means that within the new dreamlike situation occurring within the One, Spirit continues to use a body/mind system as an instrument for Its self-awakening even if there is resistance from that system's built-in mechanism of 'pseudo-self preservation.'

### 45

*prayatnad yata-manas tu / yogi samshuddha-kilbishah*
*aneka-janma-samsiddhas / tato yati param gatim*

*prayatnat* > by perseverance; *yata-manah* > subdued mind, restrained mind; *tu* > now; *yogi* > the yogi; *samshuddha* > fully purified, completely cleansed; *kilbishah* > faults; *aneka* > not one (many); *janma* > births; *samsiddhah* > thoroughly cured, fully restored; *tatah* > then; *yati* > one reaches, one attains; *param gatim* > to supreme fulfillment, to the highest refuge.

**Thus, by perseverance in subduing the mind,**
**The yogi, fully purified of faults**
**and perfected after many births,**
**Then reaches supreme fulfillment.**

Awareness remains aware of Itself, with attention simply noticing whatever thoughts arise without responding to them with any type of energetic movement either toward the thoughts, away from them, or about them. By such perseverance in subduing the *influence* of thoughts arising within the mind, the vehicle of expression known as a yogi which omnipresent Consciousness had been utilizing is fully purified of faults and is perfected after many births. The yogi expression thus reaches the supreme fulfillment of its purpose as an instrument of the One, as previously mentioned in regard to King Janaka in the notes to verse 3.20. The faults mentioned here essentially constitute egocentrism, desire, anger, fear, distortion of expression by the *rajas-guna*, obscuration of expression by the *tamas-guna*, and affinity for the higher standard of sensory experience associated with the *sattva-guna*. The characteristics of the *gunas*, the components of Nature, have been described in the notes to verse 2.39.

### 46

*tapasvibhyo 'dhiko yogi / jnanibhyo 'pi mato 'dhikah*
*karmibhyash chadhiko yogi / tasmad yogi bhavarjuna*

*tapasvibhyah* > to the ascetics practicing austerities; *adhikah* > superior; *yogi* > one practicing raja-yoga or meditation; *jnanibhyah* > to the learned ones full of scriptural knowledge; *api* > even; *matah* > considered to be;

*adhikah* > superior; *karmibhyah* > to the performers of prescribed religious rituals; *cha* > and; *adhikah* > superior; *yogi* > the yogi; *tasmat* > therefore; *yogi* > a yogi; *bhava* > you should be; *arjuna* > O Arjuna.

**The yogis — those endeavoring to realize truth by way of meditation —
are considered to be superior to the ascetics,
Superior to the performers of prescribed religious rituals,
and even superior to the learned ones rich in scriptural knowledge.
Therefore, do be a yogi, O Arjuna.**

One potential reason for the perspective on meditation which Krishna offers here is that in order to engage in the other three types of practices, something is required from the environment. Ceremonial paraphernalia, foods, flowers, and other accessories are needed for the performance of traditional religious rituals, and quite obviously, scriptures are needed in order to have scriptural knowledge. As for the practice of asceticism, the environment is required to be of a particular type which will stave off sensations of pleasure or feelings of comfort. All that is involved in exploring awareness meditation, however, is simply noticing one's direct experience without entertaining any stories about whatever stimuli is encountered. The principle underlying this practice of meditation is actually complete surrender, which is ultimately Krishna's final message to Arjuna at the conclusion of his teachings as well — *sarva-dharman parityajya / mam ekam sharanam vraja* (verse 18.66): "Abandoning all socially and scripturally prescribed religious duties, take complete refuge in Me alone." As Krishna represents the purely contented presence of Awareness (*Sat-Chid-Ananda*), the Gita's dialogue both now and later points to the recurring theme of true Yoga referring not to a contest of accomplishment but to a reorientation of perspective.

### 47
*yoginam api sarvesham / mad-gatenantaratmana
shraddhavan bhajate yo mam / sa me yuktatamo matah*

*yoginam* > of those practicing meditation; *api* > even;
*sarvesham* > of all these; *mat-gatena* > by going to Me,
by coming to Me; *antaratmana* > with the innermost self,
with a sincere heart; *shraddhavan* > full of faith;
*bhajate* > one honors, one loves; *yah* > who; *mam* > Me;
*sah* > that one; *me* > to Me; *yuktatamah* > most aligned with,
most intent upon, most devoted to; *matah* > considered to be.

**And even among all yogis,**
**I consider those who approach Me**
**with a sincere heart full of faith and love**
**to be most aligned with Me (who am their own true nature).**

*om tat saditi srimad bhagavad-gita / supanishatsu brahma-vidyayam*
*yoga-shastre srikrishnarjuna samvade / dhyana-yogo nama shashtho 'dhyayah*

From the Ambrosial Song of God —
A conversation between Krishna and Arjuna
which is a Upanishad (confidential sharing)
of wisdom-teachings regarding the Absolute
And a scripture concerning Self-realization —
Thus ends the Sixth Chapter entitled Dhyana-yoga,
Recognizing Divine Unicity By Way of Meditation.

## Chapter Seven

# Jnana-vijnana-yoga
### (Recognizing Divine Unicity By Way of
### Higher Knowledge and Discernment)

"What we call 'reality' literally changes moment to moment....Yet our usual mental activity is to label things, which turns them into objects for us. The same thing happens with emotions and sensations. We label them, and then we believe they are real and that this is the way Reality actually is. The labeling produces a sense of subject and object, and hence a sense of separation. Then we project that we know what will fix this sense of separation, and off we go. If you actually look, there are no boundaries to objects; there is only the labeling, which is a perceptional framework imposed on that instant, depending on your cultural conditioning and your mood at the time. For example, we have the idea that our body is a separate entity. Without air, how long can the body continue?....If you really look at it, you can see that it can't exist by itself, not even for a moment. The next breath is coming into this body and is becoming part of the cellular structure of this body; now this breath is going out. Where is my body ending? Is it this next breath coming in? When do I freeze-frame it and say 'This is my body'? It is a complete living organism that involves all of creation, everything that produces the air.

"Through labeling, we create two objects — body and air — and yet there is no division except in our thinking. When you are operating from the sense of self, Reality seems to be a certain way, and everybody lives in a very different world. But once this activity of labeling is noticed, and there is a recognition of the painfulness of this activity, it falls away by itself. Then you can't say that anything has a beginning or an end; there is only a constant rearrangement of atoms. Everything is a fluid, ongoing play of Consciousness, and there is nobody that is separate from it."

— Isaac Shapiro

### 1
*sri bhagavan uvacha:*
*mayy asakta-manah partha / yogam yunjan madashrayah*
*asamshayam samagram mam / yatha jnasyasi tach chrinu*

*sri bhagavan uvacha* > the venerable one (Krishna) said; *mayi* > to Me;
*asakta-manah* > one whose mind is intent upon or attentive to;
*partha* > O son of Pritha (Arjuna); *yogam* > the practice of meditation;

*yunjan* > conjoining with; *mat-ashrayah* > completely relying or depending upon Me, taking complete refuge in Me; *asamshayam* > without doubt; *samagram* > fully; *mam* > Me; *yatha* > how; *jnasyasi* > you shall know; *tat* > that; *shrinu* > do hear.

**The venerable Krishna said:**
**Now hear with an attentive mind, O Arjuna,**
**How by taking complete refuge in Me**
**in conjunction with the practice of meditation [which I described to you]**
**You shall come to fully know Me without any doubt.**

**2**

*jnanam te 'ham savijnanam / idam vakshyamyasheshatah*
*yaj jnatva neha bhuyo 'nyaj / jnatavyam avashishyate*

*jnanam* > higher knowledge; *te* > to you; *aham* > I;
*sa* > containing, along with; *vijnanam* > discernment; *idam* > this;
*vakshyami* > I shall speak; *asheshatah* > fully, without remainder;
*yat* > which; *jnatva* > having comprehended; *na* > not;
*iha* > here in this world; *bhuyah* > further; *anyat* > other;
*jnatavyam* > to be known; *avashishyate* > it remains.

**I shall fully impart to you higher knowledge**
**which includes discernment [of the absolute from the relative].**
**Having comprehended this,**
**nothing further remains to be known in this world.**

**3**

*manushyanam sahasreshu / kashchid yatati siddhaye*
*yatatam api siddhanam / kashchin mam vetti tattvatah*

*manushyanam* > among humankind; *sahasreshu* > out of thousands;
*kashchit* > someone; *yatati* > one endeavors; *siddhaye* > toward
perfection; *yatatam* > from among those who endeavor; *api* > even;
*siddhanam* > of the perfected; *kashchit* > someone; *mam* > Me;
*vetti* > one knows; *tattvatah* > in truth (here meaning 'in fullness').

**Out of thousands among humankind,**
**perhaps someone may endeavor to reach perfection;**
**And among those who endeavor —**
**Even among the perfected —**
**Perhaps someone may actually know Me (the Absolute) fully.**

Those within whom there is the realization of being formless Awareness are unquestionably *siddhas*, perfected ones who know the truth. So what is meant here by *vetti tattvatah* is a more complete knowing of the truth which includes realizing the aggregate of forms in existence to also be a unique expression of one's true Self, the nondual Spirit-Presence, as well. Krishna begins discussing this principle in the next verse, which continues through his later mention of *adhibhuta* and *adhidaiva* in verses 7.30 and 8.4, and culminates in his elegant elaboration of this principle in verses 20 through 39 of Chapter Ten. We may also recall Krishna's statement in verse 1 that "You shall come to fully (*samagram*) know Me without any doubt."

### 4
*bhumir apo 'nalo vayuh / kham mano buddhir eva cha*
*ahamkara itiyam me / bhinna prakritir ashtadha*

*bhumih* > earth; *apah* > water; *analah* > fire; *vayuh* > air; *kham* > ether, space, sky; *manah* > mind; *buddhih* > intellect; *eva* > indeed; *cha* > and; *ahamkarah* > egoism, 'I am the doer'; *iti* > thus; *iyam* > this; *me* > My; *bhinna* > divided; *prakritih* > Nature; *ashtadha* > into eight.

**Earth, water, fire, air, ether,**
**mind, intellect, and egoism —**
**My Nature is thus [categorically] divided**
**into these eight [classifications].**

### 5
*apareyam itas tvanyam / prakritim viddhi me param*
*jiva-bhutam mahabaho / yayedam dharyate jagat*

*apara* > lower; *iyam* > this; *itah* > here, in this world; *tu* > but; *anyam* > other; *prakritim* > Nature; *viddhi* > please know; *me* > my; *param* > superior; *jiva* > the animating or vivifying capability; *bhutam* > consisting of; *maha-baho* > O mighty-armed one; *yaya* > by which; *idam* > this; *dharyate* > it is sustained; *jagat* > the world, the universe.

**This is the lower aspect of My Nature**
**[which appears] as the form of this world;**
**But know also the other, superior aspect of My Nature**
**which consists of the animating capability**
**by which this world is sustained, O mighty-armed one.**

### 6
*etadyonini bhutani / sarvan' ityupadharaya*
*aham kritsnasya jagatah / prabhavah pralayas tatha*

*etat* > this (superior aspect of Nature); *yonini* > source, origin;
*bhutani* > created beings, creative expressions of Being; *sarvani* > all;
*iti* > thus; *upadharaya* > please understand, please consider;
*aham* > the sense of 'I-ness' ('I am'); *kritsnasya* > in its entirety;
*jagatah* > of the world, of the universe; *prabhavah* > the origin;
*pralayah* > dissolution; *tatha* > and thus, and likewise.

**This superior aspect of My Nature
is the source from which all creative expressions of Being originate.
Thus, understand that the sense of 'I-ness' ('I am')
is the source of this entire world-appearance,
and is likewise [the source of] its dissolution.**

As mentioned in the notes to verse 3.10, when infinite Consciousness becomes aware of Its own existence ('I am'), Its creative Power instantaneously manifests a conceptual space for It to exist in, and an infinite number of variegated body/mind vehicles for It to exist through and appear as. This apparent coming into being as the universe occurs in a dreamlike way; the Unmanifest does not actually transform into the manifest, as will be confirmed in upcoming verse 24. Regardless of any innocent identification with the organic vehicle being lived through, it is still only the same one infinite Reality appearing as the assumed finite identity. There is never something else existing other than undivided Existence Itself, as will be confirmed in upcoming verse 19. Its lower relative Nature is the perceived, that which is born; and Its superior (true) Nature is the unperceived, perennially unborn. When within infinite Consciousness there is the absence of the sense that 'I am,' as reflected in the body/mind's states of deep, dreamless sleep or *asamprajnata samadhi* (Awareness without contents to be aware of), the universe dissolves.

Although Spirit is omnipresent throughout every atom of the universe and the space between atoms as well, what appears as an inanimate object like a chair or a table does not have either physical or subtle senses for Spirit to function through. Such objects are permeated by *tamas-guna*, the component of inertia, and are not endowed with the aliveness mentioned in the previous verse which enables the animation of the elements. The superior Nature which enables the animation of the lower Nature is known as *jiva*.

**7**

*mattah parataram nanyat / kinchid asti dhananjaya
mayi sarvam idam protam / sutre mani-gana iva*

*mattah* > than Me; *parataram* > superior; *na* > not; *anyat kinchit* > anything else whatsoever; *asti* > there is; *dhananjaya* > O winner of wealth; *mayi* > upon Me; *sarvam* > all; *idam* > this; *protam* > strung; *sutre* > on a thread; *mani-ganah* > a group of pearls or gems; *iva* > like.

> **There is nothing whatsoever**
> **which is superior to Me (absolute Consciousness),**
> **O winner of wealth.**
> **All of this [which you perceive] is strung upon Me,**
> **as is a collection of gems on a thread.**

Interestingly, one of the definitions of *mani* in the Tamil language of India is 'knot.' An analogy of knots on a string would have also been quite fitting for Krishna to use, as the knots are composed entirely of the string alone and nothing else.

8

*raso 'ham apsu kaunteya / prabhasmi shashi-suryayoh*
*pranavah sarva-vedeshu / shabdah khe paurusham nrishu*

*rasah* > flavor; *aham* > the sense of 'I-ness'; *apsu* > in water;
*kaunteya* > O son of Kunti; *prabha* > the radiance; *asmi* > I am;
*shashi-suryayoh* > of the sun and the rabbit-marked moon;
*pranavah* > the sacred syllable Om; *sarva-vedeshu* > in all
the Vedas; *shabdah* > sound; *khe* > in the ether;
*paurusham* > virility, masculine temperament; *nrishu* > in men.

> **The sense of 'I-ness' is the pure flavor of water, O son of Kunti;**
> **It is the radiance of the sun and of the rabbit-marked moon,**
> **The sacred syllable Om in all the Vedas,**
> **Sound in the ether,**
> **And the masculine characteristics of men.**

Just as in some cultures of the world observers of the moon see something resembling a man's face upon it, in many others a rabbit sitting up on its hind legs in front of a smaller pot-like object is observed. Along with the culture of India, the 'rabbit in the moon' is spoken of in the folklore of the Chinese, Japanese, Korean, Aztec, Mesoamerican, and Native American cultures. Yet when the Absolute is unaware that It exists as an 'I,' there is no moon to give radiance to, no water to give flavor to, and so forth.

**9**

*punyo gandhah prithivyam cha / tejas chasmi vibhavasau*
*jivanam sarva-bhuteshu / tapas chasmi tapasvishu*

*punyah* > pure; *gandhah* > fragrance; *prithivyam* > in the earth; *cha* > and;
*tejah* > energetic splendor; *cha* > and; *asmi* > I am; *vibhavasau* > in flame;
*jivanam* > causing to live, the life-giving or animating principle;
*sarva-bhuteshu* > in all beings; *tapah* > austerity; *cha* > and;
*asmi* > I am; *tapasvishu* > in the ascetics.

**'I am' is the pure fragrance of earth**
**and the energetic splendor of fire.**
**It is the life-giving principle in all beings,**
**and the austerity of the ascetics.**

**10**

*bijam mam sarva-bhutanam / viddhi partha sanatanam*
*buddhir buddhi-matam asmi / tejas tejasvinam aham*

*bijam* > seed, primary cause; *mam* > Me; *sarva-bhutanam* > of all living beings;
*viddhi* > please know; *partha* > O son of Pritha; *sanatanam* > original, primeval;
*buddhih* > intelligence; *buddhi-matam* > of those who are intelligent;
*asmi* > I am; *tejah* > potency; *tejasvinam* > of the potent; *aham* > I.

**Know Me to be the primeval seed**
**of all living beings, O son of Pritha;**
**I am the Intelligence of the intelligent**
**and the Potency of the potent.**

**11**

*balam balavatam chaham / kamaraga-vivarjitam*
*dharma 'viruddho bhuteshu / kamo 'smi bharatarshabha*

*balam* > strength; *balavatam* > of the strong; *cha* > and; *aham* > I;
*kamaraga* > impassioned desire; *vivarjitam* > devoid of; *dharma-aviruddhah* >
not contrary to living consciously according to Life-centered values;
*bhuteshu* > in living beings; *kamah* > desire; *asmi* > I am; *bharata-rishabha* >
O best of the Bharata dynasty who possesses the strength of a bull.

**O best of the Bharatas with bull-like strength,**
**'I am' is the strength of the strong devoid of impassioned desire,**
**And it is also any desire within beings which is not contrary**
**to living consciously according to Life-centered values.**

**12**

*ye chaiva sattvika bhava / rajasas tamasash cha ye*
*matta eveti tan viddhi / na tvaham teshu te mayi*

*ye* > which; *cha* > and; *eva* > indeed; *sattvikah* > imbued with the
nature of clarity and balance; *bhavah* > coming into being; *rajasah* > imbued
with the nature of activation and distortion; *tamasah* > imbued with the
nature of darkness and inertia; *cha* > and; *ye* > which; *mattah* > from Me;
*eva* > indeed; *iti* > thus; *tan* > them; *viddhi* > please know; *na* > not;
*tu* > however; *aham* > I; *teshu* > in them; *te* > they; *mayi* > in Me.

**Indeed, anything whatsoever which comes into being—**
**Whether imbued with the nature of clarity and balance (sattva),**
**coloration and intensification (rajas), or darkness and inertia (tamas) —**
**It proceeds from Me (the One without a second).**
**Please know, however, that I am not in those things; they are in Me.**

It is often thought that an infinitesimal particle of Spirit is hidden deep inside
the considerably larger body/mind vessel like some needle in a haystack,
yet here Krishna states that the truth is exactly the opposite.

**13**

*tribhir guna-mayair bhavair / ebhih sarvam idam jagat*
*mohitam nabhijanati / mam ebhyah param avyayam*

*tribhih guna-mayaih* > produced by the three components of Nature (sattva,
rajas, and tamas); *bhavaih* > by that which comes into being; *ebhih* > by these;
*sarvam* > all; *idam* > this; *jagat* > world, universe; *mohitam* > confused;
*na* > not; *abhijanati* > it recognizes; *mam* > Me; *ebhyah* > than these;
*param* > higher; *avyayam* > changeless, imperishable.

**Confused by that which comes into being**
**produced by these three components of Nature,**
**This entire world does not recognize Me (its own true nature),**
**who am above those components and changeless.**

**14**

*daivi hy esha gunamayi / mama maya duratyaya*
*mam eva ye prapadyante / mayam etam taranti te*

*daivi* > divine; *hi* > truly; *esha* > this; *guna-mayi* > produced by the components
of Nature; *mama* > My; *maya* > artistic magical illusion; *duratyaya* > difficult to

pass beyond (see through); *mam eva* > Me alone; *ye* > who; *prapadyante* >
they take refuge, they embrace; *mayam* > creative illusory imagery;
*etam* > this; *taranti* > they get through, they cross over; *te* > they.

**Truly divine and challenging to see through
Is this artistic magical illusion
produced by the components of My Nature;
Yet those who take refuge in Me alone
see through this creative imagery.**

The very first definition for *maya* in both Monier-Williams' and Capeller's
Sanskrit-English dictionaries is 'art.' And another meaning of *prapadyante*
is 'to throw one's self down,' which connotes relinquishing the sense of
pseudo-selfhood. The Zen master Bodhidharma stated that "To give up
yourself without regret is the greatest charity."

**15**
*na mam dushkritino mudhah / prapadyante naradhamah
mayayapahrita-jnana / asuram bhavam ashritah*

*na* > not; *mam* > Me; *dushkritinah* > performers of wicked deeds;
*mudhah* > deluded; *prapadyante* > they take refuge; *nara-adhamah* > most vile
among humankind; *mayaya* > by illusion; *apahrita* > stolen, taken away;
*jnanah* > wisdom; *asuram* > demonic; *bhavam* > temperament,
condition; *ashritah* > resorting to.

**The performers of wicked deeds —
deluded and most vile among humankind —
do not take refuge in Me.
Their wisdom having been stolen away by illusion,
they resort to a demonic temperament.**

There will be a detailed description of both the heavenly and demonic
temperaments later in Chapter Sixteen.

**16**
*chatur-vidha bhajante mam / janah sukritino'rjuna
arto jijnasur artharthi / jnani cha bharatarshabha*

*chatur-vidhah* > of four kinds; *bhajante* > they revere, they worship, they adore;
*mam* > Me; *janah* > persons; *sukritinah* > those who perform virtuous actions;
*arjuna* > O Arjuna; *artah* > one who is suffering; *jijnasuh* > one inquiring
into truth; *artha-arthi* > one seeking prosperity; *jnani* > one who has realized

the truth; *cha* > and; *bharata-rishabha* > O best amongst the descendants of Bharata who possesses the strength of a bull.

**O Arjuna, best of the powerful Bharata dynasty,**
**Four kinds of persons who perform beneficent activities worship Me:**
**One who is suffering,**
**One who is seeking prosperity,**
**One inquiring into truth,**
**And one who has realized the truth.**

## 17

*tesham jnani nityayukta / ekabhaktir vishishyate*
*priyo hi jnanino 'tyartham / aham sa cha mama priyah*

*tesham* > of them; *jnani* > one who has realized the Truth; *nitya-yuktah* > ever endowed or aligned with; *eka-bhaktih* > devotion to the One; *vishishyate* > that one is foremost; *priyah* > dear; *hi* > indeed; *jnaninah* > of the realized one; *atyartham* > exceedingly; *aham* > I; *sah* > that one; *cha* > and; *mama* > to Me; *priyah* > dear.

**Among them, foremost is he or she who has realized the truth**
**and is thus ever endowed with devotion to the One.**
**I am exceedingly dear to that realized one,**
**And that jnani is dear to Me.**

## 18

*udarah sarva evaite / jnani tvatmaiva me matam*
*asthitah sa hi yuktatma / mam evanuttamam gatim*

*udarah* > noble; *sarve* > all (refers to the four types of virtuous persons mentioned in verse 16); *eva* > certainly; *ete* > these; *jnani* > one who has realized his or her true nature; *tu* > but; *atma* > self; *eva* > truly; *me* > My; *matam* > considered to be; *asthitah* > abiding in; *sah* > that one; *hi* > truly; *yukta-atma* > whose inner fourfold subtle body is aligned; *mam* > Me; *eva* > indeed; *anuttamam* > highest, supreme; *gatim* > way of being, manner of going.

**All of these [types of worshippers I mentioned] are certainly noble,**
**But I consider the one wherein there is realization**
**to be My very self,**
**For the inner subtle body of that one**
**is truly abiding in alignment with Me (absolute truth),**
**which is indeed the highest way of being.**

**19**

*bahunam janmanam ante / jnanavan mam prapadyate*
*vasudevah sarvam iti / sa mahatma sudurlabhah*

*bahunam janmanam* > of many births; *ante* > at the end, finally; *jnanavan* > one who has recognized the divine unicity of Life; *mam* > Me; *prapadyate* > that one takes refuge in; *vasudevah* > divine Omnipresence; *sarvam* > all that exists; *iti* > thus (perceiving); *sah* > this; *maha-atma* > a great expression of the Spirit-Self; *sudurlabhah* > very difficult to come by, rare.

**After the births of many [body/mind instruments for Self-awakening],**
**Within one of them there is recognition of the unicity of Life,**
**And that [expression of the] One takes refuge in Me (the truth of Itself),**
**Perceiving that all that exists is [Itself as] divine Omnipresence.**
**Such a great self-expression of Life is rarely found.**

**20**

*kamais taistair hrita-jnanah / prapadyante 'nyadevatah*
*tamtam niyamam asthaya / prakritya niyatah svaya*

*kamaih* > by desires; *taih taih* > by such-and-such; *hrita* > stolen away; *jnanah* > wisdom; *prapadyante* > they resort to; *anya* > an other one, a different one; *devatah* > the celestials (expressions of the One in subtler dimensions of Consciousness); *tam tam* > this or that; *niyamam* > observances, obligatory rites, rules; *asthaya* > following; *prakritya* > by their acquired (relative) nature; *niyatah* > suppressed, constrained; *svaya* > by their own.

**Those [expressions of the One]**
**wherein wisdom has been stolen away by such-and-such desires**
**Resort to [the worship of what is perceived as] an 'other'**
**among the celestials**
**And follow this or that obligatory rite,**
**constrained by their own acquired natures.**

**21**

*yo yo yam yam tanum bhaktah / shraddhay'-architum ichchati*
*tasya tasya-'chalam shraddham / tam eva vidadhamyaham*

*yah yah* > whoever; *yam yam* > whatever; *tanum* > form, embodiment; *bhaktah* > devotee; *shraddhaya* > with faith; *architum* > to worship; *ichchati* > that one wishes; *tasya tasya* > of each one accordingly, upon whoever this one may be; *achalam* > unshakeable; *shraddham* > faith; *tam* > this; *eva* > certainly, just so; *vidadhami* > I bestow, I provide; *aham* > I.

Whatever form of deity
any devotee wishes to faithfully worship—
Just so, I accordingly bestow upon each worshipper
unwavering faith in that particular form.

22

*sa taya shraddhaya yuktas / tasya-'radhanam ihate*
*labhate cha tatah kaman / mayaiva vihitan hi tan*

*sah* > this one (the worshipper); *taya* > with this; *shraddhaya* > by faith; *yuktah* > endowed, aligned; *tasya* > of that (form of deity); *aradhanam* > performance of worship; *ihate* > one longs for, one aspires for; *labhate* > one obtains; *cha* > and; *tatah* > thereby, then; *kaman* > desired objects or objectives; *maya* > by Me; *eva* > alone; *vihitan* > provided; *hi* > surely; *tan* > them.

Endowed with such faith,
One worships that form
and thereby obtains what he or she aspired for,
The desired object or objective
being of course provided by Me alone.

23

*antavat tu phalam tesham / tad bhavatyalpa-medhasam*
*devan devayajo yanti / madbhakta yanti mam api*

*antavat* > that which ends, that which is limited and temporary; *tu* > but; *phalam* > fruit (the obtained objects or objectives mentioned in the previous verse); *tesham* > of them; *tat* > that; *bhavati* > it is; *alpa-medhasam* > of those with little comprehension; *devan* > to the celestials; *deva-yajah* > the worshippers of the celestials; *yanti* > they go; *mat-bhaktah* > those devoted to Me; *yanti* > they proceed, they reach; *mam* > to Me; *api* > even so, so also.

But limited and temporary is the resulting gain
of those with little comprehension [of the underlying truth].
The worshippers of the celestials go to the celestials;
so also do those devoted to Me come to Me.

Within absolute Consciousness there is the experiencing of whatever is desired ("Thy Will be done") in a dreamlike way; so when there is the sense of separate self and other, that dream simply continues after the 'death' of the body/mind instrument. When there is realization of unitary wholeness, however, that dream ceases, and the words *yanti mam* ('they reach Me') represent the cessation of that illusion of separation.

**24**

*avyaktam vyaktim apannam / manyante mam abuddhayah*
*param bhavam ajananto / mama-'vyayam anuttamam*

*avyaktam* > the Unmanifest; *vyaktim* > appearance as a visible manifestation,
appearance as an individual personality; *apannam* > changed into, entered
into, or fallen into misfortune; *manyante* > they think, they consider;
*mam* > Me; *abuddhayah* > those lacking awakened perception; *param* > highest;
*bhavam* > state of Being; *ajanantah* > not knowing; *mama* > My;
*avyayam* > immutable, not subject to change; *anuttamam* > incomparable.

**Not knowing My highest state of Being**
**which is immutable and incomparable,**
**Those lacking awakened perception think that I, the Unmanifest,**
**have fallen into misfortune by My appearing as an individual personality.**

Krishna's immutable 'state' is not a *stasis* or stationariness as might be
construed by the human intellect. The one all-pervasive, unmanifest Stillness
dynamically continues manifesting as all that is, yet is not altered in the
slightest by Its *appearing* as 'the ten thousand things,' just as a small twisted
tree stump is not altered by its appearing as some kind of animal when seen
in the dark. Therein lies the immutability which, as a concept, was initially
introduced in the Gita in verses 2.21 and 2.25.

**25**

*naham prakashah sarvasya / yogamaya-samavritah*
*mudho 'yam nabhijanati / loko mam ajam avyayam*

*na* > not; *aham* > I; *prakashah* > evident, revealed (by intuition or
apperception); *sarvasya* > to all; *yoga-maya* > conjoining with the
creative Power which produces miraculous illusions, by the
application of supernatural artistry; *samavritah* > covered all over
(like clothing), wrapped in; *mudhah* > confused; *ayam* > this;
*na* > not; *abhijanati* > it recognizes; *lokah* > world of human beings;
*mam* > Me; *ajam* > unborn; *avyayam* > imperishable.

**I am not evident to all [expressions of Myself],**
**Clad as I am in the artistic fashionings of My creative Power**
**which produces miraculous illusions.**
**Hence humankind does not recognize Me,**
**the birthless and deathless [Everpresence].**

**26**
*vedaham samatitani / vartamanani charjuna*
*bhavishyani cha bhutani / mam tu veda na kashchana*

*veda aham* > I know; *samatitani* > those who have passed beyond
or crossed over; *vartamanani* > those who are turning or moving;
*cha* > and; *arjuna* > O Arjuna; *bhavishyani* > those who are yet to be;
*cha* > also; *bhutani* > living beings; *mam* > Me; *tu* > but;
*veda* > one knows; *na* > not; *kashchana* > anyone.

**I know those living beings (thought-forms) which have passed,**
**those which are currently moving about,**
**and those which are yet to be, O Arjuna;**
**But no one knows Me.**

As absolute Consciousness is One without a second, there is no other for It to
be known by. And as mentioned in the notes to verse 4.5, only Consciousness
can know the ideational constructs appearing within It; the thoughts
themselves cannot be knowers of Consciousness.

**27**
*ichcha-dvesha-samutthena / dvandva-mohena bharata*
*sarva-bhutani sammoham / sarge yanti parantapa*

*ichcha* > wish, inclination; *dvesha* > hatred, aversion; *samutthena* > by the
arising; *dvandva* > of the pairs of opposites (such as heat and cold, pleasure
and pain, honor and dishonor, etc.); *mohena* > by the distraction, by the
infatuation; *bharata* > O scion of Bharata; *sarva* > all; *bhutani* > living
beings; *sammoham* > bewilderment, astonishment; *sarge* > at the time of
coming forth into manifestation, at the time of being emitted;
*yanti* > they fall into; *parantapa* > O conqueror of foes.

**O scion of Bharata, conqueror of foes,**
**Due to distraction by [and infatuation with] the pairs of opposites**
**caused by the arising of attraction and aversion to them,**
**All living beings fall into bewilderment**
**at the time of their coming forth into manifestation.**

The four types of manifestation are: (1) *jarayuja* — born from a womb, such as
humans and animals; (2) *andaja* — born from an egg, such as birds, fish, and
reptiles; (3) *bijya* — sprung from a seed, such as plants, trees, and vegetables;
and (4) *svedaja* — produced from hot moisture, such as lice and worms.

**28**

*yesham tvanta-gatam papam / jananam punya-karmanam*
*te dvandva-moha-nirmukta / bhajante mam dridha-vratah*

*yesham* > of whom; *tu* > but; *anta-gatam* > come to an end; *papam* > misfortune,
trouble; *jananam* > of those persons; *punya-karmanam* > whose actions are
virtuous or auspicious; *te* > they; *dvandva* > the pairs of opposites;
*moha* > confusion, deception; *nirmuktah* > freed from;
*bhajante* > they worship; *mam* > Me; *dridha* > firm; *vratah* > vows.

**But those persons whose misfortune has come to an end —**
**The performers of virtuous actions**
**who are free from the confusing effects of the pairs of opposites —**
**Worship Me (absolute truth) with firm vows.**

**29**

*jara-marana-mokshaya / mam ashritya yatanti ye*
*te brahma tad viduh kritsnam / adhyatmam karma chakhilam*

*jara* > old age; *marana* > dying; *mokshaya* > toward freedom;
*mam* > Me; *ashritya* > taking refuge in; *yatanti* > they are intent upon;
*ye* > who; *te* > they; *brahma* > Brahman, the Absolute; *tat* > that;
*viduh* > they recognize; *kritsnam* > fully; *adhyatmam* > that which pertains
to Atman or the universal principle of selfhood in all sentient beings;
*karma* > action; *cha* > and; *akhilam* > in its entirety, without any separation.

**Those who take refuge in Me,**
**Intent upon freedom from [the experiencing of] old age and dying,**
**Come to fully recognize That which is Brahman, the Absolute;**
**What is Atman, the universal principle of selfhood in all sentient beings;**
**And the role of action in its entirety.**

**30**

*sadhibhut'-adhidaivam mam / sadhiyajnam cha ye viduh*
*prayanakale 'pi cha mam / te vidur yukta-chetasah*

*sa* > along with; *adhibhuta* > that which pertains to the aggregate
of material elements comprising the physical plane of being;
*adhidaivam* > that which pertains to the aggregate of subtle phenomena
comprising the celestial dimension of being; *mam* > Me; *sa* > along with;
*adhiyajnam* > that which pertains to the principle of sacrifice; *cha* > and;

*ye* > who; *viduh* > they recognize; *prayana-kale* > 'on the journey' (refers to Awareness dissociating from the body at the time of the body's death); *api* > even; *cha* > and; *mam* > Me; *te viduh* > they recognize; *yukta-chetasah* > those with deeply absorbed attention.

**Those who recognize Me**
**(one's own true nature as the purely contented presence of Awareness)**
**Within the context of the physical plane of being,**
**The celestial dimension of being,**
**And the principle of sacrifice**
**Continue to retain recognition of Me with deeply absorbed attention**
**even at the hour of the body's death.**

The word *adhiyajnam* here invites recollection of Krishna's statement in verse 3.15 that "The omnipresent Truth eternally dwells in expressions of sacrifice," which encompasses reciprocal giving and serving.

*om tat saditi srimad bhagavad-gita / supanishatsu brahma-vidyayam*
*yoga-shastre srikrishnarjuna samvade / jnana-vijnana-yogo nama saptamo 'dhyayah*

From the Ambrosial Song of God —
A conversation between Krishna and Arjuna
which is a Upanishad (confidential sharing)
of wisdom-teachings regarding the Absolute
And a scripture concerning Self-realization —
Thus ends the Seventh Chapter entitled Jnana-vijnana-yoga,
Recognizing Divine Unicity By Way of Higher Knowledge and Discernment.

# Chapter Eight

---

# Akshara-brahma-yoga
### (Recognizing Divine Unicity By Way of the Syllable Om
### Representing the Imperishable Absolute)

"The syllable Aum is this entire Creation. It may be succinctly described as all
that has passed, all that is now present, all that is yet to come, and whatever is
beyond the three phases of time as well. All of that is verily Aum."
— Mandukya Upanishad, verse 1

"Pippalada said: O Satyakama, the syllable Om is Brahman, both with and
without qualities. Therefore, one who, with Its support, realizes Om as such,
reaches realization of one aspect of Brahman or the other."
— *Prashna Upanishad*, verse 5.2

"When the body/mind is utilized as the lower piece of kindling wood and
the syllable Om is the upper piece, the practice of meditation becomes the
friction which draws out intuitive apperception of the luminous Self, which
is as ever-present as dormant fire is within wood."
— *Shvetashvatara Upanishad*, verse 1.14

"By looking for It, It cannot be seen; therefore It is called invisible.
By listening for It, It cannot be heard; therefore It is called inaudible.
By reaching for It, It cannot be touched; therefore It is called intangible.
It eludes these three attempts because It is one homogeneous Mystery.
There is no upper region of this One which is brightened by exaltation.
There is no lower region of this One which is darkened due to exclusion.
Perpetually evading definition, It continually returns to the state
prior to *things*.
This state is not a state, just as Its image is unimaginable. Such is Its subtlety.
Confronting It, Its front is not found; following after It, Its back is not found.
Therefore, by abiding as what is most ancient,
one is effective in attending to what is most immediate.
This knowing what preceded the beginning of things
is the essence of the Way."    — *Tao Te Ching*, Chapter 14

**1**
*arjuna uvacha:*
*kim tad brahma kim adhyatmam / kim karma purushottama*
*adhibhutam cha kim proktam / adhidaivam kim uchyate*

*arjunah uvacha* > Arjuna said; *kim* > what; *tat* > that; *brahma* > Brahman,
the Absolute; *kim* > what; *adhyatmam* > that which pertains to Atman or
the universal principle of selfhood in all sentient beings; *kim* > what;
*karma* > action; *purusha-uttama* > O best of men; *adhibhutam* > that which
pertains to the aggregate of elements comprising the physical plane of being;
*cha* > and; *kim* > what; *proktam* > said to be; *adhidaivam* > that which
pertains to the aggregate of celestial phenomena comprising the
subtle dimension of being; *kim* > what; *uchyate* > it is said to be.

**Arjuna inquired:**
**What *is* that Absolute?**
**What is the universal principle of selfhood in all sentient beings?**
**What *is* the role of action, O best of men?**
**And what is said to be the context**
**in which you pertain to the physical plane of being**
**and the subtle dimension of being?**

**2**
*adhiyajnah katham ko 'tra / dehe 'smin madhusudana*
*prayanakale cha katham / jneyo 'si niyatatmabhih*

*adhiyajnah* > that which pertains to the principle of sacrifice; *katham* > how;
*kah* > who; *atra* > here; *dehe asmin* > in this body; *madhusudana* > O slayer
of the demon Madhu; *prayana-kale* > at the hour of death; *cha* > and;
*katham* > how; *jneyah* > to be known, to be perceived; *asi* > you are;
*niyata-atmabhih* > by those who are self-controlled.

**Who dwells here in this body,**
**and how does that one pertain to the principle of sacrifice,**
**O slayer of the demon Madhu?**
**And at the hour of death,**
**how are you to be recognized by those who are self-controlled?**

**3**
*sri bhagavan uvacha:*
*aksharam brahma paramam / svabhavo 'dhyatmam uchyate*
*bhuta-bhavodbhava-karo / visargah karma-samjnitah*

*sri bhagavan uvacha* > the radiant one (Krishna) said; *aksharam* > imperishable;
*brahma* > Brahman, the Absolute; *paramam* > supreme; *svabhavah* > inherent
disposition, natural state, spontaneous impulse; *adhyatmam* > that which
pertains to Atman or the universal principle of selfhood in all sentient beings;

*uchyate* > it is said; *bhuta-bhava* > the 'becoming' (development and subsequent dissolution) of beings; *udbhava* > origin, production; *karah* > causing; *visargah* > sending forth, emitting, or emanating of creative vibratory energy; *karma* > action; *samjnitah* > meant by, known as.

**The radiant Krishna replied:**
**The Absolute is the imperishable Supreme;**
**Selfhood [or 'selfing'] is said to be Its spontaneous impulse universally;**
**And what is known as action is Its [subsequently also spontaneous]**
**emission of creative vibratory energy**
**Which causes the production, development,**
**and dissolution of all beings.**

As mentioned in verse 7.6, the movement to 'I am' within absolute Consciousness is the genesis of the entire world-appearance. Yet this movement is not really a movement inasmuch as when one is sitting motionlessly and suddenly becomes aware of something, no movement has actually taken place. Therefore the Absolute can remain 'firmly immovable and unmoving' (verse 2.24) while continually becoming aware of Its existence in each of Its manifest expressions wherever a body/mind instrument for such self-awareness is available. And the word *visargah* here is considered to be synonymous with the 'unstruck' (uncaused) sound vibration of the revered mystic syllable Om, which in the Upanishads is said to be the initiating factor of the created universe.

**4**
*adhibhutam ksharo bhavah / purushash chadhidaivatam*
*adhiyajno 'ham evatra / dehe deha-bhritam vara*

*adhibhutam* > that which pertains to the aggregate of material elements comprising the physical plane of being; *ksharah* > perishable; *bhavah* > the state of becoming; *purushah* > the universal potential for expression via personification; *cha* > and; *adhidaivatam* > that which pertains to the aggregate of subtle phenomena comprising the celestial dimension of being; *adhiyajnah* > that which pertains to the principle of sacrifice; *aham* > I; *eva* > alone; *atra* > here; *dehe* > in the body; *deha-bhritam* > of the embodied; *vara* > O best.

**Within the physical plane of being,**
**The aggregate of material elements**
**is the perishable state of becoming (transformation);**

Within the celestial dimension of being,
The aggregate of subtle phenomena
is the universal potential for expression via personification;
And I alone (unconditioned unconditional Love)
am the principle of sacrifice here in the body,
O best of embodied beings.

The Love alluded to here has been briefly described in the notes to 6.24-25.

### 5

*anta-kale cha mam eva / smaran muktva kalevaram*
*yah prayati sa mad-bhavam / yati nastyatra samshayah*

*anta-kale* > at the time of ending (refers to the body's duration of functioning); *cha* > and; *mam* > Me; *eva* > alone; *smaran* > remembering; *muktva* > having cast aside or dissociated from; *kalevaram* > the body; *yah* > who; *prayati* > one goes forth, one departs; *sah* > that one; *mat-bhavam* > My state of being; *yati* > one reaches, one attains; *na* > not; *asti* > there is; *atra* > in this matter; *samshayah* > doubt, uncertainty.

**And one who, at the end of the body's duration of functioning,**
**Dissociates from the body and 'goes forth' remembering Me alone**
**reaches My state of being;**
**There is no uncertainty in this matter.**

The phrase *mad-bhavam* here refers to the 'stateless' state of purely being without doing, which is distinguished from the 'coming into being' (appearing as a form) discussed in relation to verses 6, 12, 13, 24, and 27 of Chapter Seven.

### 6

*yam yam vapi smaran bhavam / tyajatyante kalevaram*
*tam tam evaiti kaunteya / sada tadbhava-bhavitah*

*yam yam* > whatever; *va api* > moreover; *smaran* > remembering; *bhavam* > being; *tyajati* > one relinquishes; *ante* > at the end; *kalevaram* > the body; *tam tam* > at that; *eva* > just so; *eti* > one arrives; *kaunteya* > O son of Kunti; *sada* > ever; *tadbhava* > becoming that; *bhavitah* > absorbed in.

**Moreover, whatever being one remembers**
**upon relinquishing the body at the end of its duration —**
**Just so, one arrives at that, O son of Kunti,**
**ever becoming that which one is absorbed in.**

Insofar as the word *bhavam* ('being') here could refer either to a state of being or to a particular living being, the second reading would predominantly connote becoming like one's preferred deity within subtler realms beyond the physical. In either case, however, Arjuna would have been completely justified had he inquired at this point: "Krishna, you said that all that exists is the one divine Omnipresence (in verse 7.19). So where can That which is everywhere *go* at the end of a particular body's duration?" To which Krishna could have responded: "*That* doesn't go anywhere, but *within* That there can be a dreamlike *experience* of going somewhere." This idea will be developed further in upcoming verses 24 and 25.

## 7

*tasmat sarveshu kaleshu / mam anusmara yudhya cha*
*mayy arpita-manobuddhir / mam evaishyasyasamshayah*

*tasmat* > therefore; *sarveshu kaleshu* > at all times; *mam anusmara* > remember Me; *yudhya* > do fight; *cha* > and; *mayi* > to Me; *arpita* > entrusted; *manah* > mind; *buddhih* > intellect; *mam* > Me; *eva* > alone; *eshyasi* > you will come; *asamshayah* > without a doubt.

**Therefore, remember Me at all times,**
**and fight [in the confrontation with the Kauravas here as is your duty].**
**With your mind and intellect entrusted to Me,**
**you will come to Me alone without a doubt**
**[upon dissociation from the physical body].**

## 8

*abhyasa-yoga-yuktena / chetasa nanya-gamina*
*paramam purusham divyam / yati partha-'nuchintayan*

*abhyasa-yoga-yuktena* > by the repetition of engagement in dhyana-yoga (meditation); *chetasa* > by the attention; *na anya-gamina* > by not going elsewhere; *paramam purusham* > to the supreme personification of Spirit; *divyam* > divine; *yati* > one goes; *partha* > O son of Pritha; *anuchintayan* > recollecting, meditating upon.

**By the repetition of this type of engagement in meditation**
**with one's attention not going elsewhere, O Partha,**
**One goes to the supreme divine personification of Spirit**
**that one has been recollecting.**

**9**

*kavim puranam anushasitaram / anor aniyamsam anusmared yah*
*sarvasya dhataram achintya-rupam / aditya-varnam tamasah parastat*

*kavim* > the omniscient seer-poet; *puranam* > ancient; *anushasitaram* > the
sovereign; *anoh aniyamsam* > smaller than smallest, subtler than the subtlest;
*anusmaret* > let one remember, let one meditate upon; *yah* > who;
*sarvasya* > of all; *dhataram* > the sustainer; *achintya-rupam* > whose form is
incomprehensible; *aditya-varnam* > whose effulgence is like that
of the sun; *tamasah* > than darkness; *parastat* > beyond.

**Let one remember the omniscient Seer-poet —**
**The ancient Sovereign who is subtler than the subtlest**
**yet is the sustainer of all —**
**Whose form is incomprehensible and resplendent like the sun,**
**beyond all darkness.**

**10**

*prayana-kale manasa-'chalena / bhaktya yuktoyoga-balena chaiva*
*bhruvor madhye pranam aveshya samyak / sa tam param purusham upaiti divyam*

*prayana-kale* > 'on the journey' (refers to Awareness dissociating from the
body at the time of the body's death); *manasa achalena* > with an unmoving
mind; *bhaktya* > with a devotional temperament; *yuktah* > endowed;
*yoga-balena* > by the power developed through the practice of raja-yoga;
*cha* > and; *eva* > indeed; *bhruvoh* > of the two eyebrows; *madhye* > in
the middle; *pranam* > the vital life-airs; *aveshya* > having directed
towards, having caused to enter; *samyak* > completely, accurately;
*sah* > that one; *tam* > this; *param purusham* > the Supreme Person;
*upaiti* > one reaches; *divyam* > heavenly, divine.

**For at the time of the body's death,**
**Endowed with an unmoving mind,**
**a devotional temperament,**
**and power developed through the practice of raja-yoga,**
**One whose vital life-airs are accurately directed**
**to enter between the eyebrows**
**Reaches this divine Supreme Person.**

Verses 9 through 13 specifically pertain to those with a natural penchant for
the way of raja-yoga, which of course requires great selflessness and
devotion. At the same time, for those lacking this particular affinity or ability,

the way of selfless devotional action which is not dependent upon all the other components of raja-yoga will be delineated by Krishna in verses 26 through 34 of Chapter Nine. Also, it may be noted that although the term *raja-yoga* used throughout this particular presentation of the Gita does refer to a specific combination of practices, it does not refer to the systematized teachings given by Patanjali, as the presumed initial recitation of the Bhagavad-Gita predates the *Yoga-Sutras* by perhaps 800 years. This same principle applies to the term *Sankhya* used herein — it refers to the process of empirical analysis, yet not to the specific system established in literary form some 1200 years later as the *Sankhya-Karika*.

When reciting this verse in the alternate metre known as *trishtubh*, the second segment of the second line has one additional syllable.

### 11
*yad aksharam vedavido vadanti / vishanti yad yatayo vitaragah*
*yad ichchanto brahmacharyam charanti / tat te padam sangrahena pravakshye*

*yat* > which; *aksharam* > the sacred syllable; *veda-vidah* > those who know
the Vedas; *vadanti* > they speak of; *vishanti* > they enter into; *yat* > which;
*yatayah* > the ascetics; *vita-ragah* > free from impassionment; *yat* > which;
*ichchantah* > wishing for; *brahmacharyam* > a lifestyle embracing abstinence,
continence, or celibacy; *charanti* > they follow; *tat* > that; *te* > to you;
*padam* > the steps; *sangrahena* > in brief; *pravakshye* > I shall speak about.

**Wishing to enter into [the mystery of] that sacred syllable**
**which those who know the Vedas speak of,**
**The ascetics embrace a life of continence free from impassionment.**
**I shall briefly describe to you the steps which they follow.**

### 12-13
*sarva-dvarani samyamya / mano hridi nirudhya cha*
*murdhnyadhay'-atmanah pranam / asthito yoga-dharanam*

*om ityekaksharam brahma / vyaharan mam anusmaran*
*yah prayati tyajan deham / sa yati paramam gatim*

*sarva* > all; *dvarani* > the gateways of the body (refers to the senses);
*samyamya* > closing; *manah* > the mind; *hridi* > in the heart; *nirudhya* >
insulating; *cha* > and; *murdhni* > within the head (meaning between the
eyebrows, as stated in verse 10); *adhaya* > placing; *atmanah* > of oneself, of
one's own; *pranam* > the vital life-airs; *asthitah* > established; *yoga-dharanam* >
the holding of focused attention, absorption in concentration;

*om* > the sound vibration Om; *iti* > in this way; *eka-aksharam* > a single syllable; *brahma* > infinite Spirit; *vyaharan* > uttering; *mam* > Me; *anusmaran* > remembering; *yah* > who; *prayati* > one goes forth; *tyajan* > abandoning; *deham* > the body; *sah* > that one; *yati* > one goes; *paramam* > to the supreme; *gatim* > refuge.

**Closing all the sense-gateways of the body,**
**Cloistering the mind within the heart-sanctuary,**
**and reposing the vital life-airs within one's forehead;**
**Established in holding attention there,**
**Uttering 'Om,' the sound vibration representing infinite Spirit**
**as a single syllable,**
**and remembering Me —**
**One who goes forth abandoning the body in this way**
**goes to the supreme refuge.**

In 'Om,' also spelled 'Aum,' the letter A represents the Vaishvanara Atman or universal aspect of the Self which witnesses the *jagat avastha* (physical waking state); the letter U represents the Taijasa Atman or luminous aspect of the Self which witnesses the *svapna avastha* (subtle dreaming state); and the letter M represents the Prajna Atman or aspect of the Self as intuitive intelligence which witnesses the *sushupti avastha* (causal deep sleep state). The Turiya (fourth part) of Aum represents the completely transcendent aspect of the Self as pure Awareness which is prior to and independent of witnessing any states at all.

*Mano hridi nirudhya*, 'insulating the mind within the heart,' may simply mean protecting one's attention from becoming distracted by environmental stimuli, or it could be a reminder that "those yogis who approach Me with a loving heart are most aligned with Me" (verse 6.47).

**14**
*ananya-chetah satatam / yo mam smarati nityashah*
*tasyaham sulabhah partha / nitya-yuktasya yoginah*

*ananya-chetah* > having no other thought, interest, or intention; *satatam* > ever; *yah* > who; *mam* > Me; *smarati* > one remembers; *nityashah* > constantly; *tasya* > for that one; *aham* > I; *su-labhah* > very easy to reach; *partha* > O son of Pritha; *nitya-yuktasya* > of one who is continuously attentive; *yoginah* > for the yogi.

**For that yogi who is attentive
to remembering Me constantly,
ever without other interests,
I am very easy to reach, O son of Pritha.**

### 15

*mam upetya punar janma / duhkha-'layam ashashvatam
napnuvanti mahatmanah / samsiddhim paramam gatah*

*mam* > Me; *upetya* > approaching; *punah* > again; *janma* > birth;
*duhkha* > misery; *alayam* > abode; *ashashvatam* > impermanent, transitory;
*na* > not; *apnuvanti* > they undergo, they come upon, they meet with;
*maha-atmanah* > great expressions of the Spirit-Self, the great-hearted ones;
*samsiddhim* > to perfection; *paramam* > supreme; *gatah* > arrived at.

**By approaching Me,
The great-hearted ones do not again undergo [the dream of] birth
in the transitory abode of misery,
Because they have arrived at the supreme perfection
[of their utility as instruments for Self-awakening].**

### 16

*abrahma-bhuvanal lokah / punar avartino'rjuna
mam upetya tu kaunteya / punar janma na vidyate*

*abrahma-bhuvanat* > up to and including the abode of the
Creator aspect of the One; *lokah* > worlds; *punah* > again;
*avartinah* > revolving, returning, repeating; *arjuna* > O Arjuna;
*mam* > Me; *upetya* > approaching; *tu* > but; *kaunteya* > O son of Kunti;
*punah* > again; *janma* > birth; *na* > not; *vidyate* > it is experienced.

**Up to and including the abode of Lord Brahma the Creator,
there is a recurrence of all the worlds, Arjuna;
But one who approaches Me, O son of Kunti,
does not experience [the dream of] birth again.**

### 17

*sahasra-yuga-paryantam / ahar yad brahmano viduh
ratrim yuga-sahasrantam / te 'horatra-vido janah*

*sahasra-yuga* > one thousand cycles of the combined four ages of
universal time; *paryantam* > extending; *ahah* > day; *yat* > which;

*brahmanah* > of the creative aspect of Spirit personified as Lord Brahma;
*viduh* > they know; *ratrim* > night; *yuga-sahasra-antam* > ending
after one thousand cycles of the combined four ages; *te* > they;
*ahah-ratra* > day and night; *vidah* > those who know; *janah* > people.

**Those who know that Brahma's day extends for one thousand cycles
of the combined four ages of time,
And that his night ends also after one thousand such cycles,
Are those persons who know [the true definition of] day and night.**

The four ages of the universal time-cycle are said to be Satya-yuga ('the age
of truth'), Treta-yuga ('the age of three sacred fires'), Dvapara-yuga ('the age
of uncertainty'), and Kali-yuga ('the age of discord'). According to the
astronomical calculations of Swami Sri Yukteswar, the spiritual preceptor of
Paramahansa Yogananda, the Earth is currently in the phase of an ascending
Dvapara-yuga which commenced at around the beginning of the eighteenth
century. Indeed, we have in fact witnessed an astounding acceleration in the
development of human potential since that time, not merely in regard to
technological advancement, but in the areas of intensive interest in social
justice, civil rights, political reform, world peace, global unity, and spiritual
awakening. At the same time, it is also witnessed that regardless of whatever
age one is living in, one's experience of the world will predominantly be
based on the degree to which pure Consciousness identifies Itself with one
particular body/mind system and its conditioned patterns of thought.

When within Consciousness there is complete freedom from identification
with an assumed self, there is the experiencing of Satya-yuga; when there is
some identification, there is the experiencing of Treta-yuga; when there is
much identification, there is the experiencing of Dvapara-yuga; and when
there is complete absorption in the hypnotic trance of misidentification,
there is the experiencing of Kali-yuga. Such experiences can change at any
time in accordance with the depth of one's awakening to one's true nature,
or the degree to which one's fourfold inner faculty (*antahkarana*) is clear
(predominated by *sattva*) and free from either distortion or obstruction
(predominance by *rajas* or *tamas*). In verse 51 of The Gospel of Thomas, the
apostles ask Jesus: "When will the new world come?", to which he replies:
"What you look forward to has already come, but you do not recognize it."
Later in verse 113 they again ask: "When will the Kingdom come?", and Jesus
replies: "It will not come by waiting for it. It will not be a matter of saying
'Behold, here it is' or 'Look, there it is.' Rather, the kingdom of the Father is
spread out upon the Earth, and men do not see it."

**18**

*avyaktad vyaktayah sarvah / prabhavantyahar-agame*
*ratryagame praliyante / tatraiva-'vyakta-samjnake*

*avyaktat* > from the Unmanifest; *vyaktayah* > appearances, manifestations;
*sarvah* > all; *prabhavanti* > they spring forth, they emerge; *ahah-agame* > at the
arrival of (Brahma's) day; *ratri-agame* > at the arrival of (Brahma's) night;
*praliyante* > they are dissolved, they are reabsorbed into; *tatra* > therein,
in that; *eva* > alone; *avyakta* > the Unmanifest; *samjnake* > is known as.

**From the Unmanifest,
all appearances emerge at the dawn of Brahma's day;
And at the advent of his night they dissolve,
being reabsorbed into That alone which is known as the Unmanifest.**

**19**

*bhuta-gramah sa evayam / bhutva bhutva praliyate*
*ratryagame 'vashah partha / prabhavatyahar-agame*

*bhuta-gramah* > aggregate of beings; *sah eva ayam* > this very same;
*bhutva bhutva* > comes into being or appears again and again;
*praliyate* > it is dissolved; *ratri-agame* > at the arrival of (Brahma's)
night; *avashah* > unwillingly, not having independent will;
*partha* > O son of Pritha; *prabhavati* > it arises, it emerges;
*ahah-agame* > upon the arrival of (Brahma's) day.

**This very same aggregate of beings
appears again and again, O son of Pritha,
Becoming dissolved at the arrival of Brahma's night
And again arising at the dawn of his day,
with no independent will [in these proceedings].**

Interestingly, in this verse the phrase *bhuta-gramah sa evayam* ('this very same
aggregate of beings') refers to that which was called *vyaktayah* ('appearances')
in the previous verse. This alludes to the principle that as there is no birth
for the singular undivided Consciousness appearing as all that is (*na jayate
mriyate va kadachin*, verse 2.20), there are subsequently no 'victims' of the
recurring dream described here which arises and dissipates.

**20**

*paras tasmat tu bhavo 'nyo / 'vyakto 'vyaktat sanatanah*
*yah sa sarveshu bhuteshu / nashyatsu na vinashyati*

*parah* > higher; *tasmat* > than this; *tu* > but; *bhavah* > condition, state; *anyah* > other; *avyaktah* > unmanifest; *avyaktat* > than the unmanifest; *sanatanah* > everlasting, permanent; *yah* > which; *sah sarveshu* > in all this; *bhuteshu nashyatsu* > in the perishing of beings; *na vinashyati* > it does not perish.

**But higher than this state-related Unmanifest
(Nature, Prakriti, with Its continually alternating states
of being manifest and not being manifest),
There is another, permanent Unmanifest
which does not perish amidst all this perishing of beings.**

### 21
*avyakto 'kshara ityuktas / tam ahuh paramam gatim
yam prapya na nivartante / tad dhama paramam mama*

*ayvaktah* > unmanifest; *aksharah* > imperishable; *iti uktah* > it is said; *tam* > this; *ahuh* > they regard, they consider; *paramam* > supreme; *gatim* > refuge; *yam* > which; *prapya* > reaching; *na* > not; *nivartante* > they return; *tat* > that; *dhama* > abode, home; *paramam* > supreme; *mama* > My.

**That which is called the imperishable Unmanifest
is regarded as the supreme refuge,
For upon reaching [the realization of being] That,
One does not return [to the dream of dissolving and re-arising].
That is My supreme abode (My natural 'stateless state').**

### 22
*purushah sa parah partha / bhaktya labhyas tvananyaya
yasyantah-sthani bhutani / yena sarvam idam tatam*

*purushah sah parah* > this Supreme Person; *partha* > O son of Pritha; *bhaktya* > by devotion, by love; *labhyah* > able to be found, capable of being reached; *tu* > indeed, now; *ananyaya* > not by another; *yasya* > of whom; *antah-sthani* > abiding within; *bhutani* > all beings; *yena* > by whom; *sarvam idam* > all this (manifestation); *tatam* > extended, pervaded.

**This Supreme Person within whom all living beings abide
and by whom all these manifest worlds are pervaded
Is able to be discovered only by sincere devotion,
and indeed not by any other way, O son of Pritha.**

As mentioned in the Preface to this edition, the same one nondual Reality is both with and without form, and not merely one way only to the exclusion of the other. This paradox (the Supreme Unmanifest of verse 21 being the Supreme Person of verse 22) cannot be understood by the intellect, and so it has been referred to as *achintya bhedabheda tattva*, 'the truth of inconceivable simultaneous distinction and non-distinction.' Among the other definitions of *bheda* are 'expanding,' 'blossoming,' and 'altering,' yet the Absolute is also *abheda* — neither expanding, nor blossoming, nor altering in any way whatsoever. This truth which transcends the either/or paradigm to accommodate both/and is also indicated in verse 2 of Mahayana Buddhism's *Prajnaparamita-Hridaya Sutra* (The Heart Sutra): "Form is non-different from Emptiness; Emptiness is non-different from Form. Form Itself *is* Emptiness, and Emptiness Itself *is* Form."

In regard to the term *shunyata* ('emptiness'), the widely-acclaimed author, translator, and professor of Buddhist philosophy D. T. Suzuki has mentioned in his writings that the concept of emptiness utilized in Mahayana philosophy is one of the most misunderstood by non-Buddhists. He explains that *shunyata* does not mean nothingness in the sense of an absence or lack of something, but that it rather points to the existence of something altogether unconditioned and transcendental in nature which he refers to as 'the Absolute.' A Buddhist stating that all things are empty is not advocating a nihilistic view, but quite the contrary — he or she is hinting at an ultimate reality which is not classifiable in any category based upon logic. Professor Suzuki goes on to say that when the *Shingyo Sutra* speaks of the five *skandhas* or aggregates of phenomena having the character of emptiness — that in emptiness there is no creation or destruction, no contamination or purity, and so forth — the sense conveyed is that no limitations can be attributed to the Absolute. Although It is immanent within all material objects, It is not in Itself definable.

**23**

*yatra kale tvanavrittim / avrittim chaiva yoginah*
*prayata yanti tam kalam / vakshyami bharatarshabha*

*yatra kale* > where in time; *tu* > now; *anavrittim* > not returning; *avrittim* > return; *cha* > and; *eva* > indeed; *yoginah* > the karma-yogis, dhyana-yogis, and raja-yogis; *prayatah* > departing (from the experiencing of this world); *yanti* > they go; *tam* > this; *kalam* > times; *vakshyami* > I shall speak about; *bharata-rishabha* > O best of the Bharatas who is as mighty as a bull.

**The movements through time of the yogis**
**Which lead to their either returning or not returning**
**after departing from the experiencing of this world —**
**I shall now speak about that, O best among the mighty Bharatas.**

Verses 23 through 27 are among those which a number of Gita research scholars feel were a later addition to the text by the brahmin community. In one of the earliest English translations of the Bhagavad-Gita — *The Song Celestial*, published in 1885 — Sir Edwin Arnold presents ellipsis (...) in this section with the footnote: "I have discarded ten lines of Sanskrit text here as an undoubted interpolation by some Vedantist." Nevertheless, with all due respect, these verses have been treated in the same manner as any other verse in the present edition, and any assessment of their authenticity as part of the original scripture will be left to the reader's intuition.

The words *yatra kale* and *kalam* refer to movements of attention along two different dreamlike pathways through conceptual time, one in light and one in darkness. These movements are based not as much upon external conditions as upon internal disposition at the time when Consciousness dissociates from a particular body carrying with It a localized sense of presence. That specific points in time are not exclusively being referred to herein will be confirmed in upcoming verse 26 by the phrase *shuklakrishne gati hyete* ('these two *paths* of light and dark'), and in verse 27 by the words *ete sriti janan* ('knowing these two *courses*'). As previously mentioned in verse 2.69: "The self-regulated ones are awake to their own intuitive wisdom, which is *like* nighttime for all sentient beings; and the inherited doctrine and dogma which all sentient beings are awake to is *like* the darkness of night for the sages and sagesses who perceive [truth]."

Upcoming verses 24 and 25 are based on passages in the Upanishads wherein a distinction is drawn between those yogis who, "living in the forest, meditate with faith upon Satya Brahman (absolute Reality)," and those who are engaged in the performance of religious rituals specifically "with a view to going to other worlds." *Brihad-aranyaka Upanishad* 6.2.9-16 describes how the concept or conception of a human being begins as a libation of faith by the celestials in the subtler dimension of Consciousness, and through Parjanya (Indra), the deity presiding over rain, that oblation moves down to this world through the rain into food. From food it moves into man, and then from the man's semen into woman wherein the new expression of Life develops.

According to other passages in the ancient texts, if that new expression of Life unfolds as a disciplined and contemplative one predominated by *sattvic* characteristics, then at the time when Consciousness dissociates from that body/mind vehicle, whatever sense of selfhood remains elicits the next sequence of experiences culminating in the highest heavenly abode of Lord Brahma. After an incalculable period of time immersed in unfathomable joy, there is cessation of that pseudo-self with no return to manifestation. This is known as the ascending path of light.

*Brihad-aranyaka Upanishad* then goes on to state: "But those who *conquer* the worlds through sacrifices, charity, and austerity — they reach the deity of smoke, of night...", etc. So in contrast to the after-death experiences of those yogis who are internally surrendered to the unknown and intent upon liberation, there is a different scenario depicted for those who are more inclined toward exerting personal effort and intent upon gaining heavenly pleasures. For them, after the death of the body the next sequence of experiences is said to include passage through the subtle world of the manes (deceased ancestors) and culminate in the celestial realm of Chandra (also known as Soma), the moon-god. After a period of time such yogis are said to then re-enter the rain and return to Earth through food, man, and woman, this descending course being called the one of darkness. Considering Krishna's solace-giving declaration in verses 6.44-45, however ("As a result of one's prior yoga practice, one is carried onward to supreme fulfillment, even unwillingly"), the path of darkness may perhaps be viewed as simply a different, somewhat longer path of light. This perspective is especially well-supported by Krishna's use of the word *jyotir*, 'brightly luminous,' when describing the lunar region, the yogi's alternate stopover. Yet in any case, Krishna has already stated twice in this chapter — first in verse 15, and then again in verse 16 — that "one who approaches Me does not experience [the dream of] birth again."

### 24

*agnir jyotir ahah shuklah / shanmasa uttarayanam*
*tatra prayata gachchanti / brahma brahmavido janah*

*agnih* > fire or Agni the fire-god; *jyotih ahah* > the light of day;
*shuklah* > the bright lunar fortnight; *shat-masah* > six months;
*uttara-ayanam* > the northward journey of the sun; *tatra* > there;
*prayatah* > departing (from the experience of this world);
*gachchanti* > they pass through, they visit, they meet with;
*brahma* > Lord Brahma the Creator; *brahma-vidah* > those
who 'know Brahman'; *janah* > persons.

Those persons who 'know Brahman'
(Who conceive of the Absolute as an 'other'
which is an object of knowledge)
Depart from the experience of this world
along a course that passes through [the celestial domains
of the deities associated with] fire (Agni),
Daylight (the sun-god Surya),
The fortnight of the waxing moon,
and the six months when the sun makes its northward journey;
And lastly they visit [the abode of] Brahma
[before cessation of the assumed self in Brahman].

Here, as previously in verse 5.20, a subtle distinction is made between those who 'know Brahman' and those who know themselves to *be* Brahman. For the latter there would be nowhere to 'go' upon dissociation from the body, as discussed in the notes to verse 8.6.

### 25

*dhumo ratris tatha krishnah / shanmasa dakshinayanam*
*tatra chandramasam jyotir / yogi prapya nivartate*

*dhumah* > smoke; *ratrih* > night; *tatha* > in such a manner (refers to the yogi's alternate pathway of passage, as will be confirmed in the following two verses); *krishnah* > the dark lunar fortnight; *shat-masah* > six months; *dakshina-ayanam* > 'in the direction of the right hand' (refers to the southward journey of the sun because when one faces the sun rising in the east, one's right hand is to the south); *tatra* > there; *chandramasam* > in relation to the moon or its deity Chandra; *jyotih* > brightness, luminosity; *yogi* > the yogi; *prapya* > reaching; *nivartate* > one returns (to the experience of this world).

[However,] the yogi moving along the course
passing through [the realms of the deities associated with] smoke, night,
The fortnight of the waning moon,
and the six months when the sun travels southward
Reaches the brightly luminous [domain of the] moon-god Chandra
and thereafter returns to the experience of this world.

### 26

*shukla-krishne gati hyete / jagatah shashvate mate*
*ekaya yatyanavrittim / anyaya-'vartate punah*

*shukla-krishne* > light and darkness; *gati* > paths; *hi* > truly; *ete* > these two; *jagatah* > of the universe; *shashvate* > constant; *mate* > considered to be, regarded as, believed to be; *ekaya* > by one; *yati* > one reaches; *anavrittim* > to non-return; *anyaya* > by the other; *avartate* > one returns; *punah* > again.

**These two paths of light and darkness
are verily regarded as universal constants.
By one course one reaches non-return;
By the other, one again returns.**

### 27

*naite sriti partha janan / yogi muhyati kashchana*
*tasmat sarveshu kaleshu / yoga-yukto bhavarjuna*

*na* > not; *ete* > these two; *sriti* > courses; *partha* > Arjuna, the son of Pritha; *janan* > knowing; *yogi* > the yogi; *muhyati* > one is confused; *kashchana* > in any way whatsoever; *tasmat* > therefore; *sarveshu kaleshu* > at all times; *yoga-yuktah bhava* > be endowed with steady engagement; *arjuna* > O Arjuna.

**The yogis who know about these two courses
are not confused [about their duty] in any way whatsoever.
Therefore, at all times be endowed with steady engagement
[in one of the ways which I have described to you], O Arjuna.**

In this chapter, Krishna slightly modifies His presentation of two spiritual practices which He had discussed with Arjuna in earlier chapters—selfless work and meditation—by adding the detail of remembering Him in conjunction with these practices beginning in verse 5. In verse 7 there is the exhortation to "Remember Me at all times and do your duty," by which "one goes to the supreme divine personification of Spirit" (verse 8); and in verses 12-13 we find: "Closing all the sense-gateways of the body...reposing the vital life-airs within one's forehead...uttering 'Om'...and remembering Me...one goes to the supreme refuge." The results of both of these approaches had already been established to be the same in verses 7.21-22, reminding us of another one of Krishna's earlier statements in verse 5.4 that in regard to the practice of either Sankhya or karma-yoga, "even one of these practiced wholeheartedly yields the fruit of both."

## 28

*vedeshu yajneshu tapahsu chaiva / daneshu yat punya-phalam pradishtam*
*atyeti tat sarvam idam viditva / yogi param sthanam upaiti chadyam*

*vedeshu* > in studying the Vedas; *yajneshu* > in the performance of sacrificial rituals; *tapahsu* > in the undertaking of austerities; *cha* > and; *eva* > indeed; *daneshu* > in the giving of charity; *yad* > whatever; *punya-phalam* > auspicious fruits (results), rewards for virtuous actions; *pradishtam* > allotted, ordained, decreed; *atyeti* > one surpasses; *tat* > that; *sarvam idam viditva* > knowing all of this (refers to all that Krishna imparted throughout the chapter in response to the questions which Arjuna asked in verses 1 and 2); *yogi* > the yogi; *param sthanam* > the supreme state of Being; *upaiti* > one reaches; *cha* > and; *adyam* > primordial, original.

**Whatever has been decreed to be the auspicious result**
**of one's having studied the Vedas,**
**Performed sacrificial rituals,**
**Undertaken austerities,**
**And given charity—**
**That is surpassed by one who knows all of this**
**[which I have imparted to you in response to your questions],**
**And that yogi reaches [the cessation of all illusion in]**
**the supreme primordial state of Being.**

*om tat saditi srimad bhagavad-gita / supanishatsu brahma-vidyayam / yoga-shastre*
*srikrishnarjuna samvade / akshara-brahma-yogo nama 'shtamo 'dhyayah*

From the Ambrosial Song of God—
A conversation between Krishna and Arjuna
which is a Upanishad (confidential sharing)
of wisdom-teachings regarding the Absolute
And a scripture concerning Self-realization—
Thus ends the Eighth Chapter entitled Akshara-brahma-yoga,
Recognizing Divine Unicity By Way of the Syllable Om
Representing the Imperishable Absolute.

# Chapter Nine

---

# Rajavidya-rajaguhyam-yoga
## (Recognizing Divine Unicity
## By Way of the King Among Secret Teachings)

"If you cannot find the truth right where you are, where else do you expect to find it?"

"To study the self is to forget the self. To forget the self is to be enlightened by the ten thousand things."   —Dogen

"If you use your mind to study Reality, you won't understand either your mind or Reality. If you study Reality without using your mind, you'll understand both."

"When we're deluded there's a world to escape. When we're aware, there's nothing to escape."   —Bodhidharma

"Perceiving that subject and object are one comes as suddenly as blinking the eyes, and this leads to a greatly mysterious, wordless realization which awakens one to the truth. ...Searching for the truth by way of intellectual or academic efforts merely places one further away from it. Not until your thoughts stop extending outward in all directions; not until you relinquish all tendencies to seek for something; not until your mind is as unmoving as a stone will you be on the correct path to 'the [gateless] gate.'"

"You do not lose your true nature during times of delusion, nor do you gain it at the time of awakening....It is not dependent on or attached to anything at any time. It is omnipresent, stainless beauty—the self-existing, unborn Absolute...a priceless jewel indeed!"   —Huang Po

### 1
*sri bhagavan uvacha:*
*idam tu te guhyatamam / pravakshyamyanasuyave*
*jnanam vijnana-sahitam / yaj jnatva mokshyase 'shubhat*

*sri bhagavan uvacha* > the glorious one (Krishna) said; *idam* > this; *tu* > but (a continuation from Krishna's last statement at the end of Chapter Eight); *te* > to you (Arjuna); *guhyatamam* > most confidential, most mysterious;

*pravakshyami* > I shall impart, I shall teach; *anasuyave* > to one who harbors no ill will; *jnanam* > knowledge; *vijnana* > realization, discernment; *sahitam* > together with; *yat* > which; *jnatva* > knowing; *mokshyase* > you will be freed; *ashubhat* > from evil, from misfortune.

**The glorious Krishna said:**
**...But to you, Arjuna, who harbors no ill will toward anyone,**
**I shall now impart the most confidential of all knowledge,**
**together with [the means for] its realization.**
**Knowing this, you will be freed from [your fear of creating] evil**
**[by your participation in the battle].**

### 2
*rajavidya raja-guhyam / pavitram idam uttamam*
*pratyaksha-'vagamam dharmyam / susukham kartum avyayam*

*raja-vidya* > the king of teachings; *raja-guhyam* > the king of secrets; *pavitram* > the purifier; *idam* > this (the knowledge mentioned in the previous verse); *uttamam* > highest, best; *pratyaksha* > direct perception, immediate visibility; *avagamam* > comprehension (confirmation); *dharmyam* > righteous; *su-sukham* > very pleasant, easy, comfortable; *kartum* > to utilize, to apply; *avyayam* > everlasting.

**This knowledge,**
**which is the king of all secret teachings and the best of all purifiers,**
**is immediately confirmed by your direct perception.**
**Its application is righteous and very pleasant,**
**and [its benefit] is everlasting.**

### 3
*ashraddadhanah purusha / dharmasyasya parantapa*
*aprapya mam nivartante / mrityu-samsara-vartmani*

*ashraddadhanah* > not having faith; *purushah* > persons; *dharmasya* > of the basis for conscious living and Life-centered values; *asya* > of this (the knowledge and its practical application); *parantapa* > O scourge of foes; *aprapya* > not finding, not reaching; *mam* > Me; *nivartante* > they return; *mrityu* > death; *samsara* > the experiencing of a dreamlike sequence of states; *vartmani* > on the path.

As this knowledge and its practical application is the basis
for conscious living and Life-centered values,
Persons without faith in it do not discover Me (their true nature),
O scourge of foes,
But return onto the path of experiencing a dreamlike sequence of states,
including 'death.'

The path mentioned here is the one described in verse 8.25.

**4**

*maya tatam idam sarvam / jagad avyakta-murtina*
*matsthani sarva-bhutani / na chaham teshvavasthitah*

*maya* > by Me; *tatam* > extended, spread, pervaded; *idam* > this;
*sarvam* > entire; *jagat* > universe; *avyakta-murtina* > in My unmanifest aspect;
*mat-sthani* > situated within Me; *sarva-bhutani* > all living beings; *na* > not;
*cha* > and; *aham* > I; *teshu* > in them; *avasthitah* > abiding.

This entire universe is pervaded by Me (the Absolute)
in My unmanifest aspect.
All living beings are situated within Me,
yet I am not abiding in them.

**5**

*na cha matsthani bhutani / pashya me yogam aishvaram*
*bhutabhrin na cha bhutastho / mamatma bhuta-bhavanah*

*na* > not; *cha* > and; *mat-sthani* > situated within Me; *bhutani* > living beings;
*pashya* > behold; *me* > My; *yogam aishvaram* > mystic potency, supernatural
power; *bhuta-bhrit* > sustaining beings; *na* > not; *cha* > and;
*bhuta-sthah* > abiding within beings; *mamatma* > My sense of self;
*bhuta-bhavanah* > bringing beings into manifestation.

And [at the same time, from another perspective,]
there are not living beings situated within Me.
Behold My mystic potency of sustaining beings without abiding in them—
My sense of self (knowing that *I am*)
is what brings all beings into manifestation.

As previously discussed in relation to verses 3.10 and 7.6, when within
infinite Consciousness there is the subtle movement from being *existing*
*Awareness* to being *aware of Itself existing* ('I am'), this creates the entire

appearance of a universe filled with an abundance of phenomena, including the forms of all living beings. So from one perspective, all of those beings are indeed situated within the one undivided Consciousness as illusory images. Yet an illusion is something that's not actually there, like the water puddles which are seen in a mirage on the highway during hot, sunny days; thus, in that sense, "there are not living beings situated within Me." And in regard to "I am not abiding in them" — again, is the pavement actually abiding in the water of a mirage?

### 6

*yathakasha-sthito nityam / vayuh sarvatrago mahan*
*tatha sarvani bhutani / mat-sthanityupadharaya*

*yatha* > just as; *akasha-sthitah* > situated in the sky; *nityam* > always; *vayuh* > the wind; *sarvatra-gah* > going everywhere; *mahan* > mighty; *tatha* > in this way; *sarvani bhutani* > all living beings; *mat-sthani* > situated in Me; *iti upadharaya* > contemplate this, reflect on this.

**Just as the mighty wind, moving everywhere,**
**is always situated in the sky,**
**So also in that way are all living beings situated in Me.**
**Reflect on this....**

### 7

*sarva-bhutani kaunteya / prakritim yanti mamikam*
*kalpa-kshaye punas tani / kalpadau visrijamyaham*

*sarva-bhutani* > all living beings; *kaunteya* > O son of Kunti; *prakritim* > into Nature; *yanti* > they go to, they enter into; *mamikam* > My own; *kalpa-kshaye* > at the termination of a full day of Brahma; *punah* > again; *tani* > them; *kalpa-adau* > at the beginning of a new day of Brahma; *visrijami aham* > I emanate, I send flowing forth.

**All beings enter into My own Nature**
**at the end of Brahma's day, O son of Kunti,**
**And I again emanate them**
**at the beginning of Brahma's new day.**

Based on what Krishna stated in verse 8.17, a full day of Brahma would amount to two thousand rotations of the combined four ages of the universal time-cycle.

**8**

*prakritim svam avashtabhya / visrijami punah punah*
*bhuta-gramam imam kritsnam / avasham prakriter vashat*

*prakritim* > Nature; *svam* > own; *avashtabhya* > resting upon, supported by;
*visrijami* > I emit, I send flowing forth; *punah punah* > again and again;
*bhuta-gramam* > the multitude of living beings; *imam* > this;
*kritsnam* > entire; *avasham* > not willfully, not having
independent will; *prakriteh* > of Nature; *vashat* > by the power.

**Resting upon My own Nature,**
**I again and again emit the entire multitude of living beings.**
**This is not done willfully,**
**but happens by the sheer force of Nature.**
_____ Or: _____
**Resting upon My own Nature,**
**By Its sheer force**
**I again and again emit the entire multitude of living beings,**
**which are without independent will.**

The first reading of this verse would be in support of verse 5.14's statement
*svabhavas tu pravartate* (all actions proceed by the spontaneity of Nature).
The connotation is that the emission of beings is not done deliberately to
fulfill a specific desire, just as one may awaken from sleep to discover that
perspiration had unintentionally been emitted during the night. The second
reading would essentially reiterate what was presented in verse 8.19,
whereby the emanated ones would be without independent will because they
are merely memory-impressions arising within the singular all-pervasive
Consciousness and have no capacity to formulate independent agendas.

**9**

*na cha mam tani karmani / nibadhnanti dhananjaya*
*udasinavad asinam / asaktam teshu karmasu*

*na* > not; *cha* > and; *mam* > Me; *tani* > these; *karmani* > actions;
*nibadhnanti* > they bind up; *dhananjaya* > O winner of wealth;
*udasina-vat* > impartially, neutrally; *asinam* > sitting;
*asaktam* > unattached; *teshu karmasu* > in these actions.

**And these actions do not bind Me,
O winner of wealth;
For I sit neutrally,
unattached to them.**

### 10

*maya-'dhyakshena prakritih / suyate sacharacharam
hetunanena kaunteya / jagad viparivartate*

*maya* > with Me; *adhyakshena* > as a witness, as an overseer; *prakritih* > Nature;
*suyate* > it generates, it begets; *sa* > both; *chara-acharam* > the moving and the
unmoving; *hetuna anena* > for this reason, because of this; *kaunteya* > O son
of Kunti; *jagat* > the world, the universe; *viparivartate* > it revolves.

**With Me as the witnessing Presence,
Nature generates all things, both moving and unmoving.
It is because of this, O son of Kunti,
that all the worlds revolve.**

### 11

*avajananti mam mudha / manushim tanum ashritam
param bhavam ajananto / mama bhuta-maheshvaram*

*avajananti* > they disrespect, they look upon with contempt; *mam* > Me;
*mudhah* > the confused ones; *manushim tanum* > a human body;
*ashritam* > utilizing, occupying; *param* > supreme;
*bhavam* > existence, nature; *ajanantah* > not knowing;
*mama* > My; *bhuta-maha-ishvaram* > the great Lord of beings.

**Confused persons disrespect Me
when I assume a human form,
Not knowing My supreme nature
as the great Lord of beings.**

From the perspective of the one Life assuming all human as well as other
forms, then disrespect for any form of Life is actually disrespect for the
Totality as well as Its expression as oneself.

### 12

*moghasha mogha-karmano / mogha-jnana vichetasah
rakshasim asurim chaiva / prakritim mohinim shritah*

*mogha-ashah* > those whose hopes are futile or useless; *mogha-karmanah* > those whose activities are futile or useless; *mogha-jnanah* > those whose knowledge is futile or useless; *vichetasah* > bereft of good sense; *rakshasim* > fiendish, malefic, murderous; *asurim* > demonic (suggests the legendary opponents of the celestials who sometimes usurp their kingdom); *cha* > and; *eva* > indeed; *prakritim* > nature, character; *mohinim* > infatuated, unconscious; *shritah* > adopting.

**Futile indeed
are all of the hopes, knowledge, and activities of such persons.
Unconscious and bereft of good sense,
They adopt the [tamasic] nature of murderers
and [the rajasic nature of] plunderers.**

In the classic literary epics of ancient India, the *rakshasas* are generally portrayed as being predominated by the darkening quality of the *tamas-guna* and thus prone to committing wanton acts of violence — mostly taking others' lives indiscriminately, though sometimes with cannibalistic intent. *Asuras*, on the other hand, being predominated by the distorting quality of the *rajas-guna*, are depicted as having a marked preference for seizing power over others, enslaving them, stealing their wealth, and sexually violating them.

**13**
*mahatmanas tu mam partha / daivim prakritim ashritah
bhajantyananya-manaso / jnatva bhutadim avyayam*

*maha-atmanah* > the great expressions of the Spirit-Self, the great-hearted ones; *tu* > but; *mam* > Me; *partha* > O son of Pritha; *daivim prakritim* > a godly nature; *ashritah* > taking refuge in, dwelling or resting within; *bhajanti* > they lovingly worship; *ananya-manasah* > whose minds are without another; *jnatva* > knowing; *bhuta-adim* > the origin of living beings; *avyayam* > imperishable, immutable.

**But the great-hearted ones take shelter
in the godly (sattvic) nature, O son of Pritha,
their minds not considering any other recourse.
They worship Me lovingly,
knowing Me to be the imperishable origin of living beings.**

The *mahatmas*, being predominated by the clarifying quality of the *sattva-guna*, are generally inclined toward actions intended to improve the quality of others' lives in some capacity.

**14**

*satatam kirtayanto mam / yatantash cha dridha-vratah*
*namasyantash cha mam bhaktya / nitya-yukta upasate*

*satatam* > continually; *kirtayantah* > glorifying, reciting, celebrating;
*mam* > Me; *yatantah* > endeavoring; *cha* > and; *dridha-vratah* > those
who observe strict vows; *namasyantah* > worshipping, offering
veneration; *cha* > and; *mam* > Me; *bhaktya* > with loving devotion;
*nitya-yuktah* > perpetually aligned; *upasate* > they adore.

**Ever reciting and celebrating My glories,**
**endeavoring to observe strict vows,**
**and offering devotional worship,**
**They are perpetually aligned with Me by their love.**

This verse refers to those for whom Krishna is an *ishtadeva* (preferred deity)
from among the many divine personifications of Spirit, the Supreme
Person mentioned in verse 8.22. There will be some further discussion of
bhakti-yoga, this type of approach toward Krishna with loving devotional
sentiments, in later portions of the Gita.

**15**

*jnana-yajnena chapyanye / yajanto mam upasate*
*ekatvena prithaktvena / bahudha vishvato-mukham*

*jnana-yajnena* > by the sacrifice of focusing exclusively on the discovery
of one's own innate knowing of absolute truth; *cha* > and; *api* > however;
*anye* > others; *yajantah* > offering; *mam* > Me; *upasate* > they worship;
*ekatvena* > as the One; *prithaktvena* > as the many; *bahudha* > variously
manifested; *vishvatah-mukham* > facing in all directions.

**Others, however,**
**Offering the sacrifice of focusing exclusively on discovering**
**their own innate knowing of absolute truth,**
**Worship Me as the One variously manifested as the many**
**and facing in all directions.**

**16**

*aham kratur aham yajnah / svadhaham aham aushadham*
*mantro 'ham aham evajyam / aham agnir aham hutam*

*aham* > I; *kratuh* > intention, inspiration, ritual ceremony; *aham* > I;
*yajnah* > sacrifice; *svadha* > the offering of a food item in a ritual ceremony
(such as the compressed balls of rice offered to departed ancestors mentioned
in verse 1.42); *aham* > I; *aham* > I; *aushadham* > herbal medicine (refers to soma,
as mentioned in upcoming verse 20); *mantrah* > sacred litany; *aham* > I;
*aham* > I; *eva* > only, alone; *ajyam* > clarified butter (ghee); *aham* > I;
*agnih* > fire; *aham* > I; *hutam* > the pouring of the oblation.

**I (the One) am the ritual ceremony,**
**the inspiration to perform sacrifice,**
**and the food items offered in such rites;**
**I am the herbal medicine soma [ingested at such ceremonies]**
**and the sacred litany [chanted thereat];**
**And it is I alone who am the clarified butter,**
**the pouring of that oblation,**
**and the fire into which the ghee is poured.**

This verse is essentially a rephrased reiteration of verse 4.24 in its delineating
various components of a ceremonial *yajna* for presenting a perspective of
beholding 'the One variously manifested as the many.' The distinction here is
in Krishna's speaking to Arjuna from the standpoint of being that very
Brahman mentioned in the earlier verse.

In regard to the herbal medicine mentioned here, for at least three hundred
years researchers have been formulating theories as to the identity of the
soma plant based on descriptions of it in the ninth section of the Rig Veda.
Many presume that the pressed and strained liquid traditionally associated
for several thousand years with the ritual ceremonies prescribed in the Vedas
was made from the amanita muscaria mushroom. This seems somewhat
unlikely, however, as mushrooms are even still to this day regarded as
a *tamasic* or impure food which is unacceptable for religious offerings in
orthodox Hinduism. Other researchers contend that soma was instead
ephedra sinica, which is even more unlikely, since whether ephedra actually
contains any of the entheogenic properties attributed to soma is debatable
to begin with. Moreover, ephedra's documented history of causing adverse
effects and death is not exactly congruous with soma's reputation as 'the
elixir of immortality.' One of the more plausible candidates proposed for
speculation regarding soma is the healing entheogen ayahuasca, yet so far
to date no conclusive determination has been arrived at, and the mystery
surrounding the legendary sacrament has sportively remained intact.

The *mantras* mentioned here comprise single phrases, stanzas, and entire compositions divided into four categories. Invocations and glorifications drawn from the Rig Veda are chanted by the *hotri* priest who offers all the sacrificial items into the fire. Supplications and benedictions drawn from the Yajur Veda are chanted by the *adhvaryu* priest who makes all the initial preparations for the ceremony. Melodic hymns largely in relation to the soma plant drawn from the Sama Veda are sung by the *udgatri* ('chanter') priest. And mystical formulae and incantations drawn from the Atharva Veda are chanted by the *brahmana* priest who oversees the ceremony and corrects any mistakes made in its performance.

### 17

*pitaham asya jagato / mata dhata pitamahah*
*vedyam pavitram omkara / rik sama yajur eva cha*

*pita* > father; *aham* > I; *asya* > of this; *jagatah* > of the universe;
*mata* > mother; *dhata* > sustainer, supporter; *pitamahah* > grandfather;
*vedyam* > that which is to be known, understood, or recognized;
*pavitram* > the purifier; *omkara* > the sacred syllable Om; *rik* > the Rig Veda;
*sama* > the Sama Veda; *yajuh* > the Yajur Veda; *eva* > certainly; *cha* > and.

**I am the father of this universe (Lord Shiva),**
**The mother (Goddess Adi Shakti),**
**The sustainer (Lord Vishnu),**
**The grandfather (Lord Brahma),**
**And that which is to be recognized**
**[as the unicity underlying all manner of divine expression].**
**I am the purifying syllable Om,**
**and of course the Rig, Sama, and Yajur Vedas as well.**

From a chronological standpoint, the fourth Veda, Atharva, is said to have been the last one composed, and Krishna's omission of it here suggests that it was not yet fully compiled at the time of the Gita's recitation. Another possibility is that it was available, but was not yet widely known throughout the brahmin community or accepted by them as being authoritative enough to be utilized at *yajnas* and religious ceremonies. Some other names for the supreme feminine principle or Divine Mother of all the worlds are Mahadevi, Bhagavati, Bhuvaneshvari, Parameshwari, Jagadamba, and Vishvamata.

### 18

*gatir bharta prabhuh sakshi / nivasah sharanam suhrit*
*prabhavah pralayah sthanam / nidhanam bijam avyayam*

*gatih* > the way; *bharta* > preserver, protector; *prabhuh* > master,
Lord; *sakshi* > witness; *nivasah* > home; *sharanam* > shelter;
*suhrit* > well-wishing friend; *prabhavah* > source,
origin; *pralayah* > dissolution; *sthanam* > foundational support;
*nidhanam* > repository, treasure-house; *bijam* > seed; *avyayam* > imperishable.

**[I am] the way, the protector, the master, the witness,**
**The home, the shelter, the well-wishing friend,**
**The origin, the dissolution, the foundational support,**
**The treasure-house and the imperishable seed [within it].**

'The treasure-house and the imperishable seed' may be interpreted as the
treasure-house of freedom waiting to be realized and the imperishable
seed of the longing for freedom within one's heart. Or perhaps the
treasure-house is pure Sat-Chid-Ananda and the imperishable seed within
It is the spontaneous impulse of Reality to 'taste Its own sweetness' via
personification, as indicated in verses 8.3-4.

**19**
*tapamyaham aham varsham / nigrihnamyutsrijami cha*
*amritam chaiva mrityush cha / sad asach chaham arjuna*

*tapami* > I provide heat; *aham* > I; *aham* > I; *varsham* > rain;
*nigrihnami* > I withhold; *utsrijami* > I send forth; *cha* > and;
*amritam* > immortality; *cha* > and; *eva* > indeed; *mrityuh* > death;
*cha* > and; *sat* > the real; *asat* > the dreamlike;
*cha* > and; *aham* > I; *arjuna* > O Arjuna.

**I provide heat,**
**and I either send forth the rains or withhold them.**
**O Arjuna, I am both immortality and death,**
**The Real and the dreamlike.**

**20**
*traividya mam somapah putapapa / yajnair ishtva svargatim prarthayante*
*te punyam asadya surendra-lokam / ashnanti divyan divi deva-bhogan*

*trai-vidyah* > those who learned the contents of the three Vedas
(minus Atharva, as discussed in the notes to verse 17); *mam* > Me;
*soma-pah* > those who drink the soma juice (discussed in the notes
to verse 16); *puta* > purified; *papah* > of wickedness; *yajnaih* > by the
performance of ritual sacrifices; *ishtva* > having worshipped;

*svah-gatim* > arriving in heaven; *prarthayante* > they have the motive or aspiration; *te* > they; *punyam* > pure, auspicious, meritorious; *asadya* > going to, meeting with, reaching; *sura-indra* > chief of the celestials; *lokam* > the world; *ashnanti* > they enjoy; *divyan divi* > in the divine subtle region; *deva-bhogan* > the pleasures of the celestials.

**Those who become purified of all wickedness**
**by learning the contents of the three Vedas and drinking the soma juice**
**Worship Me by the performance of ritual sacrifices,**
**aspiring for entrance into heaven.**
**They reach the meritorious world of Indra, chief of the celestials,**
**And there in the divine subtle region [of Consciousness]**
**they enjoy the pleasures of the gods.**

**21**
*te tam bhuktva svarga-lokam vishalam / kshine punye martya-lokam vishanti*
*evam trayi-dharmam anuprapanna / gatagatam kama-kama labhante*

*te* > they; *tam* > this; *bhuktva* > having enjoyed; *svarga-lokam* > the heavenly region; *vishalam* > vast, extensive; *kshine* > in becoming exhausted, in wasting away; *punye* > in the merits, in the prosperity (the rewards accrued from the performance of virtuous actions); *martya-lokam* > the world of mortality; *vishanti* > they enter; *evam* > in this way; *trayi-dharmam* > the religious injunctions of the three Vedas; *anuprapannah* > following, abiding by, conforming to; *gata-agatam* > coming and going; *kama-kamah* > desiring sensory pleasures; *labhante* > they obtain.

**Having enjoyed this extensive heavenly region,**
**They reenter the world of mortality**
**when the rewards accrued from their performance of virtuous actions**
**have been exhausted.**
**In this way,**
**Those who conform to the religious injunctions of the Vedas**
**with a desire for [nothing more than] sensory pleasures**
**Simply obtain that which comes and goes.**

As previously discussed in relation to verses 8.23-26, this dreamlike experience occurs within undivided omnipresent Awareness when there is identification with one particular character appearing within the infinitude of creative expression.

**22**
*ananyash chintayanto mam / ye janah paryupasate*
*tesham nitya-'bhiyuktanam / yoga-kshemam vahamyaham*

*ananyah* > without distraction, having no other; *chintayantah* > considering, meditating upon, focusing attention upon; *mam* > Me; *ye* > who; *janah* > persons; *paryupasate* > they worship, they venerate, they adore; *tesham* > to them; *nitya* > continuously; *abhiyuktanam* > of those who are adhering, of those who are aligned; *yoga-kshemam* > in regard to the acquiring and protecting of life's necessities, in regard to the realization of unicity (yoga) and final emancipation (kshema); *vahami aham* > I Myself bring.

**[But] to those persons who ever adhere to Me
by their adoration,
Considering that they have no other [to rely upon],
I Myself provide and protect their life's necessities.**
_____ Or: _____
**[But] to those persons whose attention is focused upon Me
without distraction,
Worshipping Me by their alignment [with truth],
I Myself bring them to Self-realization and liberation.**

In the first reading the word *kshema* conveys the sense of giving safety and security; in the second reading it represents cessation of the feeling of needing safety and security.

### 23
*ye 'pyanya-devata-bhakta / yajante shraddhayanvitah
te 'pi mam eva kaunteya / yajantyavidhi-purvakam*

*ye* > who; *api* > even; *anya* > others; *devata* > the celestials; *bhaktah* > devoted to; *yajante* > they worship; *shraddhaya anvitah* > endowed with faith, attended by faith; *te* > they; *api* > also; *mam* > Me; *eva* > only; *kaunteya* > O son of Kunti; *yajanti* > they worship; *avidhi-purvakam* > not in accordance with anciently established precepts (which in verse 8.26 are 'regarded as universal constants' for experiencing the path of light and non-return after dissociation from the body as described in verse 8.24).

**Even those who are devoted to others — to the celestials —
and worship them endowed with great faith —
They, too, are only worshipping Me alone, O son of Kunti;
Though not in accordance with anciently established precepts
[regarding non-return to the experience of being human].**

**24**

*aham hi sarva-yajnanam / bhokta cha prabhur eva cha*
*na tu mam abhijananti / tattvenatash chyavanti te*

*aham* > I; *hi* > truly; *sarva-yajnanam* > of all sacrifices; *bhokta* > the experiencer, the enjoyer; *cha* > and; *prabhuh* > lord; *eva* > only; *cha* > and; *na* > not; *tu* > but; *mam* > Me; *abhijananti* > they recognize, they perceive; *tattvena* > in truth; *atah* > therefore; *chyavanti te* > they descend (referring to the path of darkness and return described in verse 8.25).

**I am truly the only enjoyer and Lord of all sacrifices,**
**but they do not recognize this truth about Me,**
**And therefore they descend**
**[back into the experiencing of this world**
**after 'visiting' the heavenly domain].**

This verse is the opposite approach of the same idea previously expressed in verse 5.29 ("Knowing Me [omnipresent Spirit] to be the enjoyer of all sacrifices and great Lord...one attains everlasting peace"). Again, Self-realization does not remove a separation between two things; it removes the idea or *sense* of separation within that One which never becomes divided up into segments at any time (*achchedyo 'yam*, 'this Presence is indivisible,' verse 2.24).

**25**

*yanti deva-vrata devan / pitrin yanti pitri-vratah*
*bhutani yanti bhutejya / yanti mad-yajino 'pi mam*

*yanti* > they go, they reach; *deva-vratah* > those who are devoted to the celestials, those who observe religious vows (vratas) in relation to the celestials; *devan* > to the celestials; *pitrin* > to the departed ancestors; *yanti* > they go, they reach; *pitri-vratah* > those who are devoted to or observe religious vows in relation to their departed ancestors; *bhutani* > to the elementals; *yanti* > they go, they reach; *bhuta-ijyah* > those who revere, worship, or make offerings to the elementals; *yanti* > they go, they reach; *mat-yajinah* > those who make offerings to Me, those whose sacrifices are made for Me; *api* > surely; *mam* > to Me.

**Those who are devoted to the celestials go to the celestials;**
**Those who observe religious vows in relation to their departed ancestors**
**go to their ancestors;**
**Those who worship the elementals reach the elementals;**
**And those whose offerings and sacrifices are made for Me**
**surely reach Me.**

Elementals are here distinguished from celestials in that they are subtle expressions of Being in the earthly rather than the heavenly region of infinite Consciousness. And there are two readings possible in regard to *yanti mad-yajino 'pi mam*. One is of course that those whose offerings and sacrifices are made exclusively for the sake of knowing their true nature surely reach recognition of unitary wholeness. Another reading would be that just as those who are devoted to a particular celestial, elemental, or ancestor reach their respective preferred deity, so also would a devotee of Krishna reach Him in His celebrated abode. One statement by Krishna to Arjuna in the latter portion of the Mahabharata, in Shanti Parva, section 12.343, is: "O son of Kunti, by assuming diverse forms, I rove at will throughout the Earth, the region of Brahma, and that other high and eternal region of felicity called Goloka ('the world of many cows')." In the epic's Anusasana Parva, section 13.83, we also find: "In a region higher than the three worlds known to all by the name of Goloka...neither death, nor decrepitude, nor fire can overcome its denizens. No ill fortune exists there. Many delightful forests and beautiful features may be seen there." This is yet another manifestation composed entirely of all-pervasive Consciousness.

### 26

*pattram pushpam phalam toyam / yo me bhaktya prayachchati*
*tad aham bhaktyupahritam / ashnami prayatatmanah*

*pattram* > a leaf; *puspam* > a flower; *phalam* > a fruit; *toyam* > water;
*yah* > who; *me* > to Me; *bhaktya* > with devotion; *prayachchati* > one offers,
one presents; *tat* > that; *aham* > I; *bhakti-upahritam* > brought near
out of devotion, offering of love; *ashnami* > I partake of, I enjoy;
*prayata-atmanah* > from the pure-minded one, from the sincere-hearted one.

**If one with devotion offers Me**
**a leaf, a flower, a fruit, or water,**
**I accept such an offering of love**
**from that sincere-hearted one.**

### 27

*yat karoshi yad ashnasi / yaj juhoshi dadasi yat*
*yat tapasyasi kaunteya / tat kurushva mad-arpanam*

*yat* > what; *karoshi* > you do; *yat* > what; *ashnasi* > you eat; *yat* > what;
*juhoshi* > you offer in sacrifice; *dadasi* > you give to others; *yat* > what;
*yat* > what; *tapasyasi* > the austerities which you undergo; *kaunteya* > O son
of Kunti; *tat* > that; *kurushva* > do; *mat* > to Me; *arpanam* > as an offering.

> O Kaunteya, whatever you do —
> Whether it be eating,
> Performing some type of sacrifice,
> Giving of charity,
> Or undergoing some kind of austerity —
> Do all of these as an offering to Me.

This verse brilliantly demonstrates an approach in Krishna's instruction to Arjuna which is virtually the opposite of his approach earlier in the Gita, yet nonetheless arrives at exactly the same message. Back in Chapter Three, Krishna informed Arjuna that to believe oneself to be the doer of actions is confusion (verse 27), and that actions simply happen due to the components of Nature stirring each other as both the senses and the sense-objects (verse 28). Thus, in verse 3.30 he was essentially saying: "Look, you're not the doer, so just entrust all of your actions to Me (omnipresent Spirit) and 'let go' in that way." Whereas here in the present verse, it appears that upon seeing that Arjuna is as yet unable to release the ideas of independent selfhood and personal doership, Krishna is therefore saying: "Alright, then, whatever you *do*, do as an offering to Me and 'let go' in *that* way."

### 28

*shubhashubha-phalair evam / mokshyase karma-bandhanaih*
*sannyasa-yoga-yuktatma / vimukto mam upaishyasi*

*shubha-ashubha* > auspicious and inauspicious, agreeable and disagreeable, fortunate and unfortunate; *phalaih* > from the fruits (results); *evam* > thus; *mokshyase* > you shall be freed; *karma-bandhanaih* > from the binding effects of actions; *sannyasa* > renunciation; *yoga* > manner, application; *yuktatma* > wholly intent upon; *vimuktah* > liberated; *mam upaishyasi* > you shall come to Me.

> Wholly intent upon this manner of renunciation,
> You will thus be freed from the binding effects of actions
> as well as from the agreeable and disagreeable results
> [which actions produce].
> You shall be liberated and come to Me
> [upon dissociation from the body/mind vehicle].

### 29

*samo 'ham sarva-bhuteshu / na me dveshyo 'sti na priyah*
*ye bhajanti tu mam bhaktya / mayi te teshu chapyaham*

*samah* > equal, impartial; *aham* > I; *sarva-bhuteshu* > to all living beings; *na* > not; *me* > by Me; *dveshyah* > hated, disfavored; *asti* > there is; *na* > nor; *priyah* > dear, favored; *ye* > who; *bhajanti* > they revere, they worship; *tu* > but; *mam* > Me; *bhaktya* > with loving devotion; *mayi* > in Me; *te* > they; *teshu* > in them; *cha* > and; *api* > also; *aham* > I.

**I am equal and impartial toward all living beings;**
**There is no one either hated or especially favored by Me.**
**But those who worship Me with loving devotion**
**are in [alignment with] Me,**
**And I am also [clearly reflected] in them.**

As the one undivided Spirit expresses Itself as all forms of Life, It does not offer greater access to Itself in certain forms and restrict access to Itself in other forms. At the same time, it is also only natural that truth is more closely aligned with and more clearly reflected in those forms wherein there is an intense interest in embodying truth.

### 30
*api chet suduracharo / bhajate mam ananya-bhak*
*sadhur eva sa mantavyah / samyag vyavasito hi sah*

*api* > even; *cet* > if; *suduracharah* > performer of very wicked deeds; *bhajate* > one reveres, one worships; *mam* > Me; *ananya-bhak* > devoted to nothing else; *sadhuh* > saintly, virtuous; *eva* > indeed; *sah* > that one; *mantavyah* > to be regarded; to be considered; *samyanch* > wholly, one-pointedly, correctly; *vyavasitah* > resolved; *hi* > truly; *sah* > that one.

**Even one who had [previously] performed very wicked deeds**
**is to be regarded as saintly**
**If he or she truly becomes wholeheartedly resolved**
**in regard to worshipping Me with unalloyed devotion.**

### 31
*kshipram bhavati dharmatma / shashvach-chantim nigachchati*
*kaunteya pratijanihi / na me bhaktah pranashyati*

*kshipram* > quickly; *bhavati* > one becomes; *dharmatma* > one who embodies Life-centered values; *shashvat* > everlasting; *shantim* > peace; *nigachchati* > one settles into, one is brought into; *kaunteya* > O son of Kunti; *pratijanihi* > proclaim it; *na* > not; *me* > of Me; *bhaktah* > worshipper, devotee; *pranashyati* > one is lost, one is ruined.

That one quickly becomes a veritable embodiment of Life-centered values
and settles into everlasting peace.
O son of Kunti, let it be known
that one who is devoted to Me is never lost.

### 32

*mam hi partha vyapashritya / ye 'pi syuh papa-yonayah*
*striyo vaishyas tatha shudras / te 'pi yanti param gatim*

*mam* > Me; *hi* > surely; *partha* > O son of Pritha; *vyapashritya* >
taking refuge in; *ye* > who; *api* > even; *syuh* > they happen to be;
*papa-yonayah* > those born in a rough-hewn or a wicked family;
*striyah* > women; *vaishyah* > merchants and farmers; *tatha* > thus;
*shudrah* > craftspeople, skilled laborers, and life-assistants; *te* > they;
*api* > also; *yanti* > they proceed; *param gatim* > to the highest
course (of non-return described in verse 8.24).

O son of Pritha, all those who take refuge in Me,
whether man or woman —
Be they merchants, farmers, laborers, or life-assistants —
Even if they happen to be born in a rough-hewn or a wicked family —
All of them also surely proceed to the highest course
[of non-return to the illusion of separation].

### 33

*kim punar brahmanah punya / bhakta rajarshayas tatha*
*anityam asukham lokam / imam prapya bhajasva mam*

*kim punah* > then how much more so, what then to speak of;
*brahmanah* > teachers and priests; *punyah* > pure-hearted, of virtuous
character; *bhaktah* > devout; *raja-rishayah* > sages and seer-poets among
the royal order; *tatha* > also; *anityam* > ephemeral, unstable;
*asukham* > unhappy; *lokam* > world; *imam* > this; *prapya* > obtaining,
finding, arriving at; *bhajasva* > worship, serve; *mam* > to Me.

What, then, to speak of the teachers and priests of virtuous character
and the devout sages and seer-poets among the royal order.
Having obtained [a taste of] this ephemeral world
fraught with unhappiness and instability,
Dedicate yourself to Me.

**34**

*manmana bhava madbhakto / madyaji mam namaskuru*
*mam evaishyasi yuktvaivam / atmanam mat-parayanah*

*mat-manah* > with attention focused upon Me, with a mind clearly
reflecting Me (Sat-Chid-Ananda); *bhava mat-bhaktah* > be wholeheartedly
devoted to Me; *mat-yaji* > making sacrifices for Me; *mam* > to Me;
*namaskuru* > bow in obeisance, offer reverential salutation;
*mam* > to Me; *eva* > surely; *eshyasi* > you will come;
*yuktva* > drawn by, attuned to; *evam* > thus;
*atmanam* > yourself, the true Self, the Spirit-Self;
*mat-parayanah* > accepting Me as the supreme refuge.

**With your attention focused upon Me**
**(the purely contented presence of Awareness),**
**Offer Me your wholehearted devotion**
**along with your obeisances and sacrifices.**
**Thus you will surely come to Me,**
**Being drawn by your acceptance of Me, your own true nature,**
**as your supreme refuge.**

As discussed hereinbefore in the notes to verse 25, *madyaji* ('making sacrifices
for Me') may be taken to mean either Arjuna's making sacrifices for the
sake of realizing the truth of unicity, or his doing so in connection with
recognizing Krishna to be his preferred personification of the One. Similarly,
both here as well as previously in verses 8.7 and 9.28, the phrase 'you will
come to Me' could be taken to mean "you will come to recognize your true
nature while still with the physical body" as easily as "you will come to my
personal abode upon dissociation from the physical body." Either way,
however, the general tenor of Krishna's advice beginning from verse 8.7 up
to this midpoint in the Gita indeed seems to be for Arjuna to investigate the
possibility that his most naturally available resource for spiritual awakening
may be a more heart-centered manner of approach.

At the same time, in regard to spiritual approaches in the Gita which are,
energetically speaking, more mind-, intellect-, or physical body-centered,
*bhakti* or devotion is presented as integral to them as well, as evidenced by
verses such as 3.3, 5.17, 6.14, 7.17, 8.10, and 13.10. So in Arjuna's preparation
for attending to his immediate situation at Kurukshetra, the most pertinent
internal inquiry he could make at this point doesn't really appear to be
"Should I be devoted *instead of* [fill in the blank]," but rather "What am I
actually devoted *to*?" Moreover, within the purest form of karma-yoga

there is a willingness to act without the expectation of obtaining any personal rewards either on Earth or in heaven. Similarly, within the purest form of bhakti-yoga there is a willingness to love without even the expectation of attaining Self-realization or liberation as some kind of reward.

In the words of Adyashanti: "It would be a mistake to equate oneness and equalness and seeing the same everywhere — seeing God in all things — with a lack of diversity or a lack of uniqueness. It's just the opposite. The perception of oneness releases Existence to truly be what It can be. If this doesn't make sense to you, don't worry; it doesn't matter. At some point you'll end up living it whether it makes sense or not. It's the destiny of all beings at some point or another. You can't avoid yourself forever."

*om tat saditi srimad bhagavad-gita / supanishatsu brahma-vidyayam / yoga-shastre srikrishnarjuna samvade / rajavidya-rajaguhya-yogo nama navamo 'dhyayah*

From the Ambrosial Song of God —
A conversation between Krishna and Arjuna
which is a Upanishad (confidential sharing)
of wisdom-teachings regarding the Absolute
And a scripture concerning Self-realization —
Thus ends the Ninth Chapter entitled Rajavidya-rajaguhya-yoga,
Recognizing Divine Unicity By Way of the King Among Secret Teachings.

# Chapter Ten

# Vibhuti-yoga
### (Recognizing Divine Unicity By Way of
### Its Manifest Expressions)

"....It is absolutely necessary for everyone to believe in nothing. But I do not mean voidness. There is something, but that something is something which is always prepared for taking some particular form, and it has some rules, or theory, or truth in its activity. This is called Buddha nature, or Buddha himself."

"Oneness is valuable, but variety is also wonderful. Ignoring variety, people emphasize the one absolute existence, but this is a one-sided understanding. In this understanding, there is a gap between variety and oneness. But oneness and variety are the same thing, so oneness should be appreciated in each existence. That is why we emphasize everyday life rather than some particular state of mind. We should find the reality in each moment, and in each phenomenon."   —Shunryu Suzuki Roshi

"God is without form, without quality, as well as with form and quality. Watch and see with what endless variety of beautiful forms He plays the play of His *maya* with Himself alone. The *lila* [playful sport] of the all-pervading One goes on and on in this way in infinite diversity. He is without beginning and without end. He is the whole and also the part. The whole and part together make up real Perfection."   —Sri Anandamayi Ma

"To live of love, it is to know no fear; no memory of past faults can I recall;
No imprint of my sins remaineth here; the fire of Love divine effaces all.
…To live of love it is to sail afar, and bring both peace and joy where'er I be.
0 Pilot blest! love is my guiding star; in every soul I meet, Thyself I see."
                                                    —St. Therese of Lisieux

### 1
*sri bhagavan uvacha:*
*bhuya eva mahabaho / shrinu me paramam vachah*
*yat te 'ham priyamanaya / vakshyami hita-kamyaya*

*sri bhagavan uvacha* > the illustrious one (Krishna) said; *bhuyah* > once again; *eva* > indeed; *maha-baho* > O mighty-armed one (Arjuna); *shrinu* > do hear; *me* > from Me; *paramam* > supreme; *vachah* > words of advice; *yat* > which;

*te* > to you; *aham* > I; *priyamanaya* > to one who is held dear;
*vakshyami* > I shall speak; *hita-kamyaya* > with a wish for your well-being.

**The illustrious one, Krishna, said:**
**Once again, O mighty-armed Arjuna,**
**Hear these supreme words of counsel from Me,**
**Which I shall speak to you with a wish for your well-being**
**because you are very dear to Me.**

**2**
*ne me viduh sura-ganah / prabhavam na maharshayah*
*aham adir hi devanam / maharshinam cha sarvashah*

*na* > not; *me* > of Me; *viduh* > they know; *sura-ganah* > the multitudes of
celestials; *prabhavam* > origin; *na* > nor; *maha-rishayah* > the great sages;
*aham* > I; *adih* > beginning; *hi* > truly; *devanam* > of the celestials;
*maha-rishinam* > of the great sages; *cha* > and; *sarvashah* > in every respect.

**Neither the multitudes of celestials**
**nor the great sages know My origin,**
**For in truth I am the originator of the celestials and sages**
**in every respect.**

**3**
*yo mam ajam anadim cha / vetti loka-maheshvaram*
*asammudhah sa martyeshu / sarva-papaih pramuchyate*

*yah* > who; *mam* > Me; *ajam* > unborn; *anadim* > without beginning; *cha* > and;
*vetti* > one knows; *loka* > of the worlds; *maha-ishvaram* > the great Lord;
*asammudhah* > unconfused; *sah* > that one; *martyeshu* > among mortal beings;
*sarva-papaih* > from all sins; *pramuchyate* > that one is freed.

**One who knows Me (pure Spirit)**
**As unborn, beginningless,**
**the great Lord of all the worlds —**
**That one is unconfused among mortal beings,**
**and is freed from all [concerns regarding] sins.**

When, with a particular body, the One expressing as the All completely
relaxes out of all imagined doing and into unalloyed *being*, the space for
self-revelation is discovered to be immediately available. Upon recognizing
that one is timeless Awareness prior to all learned ideas about sin and virtue,

such words quickly lose their ability to send one spinning into a trance of misidentification in regard to the body and arising thoughts.

### 4-5

*buddhir jnanam asammohah / kshama satyam damah shamah*
*sukham duhkham bhavo 'bhavo / bhayam chabhayam eva cha*

*ahimsa samata tooshtis / tapo danam yasho 'yashah*
*bhavanti bhava bhutanam / matta eva prithag-vidhah*

*buddhih* > intelligence, insight; *jnanam* > wisdom; *asammohah* > freedom from confusion; *kshama* > patience, forbearance; *satyam* > truthfulness, sincerity; *damah* > self-discipline; *shamah* > serenity, equanimity; *sukham* > ease, comfort, happiness; *duhkham* > difficulty, distress, sorrow; *bhavah* > coming into being; *abhavah* > ceasing to be; *bhayam* > fearfulness; *cha* > and; *abhayam* > fearlessness; *eva* > indeed; *cha* > and;

*ahimsa* > nonviolence; *samata* > equability, impartiality; *tooshtih* > satisfaction; *tapah* > austereness, conservativism; *danam* > charitableness, liberality; *yashah* > fame, worthiness; *ayashah* > disgrace, unworthiness; *bhavanti* > they arise; *bhavah* > dispositions, temperaments, ways or conditions of being; *bhutanam* > of living beings; *mattah* > from Me; *eva* > alone; *prithak-vidhah* > of many varieties.

**Insightfulness, wisdom, freedom from confusion;**
**Forbearance, sincerity, self-discipline, equanimity,**
**happiness and distress—**
**Whatever comes into being and ceases to be,**
**Indeed including fear and fearlessness,**
**Nonviolence, impartiality, satisfaction,**
**Conservativism and liberality, worthiness and unworthiness—**
**All the multifarious conditions and dispositions of living beings**
**arise from Me alone (the unitary Absolute).**

The characteristics listed in these two verses appear to be directly representative of specific feelings, attitudes, and issues within Arjuna as he faces the impending conflict with his family members and other relations on the battlefield of Kurukshetra.

### 6

*maharshayah sapta purve / chatvaro manavas tatha*
*mad-bhava manasa jata / yesham loka imah prajah*

*maha-rishayah* > the great sages; *sapta* > seven; *purve* > preceding them,
earlier than them; *chatvarah* > the four; *manavah* > the Manus;
*tatha* > also; *mat-bhavah* > My essence, My perspective, My temperament;
*manasah* > sprung from the mind, conceived in the mind;
*jatah* > born; *yesham* > of whom; *loka* > the world; *imah* > these;
*prajah* > created beings, descendents, children.

**The seven great sages,**
**The four who preceded them, and the Manus**
**Were all conceived from My various perspectives and temperaments**
**present within [universal] Mind,**
**And from them were born all the created beings of the world.**

Practically no two ancient texts present the exact same list of names for
the seven great sages mentioned here, but one source, the *Brihad-aranyaka
Upanishad*, in verse 2.2.4 mentions Atri, Vasishtha, Kashyapa, Gautama,
Bharadvaja, Vishvamitra, and Jamadagni. Atri, 'the devourer,' is revered
as the father of the world's earliest known teacher of pure nondualism,
Dattatreya ('the gift of Atri'). Datta is said to be the first teacher in the
Navnath ('nine masters') spiritual lineage which descended through
Gorakhnath ('protector of the cows'). Kashyapa, 'one with black teeth,' is
celebrated as the father of all the celestials, titans, and Vamanadeva, the
'godlike dwarf' incarnation of Vishnu. Vasishtha, 'most wealthy,' is the
spiritual preceptor of Lord Ramachandra. His teachings to Rama are
presented in the epic companion volume to the Ramayana known as the
*Yoga Vasishtha*. Gautama, "the descendant of Gotama ('the largest ox')," is
the author of the *Gautama-dharma-sutra* as well as a number of hymns in
the Rig and Sama Vedas. Bharadvaja, 'one who possesses great strength,'
is the ancestor of Dronacharya. Most of the kings and princes assembled
on both sides at Kurukshetra received their military training from Drona.
Vishvamitra, 'the friend of all,' is another teacher of Sri Rama, and is said to
be the author of the sacred Gayatri mantra. Jamadagni, 'one who consumes
fire,' is the father of Parashurama, the incarnation of Vishnu who rid the
world of all the corrupt and tyrannical members of the royal *kshatriya* order
of his time.

'The four who preceded them' may be referring to four other sages
mentioned in the original Vedas — Agastya, Bhrigu, Kutsa, and Angiras —
or it may mean the four Kumaras, who were spoken of in ancient narrations
which were later compiled into what became known as the Puranas ('events
of the past'). Agastya, "the descendant of Agasti ('thrower of the mountain')),"
is the author of the *Agastya Samhita* and the *Aditya-hridayam*, the most famous

hymn to the sun-god Surya. Bhrigu, 'continual traveler,' is the father of Vedic astrology and of the titans' guru Shukracharya. Kutsa, 'thunderbolt,' is the author of most of the hymns of the Rig Veda. Angiras, 'vocal sound,' is the author of most of the Atharva Veda, and is the father of the celestials' guru Brihaspati. Lists of the seven great sages from other texts mention the names Pulastya, Pulaha, Kratu, and Marichi in conjunction with some of these preceding four and some of the aforementioned seven.

The Four Kumaras—Sanaka ('ancient'), Sanandana ('joyful'), Sanatana ('everlasting'), and Sanatkumara ('ever youthful')—are sages often depicted as resembling small children. Their teachings are found in Book Four of both the Bhagavata and Shiva Puranas, as well as in Chapter Seven of the *Chandogya Upanishad*. From them came the Hamsa spiritual lineage descended through Nimbarka. The Manus such as Vaivasvata (mentioned in Gita verse 4.1) are fourteen legendary kings of the Earth beginning with Svayambhuva described in Chapter Seventeen of the Linga Purana.

### 7

*etam vibhutim yogam cha / mama yo vetti tattvatah*
*so 'vikampena yogena / yujyate natra samshayah*

*etam* > this; *vibhutim* > manifest grandeur, manifest expression;
*yogam* > mystic power; *cha* > and; *mama* > of Mine; *yah* > who;
*vetti* > one knows; *tattvatah* > in truth; *sah* > that one;
*avikampena yogena* > in the unwavering realization
of unicity; *yujyate* > one becomes established; *na* > not;
*atra* > in regard to this; *samshayah* > doubt, uncertainty.

**One who knows the truth in regard to this manifest expression**
**and mystic power of Mine**
**Becomes established in the unwavering realization of unicity.**
**There is no doubt about this.**

### 8

*aham sarvasya prabhavo / mattah sarvam pravartate*
*iti matva bhajante mam / budha bhava-samanvitah*

*aham* > I; *sarvasya* > of all; *prabhavah* > source, origin;
*mattah* > from Me; *sarvam* > everything; *pravartate* > it proceeds,
it issues forth; *iti* > thus; *matva* > considering, reflecting upon;
*bhajante* > they worship, they honor; *mam* > Me; *budhah* > the wise
ones; *bhava* > affection; *samanvitah* > full of, accompanied by.

**I am the source of all that is;**
**Everything emanates from Me.**
**Reflecting upon this,**
**The wise worship Me with [simple, natural] affection.**

The revered Swami B.R. Sridhar Maharaj has stated that the words
*bhava-samanvitah* in this verse indicate what is known as *raganuga-bhakti*,
devotion impelled by spontaneous heartfelt affection, as distinguished
from *vaidhi-bhakti*, devotion practiced according to doctrinal injunctions.
*Vaidhi-bhakti* is generally performed in a calculated way with considerations
of personal gain and loss, or out of a sense of obligation or fear, whereas
in the natural outflowing of *raganuga-bhakti*, one's own self-interests are
altogether set aside in deference to serving the interests of the Whole. Among
all such *raganuga* devotees, Krishna's companions the *gopis* of Vrindaban
(milkmaids of 'the forest where the holy basil grows') have been praised
throughout the Puranas as being the most 'self-forgetful' of servitors, with Sri
Radha described as exemplifying this quality to the utmost degree. Followers
of the sixteenth-century spiritual teachers Sri Chaitanya and Rupa Goswami
thus consider their highest ideal to be *radha-dasyam*, serving in the same spirit
as the dedicated servitors of Sri Radha and Krishna, without even the sense
of a self which is being self-sacrificing. There are traditionally said to be five
principal types of devotional sentiments, one of which will predominate in
any serving relationship with one's *ishtadeva* or preferred personification of
the Absolute. These five are *shanta* (passive affection), *dasya* ('unembellished'
servitorship), *sakhya* (intimate friendship), *vatsalya* (parental affection), and
*madhurya* (romantic affection).

**9**

*mach-chitta madgata-prana / bodhayantah parasparam*
*kathayantash cha mam nityam / tooshyanti cha ramanti cha*

*mat-chittah* > those whose thoughts are of Me, who contemplate
upon Me, whose attention is directed to Me, who hold Me in their hearts;
*mat-gata-pranah* > those whose lives have 'gone to Me' (been given to Me);
*bodhayantah* > enlightening, awakening; *parasparam* > each other;
*kathayantah* > speaking about, conversing about, discussing; *cha* > and;
*mam* > Me; *nityam* > continuously; *tooshyanti* > they are satisfied
or comforted; *cha* > and; *ramanti* > they are delighted; *cha* > and.

**Those who have given their very lives to Me**
**and hold Me in their hearts**
**Are delighted and fulfilled by inspiring one another**
**and always conversing about Me.**

This verse depicts those who have a genuine affinity for *satsang*, gathering together to focus entirely on timeless truth. For some, *madgata-prana* could be taken to mean those within whom the entire story of 'my life' has been relaxed into the undivided wholeness of Life, or the deconstruction of a self that had been built upon the assumption of separation. For others, the very same phrase could refer to those whose lives are wholly dedicated to serving what they deeply feel has some connection with the personification of Krishna and His associates based on faith in the words of their spiritual preceptors.

### 10

*tesham satata-yuktanam / bhajatam priti-purvakam*
*dadami buddhi-yogam tam / yena mam upayanti te*

*tesham* > to them; *satata-yuktanam* > of those who are constantly engaged; *bhajatam* > of those who honor, worship, or serve; *priti-purvakam* > accompanied by love; *dadami* > I give; *buddhi-yogam* > suitability (openness) for the application of universal intuitive Intelligence; *tam* > this; *yena* > by means of which; *mam* > to Me; *upayanti te* > they come.

**To those who are constantly engaged in serving Me with love,**
**I bestow the openness**
**to the flow of universal intuitive Intelligence**
**by means of which they come to Me.**

The connotation of *buddhi-yoga* here is closer to the way the phrase *buddhi-yukta* is used in Chapter Two, indicating a natural alignment owing to complete clarity or 'emptiness.'

### 11

*tesham evanukampartham / aham ajnanajam tamah*
*nashayamyatma-bhavastho / jnana-dipena bhasvata*

*tesham* > for them; *eva* > exactly so, specifically; *anukampa* > sympathy or compassion regarding the trembling (fears); *artham* > out of concern; *aham* > I; *ajnana-jam* > born of not noticing, born of ignoring or overlooking; *tamah* > darkness; *nashayami* > I dispel; *atma-bhava-sthah* > abiding as their own true nature; *jnana-dipena* > with the lantern of direct knowing; *bhasvata* > glowing.

**Expressly out of compassionate concern about their fears,**
**I, abiding as their own true nature,**
**Dispel the darkness born of not noticing [My presence]**
**with the shining lantern of direct knowing.**

Honest introspection may reveal that some type of fear is the primary motivating factor behind most of one's thoughts, words, and actions in moving through the experiencing of the world, from basic survival right up to and including fears in regard to what may occur at the time of Self-realization. Experience has shown, however, that by welcoming fear rather than recoiling from it—and relaxing into total acceptance of it rather than trying to avoid, resist, deny, or get rid of it—the fear tends to subside by itself in due course. This total acceptance is synonymous with the surrender that Krishna ultimately requests of Arjuna at the conclusion of the Gita for moving through the different fears which Arjuna experienced during his dialogue with Krishna at Kurukshetra. Moreover, the frequency of anyone's fear arising, its intensity, and its duration are all substantially minimized when there are no judgments or stories *about* the sensation, such as: "This is very bad," "This shouldn't be happening," "I did something terribly wrong to cause this," "I deserve (or don't deserve) this," etcetera. Such ideas are simply not true and not relevant, just as they wouldn't be in relation to one's walking along the road and suddenly experiencing the sensation of wetness when rainfall occurs.

### 12
*arjuna uvacha:*
*param brahma param dhama / pavitram paramam bhavan*
*purusham shashvatam divyam / adidevam ajam vibhum*

*arjunah uvacha* > Arjuna said; *param* > supreme; *brahma* > Brahman; *param* > supreme; *dhama* > abode; *pavitram* > purifier; *paramam* > supreme; *bhavan* > Your Lordship; *purusham* > person; *shashvatam* > eternal; *divyam* > divine; *adi-devam* > the primal God; *ajam* > unborn; *vibhum* > omnipresent.

**Arjuna said:**
**Your Lordship is the Supreme Brahman,**
**the supreme abode and purifier;**
**The divine, eternal Supreme Person—**
**The unborn, omnipresent, primal God.**

### 13
*ahus tvam rishayah sarve / devarshir naradas tatha*
*asito devalo vyasah / svayam chaiva bravishi me*

*ahuh* > they say; *tvam* > You; *rishayah* > the sages; *sarve* > all; *deva-risih* > the sage among the celestials; *naradah* > Narada; *tatha* > as also; *asitah* > Asita; *devalah* > Devala; *vyasah* > Vyasa; *svayam* > Yourself; *cha* > and; *eva* > indeed, in the same manner; *bravishi* > You are saying; *me* > to me.

Narada, the sage among the celestials —
As also Vyasa, Asita, and Devala —
All the sages declare You to be so,
And indeed, now You Yourself are declaring the same to me.

Narada ('gifted to humankind') is another sage who figures prominently
in many narrations throughout the Puranas. He is the author of the
*Narada-Bhakti-Sutras* as well as the *Pancharatra*, a manual which most
priests in Hindu temples still use for performing ceremonial worship
each day at specific times from very early in the morning until late into the
evening. Vyasa, 'the compiler,' is perhaps the most revered of all the sages
in Indian history, as he is said to have compiled the four Vedas and authored
the Mahabharata and other works. He is the father of both the Pandavas'
father King Pandu and the Kauravas' father King Dhritarashtra, and in
Gita verse 18.75 he is mentioned as the spiritual teacher of the blind king's
minister Sanjaya. Asita ('dark-colored') and his son Devala ('attendant of
the celestials') were also disciples of Vyasa, and both of them subsequently
became spiritual teachers of King Janaka, whom Krishna mentions in verse
3.20. According to the *Brahma-vaivarta Purana*, Devala was also known as
Ashtavakra ('bent or twisted in eight places'), and his teachings to King
Janaka are found in the famous exposition on nondual realization called
the *Ashtavakra Gita*.

### 14
*sarvam etad ritam manye / yan mam vadasi keshava*
*na hi te bhagavan vyaktim / vidur deva na danavah*

*sarvam etat* > all of this; *ritam* > true; *manye* > I believe, I accept;
*yat* > which; *mam* > to me; *vadasi* > You tell; *keshava* > O one who is like (*va*)
an embodiment of Brahma (*ka*), Vishnu (*a*), and Shiva (*isha*) combinedly;
*na* > not; *hi* > surely; *te* > Your; *bhagavan* > O venerable one;
*vyaktim* > visible manifestations, individual personalities; *viduh* > they
know; *devah* > the celestials; *na* > nor; *danavah* > the titans.

**O one who is like an embodiment of Brahma, Vishnu,
and Shiva combinedly,
I regard as true everything which You have told me.
Surely, O venerable one, neither the celestials nor the titans
know [the extent of] Your visible manifestations.**

The Danavas (titans) are descendants of Daksha ('adept'), another one of
the early progenitors of humankind such as those mentioned in verse 6.

**15**
*svayam evatmanatmanam / vettha tvam purushottama*
*bhuta-bhavana bhutesha / devadeva jagatpate*

*svayam* > naturally, of Your own accord; *eva* > alone;
*atmana* > by Yourself; *atmanam* > Yourself; *vettha* > You know;
*tvam* > You; *purusha-uttama* > O Supreme Person; *bhuta-bhavana* > O one who
is the source of well-being for all creatures; *bhuta-isha* > O master of beings;
*deva-deva* > O God of gods; *jagat-pate* > O Lord of the universe.

**You alone naturally know Yourself by Yourself,
O Supreme Person, source of well-being for all creatures,
O master of beings, God of gods,
Lord of the universe...!**

**16**
*vaktum arhasyasheshena / divya hyatma-vibhutayah*
*yabhir vibhutibhir lokan / imams tvam vyapya tishthasi*

*vaktum* > to tell, to describe; *arhasi* > please do, may You be
pleased to; *asheshena* > without remainder; *divyah* > divine; *hi* > truly;
*atma-vibhutayah* > self-expressions; *yabhih* > whereby, through which;
*vibhutibhih* > displays of abundant potency; *lokan* > worlds;
*iman* > these; *tvam* > You; *vyapya* > permeating, spreading or
extending throughout; *tishthasi* > You are situated.

**Please tell me —
Leaving nothing untold —
Of the truly divine self-expressions
through which You permeate these worlds
situated in displays of Your abundant potency.**

**17**
*katham vidyam aham yogims / tvam sada parichintayan*
*keshu keshu cha bhaveshu / chintyo 'si bhagavan maya*

*katham* > in what way; *vidyam aham* > I shall perceive;
*yogin* > O master of great mystic powers; *tvam* > You;
*sada* > constantly; *parichintayan* > contemplating, recollecting;
*keshu keshu* > in what particular; *cha* > and; *bhaveshu* > states of being,
appearances; *chintyah* > to be contemplated, to be remembered;
*asi* > You are; *bhagavan* > O opulent one; *maya* > by me.

In what way shall I visualize You in my constant recollection of You,
O master of great mystic powers?
And in what particular forms are You to be contemplated by me,
O opulent one?

**18**
*vistarenatmano yogam / vibhutim cha janardana*
*bhuyah kathaya triptir hi / shrinvato nasti me 'mritam*

*vistarena* > specifically, in a detailed way; *atmanah* > of Yourself;
*yogam* > mystic potency; *vibhutim* > manifest expressions; *cha* > and;
*jana-ardana* > O animator of people; *bhuyah* > more, further; *kathaya* > please
speak; *triptih* > satiation; *hi* > truly; *shrinvatah* > by hearing, by listening;
*na asti* > there is not; *me* > for me; *amritam* > immortal, ambrosial.

**Please speak further about Your mystic potency and manifest expressions
in a detailed way, O animator of people,
For I truly feel no point of satiation
in listening to Your ambrosial words.**

**19**
*sri bhagavan uvacha:*
*hanta te kathayishyami / divya hyatma-vibhutayah*
*pradhanyatah kuru-shreshtha / nastyanto vistarasya me*

*sri bhagavan uvacha* > the blessed one (Krishna) said; *hanta* > listen;
*te* > to you; *kathayishyami* > I shall speak; *divyah* > divine; *hi* > just;
*atma-vibhutayah* > self-expressions; *pradhanyatah* > principal, prominent;
*kuru-shreshtha* > O best of the Kuru dynasty; *na asti* > there is not; *antah* > an
end; *vistarasya* > of the expanse in all of its detail, of the full extent; *me* > My.

**The blessed Krishna said:
Listen, O best of the Kurus:
I shall mention to you just the divine self-expressions of Mine
which are the most prominent,
because there is no end to the full extent of them.**

**20**
*aham atma gudakesha / sarva-bhutashaya-sthitah*
*aham adish cha madhyam cha / bhutanam anta eva cha*

*aham* > I; *atma* > the Self; *gudakesha* > O conqueror of sloth;
*sarva-bhuta* > all living beings, all manifestations of Being;

*ashaya-sthitah* > situated in the heart; *aham* > I, the sense of 'I-ness,' the awareness 'I am'; *adih* > origin; *cha* > and; *madhyam* > middle; *cha* > and; *bhutanam* > of all beings; *antah* > end; *eva* > indeed; *cha* > also.

**I (pure Presence) am the Self, O conqueror of sloth,**
**Situated at the very heart of every living being.**
**The awareness 'I am' is the origin and the lifespan of all beings,**
**and indeed their end as well.**

*Ashaya-sthitah*, 'situated in the heart,' means 'as the essence'; it does not mean relegated exclusively to one particular organ within the physical body. In verse 3 Krishna once again states that He is *ajam*, unborn, and in verse 12 Arjuna conveys that he regards Krishna, the absolute Reality, in the same way. These statements point toward the principle that ultimately, That which is never born cannot be defined, described, or even imagined via any words or images born within the scope of thought and language. Hence this verse is yet another among the many verses within the Gita which invites the reader to pause and reflect: "Without resorting to any thoughts or words whatsoever *about* the Self — including those offered as pointers within the Gita as well — what *is* It? What is It, really, when I don't reflexively reach for memories of what I learned about It?" This question follows along the same line of Self-inquiry as Ramana Maharshi's "Who am I?", and staying with the honest, innocent 'not knowing' of any answers drawn from memory may indeed elicit some profound insights. As noted by St. John of the Cross, "To come to the knowledge which you have not, you must go by a way in which you know not."

## 21

*adityanam aham vishnur / jyotisham ravir amshuman*
*marichir marutam asmi / nakshatranam aham shashi*

*adityanam* > of the children of Aditi ('infinity'); *aham* > I; *vishnuh* > Vishnu ('all-pervasive'); *jyotisham* > of luminaries; *ravih* > the sun; *amshuman* > radiant; *marichih* > Marichi ('ray of light'); *marutam* > of the Maruts ('the flashing ones,' the storm-gods); *asmi* > I am; *nakshatranam* > among the stars of the night; *aham* > I; *shashi* > the 'rabbit-marked' moon.

**Among the children of Aditi (Infinity) I am Vishnu;**
**Of luminaries I am the radiant sun;**
**Among the storm-gods, the Maruts, I am Marichi;**
**And among the stars of the night**
**I am the 'rabbit-marked' one, the moon.**

The incarnation of Vishnu specifically referred to here is Vamanadeva, who is said to have rescued the universe at one point in ancient times when it was under the dominion of Bali ('offering'), king of the titans. Some of the other Adityas mentioned in the Vedas are Indra, chief of the celestials; the sun-god Surya, also known as Savitri ('the vivifier'); Varuna ('all-encompassing'), the celestial king of the oceans; and Mitra ('friend'), the celestial symbolizing relationship who oversees the protection of *dharma*.

**22**

*vedanam samavedo 'smi / devanam asmi vasavah*
*indriyanam manash chasmi / bhutanam asmi chetana*

*vedanam* > among the Vedas; *sama-vedah* > the Sama Veda; *asmi* > I am; *devanam* > of the celestials; *asmi* > I am; *vasavah* > the celestial king Indra; *indriyanam* > of the senses; *manah* > the mind; *cha* > and; *asmi* > I am; *bhutanam* > of living beings; *asmi* > I am; *chetana* > Consciousness.

**Among the Vedas I am the Sama Veda;**
**Among the celestials I am their king, Indra;**
**Among the senses I am the mind;**
**And I am the faculty of Consciousness in all living beings.**

The Sama Veda is 'the knowledge of chanted verses,' the Rig Veda is 'the knowledge of praises,' the Yajur Veda is 'the knowledge of prayers,' and the Atharva Veda is 'the knowledge for priests.' *Vasavah* means 'in relation to the Vasus.' The Vasus are said to be the attendants of Indra, whose name means 'chief' as well as 'to drop' (referring to rain).

**23**

*rudranam shankarash chasmi / vittesho yaksha-rakshasam*
*vasunam pavakash chasmi / meruh shikharinam aham*

*rudranam* > among the Rudras ('the howling ones' or 'ones who cause crying'), a group of eleven celestials associated with evolution, dissolution, and renewal; *shankarah* > 'beneficent,' a name of Shiva ('auspicious'); *cha* > and; *asmi* > I am; *vitta-ishah* > Kubera, the 'lord of wealth'; *yaksha-rakshasam* > among the Yakshas (subtle beings who are attendants of the celestials with guardianship over Nature's treasures) and Rakshasas (demonic cannibals with supernatural powers); *vasunam* > among the Vasus, the 'shining dwellers' which are Nature's elements, planets, and stars; *pavakah* > fire, 'the purifier'; *cha* > and; *asmi* > I am; *meruh* > Mount Meru, legendary home of the celestials; *shikharinam* > among mountain peaks; *aham* > I.

Among the Rudras I am the beneficent Shiva;
Among the Yakshas and Rakshasas I am the lord of wealth, Kubera;
Among the Vasus, I am the purifying fire;
And among mountain peaks I am Mount Meru.

*Pavakah* could also refer to Agni, the celestial minister of fire later mentioned in verse 11.39.

### 24

*purodhasam cha mukhyam mam / viddhi partha brihaspatim*
*senaninam aham skandah / sarasam asmi sagarah*

*purodhasam* > among the priests of royal families; *cha* > and; *mukhyam* > the chief, the best; *mam* > Me; *viddhi* > please know; *partha* > O son of Pritha; *brihaspatim* > Brihaspati ('lord of prayer'); *senaninam* > among military commanders; *aham* > I; *skandah* > 'one who attacks' (a name of Karttikeya); *sarasam* > among bodies of water; *asmi* > I am; *sagarah* > the ocean.

### And, O Partha,
Know Me to be the foremost among priests of royal families —
Brihaspati (priest of the celestials).
Among military commanders I am Karttikeya,
and among bodies of water I am the ocean.

Karttikeya — known as such because he was nursed and raised by Krittika, the six sisters personifying the open star cluster Pleiades — is one of the two principal sons of Lord Shiva and Goddess Parvati, the other being the elephant-headed Ganesha ('lord of the retinue'). He is depicted in ancient literature as being the commander-in-chief of the celestials' army who leads them to victory in quelling various uprisings of the demons.

### 25

*maharshinam bhrigur aham / giram asmyekam aksharam*
*yajnanam japa-yajno 'smi / sthavaranam himalayah*

*maha-rishinam* > among the great sages; *bhriguh* > Bhrigu; *aham* > I; *giram* > among spoken words; *asmi* > I am; *ekam aksharam* > the single syllable 'Om'; *yajnanam* > among sacrifices; *japa-yajnah* > the sacrifice of murmuring a mantra; *asmi* > I am; *sthavaranam* > among immovable things; *himalayah* > 'the abode of snow,' the Himalayan mountains.

**Among the great sages I am Bhrigu;**
**Among spoken words I am the single syllable 'Om';**
**Among sacrifices I am the murmuring of a mantra;**
**And among immovable things I am the Himalayan mountains.**

A *mantra* is a particular instrument of thought utilized to 'protect' or 'rescue' one (*tra*) from other thoughts which are experienced as producing suffering, in much the same way as one thorn is used to remove another thorn embedded in one's hand.

### 26

*ashvatthah sarva-vrikshanam / devarshinam cha naradah*
*gandharvanam citrarathah / siddhanam kapilo munih*

*ashvatthah* > 'where horses stand,' the banyan tree Ficus Religiosa, also known as the 'sacred fig tree'; *sarva-vrikshanam* > among all trees; *deva-rishinam* > of the sages among the celestials; *cha* > and; *naradah* > Narada; *gandharvanam* > among the Gandharvas ('those who move as swiftly as a fragrance'); *citrarathah* > Citraratha ('one with a brightly shining chariot,' the chief of the celestial musicians); *siddhanam* > among those who are perfected; *kapilah* > Kapila, 'the tan-colored one'; *munih* > the sage.

**Among all trees I am the banyan tree;**
**Of sages among the celestials I am Narada;**
**Among the Gandharvas I am Citraratha;**
**And among perfected beings I am the sage Kapila.**

The Bodhi tree beneath which the Buddha realized enlightenment is of the same genus as the *ashvattha* mentioned in this verse. Gandharvas are celestial musicians said to sometimes act as messengers between the denizens of heaven and humankind. Kapila is the original expounder of the Sankhya philosophical system.

### 27

*uchchaih-shravasam ashvanam / viddhi mam amritodbhavam*
*airavatam gajendranam / naranam cha naradhipam*

*uchchaih-shravasam* > Indra's horse Uchchaihshravas, 'the shrill-sounding one'; *ashvanam* > among horses; *viddhi* > please know; *mam* > Me; *amrita-udbhavam* > emerged from the ocean of nectar; *airavatam* > Airavata ('full of much food'), the carrier of Indra; *gaja-indranam* > among the best of elephants; *naranam* > among humankind; *cha* > and; *nara-adhipam* > the monarch, 'ruler of humans.'

Among horses know Me to be Uchchaihshravas,
who emerged from the ocean of nectar;
Among the best of elephants I am Airavata;
And among humankind I am the monarch.

### 28

*ayudhanam aham vajram / dhenunam asmi kamadhuk*
*prajanash chasmi kandarpah / sarpanam asmi vasukih*

*ayudhanam* > among weapons; *aham* > I; *vajram* > thunderbolt;
*dhenunam* > among cows; *asmi* > I am; *kama-dhuk* > 'one from whom all
that is wished for is drawn,' sage Vasishtha's cow that yields unlimited milk;
*prajanah* > the cause of progeny, the impetus or motivation to procreate;
*cha* > and; *asmi* > I am; *kandarpah* > 'extravagant satisfaction,'
a name of Kamadeva, 'the desire-inducing celestial';
*sarpanam* > among serpents; *asmi* > I am; *vasukih* > Vasuki.

Among weapons I am the thunderbolt;
Among cows I am Kamadhuk, who fulfills all wishes;
Among impetuses for procreation I am Kamadeva,
the celestial who induces desires for extravagant satisfaction;
And among [moving] serpents I am Vasuki.

Vasuki, 'belonging to the excellent ones,' is the bejeweled king of serpents
mentioned in the Bhagavata Purana and other scriptures who is said to be
the snake worn around the neck of Lord Shiva.

### 29

*anantash chasmi naganam / varuno yadasam aham*
*pitrinam aryama chasmi / yamah samyamatam aham*

*anantah* > Ananta ('endless'); *cha* > and; *asmi* > I am; *naganam* > among naga
('unmoving') snakes; *varunah* > Varuna, the celestial king of the oceans;
*yadasam* > among aquatic beings; *aham* > I; *pitrinam* > among the deceased
ancestors; *aryama* > Aryama ('intimate friend'); *cha* > and; *asmi* > I am;
*yamah* > 'restrainer,' refers to the celestial lord of death;
*samyamatam* > among subduers; *aham* > I.

Among unmoving snakes, I am Ananta (the resting-place of Vishnu);
Among aquatic beings I am Varuna;
Among the departed ancestors I am Aryama;
And among subduers I am Yama, the celestial lord of death.

**30**

*prahladash chasmi daityanam / kalah kalayatam aham*
*mriganam cha mrigendro 'ham / vainateyash cha pakshinam*

*prahladah* > Prahlada ('joyful excitement,' one of the kings of
the titans prior to his grandson Bali); *cha* > and; *asmi* > I am;
*daityanam* > among the descendants of Diti; *kalah* > time;
*kalayatam* > among forces which impel one to monitoring and
calculation; *aham* > I; *mriganam* > among wild animals;
*cha* > and; *mriga-indrah* > the lion, 'king of beasts'; *aham* > I;
*vainateyah* > the son of Vinata ('bowing with humility'), a name
of Garuda ('one who seizes'); *cha* > and; *pakshinam* > among birds.

**Among the descendants of Diti I am Prahlada;**
**Among forces which impel one to monitoring and calculation, I am time;**
**Among wild animals I am the lion;**
**And among birds I am Garuda (the carrier of Vishnu).**

**31**

*pavanah pavatam asmi / ramah shastra-bhritam aham*
*jhashanam makarash chasmi / srotasam asmi jahnavi*

*pavanah* > the wind; *pavatam* > among purifiers; *asmi* > I am;
*ramah* > Rama ('delightful,' the kshatriya prince whose life-story
is narrated in the epic Ramayana); *shastra-bhritam* > among wielders
of weapons; *aham* > I; *jhashanam* > among fish; *makarah* > the makara;
*cha* > and; *asmi* > I am; *srotasam* > among rivers; *asmi* > I am;
*jahnavi* > the Ganges, 'daughter of Jahnu (a sage).'

**Among purifiers I am the wind,**
**Among the wielders of weapons I am Rama,**
**Among fishes I am the makara,**
**And among rivers I am the Ganges.**

The makara is a celestial sea creature with the combined characteristics of a
fish, a crocodile, and even some land mammals. It is portrayed as the carrier
of Varuna and of Ganga, the personified river Ganges.

**32**

*sarganam adir antash cha / madhyam chaivaham arjuna*
*adhyatma-vidya vidyanam / vadah pravadatam aham*

*sarganam* > of creations, of emissions; *adih* > the beginning;
*antah* > end; *cha* > and; *madhyam* > middle; *cha* > and; *eva* > also;
*aham* > I, 'I-ness'; *arjuna* > O Arjuna; *adhyatma-vidya* > knowledge
about the Atman or universal principle of selfhood in all sentient beings;
*vidyanam* > among all types of learned knowledge; *vadah* > the spoken
words; *pravadatam* > of those who speak; *aham* > I.

**'I-ness' (the most basic awareness of existing)**
**Is the beginning, the end, and also the middle**
**of whatever has been created, O Arjuna.**
**Among all the types of knowledge that are learned,**
**This 'I am' is knowledge about [Itself,]**
**the universal principle of selfhood in all sentient beings;**
**And [the same] 'I' becomes the spoken words of all who speak.**

In verse 20 Krishna stated that He (the Absolute) is the beginning, middle,
and end of every living being's lifespan; in this verse that idea is expanded to
include anything that has been created from the eight foundational elements
listed in verse 7.4. In regard to *adhyatma-vidya*, if there is deep resonance
upon hearing or reading that one's true nature is the one omnipresent
Spirit-Self appearing as all life-forms, that information (*vidya*) could
potentially function like a powerful seed which in due course flowers into
*jnana*, true experiential knowing. This flowering takes place most reliably
within the body/mind system of one who is completely free of entertaining
any mental constructs defining oneself. And an alternate poetic reading of
*vadah pravadatam aham* is: "When there is *pravadatam*—when someone is
speaking out about something, or even against something—I am *vada*, that
spoken response which contains no interest other than ascertaining what is
true regardless of who is presenting the idea." This is in contrast to *jalpa* and
*vitanda*. *Jalpa*, exactly the opposite of *vada*, is a response wherein the only
interest is asserting one's own ideas regardless of what is true. In *vitanda*,
the response entails faultfinding and complaining about whatever has been
presented without even offering an alternative idea for discussion.

**33**
*aksharanam akaro 'smi / dvandvah samasikasya cha*
*aham evakshayah kalo / dhataham vishvato-mukhah*

*aksharanam* > among letters of the alphabet; *akarah* > the letter 'A'; *asmi* > I am;
*dvandvah* > larger compound words in which the two conjoined smaller
words are of equal significance; *samasikasya* > among compound words;

*cha* > and; *aham eva* > I alone; *akshayah* > undecaying, inexhaustible; *kalah* > time; *dhata* > the establisher, the creator, the arranger; *aham* > I am; *vishvatah-mukhah* > facing everywhere (referring to Lord Brahma, who is depicted with a head facing in each direction).

> **Among letters of the alphabet I am the letter 'A,'**
> **And among compound (phraselike) words**
> **I am those in which the two conjoined words**
> **are of equal significance.**
> **I alone am [incalculable] time without end (timelessness),**
> **and I am Brahma, the Creator facing in all directions.**

This is Krishna's second statement that He is time, the first one being in verse 30. The distinction between them is that the previous statement referred to time as 'a force which impels one to monitoring and calculation,' once again specifically corresponding to the lifespan of living beings. The time mentioned in the current verse is *akshayah*, of the nature of infinitude, which is thus beyond the lifespan of all beings and subsequently beyond any possible measurement.

**34**

*mrityuh sarva-harash chaham / udbhavash cha bhavishyatam*
*kirtih srir vak cha narinam / smritir medha dhritih kshama*

*mrityuh* > death; *sarva-harah* > seizing or carrying away everything; *cha* > and; *aham* > I; *udbhavah* > source of generation; *cha* > also; *bhavishyatam* > of that which is yet to be; *kirtih* > good reputation; *srih* > beauty; *vak* > voice, speaking; *cha* > also; *narinam* > of women; *smritih* > memory; *medha* > innate wisdom; *dhritih* > stability; *kshama* > patience, tolerance.

> **I am all-seizing death,**
> **As well as the generating source of all things that are yet to be.**
> **Among [the virtues of] women I am good reputation,**
> **beauty, [fine quality in] speaking, excellent memory,**
> **innate wisdom, stability, and forbearance.**

We find a reminder here, merely five verses after it was mentioned in verse 29, that death is also a divine manifest expression of the Absolute. The reason for this may be that Krishna is preparing Arjuna for what he will behold in verses 26 through 30 of the very next chapter. And *vak* may connote not only the fineness of a woman's *choice* of words, but also of her vocal sound vibration which produces the words.

**35**
*brihat-sama tatha samnam / gayatri chandasam aham*
*masanam margashirsho 'ham / ritunam kusumakarah*

*brihat-sama* > 'the great hymn,' a song of praise to Indra in the Sama Veda;
*tatha* > also; *samnam* > among hymns; *gayatri* > the Gayatri metre of 24
syllables; *chandasam* > among rhythmic metres; *aham* > I; *masanam* > among
months; *marga-shirshah* > Margashirsha; *aham* > I; *ritunam* > among seasons;
*kusuma-akarah* > spring, the time 'abundant with flowers.'

**Among hymns I am the great song of praise to Indra,**
**and among rhythmic metres I am the Gayatri.**
**Among months I am Margashirsha,**
**and among seasons I am spring, the time abundant with flowers.**

Margashirsha, 'deer's head,' is the astrological period approximately
corresponding to Sagittarius from November 22nd to December 21st when
the full moon enters the constellation of the deer's head.

**36**
*dyutam chalayatam asmi / tejas tejasvinam aham*
*jayo 'smi vyavasayo 'smi / sattvam sattvavatam aham*

*dyutam* > gambling; *chalayatam* > of those who deceive or cheat; *asmi* > I am;
*tejah* > strength, vigor; *tejasvinam* > of the powerful; *aham* > I; *jayah* > success;
*asmi* > I am; *vyavasayah* > resolute intention; *asmi* > I am; *sattvam* > those
characteristics which demonstrate the embodying of truth; *sattva-vatam* > of
those who are predominated by the clarifying component of Nature; *aham* > I.

**I am the gambling of the deceitful**
**and the vigor of the powerful;**
**I am resolute intention, I am success,**
**And I am those characteristics which demonstrate the embodying of truth**
**in beings predominated by the clarifying component of Nature.**

The reason for Arjuna's being on the battlefield facing an impending war
with his family members was due to his elder brother Yudhisthira's losing
the Pandavas' kingdoms in a gambling match with their uncle Shakuni, who
won by cheating. So in this verse Krishna reassures Arjuna that such events
are brought about by the same One that produces the innumerable flowers
of the spring season or the unlimited milk of the wish-fulfilling cow. He
then mentions that the same One will also be the resolve to participate in

the conflict, as well as the prowess which will yield victory on this occasion for those fighting for the purpose of supporting true *dharma.*

### 37

*vrishninam vasudevo 'smi / pandavanam dhananjayah*
*muninam apyaham vyasah / kavinam ushana kavih*

*vrishninam* > among the descendants of Vrishni; *vasudevah* > Krishna, the son of Vasudeva (pronounced 'Vuhhsudev'); *asmi* > I am; *pandavanam* > among the sons of Pandu; *dhananjayah* > Arjuna, the winner of wealth; *muninam* > among powerfully inspired sages or those observing a vow of silence; *api* > also; *aham* > I; *vyasah* > Vyasa, the compiler of the Vedic scriptures; *kavinam* > among the mystic seer-poets; *ushana* > 'with enthusiasm,' a name of Shukracharya, the 'resplendently pure spiritual preceptor' of the titans; *kavih* > the mystic seer-poet.

**Among the descendants of Vrishni**
**I am the son of Vasudeva [whom you see before you],**
**And among the sons of Pandu I am yourself, O winner of wealth.**
**Among powerfully inspired sages I am Vyasa,**
**And among mystic seer-poets I am Shukracharya.**

In this chapter Krishna distinguishes between five types of sages: those who are great (*maharshinam*, verse 25); those among the celestials (*devarshinam*, verse 26); those who are perfected (*siddhanam*, verse 26); those who are powerfully inspired or observing a vow of silence (*muninam* here); and those who are mystic seer-poets (*kavinam* here).

### 38

*dando damayatam asmi / nitir asmi jigishatam*
*maunam chaivasmi guhyanam / jnanam jnana-vatam aham*

*dandah* > the law-enforcing scepter; *damayatam* > of conquering rulers; *asmi* > I am; *nitih* > provision for moral guidance in regard to politics and diplomacy; *asmi* > I am; *jigishatam* > among those with military or political ambitions; *maunam* > silence; *cha* > and; *eva* > certainly; *asmi* > I am; *guhyanam* > of secrets; *jnanam* > wisdom; *jnana-vatam* > of those who are wise; *aham* > I.

**I am the law-enforcing scepter of conquering rulers**
**As well as the codes of ethical conduct**
**for those who have ambitions to conquer and rule.**
**And I am certainly the secret of silence**
**as also the wisdom of the wise.**

In this section of the text there are a few extra lines in several different Gita recensions, the essence of which is represented in the following verse.

### '38-A'

*aushadhinam yavash chasmi / dhatunam asmi kanchanam*
*snehanam sarpir apyaham / trina-jatinam darbho'ham*

*aushadhinam* > among plant-based medicines; *yavah* > barley; *cha* > and; *asmi* > I am; *dhatunam* > among minerals or metals; *asmi* > I am; *kanchanam* > gold, that which is composed of gold; *snehanam* > among unctuous substances; *sarpih* > clarified butter (ghee); *api* > assuredly; *aham* > I; *trina-jatinam* > among different kinds of grass; *darbha* > darbha grass (Desmostachya Bipinnata); *aham* > I.

**Among plant-based medicines I am barley,**
**and among minerals I am gold.**
**Among unctuous substances I am assuredly ghee,**
**and among varieties of grass I am darbha.**

Many contemporary practitioners of naturopathic and Ayurvedic healing modalities state that barley water, if prepared properly, can potentially be an effective remedy for a wide variety of physical ailments. Darbha grass has traditionally been used in Vedic ritual ceremonies since ancient times, and it is said that the Buddha's seat under the Bodhi tree was made from darbha grass.

### 39

*yach chapi sarva-bhutanam / bijam tad aham arjuna*
*na tad asti vina yat syan / maya bhutam characharam*

*yat* > whatever; *cha* > and; *api* > moreover; *sarva-bhutanam* > of all that has gone, of all that existed in the past; *bijam* > original seed, primary cause, source; *tat* > that; *aham* > I; *arjuna* > O Arjuna; *na* > not; *tat* > that; *asti* > there is; *vina* > except, besides, unless; *yat* > which; *syat* > it can be; *maya* > by Me; *bhutam* > that which happens, that which exists; *chara-acharam* > moving or unmoving.

**And moreover, whatever has existed in the past —**
**I am the source of all that as well, O Arjuna.**
**There is nothing either moving or unmoving**
**which can exist unless it is by way of Me**
**[absolute Consciousness appearing as that particular thing].**

As Krishna had already stated that He is the source of all that *is* (present tense) in seven previous verses (7.6, 7.10, 9.13, 9.18, 10.2, 10.8, and 10.20), the definition of *bhuta* as 'that which had formerly been' has been favored here in support of all the prior manifestations which Krishna mentioned such as King Ramachandra in verse 31.

### 40

*nanto 'sti mama divyanam / vibhutinam parantapa*
*esha tuddeshatah prokto / vibhuter vistaro maya*

*na* > not; *antah* > end; *asti* > there is; *mama* > My; *divyanam* > of the divine; *vibhutinam* > manifest expressions; *parantapa* > O vanquisher of foes; *eshah* > this; *tu* > but; *uddeshatah* > briefly through examples; *proktah* > mentioned; *vibhuteh* > of the abundant potency; *vistarah* > the extent; *maya* > by Me.

**There is no end to My divine manifest expressions,**
**O vanquisher of foes.**
**What I have briefly mentioned are but a few examples**
**of the extent of My abundant potency.**

### 41

*yad yad vibhutimat sattvam / srimad urjitam eva va*
*tat tad evavagachcha tvam / mama tejo'msha-sambhavam*

*yat yat* > whatever; *vibhutimat* > manifest expressions; *sattvam* > demonstrating a purity of nature; *srimat* > glorious; *urjitam* > mighty; *eva* > very; *va* > or; *tat tat* > this and that (connoting 'all of that'); *eva* > even; *avagachcha* > please understand; *tvam* > you; *mama* > My; *tejah* > energetic power, splendor; *amsha* > a portion, a fraction; *sambhavam* > arisen from, produced from.

**Whatever manifest expressions are very mighty or glorious**
**or demonstrate a purity of nature —**
**Please understand that even all of those have arisen**
**from but a fraction of My energetic power.**

### 42

*athava bahunaitena / kim jnatena tavarjuna*
*vishtabhyaham idam kritsnam / ekamshena sthito jagat*

*athava* > but on the other hand, but then again; *bahuna* > with so much; *etena* > with this; *kim* > what; *jnatena* > by that which is known; *tava* > to you; *arjuna* > Arjuna; *vishtabhya* > supporting; *aham* > I; *idam* > this; *kritsnam* > entire; *eka-amshena* > by one single portion; *sthitah* > continuing; *jagat* > universe.

**But then again, what [is the need]**
**of your knowing so much of this, Arjuna?**
**I continue supporting this entire universe**
**with the merest portion [of My potential].**

*om tat saditi srimad bhagavad-gita / supanishatsu brahma-vidyayam yoga-shastre srikrishnarjuna samvade / vibhuti-yogo nama dashamo 'dhyayah*

From the Ambrosial Song of God —
A conversation between Krishna and Arjuna
which is a Upanishad (confidential sharing)
of wisdom-teachings regarding the Absolute
And a scripture concerning Self-realization —
Thus ends the Tenth Chapter entitled Vibhuti-yoga,
Recognizing Divine Unicity By Way of Its Manifest Expressions.

# Chapter Eleven

## Vishvarupa-darshana-yoga
### (Recognizing Divine Unicity By Way of Beholding
### Its Universal Form)

"I have been blessed with a vision of Your holy feet, my Lord.
Where can my thinking mind run now?
The feeling of being separate from You has totally disappeared,
and so has the idea that I have separate free will.
There is peace.
A great joy is felt in embracing Your lotus feet.
The tongue enjoys the continuous reciting of Your name.
We who have found peace at the feet of the Lord
are not infatuated by earthly pleasures."   —Tukaram

"If God wants to act in the soul, He Himself must be the place in which
He acts."   —Meister Eckhart

"The Buddha-mind (universal Intelligence) is unborn, having the wondrous
quality of illuminating wisdom. In the Unborn, everything falls right into
alignment and settles into perfect harmony. By doing everything in
alignment with the Unborn, the eye to see others as they truly are becomes
opened in you, and within yourself you know that every sentient being that
you see is a living Buddha. ...Once you understand the great value of the
Buddha-mind, you cannot again forsake it for illusion."   —Bankei

"You are the infinite ocean [of Consciousness]; thus you can simply allow
the waves known as the universe to rise and fall within you, as this
phenomenon presents no gain or loss to you whatsoever. Dear one, you are
pure Intelligence Itself. As this universe is not something else apart from you,
how can there be any ideas about accepting it or rejecting it? For you who are
the one changelessly pure, still space of Awareness, where is birth, activity,
or the sense of 'I am the doer'? You alone appear as whatever you perceive.
Do bracelets, armlets, and anklets made of gold appear different from raw
gold? Completely give up such distinctions as 'I am That' and 'I am not this.'
Consider all as the Self and be happy, free from imaginings. ...For you there
is neither bondage nor liberation."
                —Ashtavakra to King Janaka, *Ashtavakra Gita* 15.11-15, 18

**1**
*arjuna uvacha:*
*mad-anugrahaya paramam / guhyam adhyatma-samjnitam*
*yat tvayoktam vachas tena / moho 'yam vigato mama*

*arjunah uvacha* > Arjuna said; *mat-anugrahaya* > out of kindness
to me, for my benefit; *paramam guhyam* > the supreme secret;
*adhyatma* > the one omnipresent Spirit-Self appearing as all life-forms;
*samjnitam* > communicated, made known; *yat* > which; *tvaya* > by You;
*uktam* > spoken, taught; *vachah* > words; *tena* > by this (hearing);
*mohah* > confusion; *ayam* > this; *vigatah* > gone; *mama* > my.

**Arjuna said:**
**Out of kindness to me,**
**For my benefit You have shared the supreme secret**
**about the one omnipresent Spirit-Self appearing as all life-forms.**
**By hearing these teachings imparted by You,**
**my confusion is gone.**

When reciting this verse, the first segment of the first line has one extra
syllable.

**2**
*bhavapyayau hi bhutanam / shrutau vistarasho maya*
*tvattah kamala-pattraksha / mahatmyam api chavyayam*

*bhava* > arising, coming into being; *apyayau* > entering into,
vanishing; *hi* > indeed; *bhutanam* > of living beings;
*shrutau* > both heard; *vistarashah* > extensively, in full detail;
*maya* > by me; *tvattah* > from You; *kamala-pattra-aksha* > whose eyes
are like lotus petals; *mahatmyam* > glories; *api* > also;
*cha* > and; *avyayam* > imperishable.

**From You, whose eyes are like lotus petals,**
**I have heard in full detail**
**about both the arising and the vanishing of living beings,**
**and also about Your inexhaustible glories.**

**3**
*evam etad yathattha tvam / atmanam parameshvara*
*drashtum ichchami te rupam / aishvaram purushottama*

*evam* > in the same way; *etat* > now, at this time;
*yatha* > just as; *attha tvam* > You declare; *atmanam* > Yourself;
*parama-ishvara* > O Supreme Lord; *drashtum* > to see; *ichchami* > I wish;
*te* > Your; *rupam* > form; *aishvaram* > almighty majesty;
*purusha-uttama* > O best, foremost, or highest of persons.

**Now, O Supreme Lord and best of persons,
At this time I wish to see Your form of almighty majesty
In just the same way
as You Yourself have declared it to be.**

**4**

*manyase yadi tach chakyam / maya drashtum iti prabho
yogeshvara tato me tvam / darshayatmanam avyayam*

*manyase* > You think; *yadi* > if; *tat* > that; *shakyam* > possible;
*maya* > by me; *drashtum* > to see; *iti* > in this way (as mentioned in
verse 1); *prabho* > O Lord; *yoga-ishvara* > O master of all mystic abilities;
*tatah* > then; *me* > to me; *tvam* > You; *darshaya* > please reveal;
*atmanam* > the Self; *avyayam* > imperishable.

**If You think that it is possible for me to see the imperishable Self
in that way (appearing as all life-forms),
Then, O Lord and master of all mystic abilities,
please reveal that to me.**

**5**

*sri bhagavan uvacha:
pashya me partha rupani / shatasho 'tha sahasrashah
nana-vidhani divyani / nana-varnakritini cha*

*sri bhagavan uvacha* > the glorious one (Krishna) said;
*pashya* > behold; *me* > My; *partha* > O son of Pritha; *rupani* > forms;
*shatashah* > by the hundreds; *atha* > or rather; *sahasrashah* > by the thousands;
*nana-vidhani* > of various types; *divyani* > divine; *nana* > diverse;
*varna* > colors; *akritini* > shapes; *cha* > and.

**The glorious Krishna said:
Behold, O Partha,
My hundreds — or rather, thousands —
of various divine forms of diverse colors and shapes.**

**6**

*pashyadityan vasun rudran / ashvinau marutas tatha*
*bahunyadrishta-purvani / pashyashcharyani bharata*

*pashya* > behold; *adityan* > the Adityas; *vasun* > the Vasus;
*rudran* > the Rudras; *ashvinau* > the two Ashvins ('mounted on horses'
or 'drawn by horses [in a chariot]'); *marutah* > the Maruts; *tatha* > also;
*bahuni* > many; *adrishta* > not seen; *purvani* > before; *pashya* > behold;
*ashcharyani* > astonishing things; *bharata* > O descendent of Bharata.

**Behold the Adityas, the Vasus, the Rudras,**
**the two Ashvins, the Maruts,**
**And also many astonishing things which have not been seen before,**
**O descendent of Bharata.**

The Ashvins are described in the Vedas as being the primary healers among
the celestials, the twin sons of the sun-god Vivasvan mentioned in verse 4.1
and his wife Saranya.

**7**

*ihaika-stham jagat kritsnam / pashyadya sacharacharam*
*mama dehe gudakesha / yach chanyad drashtum ichchasi*

*iha* > here; *eka-stham* > standing as one, abiding as a unitary whole;
*jagat* > universe; *kritsnam* > entire; *pashya* > behold; *adya* > today; *sa* > with;
*characharam* > the moving and the unmoving; *mama dehe* > in My body;
*gudakesha* > O conqueror of slumber; *yat* > whatever; *cha* > and;
*anyat* > else; *drashtum* > to see; *ichchasi* > you wish.

**O conqueror of slumber,**
**Today behold the entire universe**
**with all of its moving and unmoving features**
**abiding here in My body as a unitary whole...**
**And whatever else you wish to see.**

**8**

*na tu mam shakyase drashtum / anenaiva sva-chakshusha*
*divyam dadami te chakshuh / pashya me yogam aishvaram*

*na* > not; *tu* > but; *mam* > Me; *shakyase* > you are able; *drashtum* > to see;
*anena* > with this; *eva* > alone; *sva-chakshusha* > the power of your
own eyesight; *divyam* > supernal; *dadami* > I confer; *te* > to you;
*chakshuh* > eyes, vision; *pashya* > behold; *me* > My;
*yogam* > mystic power; *aishvaram* > almighty majesty.

> ...But you are not able to see Me
> with the power of your own eyesight alone;
> Therefore I confer supernal vision upon you.
> Behold My mystic power and almighty majesty........

This conferring of supernal vision did not entail adding something additional to Arjuna's eyes, but rather removing the concepts of time and space from his mind.

### 9

*sanjaya uvacha:*
*evam uktva tato rajan / maha-yogeshvaro harih*
*darshayam asa parthaya / paramam rupam aishvaram*

*sanjayah uvacha* > Sanjaya said; *evam* > thus; *uktva* > having spoken; *tatah* > then; *rajan* > O king; *maha-yoga-ishvarah* > the great master of all mystic perfections; *harih* > Krishna, 'the remover of miseries'; *darshayam asa* > He revealed; *parthaya* > to Arjuna, the son of Pritha; *paramam* > most excellent; *rupam* > form; *aishvaram* > omnipotent grandeur.

**Sanjaya said [to Dhritarashtra]:**
**Having spoken thus, O king,**
**Sri Krishna, the remover of miseries**
**and great master of all mystic perfections,**
**Then revealed to Arjuna His most excellent form of omnipotent grandeur.**

### 10-11

*aneka-vaktra-nayanam / anekadbhuta-darshanam*
*aneka-divya-'bharanam / divya-'nekodyata-'yudham*

*divya-malyambara-dharam / divya-gandha-'nulepanam*
*sarvashcharya-mayam devam / anantam vishvato-mukham*

*aneka* > not just one (many); *vaktra* > mouths; *nayanam* > eyes; *aneka* > many; *adbhuta* > wondrous; *darshanam* > aspects to see; *aneka* > many; *divya* > divine; *abharanam* > adornments (jeweled crowns, earrings, necklaces, etc.); *divya* > divine; *aneka* > many; *udyata* > upraised; *ayudham* > weapons (maces, swords, spinning discs, etc.);

*divya* > divine; *malya* > flower garlands; *ambara* > garments; *dharam* > wearing; *divya* > divine; *gandha* > perfumes; *anulepanam* > anointment of the body with tilaka, ornamental markings made from either clay, sandalwood paste, or vermillion;

*sarvashcharya-mayam* > composed entirely of wonders; *devam* > celestial;
*anantam* > infinite, unending; *vishvatah-mukham* > facing all directions.

**Displaying many wondrous features to see —
Many mouths and eyes,
Many divine adornments and upraised weapons —
Wearing divine garments and flower garlands,
divine ornamental markings and perfumes —
That form was composed entirely of celestial wonders
extending infinitely and facing in all directions.**

### 12

*divi surya-sahasrasya / bhaved yugapad utthita*
*yadi bhah sadrishi sa syad / bhasas tasya mahatmanah*

*divi* > in the heavens (sky); *surya-sahasrasya* > of a thousand suns;
*bhavet* > there would be; *yugapat* > at the same time; *utthita* > arisen; *yadi* > if;
*bhah* > brilliance; *sadrishi* > similar; *sa* > this; *syat* > it might be; *bhasah* > of the
radiance; *tasya* > of that; *maha-atmanah* > exalted one, universal Self.

**If a thousand suns
were to rise into the sky at the same time,
Their combined brilliance might be similar to the radiance
of that universal Self.**

### 13

*tatraika-stham jagat kritsnam / pravibhaktam anekadha*
*apashyad deva-devasya / sharire pandavas tada*

*tatra* > there; *eka-stham* > situated as a unitary whole; *jagat* > universe;
*kritsnam* > entire; *pravibhaktam* > having distinction or diversity;
*anekadha* > in not merely one way (but many ways); *apashyat* > he beheld;
*deva-devasya* > of the God of gods; *sharire* > in the body;
*pandavah* > the son of Pandu; *tada* > at that time.

**At that time
The son of Pandu beheld the entire universe
situated as a unitary whole yet diversified in many ways
There within the body of the God of gods.**

### 14

*tatah sa vismayavishto / hrishta-roma dhananjayah*
*pranamya shirasa devam / kritanjalir abhashata*

*tatah* > then; *sah* > he (Arjuna); *vismaya-avishtah* > overwhelmed with astonishment; *hrishta-roma* > with hairs bristling in rapture; *dhananjayah* > Arjuna, the winner of wealth; *pranamya* > bowing in obeisance; *shirasa* > with the head; *devam* > the deity; *krita-anjalih* > making a reverential gesture of conjoining the palms at the forehead; *abhashata* > he addressed.

**Then Arjuna became overwhelmed with astonishment,**
**his hairs bristling in rapture.**
**He bowed his head in obeisance,**
**And with a reverential gesture of conjoined palms**
**he addressed the deity [which he beheld].**

### 15
*arjuna uvacha:*
*pashyami devams tava deva dehe / sarvams tatha bhuta-vishesha-sanghan*
*brahmanam isham kamalasana-stham / rishimsh cha sarvan uragamsh cha divyan*

*arjunah uvacha* > Arjuna said; *pashyami* > I see; *devan* > the celestials; *tava* > Your; *deva* > O God; *dehe* > in the body; *sarvan* > all; *tatha* > also; *bhuta-vishesha* > beings of different kinds; *sanghan* > assembled; *brahmanam isham* > Lord Brahma, the Creator aspect of Brahman; *kamala-asana* > lotus-flower seat; *stham* > situated upon; *rishin* > the sages; *cha* > and; *sarvan* > all; *uragan* > 'going on the bosom' (refers to serpents, which ornament the body of Lord Shiva); *cha* > also; *divyan* > divine.

**Arjuna said:**
**I see...the celestials in Your body, my Lord...**
**along with all different kinds of other beings assembled there.**
**...Lord Brahma sitting on his lotus-flower seat,**
**as well as all the sages and divine serpents.**

### 16
*aneka-bahudara-vaktra-netram / pashyami tvam sarvato 'nanta-rupam*
*nantam na madhyam na punas tavadim / pashyami vishveshvara vishvarupa*

*aneka* > not just one (many); *bahu* > arm; *udara* > belly; *vaktra* > mouth; *netram* > eye; *pashyami* > I see; *tvam* > You; *sarvatah* > in every direction; *ananta-rupam* > infinite form; *na antam* > no end; *na madhyam* > nor middle; *na* > nor; *punah* > moreover; *tava* > Your; *adim* > beginning; *pashyami* > I see; *vishva-ishvara* > O omnipresent Lord; *vishva-rupa* > whose form is all forms comprising the universe.

I see Your infinite form extended in every direction
with many arms, bellies, mouths, and eyes.
I see no end, no middle, nor even any beginning of it,
O omnipresent Lord whose form is all forms comprising the universe.

### 17

*kiritinam gadinam chakrinam cha / tejorashim sarvato dipti-mantam*
*pashyami tvam durnirikshyam samantad / diptanalarka-dyutim aprameyam*

*kiritinam* > wearing crowns; *gadinam* > armed with maces;
*chakrinam* > wielding discs; *cha* > and; *tejah-rashim* > a mass of radiance;
*sarvatah* > all throughout; *dipti-mantam* > full of brightness; *pashyami* > I see;
*tvam* > You; *durnirikshyam* > difficult to look at; *samantat* > on all sides,
all around; *dipta-anala-arka* > the blazing flames of the sun;
*dyutim* > effulgence; *aprameyam* > immeasurable.

I see You wearing crowns,
armed with maces and wielding discs....
A mass of radiance full of brightness all throughout,
Difficult to look at with Your immeasurable effulgence
all around me like the blazing flames of the sun.

### 18

*tvam aksharam paramam veditavyam / tvam asya vishvasya param nidhanam*
*tvam avyayah shashvata-dharma-gopta / sanatanas tvam purusho mato me*

*tvam* > You; *aksharam* > unalterable; *paramam* > supreme; *veditavyam* > that
which is to be known or recognized; *tvam* > You; *asya vishvasya* > of this entire
universe; *param* > ultimate; *nidhanam* > home, treasure-house; *tvam* > You;
*avyayah* > imperishable; *shashvata-dharma* > the eternal laws or religious
principles, the eternal principles of fully conscious whole-life-centered living;
*gopta* > protector, guardian; *sanatanah* > primeval; *tvam* > You; *purushah* >
person, personification of Spirit; *matah* > regarded; *me* > by me.

You are the changeless Supreme to be realized —
The ultimate home for the entire universe.
You are the immortal guardian
of the eternal principles of whole-life-centered living,
and I regard You as the most primeval Person.

### 19

*anadi-madhyantam ananta-viryam / ananta-bahum shashi-surya-netram*
*pashyami tvam dipta-hutasha-vaktram / sva-tejasa vishvam idam tapantam*

*anadi* > without beginning; *madhya* > middle; *antam* > or end;
*ananta* > unlimited; *viryam* > power; *ananta* > endless; *bahum* > arms;
*shashi* > the moon; *surya* > the sun; *netram* > eyes; *pashyami* > I see;
*tvam* > You; *dipta* > blazing; *hutasha* > fire, the 'eater of oblations';
*vaktram* > mouth; *sva-tejasa* > by Your own radiance;
*vishvam idam* > this entire universe; *tapantam* > consuming.

**You are without beginning, middle, or end,**
**possessing unlimited power and innumerable arms.**
**The sun and moon are Your eyes,**
**And I see this entire universe being consumed by Your radiance,**
**As if it were an oblation**
**offered into the blazing fire of Your mouth.**

### 20

*dyava-prithivyor idam antaram hi / vyaptam tvayaikena dishash cha sarvah*
*drishtvadbhutam rupam ugram tavedam / loka-trayam pravyathitam mahatman*

*dyava-prithivyoh* > of heaven and Earth; *idam* > this; *antaram* > intermediate
space; *hi* > indeed; *vyaptam* > pervaded; *tvaya* > by You; *ekena* > alone;
*dishah* > directions, regions; *cha* > and; *sarvah* > all; *drishtva* > seeing;
*adbhutam* > extraordinary, wonderful; *rupam* > form; *ugram* > formidable,
fierce; *tava* > Your; *idam* > this; *loka-trayam* > the inhabitants of
the three worlds; *pravyathitam* > terrified, distressed;
*mahatman* > O exalted one, O high-minded one, O great-hearted one.

**The space between heaven and Earth**
**is indeed pervaded by You alone in all directions;**
**And upon seeing this extraordinary, fierce form of Yours,**
**The inhabitants of the three worlds are terrified, O exalted one.**

### 21

*ami hi tvam sura-sangha vishanti / kechid bhitah pranjalayo grinanti*
*svasti 'tyuktva maharshi-siddha-sanghah / stuvanti tvam stutibhih pushkalabhih*

*ami* > these; *hi* > indeed; *tvam* > You; *sura-sanghah* > groups of celestials;
*vishanti* > they enter; *kechit* > some; *bhitah* > worried, frightened;
*pranjalayah* > offering reverential gestures, conjoining the palms;
*grinanti* > they sing praises; *svasti* > "Blessed be," "May all
be well," or "All glory to You"; *iti* > thus; *uktva* > saying;
*maharshi* > the great sage; *siddha* > perfected one; *sanghah* > multitudes;
*stuvanti* > they praise; *tvam* > You; *stutibhih* > with hymns;
*pushkalabhih* > numerous, resounding, eloquent.

> Indeed, groups of celestials are entering into You —
> Some of them fearfully —
> Offering reverential gestures and singing Your glories.
> Saying "May all be well!",
> Multitudes of great sages and perfected ones
> praise You with eloquent hymns.

In this verse we find some of the celestials entering into the manifestation of the universal Self fearfully in what may be viewed as representing either their surrendering the idea of separate selfhood, or their unexpected discovery that the separate self never existed as anything other than merely an idea. Although it is not a certainty that fear will arise, it's entirely natural and typical for some fear to be temporarily experienced when one suddenly, penetratingly realizes that one is not what one had for a very long time believed oneself to be.

### 22

*rudraditya vasavo ye cha sadhya / vishve 'shvinau marutash choshmapash cha*
*gandharva-yakshasura-siddha-sangha / vikshante tvam vismitash chaiva sarve*

*rudra* > the Rudras; *adityah* > the Adityas; *vasavah* > the Vasus; *ye* > who (connoting 'those who are known as'); *cha* > and; *sadhyah* > the Sadhyas; *vishve* > the Vishvedevas; *ashvinau* > the two Ashvins; *marutah* > the Maruts; *cha* > and; *ushmapah* > the Ushmapa manes; *cha* > and; *gandharva* > of the Gandharvas; *yaksha* > the Yakshas; *asura* > the demons; *siddha* > the perfected ones; *sanghah* > assemblies; *vikshante* > they behold; *tvam* > You; *vismitah* > astonished; *cha* > and; *eva* > indeed; *sarve* > all.

> The Rudras, the Adityas, the Vasus,
> Those who are known as the Sadhyas,
> The Vishvedevas, the two Ashvins, the Maruts, the Ushmapas,
> And assemblies of Gandharvas, Yakshas, demons, and perfected ones
> all indeed behold You with astonishment.

Sadhyas, 'those to be cultivated,' are 'siddhas (perfected ones)-in-progress,' the Sanskrit root of their name being the same as for the word *sadhaka*, which indicates one engaged in spiritual practices. They're said to be celestial descendants of the *pitris*, the spectres of departed ancestors, and one particular class of *pitri* are known as *ushmapas*, 'steam inhalers,' those who draw in the steam rising from the hot food utilized in ritual offerings. Regarding the Vishvedevas, 'containing all the gods,' it appears from references in the Vedas that they are an integrated collective representing all the groups of celestials, just as their name implies.

**23**

*rupam mahat te bahu-vaktra-netram / mahabaho bahu-bahuru-padam*
*bahudaram bahu-damshtra-karalam / drishtva lokah pravyathitas tathaham*

*rupam* > form; *mahat* > colossal; *te* > of You; *bahu* > many; *vaktra* > mouths;
*netram* > eyes; *maha-baho* > O mighty-armed one; *bahu* > many; *bahu* > arms;
*uru* > thighs; *padam* > feet; *bahu-udaram* > many bellies; *bahu-damshtra* > many
tusks or fangs; *karalam* > dreadful; *drishtva* > seeing; *lokah* > the worlds;
*pravyathitah* > disturbed, trembling; *tatha* > also; *aham* > I.

**O mighty-armed one,**
**Seeing Your colossal form of many mouths and eyes,**
**Many arms, thighs, and feet,**
**Many bellies and many dreadful fangs,**
**All the worlds are disturbed, as am I.**

**24**

*nabhah-sprisham diptam aneka-varnam / vyattananam dipta-vishala-netram*
*drishtva hi tvam pravyathit'-antaratma / dhritim na vindami shamam cha vishno*

*nabhah-sprisham* > touching the sky; *diptam* > blazing;
*aneka-varnam* > multicolored; *vyatta* > gaping; *ananam* > mouths;
*dipta* > flaming; *vishala* > enormous, extensive; *netram* > eyes;
*drishtva* > seeing; *hi* > truly; *tvam* > You; *pravyathita* > trembling;
*antar-atma* > inner soul (heart); *dhritim* > steadiness; *na* > not;
*vindami* > I find; *shamam* > tranquility; *cha* > and; *vishno* > O Vishnu.

**Seeing You touching the sky —**
**Blazing, multicolored,**
**With gaping mouths and enormous flaming eyes —**
**Verily my heart trembles,**
**and I can find no steadiness or tranquility, O Vishnu.**

**25**

*damshtra-karalani cha te mukhani / drishtvaiva kalanala-sannibhani*
*disho najane na labhe cha sharma / prasida devesha jagan-nivasa*

*damshtra* > tusks, fangs; *karalani* > terrible; *cha* > and; *te* > Your;
*mukhani* > mouths; *drishtva* > seeing; *eva* > merely; *kala-anala* > time as
the fires (of universal dissolution); *sannibhani* > like, resembling;
*dishah* > direction, region; *na* > not; *jane* > I know; *na* > not; *labhe* > I find;
*cha* > and; *sharma* > shelter, safety; *prasida* > please be merciful;
*deva-isha* > O Lord of the celestials; *jagat-nivasa* > O abode of worlds.

Just seeing Your mouths and terrible fangs
resembling the fires of universal dissolution,
I do not know any direction [in which to turn],
nor can I find any shelter anywhere.
O Lord of the celestials, abode of worlds —
Please be merciful...!

### 26-27

*ami cha tvam dhritarashtrasya putrah / sarve sahaivavani pala-sanghaih*
*bhishmo dronah suta-putras tathasau / saha-'smadiyair api yodha-mukhyaih*

*vaktrani te tvaramana vishanti / damshtra-karalani bhayanakani*
*kechid vilagna dashan'-antareshu / sandrishyante churnitair uttamangaih*

*ami cha* > and these; *tvam* > You; *dhritarashtrasya* > of King Dhritarashtra;
*putrah* > the sons; *sarve* > all; *saha* > along with; *eva* > indeed;
*avanipala* > kings, 'protectors of the Earth'; *sanghaih* > legions;
*bhishmah* > Bhishma; *dronah* > Drona; *suta-putrah* > Karna, the
'son of the charioteer'; *tatha* > so also; *asau* > there; *saha* > together;
*asmadiyaih* > with ours; *api* > as well; *yodha-mukhyaih* > with leading warriors;

*vaktrani* > mouths; *te* > Your; *tvaramanah* > quickly; *vishanti* > they enter;
*damshtra* > fangs; *karalani* > wide-open, horrible; *bhayanakani* > frightful;
*kechit* > some; *vilagnah* > clinging, hanging; *dashana-antareshu* > inbetween
the teeth; *sandrishyante* > they are seen; *churnitaih* > having been
crushed; *uttama-angaih* > heads, 'the best of limbs.'

All the sons of Dhritarashtra along with their legions of ally kings,
together with our leading warriors as well,
Are seen to be quickly entering Your frightful gaping mouths
which are full of horrible fangs.
...Bhishma, Drona...there, too, is the charioteer's son (Karna)....
Some of them are wedged between Your teeth,
their heads having been crushed.

### 28

*yatha nadinam bahavo'mbu-vegah / samudram evabhimukha dravanti*
*tatha tavami nara-loka-vira / vishanti vaktranyabhivijvalanti*

*yatha* > just as; *nadinam* > of rivers; *bahavah* > many; *ambu-vegah* > rapid
currents of water; *samudram* > ocean; *eva* > indeed; *abhimukhah* > facing
toward; *dravanti* > they flow; *tatha* > so also; *tava* > Your; *ami* > all these;

*nara-loka-virah* > heroes among the world's men, heroes of the mortal world; *vishanti* > they enter; *vaktrani* > mouths; *abhivijvalanti* > blazing forth.

**Just as the water-currents of many rivers**
**flow rapidly toward the ocean,**
**Indeed, so also do all these heroes among the world's men**
**enter into Your blazing mouths.**

**29**
*yatha pradiptam jvalanam patanga / vishanti nashaya samriddha-vegah*
*tathaiva nashaya vishanti lokas / tavapi vaktrani samriddha-vegah*

*yatha* > just as; *pradiptam* > glowing; *jvalanam* > a flame;
*patangah* > flying insects, moths; *vishanti* > they enter;
*nashaya* > to destruction; *samriddha-vegah* > very swiftly, with great speed; *tatha eva* > in exactly the same manner; *nashaya* > to annihilation; *vishanti* > they enter; *lokah* > people; *tava* > Your; *api* > thus; *vaktrani* > mouths; *samriddha-vegah* > rushing to succeed, hurrying to achieve.

**As moths swiftly enter a glowing fire**
**to meet with destruction,**
**In exactly the same manner do all these people enter Your mouths,**
**hurrying to achieve their own annihilation.**

**30**
*lelihyase grasamanah samantal / lokan samagran vadanair jvaladbhih*
*tejobhir apurya jagat samagram / bhasas tavograh pratapanti vishno*

*lelihyase* > You frequently lick; *grasamanah* > devouring; *samantat* > from one end to the other, completely; *lokan* > people; *samagran* > all; *vadanaih jvaladbhih* > with Your fiery mouths; *tejobhih* > with the radiance; *apurya* > filling; *jagat* > the world, the universe; *samagram* > the whole; *bhasah* > brightness; *tava* > Your; *ugrah* > fierce, intense; *pratapanti* > they consume with heat; *vishno* > O Vishnu.

**You are frequently licking all beings**
**before devouring them completely with Your fiery mouths.**
**O Vishnu, the intense brightness of Your radiance**
**is filling the whole universe and consuming it with its heat.**

The Sanskrit word *lih* simply means to lick; the word *leliha* connotes tasting or relishing the taste of what is licked, thereby poetically conveying the idea that the One relishes the taste of imagining Itself to be all the different people that It playfully appears as. Also, based on Krishna's statement back in verse 7 that Arjuna will see whatever he wishes to see within Him, another consideration here is that Arjuna is perceiving what he is describing based on the present condition and past conditioning of his particular body/mind system. It would thus follow that other expressions of the One perceiving the raw, all-inclusive potential of their own true nature would see and describe a great many things differently in accordance with their respective acquired natures and attendant desires.

**31**

*akhyahi me ko bhavan ugra-rupo / namo 'stu te deva-vara prasida*
*vijnatum ichchami bhavantam adyam / na hi prajanami tava pravrittim*

*akhyahi* > please tell; *me* > to me; *kah* > who; *bhavan* > Your lordship;
*ugra-rupah* > of dreadful form; *namah* > obeisances; *astu* > let there be
(conveying the sense of 'please accept this'); *te* > unto You;
*deva-vara* > whose excellence surpasses the celestials; *prasida* > please
be merciful; *vijnatum* > to understand; *ichchami* > I wish;
*bhavantam* > Your lordship; *adyam* > O primordial one; *na* > not;
*hi* > truly; *prajanami* > I comprehend; *tava* > Your; *pravrittim* > intention.

**Please tell me who You are, O Lord of dreadful form.**
**Let there be obeisances**
**unto You whose excellence surpasses all the combined celestials.**
**Please be merciful;**
**I wish to understand You, O primordial Lord,**
**because I truly cannot comprehend Your intention.**

**32**

*sri bhagavan uvacha:*
*kalo 'smi lokakshaya-krit pravriddho / lokan samahartum iha pravrittah*
*rite 'pi tvam na bhavishyanti sarve / ye 'vasthitah pratyanikeshu yodhah*

*sri bhagavan uvacha* > the resplendent Lord said; *kalah* > time; *asmi* > I am;
*loka-kshaya-krit* > the destroyer of worlds; *pravriddhah* > mighty;
*lokan* > people, community, troops; *samahartum* > to remove, to withdraw,
to annihilate; *iha* > here; *pravrittah* > set in motion, commenced, proceeding;
*rite api tvam* > even without you (meaning Arjuna's participation in
the upcoming battle); *na bhavishyanti* > they shall not exist
in the future; *sarve* > all; *ye* > who; *avasthitah* > arrayed;
*prati-anikeshu* > in the hostile opposing army; *yodhah* > warriors.

The resplendent Lord said:
I am Time, the mighty destroyer of worlds,
proceeding to remove the troops gathered here.
Even without your active participation,
None of the warriors arrayed within the hostile opposing army
shall survive [the upcoming battle].

It has been said by Martin Luther King, Jr. that "Power at its best is love implementing the demands of justice. Justice at its best is love correcting everything that stands against love."

### 33

*tasmat tvam uttishtha yasho labhasva / jitva shatrun bhunkshva rajyam samriddham*
*mayaivaite nihatah purvam eva / nimitta-matram bhava savyasachin*

*tasmat* > therefore; *tvam* > you; *uttishtha* > arise; *yashah* > fame;
*labhasva* > gain; *jitva* > conquering; *shatrun* > aggressive adversaries;
*bhunkshva* > enjoy; *rajyam* > kingdom; *samriddham* > flourishing; *maya* >
Me; *eva* > alone; *ete* > these; *nihatah* > struck down; *purvam* > already;
*eva* > indeed; *nimitta* > efficient cause, instrument; *matram* > mere;
*bhava* > do become; *savyasachin* > O ambidextrous archer.

**Therefore, arise and gain fame by conquering your aggressive adversaries**
**and enjoying a flourishing kingdom.**
**Indeed, they have already been struck down by Me alone,**
**So do just become a mere instrument [in My hands],**
**O ambidextrous archer.**

### 34

*dronam cha bhishmam cha jayadratham cha / karnam tathanyan api yodha-viran*
*maya hatams tvam jahi ma vyathishtha / yudhyasva jetasi rane sapatnan*

*dronam* > Drona; *cha* > and; *bhishmam* > Bhishma; *cha* > and;
*jayadratham* > Jayadratha ('one whose chariot brings victory,' the son-in-law
of Dhritarashtra who married his only daughter); *cha* > and; *karnam* > Karna;
*tatha* > as well; *anyan* > others; *api* > also; *yodha-viran* > warrior heroes;
*maya* > by Me; *hatan* > slain; *tvam* > you; *jahi* > slay; *ma* > do not;
*vyathishthah* > waver, hesitate; *yudhyasva* > just fight;
*jeta asi* > you will conquer; *rane* > in the battle; *sapatnan* > adversaries.

Drona and Bhishma and Jayadratha,
Karna and the other warrior heroes as well —
You will simply be slaying those who have already been slain by Me.
Therefore, do not hesitate to fight;
You will surely conquer your adversaries in battle.

### 35

*sanjaya uvacha:*
*etach chrutva vachanam keshavasya / kritanjalir vepamanah kiriti*
*namas-kritva bhuya evaha krishnam / sagadgadam bhita-bhitah pranamya*

*sanjayah uvacha* > Sanjaya said; *etat* > this; *shrutva* > having heard;
*vachanam* > words; *keshavasya* > of Krishna, the embodiment of the combined
characteristics of Brahma, Vishnu, and Shiva; *krita-anjalih* > he who
respectfully conjoined his palms; *vepamanah* > trembling; *kiriti* > Arjuna, who
wears a diadem; *namas-kritva* > making a reverential prostration; *bhuyah* >
again; *eva* > just so; *aha* > spoke; *krishnam* > to Krishna; *sa-gadgadam* > with a
faltering voice; *bhita-bhitah* > terrified; *pranamya* > bowing.

Sanjaya said:
Having heard these words of Krishna,
Arjuna respectfully conjoined his palms,
And trembling, made a reverential prostration.
Then, bowing once again in a terrified condition,
he spoke to Krishna with a faltering voice.

### 36

*arjuna uvacha:*
*sthane hrishikesha tava prakirtya / jagat prahrishyatyanurajyate cha*
*rakshamsi bhitani disho dravanti / sarve namasyanti cha siddha-sanghah*

*arjunah uvacha* > Arjuna said; *sthane* > it is befitting; *hrishika-isha* > O master of
all living beings' sense-organs; *tava* > Your; *prakirtya* > by the glories;
*jagat* > the universe; *prahrishyati* > it rejoices; *anurajyate* > it is delighted;
*cha* > and; *rakshamsi* > the demons; *bhitani* > fear-stricken, alarmed; *dishah* >
in all directions; *dravanti* > they flee; *sarve* > all; *namasyanti* > they bow in
respectful homage; *cha* > and; *siddha-sanghah* > groups of perfected beings.

Arjuna said:
It is befitting, O master of all sense-organs,
that the whole universe rejoices, delighted by Your glories.
Fear-stricken, the demons flee in all directions,
and groups of perfected beings bow in respectful homage.

What Arjuna sees before him here is a reflected portrayal of his own fear and respect.

37

*kasmach cha te na nameran mahatman / gariyase brahmano 'pyadi-kartre*
*ananta devesha jagan-nivasa / tvam aksharam sad-asat tat-param yat*

*kasmat* > why; *cha* > and; *te* > to You; *na* > not; *nameran* > they should bow in homage; *maha-atman* > O high-minded one, O magnanimous one, O noble one; *gariyase* > greater; *brahmanah* > than Lord Brahma; *api* > even; *adi-kartre* > to the original creator; *ananta* > O infinite one; *deva-isha* > O Lord of the celestials; *jagat-nivasa* > O abode of all worlds; *tvam* > You; *aksharam* > the imperishable Absolute; *sat* > that which presently exists; *asat* > that which does not exist; *tat-param yat* > which is superior to that.

**And why should they not bow in homage to You,**
**O magnanimous one who are even greater than Lord Brahma,**
**the original Creator?**
**O infinite one, Lord of the celestials, abode of all worlds —**
**As the imperishable Absolute,**
**You are that which presently exists (the manifest),**
**That which does not exist**
**(having passed away and being no longer manifest),**
**And That which is superior to both.**

38

*tvam adi-devah purushah puranas / tvam asya vishvasya param nidhanam*
*vettasi vedyam cha param cha dhama / tvaya tatam vishvam ananta-rupa*

*tvam* > You; *adi-devah* > the primal God; *purushah* > person; *puranah* > ancient; *tvam* > You; *asya vishvasya* > of this entire universe; *param* > supreme; *nidhanam* > the treasure-house; *vetta* > the knower; *asi* > You are; *vedyam* > the knowable; *cha* > and; *param* > ultimate; *cha* > and; *dhama* > home, sanctuary; *tvaya* > by You; *tatam* > permeated; *vishvam* > the whole universe; *ananta-rupa* > O one of countless forms.

**You are the primal God,**
**The most ancient person,**
**And the supreme treasure-house of this entire universe.**
**You are the knower, the knowable,**
**and the ultimate sanctuary.**
**The whole universe is permeated by You,**
**O one of countless forms.**

**39**

*vayur yamo 'gnir varunah shashankah / prajapatis tvam prapitamahash cha*
*namo namas te 'stu sahasra-kritvah / punash cha bhuyo 'pi namo namas te*

*vayuh* > Vayu, god of the air and wind; *yamah* > Yama, the celestial lord
of death; *agnih* > the fire-god Agni; *varunah* > Varuna, celestial king of
the oceans; *shasha-ankah* > 'the rabbit-marked one,' the moon-god Shashi;
*prajapatih* > 'lord of creatures' or 'master of progeny' (refers to Lord Brahma);
*tvam* > You; *prapitamahah* > the great-grandfather; *cha* > also; *namo namah* >
obeisance and obeisance; *te* > unto You; *astu* > let there be; *sahasra-kritvah* >
made a thousand times; *punah cha bhuyah* > again and again; *api* > also;
*namo namah* > repeated offering of respectful homage; *te* > unto You.

**You are Vayu, Yama, Agni, Varuna, and Shashi**
**(the air, death, fire, water, and the moon).**
**You are Lord Brahma (the 'grandfather' of all created beings),**
**and You are his father (Creator) as well.**
**Let there be obeisances made to You a thousand times!**
**Again and again I repeatedly offer my respectful homage unto You.**

**40**

*namah purastad atha prishthatas te / namo 'stu te sarvata eva sarva*
*ananta-viryamita-vikramas tvam / sarvam samapnoshi tato 'si sarvah*

*namah* > I bow; *purastat* > before, in the front; *atha* > but also;
*prishthatah* > to the back; *te* > to You; *namah astu* > let there be bowing;
*te* > to You; *sarvatah* > on every side; *eva* > indeed; *sarva* > O Totality;
*ananta* > unlimited; *virya* > valour, power; *amita* > immeasurable;
*vikramah* > power, prowess; *tvam* > You; *sarvam* > everything;
*samapnoshi* > completely concluded by You, perfectly resolved in You;
*tatah* > due to that, for that reason; *asi* > You are; *sarvah* > everything.

**I bow before You, but I also bow to Your back.**
**Indeed, let there be bowing to You on every side, O Totality!**
**O one with unlimited valour and immeasurable prowess,**
**Everything is perfectly resolved in You because You *are* everything.**

As Zen master Bankei has said, "All things are perfectly resolved in the
Unborn."

**41**

*sakheti matva prasabham yad uktam / he krishna he yadava he sakheti*
*ajanata mahimanam tavedam / maya pramadat pranayena vapi*

*sakha* > friend; *iti* > thus; *matva* > thinking, considering; *prasabham* > presumptuously; *yat* > which; *uktam* > expressed; *he krishna* > hey there, Krishna!; *he yadava* > hey there, Yadava (scion of the Yadu dynasty)!; *he sakhe* > hey there, pal!; *iti* > thus; *ajanata* > by not knowing; *mahimanam* > greatness; *tava* > Your; *idam* > this; *maya* > by me; *pramadat* > afflicted by giddiness or carelessness; *pranayena* > emboldened by love or affectionate familiarity; *va* > or; *api* > even.

**Regarding You as my friend,
I presumptuously called out to You:
"Hey there, Krishna!" "Hey, Yadava!" "Hey, pal!"
Not knowing Your greatness,
I did this afflicted by giddiness,
or even emboldened by affectionate familiarity.**

**42**

*yach chavahas'-artham asat-krito 'si / vihara-shayyasana-bhojaneshu
eko 'thava 'pyachyuta tat-samaksham / tat kshamaye tvam aham aprameyam*

*yat* > inasmuch as; *cha* > and; *avahasa-artham* > for the purpose of joking, in jest; *asat-kritah* > treated without the proper respect; *asi* > You were; *vihara* > while walking, playing, or engaging in recreation; *shayya* > lying down and resting; *asana* > sitting; *bhojaneshu* > while eating; *ekah* > alone; *atha va api* > or even; *achyuta* > O infallible one; *tat-samaksham* > before the eyes of other people; *tat* > that; *kshamaye* > I ask forgiveness; *tvam* > from You; *aham* > I; *aprameyam* > who are immeasurable.

**I joked with You and did not treat You with the proper respect
while we were engaged in recreational activities,
lying down to rest,
or sitting and eating —
Either alone together, or even in the presence of others.
O infallible, immeasurable one,
For all of that I beg forgiveness from You.**

**43**

*pitasi lokasya characharasya / tvam asya pujyas cha gurur gariyan
na tvat-samo 'styabhyadhikah kuto 'nyo / loka-traye 'pyapratima-prabhava*

*pita* > father; *asi* > You are; *lokasya* > of the entire world; *chara-acharasya* > of the moving and the unmoving; *tvam* > You; *asya* > of this; *pujyah* > to be worshipped; *cha* > and; *guruh* > spiritual preceptor;

*gariyan* > more important, more venerable; *na* > not;
*tvat-samah* > equivalent to You; *asti* > there is; *abhyadhikah* > superior;
*kutah* > how; *anyah* > other; *loka-traye* > in the three worlds;
*api* > even; *apratima-prabhava* > O one of incomparable glory.

**You are the father and worshipable spiritual preceptor**
**of the entire world of moving and unmoving beings,**
**And You are yet more venerable than that.**
**O one of incomparable glory,**
**There is no one who is Your equal anywhere in the three worlds,**
**So how can there be another who is greater?**

**44**

*tasmat pranamya pranidhaya kayam / prasadaye tvam aham isham idyam*
*piteva putrasya sakheva sakhyuh / priyah priyayarhasi deva sodhum*

*tasmat* > therefore; *pranamya* > bowing, offering of obeisance;
*pranidhaya* > prostrating; *kayam* > the body; *prasadaye tvam aham* > I request
Your grace, I beseech You for mercy; *isham* > Lord; *idyam* > praiseworthy;
*pita iva* > like a father; *putrasya* > to a son; *sakha iva* > like a friend;
*sakhyuh* > to a friend; *priyah* > a lover; *priyayah* > to a beloved;
*arhasi* > may You be pleased; *deva* > O God; *sodhum* > to tolerate, to pardon.

**Therefore, prostrating my body before You and offering obeisance,**
**I pray for Your grace, O most praiseworthy Lord.**
**As a father forgives his son,**
**As a friend forgives a friend,**
**And as a lover forgives a beloved —**
**May You also be pleased to forgive me, O Lord.**

**45**

*adrishta-purvam hrisheeto 'smi drishtva / bhayena cha pravyathitam mano me*
*tad eva me darshaya deva rupam / prasida devesha jagan-nivasa*

*adrishta-purvam* > not seen before; *hrisheetah* > delighted, thrilled;
*asmi* > I am; *drishtva* > seeing; *bhayena* > with fear; *cha* > and;
*pravyathitam* > trembling; *manah* > mind, heart; *me* > my;
*tat eva* > that very same (refers to Krishna's appearance prior to
exhibiting His universal form); *me* > to me; *darshaya* > show;
*deva* > O God; *rupam* > form; *prasida* > be gracious;
*deva-isha* > O Lord of the celestials; *jagat-nivasa* > abode of worlds.

Upon seeing what has not been seen before,
I am delighted, yet my heart still palpitates with fear.
Please be gracious and show me Your previous form,
O God, Lord of the celestials, abode of worlds...!

### 46
*kiritinam gadinam chakra-hastam / ichchami tvam drashtum aham tathaiva*
*tenaiva rupena chatur-bhujena / sahasra-baho bhava vishva-murte*

*kiritinam* > wearing a crown (meaning the particular one which Arjuna was familiar with and accustomed to seeing on Krishna in contradistinction to the innumerable different crowns he is seeing on the universal form for the first time); *gadinam* > wielding a club (meaning likewise as in regard to the crown); *chakra-hastam* > with disc in hand; *ichchami* > I wish; *tvam* > You; *drashtum* > to see; *aham* > I; *tatha eva* > in that very same manner (as Krishna was before); *tena* > that way; *eva* > only; *rupena* > with the appearance; *chatuh-bhujena* > with four arms; *sahasra-baho* > O thousand-armed one; *bhava* > become, exhibit, transform into; *vishva-murte* > O one whose form is the entire universe, O one whose form is all forms.

I wish to see You in the very same manner as You were before —
Wearing Your familiar crown,
and wielding Your usual club and disc in Your hands.
O thousand-armed one whose form is all forms,
Please exhibit that appearance with only four arms.

Arjuna previously addressed Krishna as Vishnu in verses 24 and 30, and the current verse especially indicates that seeing Krishna's four-armed form as Vishnu is as common and familiar to him as Krishna's two-armed form. One possible explanation for this may be found in earlier sections of the Mahabharata preceding the Bhagavad-Gita in which Arjuna is twice told, once by Lord Shiva and again by Krishna Himself, that he and Krishna had formerly appeared as the sages Nara and Narayana who resided together at Badrinath in the Himalayas. *Nara* means 'human,' and *Narayana* is one of the many names of Vishnu which means 'the refuge of humankind.'

### 47
*sri bhagavan uvacha:*
*maya prasannena tavarjunedam / rupam param darsheetam atma-yogat*
*tejomayam vishvam anantam adyam / yan me tvad anyena na drishta-purvam*

*sri bhagavan uvacha* > the effulgent Lord said; *maya* > by me; *prasannena* > by being pleased, by showing kindness; *tava* > toward you; *arjuna* > O Arjuna; *idam* > this; *rupam* > form; *param* > ultimate, maximum, most extreme; *darsheetam* > displayed, revealed; *atma-yogat* > by My own mystic potency; *tejah-mayam* > composed of luminous energy; *vishvam* > all-containing, all-inclusive; *anantam* > without beginning or end; *adyam* > primeval; *yat* > which; *me* > of Mine; *tvad anyena* > by anyone other than you; *na drishta-purvam* > not seen before.

**The effulgent Lord said:**
**Being pleased with you, O Arjuna,**
**I have displayed this ultimate form of Mine by My own mystic potency.**
**Composed of luminous energy,**
**It is primeval, without beginning or end, all-inclusive,**
**and has not been seen before by anyone else prior to you.**

**48**
*na veda-yajnadhyayanair na danair / na cha kriyabhir na tapobhir ugraih*
*evam-rupah shakya aham nri-loke / drashtum tvad anyena kuru-pravira*

*na* > neither; *veda-yajna* > by the sacrifice of reciting or memorizing the Vedas; *adhyayanaih* > by studying; *na* > nor; *danaih* > by the giving of charity; *na* > not; *cha* > and; *kriyabhih* > by the performance of ritual ceremonies; *na* > nor; *tapobhih* > by austerities; *ugraih* > severe; *evam-rupah* > in this particular form; *shakyah* > I can; *aham* > I; *nri-loke* > among human society; *drashtum* > to be seen; *tvad anyena* > by anyone other than you; *kuru-pravira* > O hero of the Kuru dynasty.

**Neither by studying the Vedas,**
**Nor by engaging in the sacrifice of reciting or memorizing them,**
**Nor by the giving of charity,**
**Nor by the performance of ritual ceremonies or severe austerities**
**Can I be seen in this particular form among human society**
**by anyone other than you, O hero of the Kuru dynasty.**

It may be considered that Krishna's statements in this and the previous verse are conflictive with earlier verses in the Mahabharata which describe His universal form being momentarily seen by a great many of the wicked Kauravas. It is said that when Krishna went to their court as an ambassador of peace to try to negotiate with them and prevent the war from taking place, Duryodhana and his men attempted to capture and imprison Him, but they could not do so because He exhibited some version of His universal form at that time. Additionally, Sanjaya described the universal form to King Dhritarashtra, and he later confirms in verse 18.77 that he had indeed seen it as well. So the words *evam-rupah* here, 'in this particular form,' distinguish Arjuna's unique vision of that form as he described it from what others had seen before or may currently be seeing, as also briefly indicated in the notes to verse 30. In regard to the universal form being seen by all the different varieties of celestials and demons in verses 21-22, that may be understood as part of Arjuna's particular vision as well. Yet even if that were actually happening, the phrase *nri-loke* specifies that what Arjuna was seeing could not be seen by anyone else among *human* society, this presumably being distinguished from what could be seen by the societies of the celestials and demons.

### 49

*ma te vyatha ma cha vimudha-bhavo / drishtva rupam ghoram idrin mamedam*
*vyapeta-bhih prita-manah punas tvam / tad eva me rupam idam prapashya*

*ma* > not; *te* > of you; *vyatha* > disturbed; *ma* > not; *cha* > and;
*vimudha-bhavah* > in a condition of perplexity; *drishtva* > by seeing;
*rupam* > a form; *ghoram* > terrific, terrifying, intense; *idrik* > such as this;
*mama* > of Mine; *idam* > this; *vyapeta-bhih* > with fear dispelled;
*prita-manah* > gladdened at heart; *punah* > once again; *tvam* > you;
*tat* > that; *eva* > just so, exactly so; *me rupam* > My (former)
appearance; *idam* > this; *prapashya* > behold.

**But you shall no longer be disturbed and perplexed**
**by seeing such an intense form of Mine as this.**
**Be relieved of fear and gladdened at heart**
**by once again beholding My former appearance.**

### 50

*sanjaya uvacha:*
*ityarjunam vasudevas tathoktva / svakam rupam darshayam asa bhuyah*
*ashvasayam asa cha bhitam enam / bhutva punah saumya-vapur mahatma*

*sanjayah uvacha* > Sanjaya said; *iti* > thus; *arjunam* > to Arjuna;
*vasudevah* > Krishna, the son of Vasudeva; *tatha* > in that way;
*uktva* > having spoken; *svakam rupam* > His own form;
*darshayam asa* > He revealed; *bhuyah* > once more; *ashvasayam asa* >
He comforted; *cha* > and; *bhitam* > the frightened one (Arjuna);
*enam* > this; *bhutva punah* > becoming once again, returning to;
*saumya* > gentle; *vapuh* > handsome appearance; *mahatma* > the exalted one.

Sanjaya said:
Having thus spoken to Arjuna in that way,
The exalted son of Vasudeva revealed His own [four-armed] form,
And He further comforted the frightened Arjuna
by once again returning to His gentle, handsome [two-armed] appearance.

### 51

*arjuna uvacha:*
*drishtvedam manusham rupam / tava saumyam janardana*
*idanim asmi samvrittah / sachetah prakritim gatah*

*arjunah uvacha* > Arjuna said; *drishtva* > seeing; *idam* > this;
*manusham* > humanlike; *rupam* > form; *tava* > of Yours; *saumyam* > like
Soma (referring to the cooling, pleasing effects of the moon);
*janardana* > Krishna, 'one who excites people'; *idanim* > now;
*asmi* > I am; *samvrittah* > composed; *sa-chetah* > with the mind;
*prakritim* > the natural condition or character; *gatah* > gone to.

Arjuna said:
O exciter of people,
Seeing this calming, pleasing humanlike form of Yours again,
I have now regained my composure,
with my mind restored to its normal condition.

### 52

*sri bhagavan uvacha:*
*sudurdarsham idam rupam / drishtavan asi yan mama*
*deva apyasya rupasya / nityam darshana-kankshinah*

*sri bhagavan uvacha* > the beautiful Lord (Krishna) said;
*sudurdarsham* > very difficult to look at, unpleasant or intolerable
to the eyes; *idam* > this; *rupam* > form; *drishtavan asi* > you had seen;
*yat* > which; *mama* > of Mine; *devah* > the celestials; *api* > nevertheless;
*asya rupasya* > of this very form; *nityam* > constantly;
*darshana* > a viewing of, a meeting or visit with;
*kankshinah* > wishing for, longing for.

The beautiful Lord Krishna said:
This [universal] form of Mine which you had seen
is indeed very difficult to look at;
Nevertheless, the celestials are constantly longing for a viewing
of that very form.

### 53
*naham vedair na tapasa / na danena na chejyaya*
*shakya evam-vidho drashtum / drishtavan asi mam yatha*

*na* > not; *aham* > I; *vedaih* > by study or recitation of the Vedas; *na* > not; *tapasa* > by the practice of rigorous austerities; *na* > not; *danena* > by the distribution of alms; *na* > not; *cha* > and; *ijyaya* > by the performance of ritual sacrifices; *shakyah* > I am able; *evam-vidhah* > in such a form or manner; *drashtum* > to be seen; *drishtavan asi* > you had seen; *mam* > Me; *yatha* > as.

**[Again I say that] neither by the study or recitation of the Vedas,**
**Nor by the practice of rigorous austerities,**
**Nor by the distribution of alms,**
**Nor by the performance of ritual sacrifices**
**Can I be seen in that specific [cosmic] form which you had seen Me.**

Perhaps the reason for Krishna's reiteration of verse 48 is to dissuade others who might invest a great deal of time, energy, and resources on the activities mentioned here in a futile attempt to replicate an experience which was solely Arjuna's alone.

### 54
*bhaktya tvananyaya shakya / aham evam-vidho'rjuna*
*jnatum drashtum cha tattvena / praveshtum cha parantapa*

*bhaktya* > by devotion; *tu* > but; *ananyaya* > unalloyed, undistracted; *shakyah aham* > I am able; *evam-vidhah* > in this way, whereby; *arjuna* > O Arjuna; *jnatum* > to be known; *drashtum* > to be seen; *cha* > and; *tattvena* > into the truth; *praveshtum* > to enter; *cha* > and; *parantapa* > O chastiser of foes.

**But by way of unalloyed devotion,**
**One can enter into the truth**
**whereby I am able to be seen and known,**
**O Arjuna, chastiser of foes.**

Although intense mystical experiences *could* potentially bring about inner transformation or awakening, there is no guaranteed cause-and-effect relationship between the two. Duryodhana momentarily saw some version of the universal form prior to his arrival at Kurukshetra, yet nowhere in the Mahabharata is it indicated that he became more open-hearted or gained any deeper insight into the nature of Reality as a result of that experience.

By contrast, prior to Arjuna's experience of having seen the universal form, in verse 1 of this chapter he tells Krishna: "By hearing the teachings imparted by You, my confusion is gone." Hence Krishna's recommendation in verse 4.34 is simply to "inquire sincerely from and humbly offer service to those with clear, undistorted perception."

**55**

*mat-karma-krin mat-paramo / mad-bhaktah sanga-varjitah*
*nirvairah sarva-bhuteshu / yah sa mam eti pandava*

*mat-karma-krit* > performing actions for Me; *mat-paramah* > considering Me to be supreme; *mat-bhaktah* > devoted to Me; *sanga-varjitah* > abandoning attachment; *nirvairah* > without ill will; *sarva-bhuteshu* > toward all living beings; *yah* > who; *sah* > that one; *mam* > to Me; *eti* > one comes; *pandava* > O son of Pandu.

**One who, regarding Me as supreme,**
**performs all actions for Me;**
**Who, abandoning all attachments, is devoted to Me;**
**And who is without ill will toward any living being—**
**Such a one comes to Me, O son of Pandu.**

*Mat-karma-krit*, 'performing actions for Me,' means functioning as a clear conduit for universal Intelligence in a way which is whole-life-centered rather than egoically self-centered, as amply discussed throughout Chapters Two through Five. And *mat-paramah* may be read as considering the Absolute or universal Intelligence to be the supreme principle, ideal, way, refuge, or realization.

*om tat saditi srimad bhagavad-gita / supanishatsu brahma-vidyayam / yoga-shastre*
*srikrishnarjuna samvade / vishvarupa-darshana-yogo nam' aikadasho 'dhyayah*

From the Ambrosial Song of God—
A conversation between Krishna and Arjuna
which is a Upanishad (confidential sharing)
of wisdom-teachings regarding the Absolute
And a scripture concerning Self-realization—
Thus ends the Eleventh Chapter entitled Vishvarupa-darshana-yoga,
Recognizing Divine Unicity By Way of Beholding Its Universal Form.

# Chapter Twelve

## Bhakti-yoga
### (Recognizing Divine Unicity By Way of Devotion)

"Lovers share a sacred decree — to seek the Beloved.
They roll head over heels,
rushing toward the Beautiful One like a torrent of water.
In truth, everyone is a shadow of the Beloved —
Our seeking is His seeking, our words are His words.
At times we flow toward the Beloved like a dancing stream.
At times we are still water held in His pitcher.
At times we boil in a pot turning to vapor —
that is the job of the Beloved.
He breathes into my ear until my soul takes on His fragrance.
He is the soul of my soul — how can I escape?
But why would any soul in this world want to escape from the Beloved?
He will melt your pride making you thin as a strand of hair,
Yet do not trade, even for both worlds, one strand of His hair.
We search for Him here and there while looking right at Him.
Sitting by His side we ask, 'O Beloved, where is the Beloved?'
Enough with such questions! —
Let silence take you to the core of life.
All your talk is worthless
when compared to one whisper of the Beloved."   — Jalal ad-Din Rumi

"My rich and virtuous Lord of Srirangam
Who owns this entire ocean-swept Earth and sky
Has now made His possessions complete
With the bracelet which I wore on my wrist!"   — Srimati Andal

### 1
*arjuna uvacha:*
*evam satata-yukta ye / bhaktas tvam paryupasate*
*ye chapyaksharam avyaktam / tesham ke yoga-vittamah*

*arjuna uvacha* > Arjuna said; *evam* > thus, as such; *satata* > ever, constantly; *yuktah* > absorbed, engaged, intent upon; *ye* > who; *bhaktah* > devoted; *tvam* > You; *paryupasate* > they worship; *ye* > who; *cha* > and; *api* > only; *aksharam avyaktam* > the unalterable Unmanifest; *tesham* > among them (the worshippers); *ke* > who; *yoga* > of recognizing divine unicity; *vit-tamah* > the greater understanding, the superior perspective or approach.

Arjuna inquired:
Among those who are ever engaged in devotedly worshipping You as such
(with form, as a manifest personification of Spirit)
And [those who worship] only the changeless Unmanifest,
Which type of worshipper has the superior approach
in regard to recognizing divine unicity (Yoga)?

2

*sri bhagavan uvacha:*
*mayy aveshya mano ye mam / nitya-yukta upasate*
*shraddhaya parayopetas / te me yuktatama matah*

*sri bhagavan uvacha* > the majestic Lord (Krishna) said; *mayi* > in Me;
*aveshya* > entering, absorbing, settling; *manah* > the mind; *ye* > who;
*mam* > Me; *nitya* > perpetually; *yuktah* > engaged, intent upon; *upasate* > they
worship; *shraddhaya paraya* > with the greatest faith; *upetah* > endowed;
*te* > they; *me* > to Me; *yukta-tamah* > most aligned; *matah* > considered to be.

The majestic Lord Krishna said:
Those who, with a mind absorbed in Me,
Are ever engaged in worshipping Me
endowed with the greatest faith —
They are considered to be most aligned with Me.

3-4

*ye tvaksharam anirdeshyam / avyaktam paryupasate*
*sarvatra-gam achintyam cha / kutastham achalam dhruvam*

*sanniyamyendriya-gramam / sarvatra sama-buddhayah*
*te prapnuvanti mam eva / sarva-bhuta-hite ratah*

*ye* > who; *tu* > but; *aksharam* > imperishable; *anirdeshyam* > indefinable;
*avyaktam* > unmanifest; *paryupasate* > they worship; *sarvatra-gam* > 'going
everywhere,' omnipresent; *achintyam* > inconceivable; *cha* > and;
*kutastham* > situated above or beyond all things, transcendent;
*achalam* > unmoving; *dhruvam* > stable, the unchanging constant;

*sanniyamya* > restricting, regulating; *indriya-gramam* > the collective senses;
*sarvatra* > at all times, in all situations; *sama-buddhayah* > equanimous;
*te* > they; *prapnuvanti* > they reach; *mam* > me; *eva* > certainly, alone;
*sarva-bhuta-hite* > in the welfare of all sentient beings;
*ratah* > intent upon, dedicated to, delighting in.

But those who worship the imperishable, indefinable,
unmanifest, omnipresent, inconceivable, transcendent,
unmoving, unchanging Constant —
Who, regulating their collective senses,
Are even-minded in all situations
and joyfully dedicated to the welfare of all sentient beings —
They certainly also reach Me.

### 5

*klesho 'dhikataras tesham / avyaktasakta-chetasam*
*avyakta hi gatir duhkham / dehavadbhir avapyate*

*kleshah* > affliction, distress; *adhika-tarah* > more, surpassing; *tesham* > of them;
*avyakta* > the unmanifest aspect of Spirit; *asakta* > attached; *chetasam* > of the
minds; *avyakta* > the unmanifest; *hi* > surely, indeed; *gatih* > the way, the
path, the manner of going; *duhkham* > difficult, troublesome, uncomfortable;
*deha-vadbhih* > by those identified with a body; *avapyate* > it is found.

**The tribulation is greater**
**for those whose minds are attached to the Unmanifest.**
**For those identified with a body,**
**It is found that the path to [realization of oneself as] the Unmanifest**
**is indeed difficult.**

There are certain deeply ingrained and strongly held beliefs which create
difficulty in realizing one's true nature. One of them is that realization can
occur only after one has experienced sufficient difficulty, and another is that
it is possible only after a very long period of time, perhaps even numerous
bodies. Yet if the absolute One-without-a-second is unborn, timeless, and
ever-present expressing as all that is — including as the one aspiring for
realization — then it would seem that the firm conviction that "Realization
can't happen *now*; only in the future *if I*...." would serve as a fitting enough
lynchpin for a substantial portion of the tribulation which Krishna speaks
of here. What has been experienced, however, is that such tribulation can
be considerably diminished with the gentle setting aside of all pre-conceived
ideas of what Self-realization should look like, what it should feel like,
what should cause it, how long it should take, etcetera. Realization unfolds
in a uniquely different way in each body/mind system, with no factory-
assembly-line type of replication involved.

**6-7**

*ye tu sarvani karmani / mayi sannyasya mat-parah*
*ananyenaiva yogena / mam dhyayanta upasate*

*tesham aham samuddharta / mrityu-samsara-sagarat*
*bhavami nachirat partha / mayy avesheeta-chetasam*

*ye* > who; *tu* > but; *sarvani* > all; *karmani* > actions, doings; *mayi* > to Me;
*sannyasya* > renouncing, entrusting; *mat-parah* > considering Me to be
the Absolute; *ananyena* > not directed elsewhere, without distraction,
singularly focused; *eva* > alone; *yogena* > by such engagement;
*mam* > Me; *dhyayantah* > meditating upon; *upasate* > they worship;

*tesham* > of them; *aham* > I; *samuddharta* > the extractor, the 'out-lifter'
(connoting a rescuer); *mrityu* > death; *samsara* > the dreamlike illusion
of wandering or passing from one state of being to another;
*sagarat* > from the ocean; *bhavami* > I am; *na chirat* > soon, before long;
*partha* > O son of Pritha; *mayi* > in Me; *avesheeta-chetasam* > of
those whose conscious attention is fully absorbed.

**But for those with attention fully absorbed in Me, O son of Pritha —**
**Who, considering Me to be the Absolute,**
**entrust all actions to Me,**
**Worshipping by engaging in singularly-focused meditation**
**upon Me alone —**
**For them I am soon the rescuer from the ocean of death**
**and from the dream of passing from one state of being to another.**

Some other definitions of the word *sannyasa* are 'complete exhaustion'
and 'throwing down,' connoting that when there is complete exhaustion
in the struggle to maintain the facade of separate selfhood, this struggle is
dropped. When it is devoid of any sense of calculatedly *doing* the dropping,
it represents all actions being entrusted to the Absolute.

**8**

*mayy eva mana adhatsva / mayi buddhim niveshaya*
*nivasishyasi mayy eva / ata urdhvam na samshayah*

*mayi* > in Me; *eva* > alone; *manah* > mind; *adhatsva* > keep; *mayi* > in Me;
*buddhim* > intellect; *niveshaya* > settle; *nivasishyasi* > you shall
dwell; *mayi* > in Me; *eva* > just so, in the same manner;
*atah urdhvam* > henceforth; *na samshayah* > without a doubt.

Keep your mind immersed in Me alone,
settling your intellect in Me as well.
In the same manner you will henceforth dwell in Me
[after dissociation from the body];
Of this there is no doubt.

### 9

*atha chittam samadhatum / na shaknoshi mayi sthiram*
*abhyasa-yogena tato / mam ichchaptum dhananjaya*

*atha* > or if; *chittam* > attention, observation, what is noticed;
*samadhatum* > to settle, to resolve; *na* > not; *shaknoshi* > you are able;
*mayi* > in Me; *sthiram* > firmly, calmly, lastingly; *abhyasa-yogena* > by
the repeated practice of meditation (as described in verses 6.10-14);
*tatah* > then; *mam* > Me; *ichcha* > have the wish or the intention;
*aptum* > to reach, to arrive at; *dhananjaya* > O winner of wealth.

Or if you are not able to keep your attention firmly settled in Me,
Then have the intention to reach [stability of attention in] Me
by the repeated practice of awareness meditation,
O winner of wealth.

### 10

*abhyase 'pyasamartho 'si / mat-karma-paramo bhava*
*mad-artham api karmani / kurvan siddhim avapsyasi*

*abhyase* > in that type of practice; *api* > also; *asamarthah asi* > you are unable;
*mat-karma* > My work; *paramah bhava* > become intent upon; *mat-artham* > for
fulfilling My purposes; *api* > even; *karmani* > such activities; *kurvan* > carrying
out; *siddhim* > perfection; *avapsyasi* > you will reach, you will find.

If you are also unable to engage in that type of practice,
then simply become intent upon carrying out My work,
For even by [serving as an instrument in] activities
which fulfill My purposes,
you will attain perfection.

In determining some indication of what are here referred to as Krishna's
work and purposes, in verse 4.8 He stated that they entail supporting what
is true and authentic; removing what is false and produces suffering; and
reestablishing the principles of conscious living in relationship to all of life.

He further stated in verse 11.32 that on this particular occasion, His purpose is to remove the hostile troops of Kauravas arrayed at Kurukshetra, this being 'for the sake of seeing to the maintenance and protection of the general populace' (verse 3.20). Hence His polite request that Arjuna just become an instrument in His hands in verse 11.33.

**11**

*athaitad apyashakto 'si / kartum mad-yogam ashritah*
*sarva-karma-phala-tyagam / tatah kuru yatatmavan*

*atha* > or if; *etat* > this; *api* > even; *ashaktah* > unable; *asi* > you are; *kartum* > to do; *mad-yogam* > 'My yoga' (refers to the performance of karma-yoga as taught by Krishna in Chapter Three); *ashritah* > resorting to, relying upon, taking shelter in; *sarva-karma* > of all activities; *phala* > the fruits (results); *tyagam* > giving up, leaving aside, donating, distributing; *tatah* > then; *kuru* > act; *yata-atma-van* > with self-restraint.

**Or if you are unable to do even this,**
**Then you can still rely upon engaging in karma-yoga**
**(general selfless work) in the way that I taught to you —**
**Acting with self-restraint and letting go of all [expectations**
**in regard to] the results of your activities.**

An alternate reading of the word *tyagam* here as either 'gifting,' 'donating,' or 'distributing' would mean that Arjuna and others who were unable to directly 'carry out Krishna's work' by acting in accordance with the immediate necessity of the moment could then do whatever work they wished to do and distribute in charity whatever fruits came of that work, thereby supporting the whole of life in a more general way.

**12**

*shreyo hi jnanam abhyasaj / jnanad dhyanam vishishyate*
*dhyanat karma-phala-tyagas / tyagach chantir anantaram*

*shreyah* > better; *hi* > certainly; *jnanam* > genuine inner knowing; *abhyasat* > than engaging in practices, than habitual repetition of a formalized practice; *jnanat* > than theoretical knowledge, than knowledge which has been learned but not realized; *dhyanam* > meditation (as described in verses 6.10-14); *vishishyate* > it is better; *dhyanat* > than meditation; *karma-phala-tyagah* > relinquishing the fruits (results) of actions; *tyagat* > by such giving up, by such resigning; *shantih* > peace; *anantaram* > immediately.

Genuine inner knowing is certainly better than engagement in practices
[for the achieving of something which one feels is lacking];
Yet [dedication to the practice of] awareness meditation is better
than [living with] knowledge [which has been learned but not realized].
Better than practicing meditation
[as a means to a particular result, however,]
is relinquishing [all interest in regard to] the results of actions,
For such surrendering leads to immediate peace.

### 13-14

*adveshta sarva-bhutanam / maitrah karuna eva cha*
*nirmamo nirahamkarah / sama-duhkha-sukhah kshami*

*santooshtah satatam yogi / yatatma dridha-nishchayah*
*mayy arpita-mano-buddhir / yo mad-bhaktah sa me priyah*

*adveshta* > one who is without hatred; *sarva-bhutanam* > for all living
beings; *maitrah* > friendly; *karunah* > compassionate; *eva* > truly; *cha* > and;
*nirmamah* > free from the sense of being the possessor of anything;
*nirahamkarah* > free from the sense of being the independently-
functioning doer of any actions; *sama* > poised with equanimity;
*duhkha* > in adversity; *sukhah* > in jubilance; *kshami* > patient, forgiving;

*santooshtah* > content; *satatam* > always; *yogi* > the yogi;
*yata-atma* > self-disciplined; *dridha* > stable, durable;
*nishchayah* > resolution, determination; *mayi* > to Me;
*arpita* > entrusted; *manah-buddhih* > mind and intellect;
*yah* > who; *mat-bhaktah* > devoted to Me;
*sah* > that one; *me* > to Me; *priyah* > very dear.

One who is friendly and truly compassionate to all —
Devoid of hatred for any living being,
Free from the sense of doership and proprietorship,
And poised with equanimity
whether experiencing jubilance or adversity —
Who is patient, forgiving, ever content,
Self-disciplined, firmly resolved,
And devoted to Me with mind and intellect entrusted to Me —
Such a yogi is very dear to Me.

### 15

*yasman nodvijate loko / lokan nodvijate cha yah*
*harshamarsha-bhayodvegair / mukto yah sa cha me priyah*

*yasmat* > from whom; *na* > neither; *udvijate* > one disturbs; *lokah* > the world;
*lokat* > from the world; *na* > nor; *udvijate* > one receives disturbance;
*cha* > and; *yah* > who; *harsha* > excitement; *amarsha* > impatience;
*bhaya* > fear; *udvegaih* > worrying; *muktah* > freed; *yah* > who;
*sah* > that one; *cha* > also; *me* > to Me; *priyah* > very dear.

**One who neither disturbs the world**
**nor is disturbed by the world,**
**Who is free from excitement, impatience, fear, and worrying —**
**That one is also very dear to Me.**

**16**
*anapekshah shuchir daksha / udasino gata-vyathah*
*sarvarambha-parityagi / yo mad-bhaktah sa me priyah*

*anapekshah* > free from expectations of or dependence upon people,
things, or events being a particular way; *shuchih* > pure, clear, innocent;
*dakshah* > capable of functioning well in all situations or in many different
capacities, resourceful; *udasinah* > 'sitting apart' impartially without
a vested interest, situated neutrally without a preference or prejudice;
*gata-vyathah* > free from volatility or irritability; *sarva-arambha* > all endeavors,
all self-exertion; *parityagi* > giving up, leaving; *yah* > who;
*mat-bhaktah* > devoted to Me; *sah* > that one; *me* > to Me; *priyah* > very dear.

**One who is free from dependence**
**upon life-situations being a particular way**
**And is capable of functioning well in all situations —**
**Who is innocent, impartial, free from volatility,**
**And has given up all [self-interested] endeavors**
**in favor of being devoted to Me —**
**That one is very dear to Me.**

The innocence mentioned here poetically connotes allowing each moment to
be directly experienced without 'defilement' by conditioned thought-patterns.

**17**
*yo na hrishyati na dveshti / na shochati na kankshati*
*shubhashubha-parityagi / bhaktiman yah sa me priyah*

*yah* > who; *na* > neither; *hrishyati* > one revels; *na* > nor;
*dveshti* > one despises; *na* > not; *shochati* > one laments; *na* > nor;
*kankshati* > one craves; *shubha-ashubha* > good and bad;

*parityagi* > giving up, leaving; *bhaktiman* > full of devotion;
*yah* > who; *sah* > that one; *me* > to Me; *priyah* > very dear.

**One who neither revels nor despises,**
**Who neither laments nor craves,**
**And who, full of devotion,**
**Gives up [all preconceived ideas about what is] good and bad —**
**That one is very dear to Me.**

### 18-19

*samah shatrau cha mitre cha / tatha manapamanayoh*
*sheetoshna-sukha-duhkheshu / samah sanga-vivarjitah*

*tulya-ninda-stutir mauni santooshto yena kenachit*
*aniketah sthira-matir bhaktiman me priyo narah*

*samah* > equal; *shatrau* > toward an enemy; *cha* > and; *mitre* > toward a friend;
*cha* > and; *tatha* > likewise; *mana-apamanayoh* > upon being respected or
disrespected; *sheeta* > cold; *ushna* > heat; *sukha* > ease; *duhkheshu* > difficulty;
*samah* > even-minded; *sanga-vivarjitah* > free from attachment;

*tulya* > the same; *ninda* > criticism, defamation; *stutih* > eulogy;
*mauni* > in the condition of a sage or sagess who is either altogether silent or
who is generally silent and speaks only what is necessary when necessary;
*santooshtah* > content; *yena kenachit* > with whatever is, with all
that is as it is; *aniketah* > having no singular fixed residence;
*sthira-matih* > unshakeable resolve; *bhaktiman* > filled with love;
*me* > to Me; *priyah* > very dear; *narah* > a person.

**One who views and treats alike both friend and enemy;**
**Who is the same — even-minded and free from attachment —**
**Whether experiencing heat or cold, ease or difficulty,**
**whether being respected or disrespected, praised or criticized;**
**Who speaks only what is necessary when necessary,**
**Is without a singular fixed residence,**
**and is content with all that is as it is;**
**Who is filled with love**
**and endowed with an unshakeable resolve —**
**Such a person is indeed very dear to Me.**

**20**

*ye tu dharmyamritam idam / yathoktam paryupasate*
*shraddadhana mat-parama / bhaktas te 'tiva me priyah*

*ye* > who; *tu* > but then; *dharmya-amritam* > the ambrosial principles
of righteousness or religion, the immortal principles of living consciously
in accordance with Life-centered values; *idam* > this; *yatha* > as, in that
manner; *uktam* > stated, taught; *paryupasate* > they honor, they accept;
*shraddadhanah* > fully imbued with faith or trust; *mat-paramah* > regarding
Me as the supreme authority, ideal, way, refuge, or realization;
*bhaktah te* > those devoted ones; *ativa* > exceedingly; *me* > to Me; *priyah* > dear.

**But then, all those devoted ones who, regarding Me as supreme,**
**Accept with wholehearted trust**
**these immortal principles of conscious living as I have described them**
**Are exceedingly dear to Me.**

*om tat saditi srimad bhagavad-gita / supanishatsu brahma-vidyayam*
*yoga-shastre srikrishnarjuna samvade / bhakti-yogo nama dvadasho 'dhyayah*

From the Ambrosial Song of God —
A conversation between Krishna and Arjuna
which is a Upanishad (confidential sharing)
of wisdom-teachings regarding the Absolute
And a scripture concerning Self-realization —
Thus ends the Twelfth Chapter entitled Bhakti-yoga,
Recognizing Divine Unicity By Way of Devotion.

## Chapter Thirteen

# Kshetra-kshetrajna-vibhaga-yoga
### (Recognizing Divine Unicity By Way of Discerning
### The Field of Experience From Its Perceiver)

"Knowledge is dependent on the Knower for its existence. The Knower does not require any tests for knowing Its own existence. The Knower therefore is the only Reality behind knowledge and objects. That which is self-evident without the necessity to be proved is alone real; not so other things. ...Objects and their knowledge are only reflections in the eternal, self-luminous, supreme Consciousness which is the same as the Knower and which alone is real. The doubt that the reflection should be of all objects simultaneously without reference to time and place (contrary to our experience) need not arise because time and space are themselves knowable concepts and are equally reflections. ...Therefore, prince, realize with a still mind your own true nature which is the one pure, undivided Consciousness underlying the restless mind which is composed of the whole universe in all its diversity."
— Princess Hemalekha, *Tripura Rahasya* 9.88-92

"There must be a seer for objects to be seen. Find out the seer first. Why worry yourself with what will be in the hereafter? What does it matter if the world is perceived or not? Have you lost anything when there is no such perception in your sleep? The appearance or disappearance of the world is immaterial. ...Take the instance of the cinema. There are pictures moving. Try to take hold of them. What do you hold? Only the screen. Let the picture disappear. What remains over? The screen again. So also here; even when the world appears, see to whom it appears. Hold the substratum. Once the substratum is held, what does it matter if the world appears or disappears? ...The world and the mind arise and set together as one; but of the two, the world owes its appearance to the mind alone. That alone is the Real in which this pair, the world and the mind, has its risings and settings; that Reality is the one infinite Consciousness having neither rising nor setting."
— Sri Ramana Maharshi

### 1
*arjuna uvacha:*
*prakritim purusham chaiva / kshetram kshetra-jnam eva cha*
*etad veditum ichchami / jnanam jneyam cha keshava*

*sri bhagavan uvacha:*
*idam shariram kaunteya / kshetram ityabhidhiyate*
*etad yo vetti tam prahuh / kshetrajna iti tad-vidah*

*arjunah uvacha* > Arjuna said; *prakritim* > Nature; *purusham* > Spirit expressing via personification; *cha* > and; *eva* > certainly; *kshetram* > the field (here specifically referring to the field of experience); *kshetra-jnam* > the perceiver of the field; *eva cha* > as well as; *etat* > this; *veditum* > to know; *ichchami* > I wish; *jnanam* > true wisdom; *jneyam* > that which is to be inquired about or ascertained; *cha* > and; *keshava* > O vanquisher of the Keshi demon (Krishna).

*sri bhagavan uvacha* > the exalted one (Krishna) said; *idam* > this; *shariram* > the vessel comprising the external physical body and the subtle inner body; *kaunteya* > O son of Kunti (Arjuna); *kshetram* > the field (of experience); *iti* > thus; *abhidhiyate* > it is named, it is called; *etat* > this; *yah vetti tam* > the one who knows, perceives, or experiences; *prahuh* > they call it; *kshetra-jnah* > the knower, perceiver, or experiencer of the field; *iti* > thus; *tat-vidah* > those who are versed in this subject matter.

**Arjuna said:**
**O vanquisher of the Keshi demon,**
**I wish to know more about Nature**
**and certainly about pure Spirit expressing via personification,**
**As well as about the field of experience and the perceiver of that field,**
**True wisdom, and that which is to be inquired about.**

**The exalted Krishna said:**
**This body/mind vessel is called the field of experience, O son of Kunti.**
**The one who experiences this is called the perceiver of the field**
**by those who are versed in this subject matter.**

The body/mind instrument is poetically referred to as a field because within it the seeds of actions are sown and their results are reaped.

**2**

*kshetra-jnam chapi mam viddhi / sarva-kshetreshu bharata*
*kshetra-kshetrajnayor jnanam / yat taj jnanam matam mama*

*kshetra-jnam* > the perceiver of the field; *cha* > and; *api* > assuredly; *mam* > Me; *viddhi* > please know; *sarva-kshetreshu* > in all fields of experience; *bharata* > O scion of Bharata; *kshetra* > of the field; *kshetra-jnayoh* > of the perceiver of the field; *jnanam* > knowing; *yat* > which; *tat* > that; *jnanam* > true wisdom; *matam* > considered; *mama* > by Me.

**And know Me (omnipresent Consciousness)**
**to assuredly be the Perceiver of the field in all fields of experience,**
**O scion of Bharata,**
**For I consider knowing [the truth in regard to] the field and its Perceiver**
**to be true wisdom.**

This verse recalls verse 9.24, in which Krishna says that He, the *prabhuh* (Lord, infinite Consciousness), is truly the only *bhokta* (experiencer or enjoyer) of all sacrifices. The teaching in this chapter is best assimilated with clarity by remembering Krishna's statement in verse 9.19 that *sad asach chaham arjuna —* "I am both the Real and the dreamlike, O Arjuna." This reminds us that even in the discerning of the field of experience from its Perceiver, that Perceiver never loses or deviates from Its nondual nature. That the Absolute is unchanging has already been established in numerous verses such as 2.25, 4.6, 7.13, and 7.24, and we may also note the words *abhidhiyate* ('it is called' [the field]), and *prahuh* ('they call it' [the perceiver]) used in the previous verse. From this it can be understood that what is generally referred to as the apparently dual Perceiver and perceived is actually only the singularity of *perceiving.* When, within the one omnipresent Awareness, the components of Its Nature are set in motion by the sudden discovery that 'I am,' there is then the utilization of words such as 'knower,' 'perceiver,' or 'experiencer' for discerning That which is unborn and unchanging from that which It *appears as.* When infinite Consciousness appears as the born and ever-changing universe, there aren't 'two things' present, just as in the often-cited example, there simply aren't two things present when in the darkness of night a piece of thick rope appears to be a snake.

**3**
*tat kshetram yach cha yadrik cha / yad-vikari yatash cha yat*
*sa cha yo yat-prabhavash cha / tat samasena me shrinu*

*tat* > this; *kshetram* > the field of experience; *yat* > what; *cha* > and; *yadrik* > of what nature; *cha* > and; *yat* > what; *vikari* > transformations, modifications; *yatah* > from where; *cha* > and; *yat* > what; *sah* > that one (the Perceiver); *cha* > and; *yah* > who; *yat* > what; *prabhavah* > power, influence; *cha* > and; *tat* > that; *samasena* > in brief; *me* > from Me; *shrinu* > do hear.

**What this field of experience is**
**and what its nature is —**
**What transformations it undergoes**
**and what causes them —**

Who the Perceiver of the field is
and what that one's influence is —
Do hear in brief about that from Me.

**4**
*rishibhir bahudha gitam / chandobhir vividhaih prithak*
*brahma-sutra-padaish chaiva / hetumadbhir vinishchitaih*

*rishibhih* > by the sages, by the seer-poets; *bahudha* > in many ways;
*gitam* > sung, recited; *chandobhih* > with the hymns of the Vedas;
*vividhaih* > of different kinds; *prithak* > individually, respectively;
*brahma-sutra* > in the aphorisms regarding pure Spirit (refers to passages
of the Upanishads); *padaih* > verses; *cha* > and; *eva* > indeed;
*hetu-madbhih* > accompanied by reasoning, provided with reasonable
evidence; *vinishchitaih* > with what has been conclusively
ascertained, with settled or well-established conclusions.

**The individual aspects [of this wisdom]**
**Have been recited by the sages in many ways**
**with different kinds of hymns found throughout the Vedas;**
**And verses about Brahman in passages of the Upanishads**
**are accompanied by reasoning and well-established conclusions.**

Although the words *brahma-sutra-padaih* understandably suggest 'in the
verses of the *Brahma-sutras*,' research scholars have determined, based on
that scripture's arguments with various schools of thought, that it could not
have been written before the sixth century A.D., thereby placing its date of
authorship at least 1000 years after that of the Bhagavad-Gita.

**5-6**
*maha-bhutanyahamkaro / buddhir avyaktam eva cha*
*indriyani dashaikam cha / pancha chendriya-gocharah*

*ichcha dveshah sukham duhkham / sanghatash chetana dhritih*
*etat kshetram samasena / savikaram udahritam*

*maha-bhutani* > the great elements; *ahamkarah* > egoism, the sense that 'I am
the doer'; *buddhih* > intellect; *avyaktam* > dormant Nature as pure potentiality;
*eva* > indeed; *cha* > and; *indriyani* > the sense-organs; *dasha-ekam* > these
ten plus one (the mind); *cha* > and; *pancha* > five more; *cha* > also;
*indriya-gocharah* > the scope of phenomena perceivable through the senses;

*ichcha* > attraction; *dveshah* > aversion; *sukham* > happiness; *duhkham* > misery; *sanghatah* > the aggregate of the elements' interactions; *chetana* > sentience; *dhritih* > will; *etat* > this; *kshetram* > the field of experience; *samasena* > in brief; *sa-vikaram* > along with its modifications; *udahritam* > described.

**The great elements, egoism, the intellect,**
**dormant Nature as pure potentiality,**
**The ten sense-organs and the mind,**
**The scope of [physical and subtle] phenomena perceivable**
**through the senses,**
**Attraction, aversion, happiness, misery,**
**Sentience, will (willfulness/willingness),**
**and the aggregate of interactions between all these —**
**This is a brief description of the field of experience**
**along with its modifications.**

In verse 5 we find the 24 principles which are enumerated in the Sankhya system. Krishna had previously mentioned the five 'great elements' — earth, water, fire, air, and ether — and three more — mind, intellect, and egoism — in verse 7.4. The ten sense-organs consist of five *jnanendriyas* or knowledge-gathering senses — the eyes, ears, nose, tongue, and skin; and five *karmendriyas* or organs of action, which are the hands, feet, larynx, genitals, and anus. The five *tanmatras* or subtle elements which are manifest as the scope of sense-objects are sights, sounds, smells, tastes, and sensations to the touch. These 23 plus dormant Nature as pure potentiality comprise the 24 principles of evolution. When the unconditional, joyous love known as Purusha 'embraces' Its own Nature known as Prakriti in the natural energetic momentum inherent in pure, innocent Aliveness, Its infinite potential for expression via personification manifests as every form of life.

**7-11**
*amanitvam adambhitvam / ahimsa kshantir arjavam*
*acharyopasanam shaucham / sthairyam atma-vinigrahah*

*indriyartheshu vairagyam / anahamkara eva cha*
*janma-mrityu-jara-vyadhi / duhkha-doshanudarshanam*

*asaktir anabhishvangah / putra-dara-grihadishu*
*nityam cha sama-chittatvam / ishtanishtopapattishu*

*mayi chananya-yogena / bhaktir avyabhicharini*
*vivikta-desha-sevitvam / aratir jana-samsadi*

*adhyatma-jnana-nityatvam / tattva-jnanartha-darshanam*
*etaj jnanam iti proktam / ajnanam yad ato 'nyatha*

*amanitvam* > humility; *adambhitvam* > honesty, sincerity;
*ahimsa* > nonviolence; *kshantih* > patience, forbearance;
*arjavam* > simplicity; *acharya-upasanam* > honoring and serving
those who teach about spiritual truth by fully embodying it;
*shaucham* > cleanliness, integrity; *sthairyam* > stability,
steadfastness; *atma-vinigrahah* > self-restraint;

*indriya-artheshu* > in relation to sense-objects; *vairagyam* > dispassion;
*anahamkarah* > absence of the sense of doership; *eva* > certainly;
*cha* > also; *janma* > birth; *mrityu* > death; *jara* > old age; *vyadhi* > disease;
*duhkha* > afflictions; *dosha* > detrimental effects, disadvantages,
inconveniences; *anudarshanam* > noticing, reflecting upon;

*asaktih* > non-attachment; *anabhishvangah* > absence of dependency
and the sense of proprietorship; *putra* > child; *dara* > spouse;
*griha-adishu* > beginning with the home; *nityam* > continual;
*cha* > and; *sama-chittatvam* > even-mindedness, equanimity;
*ishta* > preferred, wished-for; *anishta* > dreaded;
*upapattishu* > in encountering events which happen;

*mayi* > to Me; *cha* > and; *ananya* > no other; *yogena* > in regard to
Self-realization; *bhaktih* > devotion; *avyabhicharini* > without deviation;
*vivikta* > secluded; *desha* > place; *sevitvam* > dwelling in, frequently resorting
to; *aratih* > lack of affinity; *jana-samsadi* > for the general multitude of society;

*adhyatma-jnana* > knowing that a single omnipresent Spirit-Self animates all
sentient beings; *nityatvam* > constancy; *tattva-jnana* > directly knowing
(experiencing) the truth; *artha-darshanam* > seeing the purpose, seeing the
value; *etat* > this; *jnanam* > true wisdom; *iti* > thus; *proktam* > declared
to be; *ajnanam* > not wisdom, lacking or ignoring wisdom;
*yad* > whatever; *atah* > to this; *anyatha* > contrary.

**Humility, honesty, nonviolence, forbearance, and simplicity;**
**Honoring and serving those who teach about spiritual truth**
**by fully embodying it;**
**Cleanliness, stability, and self-restraint;**
**Dispassion in regard to the objects of the senses;**
**Absence of the sense of doership;**
**Noticing the afflictive disadvantages of birth, death, old age, and disease;**

Non-attachment;
Absence of both dependency and the sense of proprietorship
in regard to one's home, spouse, children, and the rest;
Continual even-mindedness in the face of both wished-for
and dreaded events;
Undeviating devotion to Me and no other in regard to Self-realization;
Frequently resorting to a secluded place;
Lack of affinity for [the unconscious, self-centered values
promoted throughout] the general multitude of society;
Constancy in knowing that a single omnipresent Spirit-Self
animates all sentient beings,
And clearly seeing the value of directly experiencing that truth —
All of this is thus declared to constitute true wisdom,
and anything contrary to this represents a distinct lack of wisdom.

### 12

*jneyam yat tat pravakshyami / yaj jnatva 'mritam ashnute*
*anadimat param brahma / na sat tan nasad uchyate*

*jneyam* > that which is to be inquired about or ascertained; *yat* > which;
*tat* > that; *pravakshyami* > I shall explain, I shall speak about; *yad* > which;
*jnatva* > knowing; *amritam* > immortality; *ashnute* > one reaches;
*anadimat* > beginningless; *param brahma* > the Supreme Brahman,
pure Spirit; *na* > neither; *sat* > being; *tat* > That; *na* > nor;
*asat* > non-being; *uchyate* > It is said to be.

I shall now speak about that which is to be inquired about,
knowing which one reaches [the recognition of one's] immortality.
That is the Supreme Brahman,
Which is beginningless
and is said to be neither being nor non-being.

Although Krishna stated in verse 9.19 that He is everything, both the real
and the dreamlike, here He says just the opposite — *na sat tan nasad uchyate*,
that Brahman is said to be neither being nor non-being, which is essentially
the same as saying neither real nor dreamlike. This appears to be an apparent
contradiction, yet actually both statements may be viewed as conveying
truth from different perspectives. Krishna's previous statement that "I am
everything" is true from the standpoint of omnipresent Consciousness
functioning throughout a body/mind vessel which provides It with the
facility to perceive things and produce any statements about them at all.
However, when there is no physical or subtle phenomena to be perceived,

including no sense of *aham* ('I'), then at that time similar to the state of deep dreamless sleep when there is not even the presence of something called 'time,' terms such as 'being' and 'non-being' are entirely meaningless. As it has already been established in numerous earlier Gita verses that all universal phenomena is an aggregate manifestation of the Nature of the one Absolute, if there is a sense of *aham* manifest, such 'I-ness' can only be synonymous with *everything* that is manifest. But prior to the sense of I-ness arising, for the Unmanifest there can only be *uchyate*, "*It is said* that Brahman is nothing," because the Absolute is not a *thing*, not an object, and there is not even an 'I' manifest to declare what It is or isn't. From this perspective, the statement 'neither being nor non-being' is also concordantly accommodated. As beautifully expressed by Nisargadatta Maharaj: "When I look within and see that I am nothing, that is wisdom. When I look without and see that I am everything, that is love. Between these two, my life flows."

### 13
*sarvatah pani-padam tat / sarvato 'kshi-shiro-mukham*
*sarvatah shrutimal loke / sarvam avritya tishthati*

*sarvatah* > everywhere; *pani* > hands; *padam* > feet; *tat* > That
(the Supreme Brahman); *sarvatah* > everywhere; *akshi* > eyes; *shirah* > heads;
*mukham* > faces; *sarvatah* > everywhere; *shruti-mat* > having ears; *loke* > in the
world; *sarvam* > everything; *avritya* > encompassing; *tishthati* > It abides.

**That Brahman has hands and feet everywhere,**
**Heads and faces everywhere,**
**Eyes and ears everywhere,**
**And abides encompassing everything in this world.**

### 14-15
*sarvendriya-gunabhasam / sarvendriya-vivarjitam*
*asaktam sarva-bhrich chaiva / nirgunam guna-bhoktri cha*

*bahir antash cha bhutanam / acharam charam eva cha*
*sukshmatvat tad avijneyam / durastham chantike cha tat*

*sarva-indriya* > all the senses; *guna* > of the characteristics; *abhasam* > reflected
light, appearance; *sarva-indriya* > all the senses; *vivarjitam* > devoid of;
*asaktam* > without attachment; *sarva-bhrit* > supporting, sustaining,
or nourishing all; *cha* > and; *eva* > even so, still; *nirgunam* > devoid of
qualifying attributes, without attributes acquired from the components
of Nature; *guna-bhoktri* > enjoyer of attributes; *cha* > and;

*bahih* > outside; *antah* > within; *cha* > and; *bhutanam* > of all living beings; *acharam* > unmoving; *charam* > moving; *eva* > certainly; *cha* > and; *sukshmatvat* > due to being extremely subtle; *tat* > That (Supreme Brahman); *avijneyam* > not comprehended, not perceived; *dura-stham* > situated at a distance, far away; *cha* > and; *antike* > immediately nearby; *cha* > also; *tat* > That.

**Devoid of senses,**
**Yet reflecting Its light through [and thus animating]**
**the characteristics of all the sense-faculties;**
**Sustaining and nourishing all,**
**Yet without any attachment at all;**
**Devoid of qualifying (limiting) attributes**
**Yet the enjoyer of attributes —**
**That pure Spirit is both outside and within all forms of life,**
**the moving and the unmoving.**
**It is situated far away and immediately nearby as well,**
**Yet is incomprehensible due to Its extreme subtlety.**

Again, the enjoying of attributes mentioned here can be likened to one who, while sleeping in bed at night and dreaming of eating at a banquet or sailing on the ocean, is not actually engaging in those activities at all.

**16**
*avibhaktam cha bhuteshu / vibhaktam iva cha sthitam*
*bhuta-bhartri cha taj jneyam / grasishnu prabhavishnu cha*

*avibhaktam* > undivided; *cha* > and; *bhuteshu* > among living beings; *vibhaktam* > divided; *iva* > as if; *cha* > and; *sthitam* > abiding; *bhuta* > beings, the elements, that which exists; *bhartri* > the maintainer; *cha* > and; *tat* > That (pure Spirit); *jneyam* > which is to be known; *grasishnu* > accustomed to absorbing or swallowing up; *prabhavishnu* > the autocratic source of ongoing creation; *cha* > and.

**And that Brahman is undivided,**
**yet abides as if divided among living beings.**
**It is to be known as the autocratic maintainer, absorber,**
**and re-creator of all that is.**

**17**
*jyotisham api taj jyotis / tamasah param uchyate*
*jnanam jneyam jnana-gamyam / hridi sarvasya vishthitam*

*jyotisham* > of luminaries (sun, moon, fire, lightning, etc.); *api* > even; *tat* > That (Supreme Brahman, absolute Reality); *jyotih* > light of the eyes; *tamasah* > of darkness; *param* > beyond; *uchyate* > it is said; *jnanam* > true wisdom (as delineated in verses 2 and 7 through 11); *jneyam* > that which is to be inquired into or ascertained; *jnana-gamyam* > accessible by direct knowing; *hridi* > 'in the heart' (meaning as the core essence); *sarvasya* > of all beings, of all that is; *vishthitam* > present, firmly situated, spread throughout.

**That absolute Reality is said to be beyond darkness,**
**the Light by which even the luminaries are seen.**
**It is That which is to be inquired into which is true wisdom [Itself],**
**Present as the core essence of all beings and accessible by direct knowing.**

The phrase *tamasah param uchyate* could also mean "The Absolute is said to be the supreme darkness," as It eternally remains a complete mystery to the collective capabilities of the intellect, mind, and senses. Additionally, Its unlimited nature includes the potential to appear as both supreme darkness as well as supreme light, and not merely one to the exclusion of the other.

**18**
*iti kshetram tatha jnanam / jneyam choktam samasatah*
*mad-bhakta etad vijnaya / mad-bhavayopapadyate*

*iti* > thus; *kshetram* > the field of experience; *tatha* > as well as; *jnanam* > authentic wisdom; *jneyam* > that which is to be inquired about or ascertained; *cha* > and; *uktam* > described; *samasatah* > briefly; *mat-bhaktah* > My devotee; *etat* > this; *vijnaya* > observing, ascertaining; *mat-bhavaya* > to My state of being; *upapadyate* > one is made fit, one is suitably prepared.

**Thus the field of experience,**
**As well as authentic wisdom and that which is to be inquired about,**
**have all been briefly described.**
**Ascertaining [the truth in regard to] these,**
**My devotee is suitably prepared for My state of being.**

Preparation for Krishna's state of being means preparation for fully embodying and living the truth which has been realized in regard to the world, authentic wisdom, and being pure Spirit.

**19**
*prakritim purusham chaiva / viddhyanadi ubhav api*
*vikaramsh cha gunamsh chaiva / viddhi prakriti-sambhavan*

*prakritim* > Nature; *purusham* > Spirit expressing via personification or 'selfing'; *cha* > and; *eva* > even; *viddhi* > please know; *anadi* > beginningless; *ubhau* > both; *api* > assuredly; *vikaran* > transformations; *cha* > and; *gunan* > characteristics; *cha* > also; *eva* > certainly; *viddhi* > please know; *prakriti* > Nature; *sambhavan* > arising from, originating in, produced by.

**Please know that Nature and even personification of Spirit
are both assuredly beginningless;
And know also that all the characteristics and transformations
[of the field of experience] are certainly produced by Nature.**

**20**
*karya-karana-kartritve / hetuh prakritir uchyate
purushah sukha-duhkhanam / bhoktritve hetur uchyate*

*karya* > the effect, the action to be performed; *karana* > the means, the instruments utilized to perform an action; *kartritve* > in regard to the agent of action; *hetuh* > the cause, the impulse; *prakritih* > Nature; *uchyate* > it is said; *purushah* > Spirit expressing selfhood; *sukha* > of pleasure; *duhkhanam* > and pain; *bhoktritve* > in regard to experiencing; *hetuh* > the cause, the impulse; *uchyate* > it is said.

**Nature is said to be the cause
in regard to the agent of action (the body/mind vessel),
The action to be performed,
And the instruments (senses) utilized to perform an action.
Spirit expressing as a self (animating the body/mind)
Is said to be the cause
in regard to the experiencing of pleasure and pain.**

Unless a body/mind vessel is specially endowed with the ability to experience what is occurring in other body/minds, the experiencing mentioned here is of course understood to be localized within each individual expression of the One. Even spiritual awakenings 'register' as experiences associated with particular body/mind vehicles, and this is indeed demonstrated by the fact that spiritual awakenment in one body/mind system is not automatically shared within all others. Conversely, neither do 'awakened ones' automatically share all others' experiences. Krishna will later briefly speak of this localization of experiencing, including the initial focusing of attention on affiliation with a particular life-form, in verses 7 through 9 of Chapter Fifteen.

**21**

*purushah prakriti-stho hi / bhunkte prakritijan gunan*
*karanam guna-sango 'sya / sad-asad-yoni-janmasu*

*purushah* > pure Consciousness utilizing a body/mind vessel;
*prakriti-sthah* > abiding within Nature; *hi* > verily; *bhunkte* > It experiences;
*prakriti-jan* > born of Nature, produced by Nature; *gunan* > the characteristics;
*karanam* > the cause; *guna* > the characteristics of Nature;
*sangah* > proximity to, familiar affiliation with, affectionate inclination
towards; *asya* > of this; *sat-asat* > in favorable and unfavorable;
*yoni* > wombs; *janmasu* > births (refers to the body/mind vessels).

**By abiding in Its own Nature and utilizing a body/mind vessel,**
**Pure Consciousness verily experiences the characteristics**
**born of Its Nature;**
**And Its familiar affiliation with those characteristics**
**causes the births of [new] bodies to occur**
**in [what are regarded as] favorable and unfavorable wombs.**

The familiar affiliation mentioned here is not synonymous with attachment,
as confirmed in verse 9.9 by Krishna's statement that "Actions do not bind
Me, O winner of wealth; I sit neutrally, unattached to them." And once again,
it has already been established in numerous verses from the very beginning
of Krishna's teachings that Spirit never takes birth or dies at any time (*na
jayate mriyate va kadachin*, verse 2.20).

**22**

*upadrashta-'numanta cha / bharta bhokta maheshvarah*
*paramatmeti chapyukto / dehe 'smin purushah parah*

*upadrashta* > the witness very nearby; *anumanta* > allower; *cha* > and;
*bharta* > preserver, supporter; *bhokta* > enjoyer, experiencer;
*maha-ishvarah* > the great Lord; *parama-atma* > the Supreme Self;
*iti* > thus; *cha* > and; *api* > assuredly; *uktah* > is spoken of as;
*dehe asmin* > in this body; *purushah parah* > the Supreme Person,
the Absolute expressing via personification.

**The Absolute expressing via personification in this body**
**is spoken of as being the Witness 'very nearby,'**
**The Allower, the Supporter,**
**The Experiencer, the great Lord,**
**and of course the Supreme Self.**

Just as the word *uchyate* was used in verse 12, the word *uktah*, 'is spoken of as,' is used here. And although the words *dehe asmin*, 'in this body,' imply a duality — that there's something inside of something else — this is not the case, just as a whirlpool in a body of water is composed only of the same water and nothing else.

**23**

*ya evam vetti purusham / prakritim cha gunaih saha*
*sarvatha vartamano 'pi / na sa bhuyo 'bhijayate*

*yah* > who; *evam* > thus; *vetti* > one knows; *purusham* > Spirit expressing via personification; *prakritim* > Nature; *cha* > and; *gunaih* > with Its qualities; *saha* > together; *sarvatha* > in whatever way; *vartamanah* > living, moving in the world; *api* > notwithstanding, regardless of; *na* > not; *sah* > that one; *bhuyah* > again; *abhijayate* > one is born.

**One who thus knows the truth
in regard to Spirit expressing via personification
And about Nature together with Its characteristics
is not born again,
regardless of whatever way in which that one may live.**

Even up to this point in the Gita, the opportunity for cessation of the illusory self as presented here has been offered in several different contexts, most notably in verses 24 through 28 of Chapter Five. There are still many more of such offerings to come before the Gita's conclusion — the next one being just two verses from now — and all of these certainly serve to provide most welcome encouragement for those sincerely aspiring for liberation (*moksha*). It's also worth remembering, however, that what we actually *are* is never in need of liberation; it's only that which we *believe* ourselves to be under the mistaken assumption of separation which needs to be released or 'liberated.'

**24**

*dhyanenatmani pashyanti / kechid atmanam atmana*
*anye sankhyena yogena / karma-yogena chapare*

*dhyanena* > by way of meditation; *atmani* > within the Spirit-Self; *pashyanti* > they perceive; *kechit* > some; *atmanam* > the pseudo-self; *atmana* > by oneself; *anye* > others; *sankhyena* > by way of cultivating empirical knowledge; *yogena* > by way of the raja-yoga system; *karma-yogena* > by way of performing selfless actions; *cha* > and; *apare* > others.

> Some perceive that the imaginary self
> is within the [all-pervasive] Spirit-Self
> By way of meditation by oneself
> (without having received any specific technique from a traditional teacher);
> Others [perceive the truth] by way of cultivating empirical knowledge
> or by practicing the raja-yoga system,
> And still others by performing selfless actions.

The awareness meditation described in the notes following verses 6.13-14 can be done by anyone independently of any formal training in regard to specific sitting postures, breathing techniques, use of mantras or *mudras* (hand gestures), etcetera.

### 25

*anye tvevam ajanantah / shrutva-'nyebhya upasate*
*te 'pi chatitarantyeva / mrityum shruti-parayanah*

*anye* > others; *tu* > but; *evam ajanantah* > not perceiving in this way (that the pseudo-self is simply a fleeting idea in infinite Consciousness); *shrutva* > hearing; *anyebhyah* > from others; *upasate* > they honor; *te* > they; *api* > even; *cha* > also; *atitaranti* > they transcend; *eva* > certainly; *mrityum* > death; *shruti-parayanah* > fully dedicated to the timeless truth orally communicated by awakened male and female sages.

> But even those who do not perceive in this way
> yet simply honor what they hear from others
> [In due course] also certainly transcend death
> By dint of their faith in the timeless truth
> orally communicated by awakened sages and sagesses.

'Transcending death' does not mean that the body/mind vessel does not stop functioning at a certain point; it means that one realizes oneself to be That which was never born to begin with, and is hence not subject to death.

### 26

*yavat sanjayate kinchit / sattvam sthavara-jangamam*
*kshetra-kshetrajna-samyogat / tad viddhi bharatarshabha*

*yavat* > inasmuch as; *sanjayate* > it has arisen, it has come forth, it has been generated; *kinchit* > something; *sattvam* > existence; *sthavara* > inanimate, unmoving; *jangamam* > animate, moving; *kshetra* > of the field of experience; *kshetra-jna* > and the perceiver of the field; *samyogat* > by the intimate connection; *tat viddhi* > know this; *bharata-rishabha* > O best of the Bharatas.

O best of the Bharatas,
Inasmuch as something has come forth into existence —
Whether animate or inanimate —
Know that it has arisen through the intimate connection
of the field of experience with its Perceiver.

The appearance of any *thing*, any thought-form, within perceiving
Consciousness, is due to all-pervasive Consciousness 'connecting with' —
becoming conscious of — the aggregate field of potentiality mentioned in
verse 5.

### 27

*samam sarveshu bhuteshu / tishthantam parameshvaram*
*vinashyatsvavinashyantam / yah pashyati sa pashyati*

*samam* > equally, the same; *sarveshu bhuteshu* > in all living beings;
*tishthantam* > abiding; *parama-ishvaram* > the Supreme Lord;
*vinashyatsu* > in the perishing; *avinashyantam* > not perishing;
*yah* > who; *pashyati* > one sees; *sah pashyati* > that one truly sees.

One who sees the Supreme Lord
dwelling equally in all beings —
Who sees the Imperishable in the midst of the perishing —
That one truly sees.

### 28

*samam pashyan hi sarvatra / samavasthitam ishvaram*
*na hinastyatman'-atmanam / tato yati param gatim*

*samam* > equally, the same; *pashyan* > seeing; *hi* > because;
*sarvatra* > everywhere; *samavasthitam* > equally abiding;
*ishvaram* > the Lord; *na* > not; *hinasti* > one harms; *atmana* > by the
assumed self; *atmanam* > the Spirit-Self; *tatah* > therefore;
*yati* > one goes; *param gatim* > the highest course.

Because of seeing the same [imperishable] Lord
equally abiding everywhere,
One [assuredly knows that one] cannot harm the Spirit-Self
with the imaginary self,
And therefore such a one moves along the highest course
(both while experiencing the world, and upon dissociation from the body).

In this verse and the next, Krishna reminds Arjuna that "Pure Presence neither slays nor is slain" (verse 2.19), and thus Arjuna need not have any apprehension about his necessary prescribed duty being carried out as part of the natural flow of life.

### 29

*prakrityaiva cha karmani / kriyamanani sarvashah*
*yah pashyati tathatmanam / akartaram sa pashyati*

*prakritya* > by Nature; *eva* > certainly; *cha* > and; *karmani* > actions;
*kriyamanani* > performed; *sarvashah* > completely; *yah* > who;
*pashyati* > one sees; *tatha* > thus; *atmanam* > oneself;
*akartaram* > a non-doer of action; *sah pashyati* > that one truly sees.

**And certainly, one who sees that all actions**
**are performed entirely by Nature —**
**That there is no doership in oneself**
**(either as pure Spirit or in the imagined self) —**
**That one truly sees.**

### 30

*yada bhuta-prithag-bhavam / eka-stham anupashyati*
*tata eva cha vistaram / brahma sampadyate tada*

*yada* > when; *bhuta* > of living beings; *prithak* > different; *bhavam* > states,
conditions; *eka-stham* > situated in the One; *anupashyati* > one sees;
*tatah eva* > from that place alone; *cha* > and; *vistaram* > expanding;
*brahma* > Brahman; *sampadyate* > one attains; *tada* > then.

**When one perceives the different conditions of living beings**
**as inherently situated in the One**
**and expanding from that Source alone,**
**One then attains [the recognition of being that] Brahman.**

### 31

*anaditvan nirgunatvat / paramatmayam avyayah*
*sharira-stho 'pi kaunteya / na karoti na lipyate*

*anaditvat* > due to having no beginning; *nirgunatvat* > due to having
no characteristics derived from the components of Nature;
*parama-atma* > the Supreme Self or Oversoul of the universe; *ayam* > this;

*avyayah* > immutable, imperishable; *sharira-sthah* > dwelling
within a body; *api* > although; *kaunteya* > O son of Kunti;
*na karoti* > It does not perform actions; *na lipyate* > nor is It tainted.

**O son of Kunti,**
**Because this immutable Supreme Self has no beginning**
**and no characteristics derived from the three components of Its Nature,**
**It neither performs actions nor becomes tainted**
**even though It dwells within a body.**

### 32
*yatha sarva-gatam saukshmyad / akasham nopalipyate*
*sarvatra-'vasthito dehe / tathatma nopalipyate*

*yatha* > as; *sarva-gatam* > all-pervasive; *saukshmyat* > due to being subtle;
*akasham* > the sky, the ethereal space of the outer atmosphere; *na* > not;
*upalipyate* > it is tainted; *sarvatra* > in all circumstances; *avasthitah* > dwelling;
*dehe* > within a body; *tatha* > in that manner, likewise, so also;
*atma* > the Spirit-Self; *na* > not; *upalipyate* > It is contaminated.

**Just as the all-pervasive sky**
**is never tainted by anything due to its subtle nature,**
**Likewise is the Spirit-Self dwelling within a body**
**never contaminated under any circumstances.**

### 33
*yatha prakashayatyekah / kritsnam lokam imam ravih*
*kshetram kshetri tatha kritsnam / prakashayati bharata*

*yatha* > as; *prakashayati* > it illuminates; *ekah* > one; *kritsnam* > entire;
*lokam* > universe; *imam* > this; *ravih* > sun; *kshetram* > the field of experience;
*kshetri* > the Lord of the field; *tatha* > likewise, so also; *kritsnam* > entire;
*prakashayati* > It illuminates; *bharata* > O descendant of Bharata.

**Just as one sun illuminates this entire universe,**
**Likewise does the one Lord of the field (omnipresent Consciousness)**
**illuminate the entire field of experience,**
**O descendant of Bharata.**

### 34
*kshetra-kshetrajnayor evam / antaram jnana-chakshusha*
*bhuta-prakriti-moksham cha / ye vidur yanti te param*

*kshetra* > the field of experience; *kshetra-jnayoh* > of the Perceiver of the field; *evam* > thus; *antaram* > the distinction; *jnana-chakshusha* > perceiving by way of true wisdom; *bhuta* > of living beings; *prakriti* > from Nature; *moksham* > release; *cha* > and; *ye* > who; *viduh* > they know; *yanti te* > they reach; *param* > the Supreme.

**Those who thus perceive the distinction
between the field of experience and the Perceiver of the field
by way of true wisdom,
And who know [this to be the way of] release for living beings
from [the hypnotic trance induced by] Nature —
They reach [the recognition of being Brahman,] the Supreme.**

This verse recalls the final instruction of the great sage Shukadeva to King Pariksit during the last few moments of the king's life in the Bhagavata Purana, verse 12.5.11: *aham brahma param dhama, brahmaham paramam padam / evam samikshya chatmanam, atmanyadhaya nishkale*: "'I am pure Spirit, the supreme Abode. I am the absolute Truth, the highest Way as well.' — Establish this view of yourself within yourself in an undivided manner (free of doubts)."

*om tat saditi srimad bhagavad-gita / supanishatsu brahma-vidyayam / yoga-shastre srikrishnarjuna samvade / kshetra-kshetrajna-vibhaga-yogo / nama trayodasho 'dhyayah*

From the Ambrosial Song of God —
A conversation between Krishna and Arjuna
which is a Upanishad (confidential sharing)
of wisdom-teachings regarding the Absolute
And a scripture concerning Self-realization —
Thus ends the Thirteenth Chapter entitled Kshetra-kshetrajna-vibhaga-yoga,
Recognizing Divine Unicity By Way of Discerning
The Field of Experience From Its Perceiver.

# Chapter Fourteen

# Gunatraya-vibhaga-yoga
### (Recognizing Divine Unicity By Way of Discerning Between the Three Components of Nature)

"That pure Absolute which is without beginning or end exists as experiencing Consciousness. The expansive universe is Its body, so to speak, with nothing called the intellect apart from It, and no place where It is absent. Pure experiencing is the essence of Consciousness, and so also the essence of existence. Consciousness and unconsciousness coexist, as do water and wetness. This is simply What Is, and is self-evident with no rational explanation for such coexistence, yet also no contradiction or division in Consciousness. ...Ultimate and permanent happiness is reached only by way of complete equanimity. ...O king, whatever miseries arise throughout the entirety of the three worlds are produced from desires arising within the mind. Yet to be settled in a quality of equanimity that views both the presence and absence of thought as non-different is verily to abide in the Eternal."   —Queen Chudala, *Yoga Vasishtha*


"Who is this unique warrior woman [the Divine Mother]?
Her terrifying war cry pervades the universal battleground.
Who is this incomparable feminine principle?
Contemplating her limitless nature,
the passion to possess and be gratified dissolves.
Who is this elusive wisdom-woman?
Her smooth and fragrant body of intense awareness
is like the petal of a dark blue lotus.
A single eye of knowledge shines from her noble forehead
like a moon so full its light engulfs the sun.
This mysterious Goddess, eternally sixteen, is naked brilliance,
transparent insight.
Cascades of black hair stream down her back to touch her dancing feet.
Perfect in the art of wisdom warfare she is the treasury of every excellence,
the reservoir of all that is good.
Her poet sings with unshakable assurance:
Anyone who lives consciously in the presence of this resplendent savioress
can conquer death with the drumbeat 'Ma! Ma! Ma!'"   —Ramprasad

**1**
*sri bhagavan uvacha:*
*param bhuyah pravakshyami / jnananam jnanam uttamam*
*yaj jnatva munayah sarve / param siddhim ito gatah*

*sri bhagavan uvacha* > the illustrious one (Krishna) said; *param* > supreme;
*bhuyah* > further; *pravakshyami* > I shall speak; *jnananam* > among all types
of knowledge; *jnanam* > this knowledge; *uttamam* > the best; *yat* > which;
*jnatva* > realizing; *munayah* > sages moved by inner inspiration; *sarve* > all;
*param* > supreme; *siddhim* > perfection; *itah* > from this world; *gatah* > gone.

**The illustrious Krishna said:**
**I shall speak more of this supreme knowledge —**
**The best among all types of knowledge —**
**Realizing which all of the sages moved by inner inspiration**
**have gone from [the experiencing of] this world to supreme perfection.**

**2**
*idam jnanam upashritya / mama sadharmyam agatah*
*sarge 'pi nopajayante / pralaye na vyathanti cha*

*idam* > this; *jnanam* > knowledge; *upashritya* > relying upon, taking refuge in;
*mama* > my; *sadharmyam* > similarity or sameness of nature; *agatah* > arrive at;
*sarge* > at the time of the world's creation; *api* > even; *na* > not;
*upajayante* > they are born; *pralaye* > at the time of the world's
dissolution; *na* > nor; *vyathanti* > they feel tremors; *cha* > even.

**Those who rely upon this knowledge**
**arrive at a nature similar to my own.**
**They are not born even at the time of the world's creation,**
**Nor do they feel even a tremor at the time of its dissolution.**

As briefly indicated in relation to verse 13.18, arriving at a nature similar to
Krishna's own refers to fully embodying and living realized truth beginning
right here in this world, and in verse 8.24 the experiencing of such realization
is said to continue even after departure from cognizance of this world via
'the path of light.' This *sadharmyam* is broadly viewed as corresponding to
the *sarupya* (similarity to one's preferred deity) mentioned in verse 3 of
the *Kali-santarana Upanishad* along with three other types of attainments
available to the liberated one — *salokya* (abiding in the domain of one's
preferred deity), *samipya* (having association with one's preferred deity), and
of course *sayujya* (merging homogeneously into the formless aspect of Spirit).

Both the Bhagavata Purana (verse 3.29.13) and the Shiva-Gita portion of the Padma Purana also mention a fifth possible attainment known as *sarshti* (having the same abilities or resources as one's preferred deity). Yet those embodying a spirit of selfless loving service have no interest in being rewarded with any of these spiritual gifts.

**3**

*mama yonir mahad brahma / tasmin garbham dadhamyaham*
*sambhavah sarva-bhutanam / tato bhavati bharata*

*mama* > My; *yonih* > womb, source; *mahat brahma* > the great source of all growth, expansion, evolution, and development (Prakriti); *tasmin* > in this; *garbham* > the seedlike conception; *dadhami aham* > I place; *sambhavah* > origin; *sarva-bhutanam* > of all living beings; *tatah* > from that; *bhavati* > it comes forth, it is originated, it is made possible, it is brought into existence; *bharata* > O descendant of Bharata.

**Into the womb of My Prakriti (Nature),**
**the great source of growth and evolution,**
**I place the seed concept [of all life-forms];**
**And from that, all living beings come forth into existence,**
**O descendant of Bharata.**

*Mahat brahma*'s being synonymous with Prakriti will be confirmed in upcoming verse 5.

**4**

*sarva-yonishu kaunteya / murtayah sambhavanti yah*
*tasam brahma mahad yonir / aham bija-pradah pita*

*sarva-yonishu* > in all wombs; *kaunteya* > O son of Kunti; *murtayah* > physical forms; *sambhavanti* > they are produced, they originate; *yah* > which; *tasam* > of them; *brahma* > of growth, expansion, evolution, and development; *mahat yonih* > the great womb (of Nature); *aham* > I; *bija-pradah* > seed-giving; *pita* > father.

**The physical forms which are produced in all wombs**
**Are expansions and developments**
**from the great womb of Prakriti, O son of Kunti,**
**And I am the seed-giving Father.**

Swami B.R. Sridhar Maharaj refers to this as 'the subjective evolution of Consciousness.'

**5**

*sattvam rajas tama iti / gunah prakriti-sambhavah*
*nibadhnanti mahabaho / dehe dehinam avyayam*

*sattvam* > clarity, luminosity, lightness, and balance; *rajah* > creation,
activation, coloration, and intensification; *tamah* > darkness,
heaviness, inertia, and dissolution; *iti* > thus; *gunah* > the components;
*prakriti* > Nature; *sambhavah* > originating in; *nibadhnanti* > they
confine; *maha-baho* > O mighty-armed one; *dehe* > within the body;
*dehinam* > 'the embodied one,' pure Spirit experiencing the
functioning of a body/mind vessel; *avyayam* > changeless.

**Thus the components of sattva (clarity, luminosity, lightness, and balance),**
**Rajas (creation, activation, coloration, and intensification),**
**And tamas (darkness, heaviness, inertia, and dissolution)**
**Originate from Nature, O mighty-armed one,**
**[And display the illusion of] confining changeless Spirit**
**within a body/mind vessel.**

Krishna's use of the word *avyayam*, 'unchanging,' in this particular verse is
significant in that it is a reminder that the *intimacy* of Spirit with Its own
power of creative expression does not alter the *immaculacy* of the Absolute
in the slightest. As already established in many previous verses, skylike
Brahman is all that ever *Is*, and as stated in verse 8 of the *Isha Upanishad*,
It is incorporeal. Being without material form or substance, It is therefore
not confinable; and being one without a second, there is moreover no
second thing for It to be confined by. Hence we find countless scriptural
references such as verse 6.1 of the *Katha Upanishad* stating that Brahman is
eternally free. At the same time, when the light of ever-free omnipresent
Consciousness is reflected through all the senses of a body/mind vessel
(*sarvendriya-gunabhasam*, Gita verse 13.14), this creates the illusory *appearance*
of confinement. The analogy often given in Upanishadic literature and its
commentaries is of the moon reflected in a clay pot filled with water. If,
hypothetically, one had never seen the moon in the sky and knew nothing
about the phenomenon of reflection, that person would naturally assume that
the moon was confined within the clay pot.

**6**

*tatra sattvam nirmalatvat / prakashakam anamayam*
*sukha-sangena badhnati / jnana-sangena chanagha*

*tatra* > in such circumstances; *sattvam* > the clarifying component;
*nirmalatvat* > being spotless, being pure, being transparent;

*prakashakam* > illuminating; *anamayam* > conducive to good health; *sukha* > happiness; *sangena* > by affinity, by the investment of interested attention; *badhnati* > it captures; *jnana* > knowledge; *sangena* > by affinity, by the investment of interested attention; *cha* > and; *anagha* > O sinless one.

**In such circumstances,**
**Because the clarifying component is pure and illuminating,**
**Promoting good [physical, mental, and emotional] health,**
**It captures attention**
**through the affinity for knowledge and happiness, O sinless one.**

**7**
*rajo ragatmakam viddhi / trishna-sanga-samudbhavam*
*tan nibadhnati kaunteya / karma-sangena dehinam*

*rajah* > the activating component; *raga-atmakam* > characterized by impassionment; *viddhi* > please know; *trishna* > thirst, cravings; *sanga* > attachment; *samudbhavam* > born of; *tat* > that; *nibadhnati* > it captures, it holds; *kaunteya* > O son of Kunti; *karma-sangena* > by affinity or the investment of interested attention in actions and their results; *dehinam* > a portion of undivided Consciousness which is conscious of being present throughout a body/mind system.

**Know that the activating component is characterized by impassionment**
**born of cravings and attachment, O Kaunteya.**
**It holds the attention of a portion of undivided Consciousness**
**via the interest in actions and their results.**

The impression of being a finite entity appears within an infinitesimal portion of pure infinite Being just as a tiny cloud appears within the all-pervasive sky. As indicated in relation to verse 13.20, the various influences of the components can be localized to portions of the Infinite, and this is later confirmed in verse 15.7 by the phrase *mamaivamsho,* 'verily, a portion of Myself.'

**8**
*tamas tvajnanajam viddhi / mohanam sarva-dehinam*
*pramadalasya-nidrabhis / tan nibadhnati bharata*

*tamah* > the darkening component; *tu* > but; *ajnana-jam* > born of non-cognizance; *viddhi* > please know; *mohanam* > delusion; *sarva-dehinam* > of all living beings; *pramada* > unconsciousness,

recklessness, inebriation, madness; *alasya* > laziness;
*nidrabhih* > slumber; *tat* > that (attention); *nibadhnati* > it captures,
it holds; *bharata* > O descendant of Bharata.

**But know also that the darkening component born of non-cognizance**
**deludes all living beings, O descendant of Bharata,**
**Holding attention captive**
**with unconsciousness, laziness, and slumber.**

Verses 6 through 9 provide valuable alerts regarding each *guna's* potential
to captivate one's attention. At the same time, it bears noting that all three
components of Nature are also vital to the functioning of life in the world.
That life could not function without the movement made possible by *rajas*
is obvious, but sometimes the value of *tamas* is not immediately recognized.
Without it, all inanimate objects such as tables and chairs *would* move by
themselves, and no sleep would be possible for any living being at any
time. The body/mind system could not even function if *tamas's* aspect of
non-cognizance were entirely withdrawn, because one would continually
be aware of everything happening on all levels of perception simultaneously,
from the most microscopic activity to the most cosmic. A holistic perspective
of the *gunas* is therefore essential for noticing their influences on the
body/mind with complete clarity and openness, without attaching any
interpretation of such influences to the story of an assumed self. As indicated
in verses 2.62-63, what begins with a simple investment of attention can in
due course manifest throughout the entire body/mind vessel and extend
out into the environment on all levels from the very physical to the very
subtle. Helpless dependence on experiencing the temporary knowledge and
happiness produced by the component of *sattva* is also considered an
impediment to realizing the eternally contented presence of Awareness
(*Sat-chid-ananda*) which one truly is.

**9**

*sattvam sukhe sanjayati / rajah karmani bharata*
*jnanam avritya tu tamah / pramade sanjayatyuta*

*sattvam* > the component of clarity; *sukhe* > to comfort,
to happiness; *sanjayati* > it induces addiction; *rajah* > the activating
component; *karmani* > to specific actions and their results;
*bharata* > O Arjuna, descendant of Bharata; *jnanam* > wisdom;
*avritya* > enveloping; *tu* > but; *tamah* > the component of darkness;
*pramade* > to unconsciousness; *sanjayati* > it induces attachment; *uta* > surely.

The component of clarity induces addiction to feeling good,
and the activating component, to actions and their results;
But the component of darkness, enveloping all wisdom,
surely induces addiction to unconsciousness, O Arjuna.

**10**

*rajas tamash chabhibhuya / sattvam bhavati bharata*
*rajah sattvam tamash chaiva / tamah sattvam rajas tatha*

*rajah* > activation; *tamah* > darkness; *cha* > and; *abhibhuya* > predominating;
*sattvam* > clarity; *bhavati* > it comes forth, it supersedes;
*bharata* > O Arjuna, descendant of Bharata; *rajah* > activation;
*sattvam* > clarity; *tamah* > darkness; *cha* > and; *eva* > in the same manner;
*tamah* > darkness; *sattvam* > clarity; *rajah* > activation; *tatha* > so also, as well.

Sattvic clarity comes to the forefront of expression
[through the body/mind vessel]
upon predominating over activation and darkness, O Arjuna;
So also does rajasic activation come forth
[upon prevailing] over clarity and darkness,
And tamasic darkness supersedes clarity and activation
in the same manner as well.

**11**

*sarva-dvareshu dehe 'smin / prakasha upajayate*
*jnanam yada tada vidyad / vivriddham sattvam ityuta*

*sarva-dvareshu* > in all the gates; *dehe asmin* > in this body; *prakashah* >
illumination; *upajayate* > it comes forth, it appears; *jnanam* > true wisdom;
*yada* > when; *tada* > at that time; *vidyat* > it can be ascertained, it may
be understood; *vivriddham* > become abundant, become predominant;
*sattvam* > clarity, luminosity, lightness, balance; *iti* > thus; *uta* > surely.

It may thus be understood
that when all the gates of the body
are illuminated by the dawning of true wisdom,
Clarity has surely become predominant.

**12**

*lobhah pravrittir arambhah / karmanam ashamah spriha*
*rajasyetani jayante / vivriddhe bharatarshabha*

*lobhah* > greed; *pravrittih* > strenuous exertion; *arambhah* > undertaking;
*karmanam* > of activities; *ashamah* > restlessness; *spriha* > cravings;
*rajasi* > in the component of creation, activation, coloration, intensification;
*etani* > these; *jayante* > they arise, they appear; *vivriddhe* > in the abundance,
with the predominance; *bharata-rishabha* > O best of the Bharata dynasty.

**Greed, strenuous exertion in the undertaking of activities,
restlessness, and cravings —
These [are the symptoms which] arise
with the predominance of activation [throughout the body/mind],
O best of the Bharatas.**

**13**
*aprakasho 'pravrittish cha / pramado moha eva cha
tamasyetani jayante / vivriddhe kuru-nandana*

*aprakashah* > absence of illumination (non-perception); *apravrittih* > indolence;
*cha* > and; *pramadah* > recklessness, madness; *mohah* > delusion;
*eva* > certainly; *cha* > and; *tamasi* > in the component of darkness;
*etani* > these; *jayante* > they are produced; *vivriddhe* > in the
predominance; *kuru-nandana* > O joy of the Kuru dynasty.

**And non-perception, indolence, recklessness, and delusion —
These are certainly produced
when the component of darkness is predominant,
O joy of the Kurus.**

**14**
*yada sattve pravriddhe tu / pralayam yati deha-bhrit
tadottama-vidam lokan / amalan pratipadyate*

*yada* > when; *sattve* > in Nature's component of clarity; *pravriddhe* > in the
predominance; *tu* > now then; *pralayam* > dissolution; *yati* > one departs;
*deha-bhrit* > 'carrying a body' (pure Consciousness holding the image of a
body within Itself); *tada* > at that time; *uttama-vidam* > those endowed
with the highest knowledge; *lokan* > worlds; *amalan* > pure;
*pratipadyate* > It perceives, It becomes aware of.

**Now then:
When pure Consciousness 'departs' from holding an image
of a body/mind vessel predominated by Nature's component of clarity,
At the time of that dissolution [of cognitive affiliation],
It perceives the pure worlds
of those endowed with the highest knowledge.**

### 15

*rajasi pralayam gatva / karma-sangishu jayate*
*tatha pralinas tamasi / mudha-yonishu jayate*

*rajasi* > in a state predominated by Nature's component of activation;
*pralayam* > dissolution; *gatva* > going away; *karma-sangishu* > among those
with attachment to actions and their results; *jayate* > a body is born;
*tatha* > in like manner; *pralinah* > dissolving; *tamasi* > in a condition
predominated by Nature's component of darkness; *mudha-yonishu* > in the
wombs of those who are bewildered; *jayate* > there is a birth, a body is born.

**Upon [pure Consciousness] departing**
**At the dissolution [of Its affiliation with a body/mind vehicle which is]**
**in a state predominated by Nature's component of activation,**
**A new body is born among those with an emotional investment**
**in actions and their results;**
**And upon such dissolving [of association with a form**
**which is] in a condition predominated by Nature's component of darkness,**
**A new body is born**
**in one of the wombs of those who are bewildered.**

### 16

*karmanah sukritasyahuh / sattvikam nirmalam phalam*
*rajasas tu phalam duhkham / ajnanam tamasah phalam*

*karmanah* > of actions; *su-kritasya* > performed unselfishly for the benefit
of others; *ahuh* > they say (referring to the sages); *sattvikam* > imbued with
purity; *nirmalam* > without impurity, unblemished; *phalam* > the fruit (result);
*rajasah* > of coloration; *tu* > but; *phalam* > the fruit (result); *duhkham* > distress;
*ajnanam* > nescience; *tamasah* > of darkness; *phalam* > the fruit (result).

**The sages say**
**that the results of actions performed unselfishly for the benefit of others**
**are imbued with unblemished purity (sattva),**
**Whereas rajasic actions colored [with selfish motives] result in distress,**
**and tamasic acts of darkness result in nescience.**

### 17

*sattvat sanjayate jnanam / rajaso lobha eva cha*
*pramada-mohau tamaso / bhavato 'jnanam eva cha*

*sattvat* > from clarity; *sanjayate* > it is produced; *jnanam* > wisdom;
*rajasah* > from intensification; *lobhah* > greed; *eva* > certainly; *cha* > and;

*pramada* > unconsciousness; *mohau* > delusion; *tamasah* > from darkness; *bhavatah* > they are generated; *ajnanam* > nescience; *eva* > certainly; *cha* > and.

**From the clarity of sattva, wisdom is produced;**
**From the intensification of rajas surely comes greed;**
**And the darkness of tamas generates unconsciousness, delusion,**
**and of course nescience.**

**18**
*urdhvam gachchanti sattvastha / madhye tishthanti rajasah*
*jaghanya-guna-vrittistha / adho gachchanti tamasah*

*urdhvam* > upward; *gachchanti* > they go; *sattva-sthah* > those established in clarity; *madhye* > in the middle; *tishthanti* > they remain; *rajasah* > those predominated by activation; *jaghanya-guna* > of the lowest component; *vritti-sthah* > established in that condition; *adhah* > downward; *gachchanti* > they go; *tamasah* > those permeated by darkness.

**Those established in clarity ascend**
**(experience higher dimensions within Consciousness);**
**Those predominated by activation remain in the middle**
**(earthly experience);**
**And those permeated by darkness,**
**being established in the condition of the lowest component,**
**Go downward (experience lower expressions of Consciousness).**

As previously discussed in the notes to verses 6.41, 8.6, and others, That which is omnipresent does not 'go' anywhere, yet dreamlike journeys are experienced *within* It, as this verse describes. Neither are there designated directions such as up or down or left or right for Omnipresence Itself. As stated in the *Maitri Upanishad*, verse 6.17: "For Brahman, which is infinite on all sides, there are certainly no directions such as east and so forth; no across, no above, and no below. It is unborn, spacelike, immeasurable, and unimaginable."

**19**
*nanyam gunebhyah kartaram / yada drashta 'nupashyati*
*gunebhyash cha param vetti / mad-bhavam so 'dhigachchati*

*na* > not; *anyam* > other; *gunebhyah* > than the components of Nature; *kartaram* > doer or agent of actions; *yada* > when; *drashta* > the perceiver; *anupashyati* > that one sees; *gunebhyah* > in relation to the components of Nature; *cha* > and; *param* > surpassing, superior; *vetti* > one knows, one recognizes, one experiences; *mat-bhavam* > My state of being; *sah adhigachchati* > that one reaches or attains.

> **When the perceiver [of the field of experience]**
> **sees no doer or agent of actions other than the components of Nature,**
> **And recognizes [one's true nature to be] That which is superior**
> **[to those components],**
> **Such a one reaches My state of being.**

### 20
*gunan etan atitya trin / dehi deha-samudbhavan*
*janma-mrityu-jara-duhkhair / vimukto 'mritam ashnute*

*gunan* > components; *etan* > these; *atitya* > transcending; *trin* > three; *dehi* > a portion of pure Consciousness with attention localized within one particular body; *deha* > the body; *samudbhavan* > being the source of; *janma* > birth; *mrityu* > death; *jara* > old age; *duhkhaih* > discomforts, difficulties; *vimuktah* > released; *amritam* > immortality; *ashnute* > It arrives at, It reaches.

> **Upon transcending these three components**
> **which are the source of the body,**
> **The portion of [infinite, undivided] Consciousness**
> **with attention localized within the body**
> **Is released from [the dreamlike experiencing of] the tribulations**
> **of birth, old age, and death**
> **[after dissociation from the already-existing body],**
> **Having arrived at [the recognition of Its preexisting] immortality.**

As mentioned in the notes to verse 4.22, when there is realization of one's true nature in a particular body/mind vehicle, natural sensations of heat and cold, pain and pleasure still continue to occur within that vehicle as long as it continues to function and the senses encounter their objects. The full range of sensorial experiences remains available, yet it is devoid of the suffering which generally accompanies ego-identification and the conditioned beliefs which are held in regard to the birth, old age, or death of the body.

### 21
*arjuna uvacha:*
*kair lingais trin gunan etan / atito bhavati prabho*
*kim acharah katham chaitams / trin gunan ativartate*

*arjunah uvacha* > Arjuna said; *kaih lingaih* > by what signs or characteristics; *trin* > three; *gunan* > components; *etan* > these; *atitah* > transcending; *bhavati* > one is; *prabho* > O my Lord; *kim* > what; *acharah* > behavior; *katham* > how; *cha* > and; *etan* > these; *trin* > three; *gunan* > components; *ativartate* > one crosses over, one passes beyond.

**Arjuna inquired:**
**My Lord, what are the characteristics**
**of one who has transcended these components of Nature?**
**What is the behavior of that person,**
**and how did he or she move beyond these three components?**

### 22-25
*sri bhagavan uvacha:*
*prakasham cha pravrittim cha / moham eva cha pandava*
*na dveshti sampravrittani / na nivrittani kankshati*

*udasina-vad asino / gunair yo na vichalyate*
*guna vartanta ityeva / yo 'vatishthati nengate*

*sama-duhkha-sukhah svasthah / sama-loshtashma-kanchanah*
*tulya-priyapriyo dhiras / tulya-nindatma-samstutih*

*mana-'pamanayos tulyas / tulyo mitrari-pakshayoh*
*sarvarambha-parityagi / gunatitah sa uchyate*

*sri bhagavan uvacha* > the venerable one (Krishna) said; *prakasham* > illumination; *cha* > or; *pravrittim* > exertion; *cha* > or; *moham* > delusion; *eva* > even; *cha* > and; *pandava* > O son of Pandu; *na* > neither; *dveshti* > one is averse, one is repulsed; *sampravrittani* > that which has arisen or appeared; *na* > nor; *nivrittani* > that which has ceased or disappeared; *kankshati* > one longs for, one strives for;

*udasina-vat* > 'as if sitting apart,' neutral, indifferent; *asinah* > seated (situated); *gunaih* > by the components of Nature; *yah* > who; *na* > not; *vichalyate* > one is disturbed; *gunah* > the components; *vartanta* > they move about; *iti eva* > in the certainty; *yah* > who; *avatishthati* > one remains stable or settled; *na* > not; *ingate* > one is agitated;

*sama* > even-minded; *duhkha* > in pain; *sukhah* > in pleasure; *sva-sthah* > at ease in one's natural state; *sama* > equal; *loshta* > a lump of earth or clay; *ashma* > iron; *kanchanah* > gold; *tulya* > equal; *priya* > that which is agreeable; *apriyah* > that which is disagreeable; *dhirah* > steadfast; *tulya* > equal; *ninda* > criticism; *atma-samstutih* > praise of oneself;

*mana apamanayoh* > in encountering respect and contempt; *tulyah* > equal; *tulyah* > equally; *mitra* > friends; *ari* > enemies; *pakshayoh* > toward the 'wings' (factions); *sarva* > all; *arambha* > endeavors; *parityagi* > abandoning; *guna-atitah* > transcending the components of Nature; *sah uchyate* > one is said to be.

**The venerable Krishna replied:**
**O son of Pandu, one who is not repulsed**
**by the arising of either illumination, exertion, or even delusion,**
**Nor longs for any of them when they have disappeared;**
**Who abides neutrally as if sitting apart,**
**undisturbed by the components of Nature,**
**And remains stably unagitated**
**in the certainty that only the components are moving about;**
**Who is at ease in one's natural state,**
**even-minded in both pain and pleasure;**
**Who views as equal a lump of clay, iron, or gold;**
**Who is equally disposed towards the agreeable and the disagreeable;**
**Whose equanimity is steadfast**
**in encountering either praise or criticism, respect or contempt;**
**Who treats factions of both friends and enemies alike,**
**and has abandoned all [ego-sustaining] endeavors —**
**Such a one is said to have transcended the components of Nature.**

Krishna later states in verse 18.40 that "There is not a single living being, either here on Earth or even among the celestials of heaven, who is entirely free from the three components of Nature." Therefore the word *uchyate*, 'it is said,' is once again used, here for describing that expression of the One in which the realized truth of unicity is consistently demonstrated. What such a one factually transcends is the tendency to enter a trancelike state of involvement and misidentification while witnessing the interactions of the various manifestations of Nature.

### 26
*mam cha yo 'vyabhicharena / bhakti-yogena sevate*
*sa gunan samatityaitan / brahma-bhuyaya kalpate*

*mam* > Me; *cha* > and; *yah* > whoever; *avyabhicharena* > without deviation; *bhakti-yogena* > devotion to; *sevate* > one serves; *sah* > that one; *gunan* > the components of Nature; *samatitya* > transcending; *etan* > these; *brahma-bhuyaya* > for absorption into Brahman (pure unitary Consciousness); *kalpate* > one is acclimated, one is oriented.

And whoever serves Me with undeviating devotion
is one who, transcending these components of Nature,
Becomes acclimated for absorption
into pure unitary Consciousness.

Another reading of this verse is that the portion of unitary Consciousness
which serves the whole of Itself — with undeviating devotion to remaining
awake to the truth of Itself — transcends the propensity to become fascinated
with the interactions of what is in reality Its own (the One's) Nature. And the
phrase 'absorption into pure unitary Consciousness' has two applications,
one with respect to life while still affiliated with a body/mind vessel, and one
with respect to complete dissociation from experiencing the world. As
indicated in verses 5.20-21, while still affiliated, the 'transcendent' one wholly
reflects truth with abiding serenity, clarity, and joy. Then, such a one "is not
born again upon dissociation from the present body, but comes to Me" (4.9).

### 27

*brahmano hi pratishthaham / amritasya-'vyayasya cha*
*shashvatasya cha dharmasya / sukhasyaikantikasya cha*

*brahmanah* > of Brahman; *hi* > truly; *pratishtha* > the foundational basis,
the substratum; *aham* > I; *amritasya* > of the immortal; *avyayasya* > of the
immutable; *cha* > both; *shashvatasya* > of the eternal; *cha* > and; *dharmasya* >
of the principles of conscious living; *sukhasya aikantikasya* > of perfect
and complete joy, of absolute beatitude; *cha* > and.

**That Brahman which is the immortal and immutable substratum**
**Of both absolute beatitude**
**and the eternal principles of conscious living —**
**Truly, I am That.**

*om tat saditi srimad bhagavad-gita / supanishatsu brahma-vidyayam / yoga-shastre*
*srikrishnarjuna samvade / gunatraya-vibhaga-yogo nama chaturdasho 'dhyayah*

From the Ambrosial Song of God —
A conversation between Krishna and Arjuna
which is a Upanishad (confidential sharing)
of wisdom-teachings regarding the Absolute
And a scripture concerning Self-realization —
Thus ends the Fourteenth Chapter entitled Gunatraya-vibhaga-yoga,
Recognizing Divine Unicity By Way of Discerning
Between the Three Components of Nature.

# Chapter Fifteen

## Purushottama-yoga
### (Recognizing Divine Unicity By Way of Its Aspect As the Supreme Person)

"It is undoubtedly true that God comes down to Earth in a human form, as in the case of Krishna. And it is true as well that God reveals Himself to His devotees in various forms. But it is also true that God is formless. ...*Satchidananda* is like an infinite ocean. Intense cold freezes the water into ice, which floats on the ocean in blocks of various forms. ...Water above and water below, everywhere nothing but water. ...Therefore, a prayer in the Bhagavata [Purana] says: ...'Thou walkest before us, O Lord, in the shape of a man; again, Thou hast been described in the Vedas as beyond words and thought.' But you may say that for certain devotees God assumes eternal forms. There are places in the ocean where the ice doesn't melt at all."

"Do you know what describing God as being formless only is like? It is like a man's playing only a monotone on his flute, though it has seven holes. ...Mark this: form and formlessness belong to one and the same Reality."
—Sri Ramakrishna

"To me, an atom or an electron is very intelligent. It is no less with consciousness. Dead matter cannot give birth to Buddhas, bodhisattvas, saints, and many wonderful things. To the question 'Is God a person?', the answer is yes, God can be a person, God can be a cloud, God can be a flower. By realizing this we can make peace with everything in the historical dimension." —Thich Nhat Hanh

**1**

*sri bhagavan uvacha:*
*urdhva-mulam adhah-shakham / ashvattham prahur avyayam*
*chandamsi yasya parnani / yas tam veda sa veda-vit*

*sri bhagavan uvacha* > the blessed one (Krishna) said; *urdhva* > above; *mulam* > root; *adhah* > below; *shakham* > branches; *ashvattham* > 'where horses stand,' a banyan tree; *prahuh* > they say (refers to the sages who authored scriptures such as the Upanishads); *avyayam* > imperishable; *chandamsi* > the sacred hymns of the Vedas; *yasya* > of which; *parnani* > the leaves; *yah* > who; *tam* > this; *veda* > one knows; *sah* > that one; *veda-vit* > a knower of the Vedas.

The blessed Krishna said:
The sages speak of an everlasting banyan tree
which has its root above and its branches below,
The leaves of which are the hymns of the Vedas.
One who knows [the meaning indicated
by the symbolic representation of] this tree
Is a genuine knower of the Vedas.

The place where one sees such an image as described here — a tree with its root above and branches below — is in the water of a lake which has a tree growing beside it. So just as one clearly perceives the image in the lake to simply be an inverted reflection of the real tree, one who clearly perceives the entire world to simply be a reflection of Reality in the lake of universal Mind is considered to have understood the *vedanta*, the ultimate conclusions of the vast body of teachings expounded in the four Vedas.

2

*adhash chordhvam prasritas tasya shakha / guna-pravriddha vishaya-pravalah*
*adhash cha mulanyanusantatani / karma-'nubandhini manushya-loke*

adhah > below; cha > and, both; urdhvam > above; prasritah > expansively outspread; tasya > of it; shakhah > branches; guna > by the components of Nature; pravriddhah > nurtured; vishaya > the objects of the senses; pravalah > buds; adhah > downward; cha > also; mulani > the roots; anusantatani > extended; karma anubandhini > resulting in action; manushya-loke > in the human world.

Its branches spread out expansively both below and above.
Nurtured by the components of Nature,
its buds are the objects of the senses.
Roots also extend downward,
resulting in action in the human world.

At first glance this verse may appear somewhat confusing in light of what was stated in the preceding verse, yet the following depiction may be helpful in providing some greater clarity. The main root — initial self-awareness ('I am') — is 'above' in pure infinite Consciousness, and all of the branches are below that main root. Among those branches, some branches are above others. The higher branches represent the more subtle or celestial expression of 'I-amness,' and the lower branches represent the more earthly physical expression of the same. Secondary lateral roots or rootlets — *samskaras*, memory-impressions of previous experiences—extend out of the primary sense of selfhood and 'downward' into manifestation. They appear first as rudimentary concepts in the subtle region of Consciousness, and then as action in the physical plane.

### 3

*na rupam asyeha tathopalabhyate / nanto na chadir na cha sampratishtha*
*ashvattham enam suvirudha-mulam / asanga-shastrena dridhena chittva*

*na* > not; *rupam* > the form; *asya* > of this (the tree); *iha* > here in this world; *tatha* > in this manner (as described in verses 1 and 2); *upalabhyate* > it is perceivable, it is comprehensible; *na* > not; *antah* > the ending; *na* > not; *cha* > and; *adih* > the beginning; *na* > not; *cha* > and; *sampratishtha* > support, source of sustenance; *ashvattham enam* > this banyan tree; *su-virudha* > fully developed; *mulam* > root; *asanga* > non-attachment; *shastrena* > by the cutting instrument; *dridhena* > by the solid, by the powerful; *chittva* > severing.

**The form of this tree as I have described it**
**is not perceivable here in this world;**
**Neither [can it be ascertained] when it began,**
**nor where it ends, nor how it is sustained.**
**[Nonetheless,] the fully-developed root of this banyan tree**
**can be severed by the powerful cutting tool of non-attachment.**

When reciting this verse in the alternate metre known as *trishtubh*, the first segment of the first line has one additional syllable.

### 4

*tatah padam tat parimargitavyam / yasmin gata na nivartanti bhuyah*
*tam eva chadyam purusham prapadye / yatah pravrittih prasrita purani*

*tatah* > then; *padam* > abode, standpoint, 'footing' (stability); *tat* > that; *parimargitavyam* > to be intently sought; *yasmin* > to which; *gatah* > having arrived at; *na* > not; *nivartanti* > they return; *bhuyah* > again; *tam* > to that [end], in that [regard]; *eva* > in this manner; *cha* > and; *adyam purusham* > the primordial personification of Spirit; *prapadye* > I take refuge; *yatah* > from whom; *pravrittih* > the progression of life-activity; *prasrita* > flowed forth; *purani* > from very ancient times.

**Then, that stability [in the realization of timeless truth]**
**is to be intently sought which, having arrived at,**
**no one again returns [to the trance of misperception].**

> In that regard, [one's resolution may be expressed] in this manner:
> "I take refuge in the primordial Person
> from whom the progression of all life-activity has flowed forth
> since time immemorial."

It can be said that one who is settled in the standpoint of perceiving the unitary wholeness of life does not again return to perceiving in terms of division and separation. And the expression of resolution offered here represents recognition of the futility of struggling to maintain the illusion of control by an assumed self which is incapable of controlling anything, just as a shadow cannot control the movements of the person casting it.

5

*nirmana-moha jita-sanga-dosha / adhyatma-nitya vinivritta-kamah*
*dvandvair vimuktah sukha-duhkha-samjnair*
*gachchantyamudhah padam avyayam tat*

*nirmana-mohah* > devoid of pride spawned by delusion; *jita* > subdued, overcome; *sanga* > attachment, addiction; *doshah* > detriments, afflictions; *adhyatma nityah* > ever abiding in one's true nature as the Spirit-Self; *vinivritta* > retired, turned away; *kamah* > desires; *dvandvaih* > from the pairs of opposites; *vimuktah* > freed; *sukha-duhkha* > pleasure and displeasure; *samjnaih* > known as, consensually agreed upon; *gachchanti* > they go to, they come to; *amudhah* > not infatuated, not stupefied; *padam* > abode, standpoint, footing (stability); *avyayam* > immutable; *tat* > that.

> Devoid of pride spawned by delusion,
> The affliction of attachment overcome,
> Ever abiding in one's true nature as the Spirit-Self,
> Retired from the pursuit of desires,
> And freed from [being swayed by] the pairs of opposites
> consensually agreed upon as pleasure and displeasure —
> Those who are not entranced arrive at that changeless stability.

The phrase *dvandvair vimuktah sukha-duhkha-samjnair* is significant. Depending upon one's cultural conditioning, one will experience all of life's various situations from a particular perspective which will determine whether one feels happiness or despondency in those situations. For example, it has been observed that if people have been encultured in a social environment where a certain level of financial assets and possessions are considered to represent true success and fulfillment in life, they feel great disappointment if they cannot reach that standard. Yet those who were raised in an environment with little more than the bare necessities of life feel themselves to be extremely blessed to be living so luxuriously with but a fraction of the same standard. And *dvandvaih* pertains to *all* the pairs of opposites; not just in relation to finances, but also in regard to consensually-agreed-upon standards of who is beautiful and not beautiful, intelligent and not intelligent, right and wrong, worthy and unworthy, etcetera. When we view ourselves based on certain standards that we've been taught to believe in — what should or shouldn't be — we almost always become our own most scrutinizing judges and harshest critics, and thus we miss the natural joy inherent in what *is*.

Prior to all that one learns through cultural conditioning is the primal innocence of not knowing what is supposed to bring happiness or disappointment, and so there's no basis for measuring or judging, exalting or condemning. It is observed, for example, that the very simplest little toy received with utter delight and satisfaction by an infant is generally viewed quite differently just a relatively short time later in the child's development. Moreover, a careful overview of the Gita's teachings reveals that although there are undoubtedly some verses which encourage an interest in 'upgrading' to a better assumed self — to one that is *sattvic* rather than *tamasic* or *rajasic* — the Gita's most prominently-recurring themes do not promote renovation of the pseudo-self but rather the complete deconstruction of it. This is especially clear from Krishna's final instruction to Arjuna in verse 18.66, wherein He requests Arjuna to simply surrender with trust, letting go of all of his previous ideas even about what is spiritual and what is not.

**6**

*na tad bhasayate suryo / na shashanko na pavakah*
*yad gatva na nivartante / tad dhama paramam mama*

na > not; *tat* > that (the stability mentioned in verses 4 and 5); *bhasayate* > it illuminates; *suryah* > the sun; *na* > nor; *shashankah* > the 'rabbit-marked' moon; *na* > nor; *pavakah* > fire; *yat* > which; *gatva* > reaching; *na* > not; *nivartante* > they return; *tat* > that; *dhama* > dwelling-place, state; *paramam* > supreme; *mama* > My.

**Neither the sun, nor the moon, nor fire
Illuminates that [stability in the realization of being pure Spirit]
which those who have reached do not again return from.
That is My supreme state.**

With or without Self-recognition, neither the sun nor any other external source of light illuminates the dreams we see while sleeping; they are illumined by the light of our true nature, pure Consciousness, alone. And as in a similar context mentioned in relation to verse 9.25, the words *padam* and *dhama* used in verses 4 through 6 may be read as referring to either a supreme 'state' beyond all states, or to a supreme region of infinite Consciousness where Krishna can be experienced in personified form by those who depart from this world regarding Him as their preferred deity.

### 7
*mamaivamsho jiva-loke / jiva-bhutah sanatanah*
*manah-shashthan'-indriyani / prakriti-sthani karshati*

*mama* > of Me; *eva* > verily; *amshah* > a portion; *jiva* > living, alive, composed of aliveness; *loke* > in a world; *jiva-bhutah* > becoming a living and functioning expression of pure Being; *sanatanah* > primeval, eternal; *manah* > mind; *shashthani* > the sixth; *indriyani* > senses; *prakriti* > Nature; *sthani* > abiding in; *karshati* > It draws to Itself.

**A portion of Myself**
**Verily becomes a living, functioning expression of eternal Being**
**in a world composed of aliveness**
**By drawing to Itself senses abiding in Nature —**
**[including] the sixth one, the mind.**

### 8
*shariram yad avapnoti / yach chapyutkramat'-ishvarah*
*grihitvaitani samyati / vayur gandhan ivashayat*

*shariram* > a body; *yat* > when; *avapnoti* > that one obtains; *yat* > when; *cha api* > as well as; *utkramati* > that one withdraws from; *ishvarah* > the Lord; *grihitva* > taking; *etani* > these (the senses and mind); *samyati* > that one goes; *vayuh* > the wind; *gandhan* > aromas; *iva* > just as; *ashayat* > from their place.

**Upon obtaining [affiliation with] a body,**
**As well as when withdrawing from it,**
**The Lord (omnipresent Consciousness)**
**takes these senses and mind and goes,**
**Just as the wind carries aromas from their source.**

The 'taking' of the mind and senses mentioned here refers to the retaining of memory-impressions (*samskaras*) in the repository of infinite Consciousness, and once again, the 'going' mentioned refers to a dreamlike experience occurring within It. As stated by Krishna in verse 2.24, pure Spirit is *sthanur achalo*, firmly immovable and unmoving, the foundational substratum (9.18, 14.27) of all that comes and goes.

**9**

*shrotram chakshuh sparshanam cha / rasanam ghranam eva cha*
*adhishthaya manash chayam / vishayan upasevate*

*shrotram* > the sense of hearing; *chakshuh* > sight; *sparshanam* > touch;
*cha* > and; *rasanam* > taste; *ghranam* > the sense of smell; *eva* > in this manner;
*cha* > and; *adhishthaya* > remaining situated with; *manah* > the mind;
*cha* > and; *ayam* > this one (the portion of infinite Consciousness
with attention temporarily self-localized, as described in
verses 7 and 8); *vishayan* > the respective objects of the senses;
*upasevate* > that one utilizes, that one enjoys.

**In this manner,**
**Remaining situated with the senses of hearing,**
**sight, touch, taste, smell, and the mind,**
**This portion of omnipresent Awareness with self-localized attention**
**enjoys the respective objects of the senses.**

**10**

*utkramantam sthitam vapi / bhunjanam va gunanvitam*
*vimudha nanupashyanti / pashyanti jnana-chakshushah*

*utkramantam* > stepping up, out, or away; *sthitam* > remaining;
*va api* > either, whether; *bhunjanam* > enjoying, experiencing; *va* > or;
*guna-anvitam* > accompanied by or conjoined with the components of Nature;
*vimudhah* > those who are confused; *na* > not; *anupashyanti* > they perceive;
*pashyanti* > they see; *jnana-chakshushah* > those perceiving
by way of direct inner knowing.

**Those who are confused cannot perceive [the truth of the situation]**
**Either when departing [from affiliation with a body]**
**Or remaining to experience being conjoined**
**with the components of Nature;**
**Yet those perceiving by way of direct inner knowing can do so.**

As mentioned earlier, direct knowing is always available and functions automatically when perception is not detoured and filtered through conditioned thought-patterns.

**11**
*yatanto yoginash chainam / pashyantyatmanyavasthitam*
*yatanto 'pyakritatmano / nainam pashyantyachetasah*

*yatantah* > endeavoring, diligent, watchful; *yoginah* > the yogis (primarily referring to dhyana- and raja-yogis); *cha* > also; *enam* > this (referring to the world); *pashyanti* > they perceive; *atmani* > within themselves, within the Spirit-Self; *avasthitam* > situated; *yatantah* > applying exertion; *api* > even; *akrita-atmanah* > those whose body/mind systems are unprepared; *na* > not; *enam* > this; *pashyanti* > they perceive; *achetasah* > the unconscious ones.

**Attentive yogis also come to perceive this world**
**situated within the Spirit-Self,**
**Yet those who are living unconsciously or who are as yet unprepared**
**are not able to perceive in this way**
**even when applying great exertion to do so.**

As stated in verses 5.4-5, the Self-recognition attained by the *jnanis* is also reached by the yogis, and wholeheartedly practicing one of their chosen paths yields the fruit of both. One such 'fruit,' as mentioned both in the present verse and previously in verse 4.35, is: "Upon directly perceiving what is true, you will not fall into confusion again, O son of Pandu, for by such perception you will see that the entirety of living beings are within you, the Spirit-Self, and therefore also within Me (the same one Self)."

**12**
*yad aditya-gatam tejo / jagad bhasayate 'khilam*
*yach chandramasi yach chagnau / tat tejo viddhi mamakam*

*yat* > which; *aditya-gatam* > coming forth from the sun; *tejah* > radiant light; *jagat* > the universe; *bhasayate* > it illuminates; *akhilam* > entirely; *yat* > which; *chandramasi* > in the moon; *yat* > which; *cha* > and; *agnau* > in fire; *tat* > that; *tejah* > energetic radiance; *viddhi* > please know; *mamakam* > Mine.

**The radiant light which emanates from the sun**
**and illuminates the entire universe —**
**Which is also in the moon and in fire —**
**Know that energetic radiance to be Mine.**

**13**
*gam avishya cha bhutani / dharayamyaham ojasa*
*pushnami chaushadhih sarvah / somo bhutva rasatmakah*

*gam* > the Earth (from *ga*, 'that which one moves upon or falls upon');
*avishya* > settling into; *cha* > and; *bhutani* > living beings; *dharayami aham* > I
sustain; *ojasa* > with potency, by vital energy; *pushnami* > I cause to flourish;
*cha* > and; *aushadhih* > herbs (including those that are medicinal);
*sarvah* > all; *somah* > the moon; *bhutva* > becoming;
*rasa-atmakah* > having an essence which is juicy or flavorful.

**Settling into the Earth,**
**I sustain all living beings by way of vital energy;**
**And becoming the flavor-infusing moon,**
**I cause all herbs to flourish.**

### 14
*aham vaishvanaro bhutva / praninam deham ashritah*
*pranapana-samayuktah / pachamyannam chatur-vidham*

*aham* > I; *vaishvanarah* > the universal fire of digestion; *bhutva* > becoming;
*praninam* > of those infused with the breath of life; *deham* > the bodies;
*ashritah* > dwelling within; *prana* > the outgoing breath; *apana* > the incoming
breath; *samayuktah* > conjoined with; *pachami* > I digest, 'I cook';
*annam* > food; *chatuh-vidham* > of four types.

**Dwelling within the bodies of all those infused with the breath of life,**
**I become the universal fire of digestion;**
**And conjoining with the incoming and outgoing breath,**
**I digest the four types of food.**

The five types of vital life-airs, including *prana* and *apana*, have been
discussed in the notes to verse 4.27. The four types of food are: (1) those
which require the teeth for biting and chewing; (2) those which simply
utilize the lips for drinking; (3) those which require the tongue for licking;
and (4) those which require suction on the inside of the mouth for drawing
nourishment.

### 15
*sarvasya chaham hridi sannivishto / mattah smritir jnanam apohanam cha*
*vedaish cha sarvair aham eva vedyo / vedanta-krid veda-vid eva chaham*

*sarvasya* > of all beings; *cha* > and; *aham* > I; *hridi* > in the heart;
*sannivishtah* > seated; *mattah* > from Me; *smritih* > memory;
*jnanam* > that which is known; *apohanam* > removal; *cha* > as well as;
*vedaih* > by the Vedas; *cha* > and; *sarvaih* > by all; *aham* > I; *eva* > alone;

*vedyah* > to be known; *vedanta-krit* > the author of the philosophical conclusions of the Vedas; *veda-vit* > understanding of the Vedas; *eva* > certainly; *cha* > and; *aham* > I.

**I (all-pervasive Consciousness) am seated in the heart of all beings,**
**And from Me comes the memory of what is known**
**(including what is assumed to be known)**
**As well as the withdrawal [of such memories].**
**I alone am [the ultimate truth] to be known**
**[that is spoken of] throughout all the Vedas;**
**I am the author of the philosophical conclusions presented in the Vedas,**
**And I am certainly the faculty of comprehending**
**[what is imparted in] the Vedas.**

As previously mentioned in regard to the phrase *ashaya-sthitah* in verse 10.20, the word *hridi* used here, 'in the heart,' does not mean exclusively in the physical organ within one's chest. As Consciousness flows throughout the entire body and throughout all of life, 'in the heart of all beings' means 'as the core essence of all beings.' Then, the withdrawal of memory mentioned here refers to the eradication of *samskaras*, the repository of mental impressions. This is the very basis for *nirvana*, the cessation of the dream of separate selfhood. As it is one's interpretation of and identification with remembered past experiences which alone constitutes 'bondage,' those within whom such internal activity has stopped are known as *jivanmuktas*, 'liberated while still living.' When one's moment-to-moment experiences are not filtered through memories and subsequently 'colored' by them, a profound opening can occur throughout the entire body/mind system which allows life to be lived much more fully, authentically, and harmoniously. In regard to the memory of one's true nature being temporarily withdrawn — as already discussed, it occurs in the course of 'all actions proceeding by the spontaneity of Nature' (verse 5.14), with no story of shame or blame attached to it.

**16**
*dvav imau purushau loke / ksharash chakshara eva cha*
*ksharah sarvani bhutani / kutastho 'kshara uchyate*

*dvau imau* > these two; *purushau* > persons; *loke* > in the world;
*ksharah* > perishable; *cha* > and; *aksharah* > imperishable;
*eva* > certainly; *cha* > and; *ksharah* > perishable; *sarvani* > all;
*bhutani* > beings; *kutasthah* > immovable, unchanging;
*aksharah* > imperishable; *uchyate* > one is called.

There are two types of persons in this world —
the perishable and the imperishable.
All beings are certainly perishable,
Yet those who are immovable and unchanging
[in living the realized truth of unicity]
are called imperishable.

*Kutastha*, 'standing at the top,' connotes perceiving oneself as That which is not a thing yet appears as all things. This is the perception of the *jivanmuktas*, the Self-realized ones who consistently function in the world in alignment with their eternally unborn nature. They are poetically called imperishable, yet as this verse states, their bodies cease to function in due course just the same as those without this type of perception.

### 17
*uttamah purushas tvanyah / paramatmetyudahritah*
*yo loka-trayam avishya / bibhartyavyaya ishvarah*

*uttamah* > principal, highest; *purushah* > personification of pure Spirit; *tu* > but; *anyah* > other; *paramatma* > the Supreme Self; *iti* > thus; *udahritah* > called; *yah* > who; *loka-trayam* > the three worlds; *avishya* > permeating; *bibharti* > sustains, nurtures; *avyayah* > immutable; *ishvarah* > the Lord.

But the highest personification of Spirit
is another who is called the Supreme Self —
The unchanging Lord who permeates the three worlds
and sustains them.

### 18
*yasmat ksharam atito 'ham / aksharad api chottamah*
*ato 'smi loke vede cha / prathitah purushottamah*

*yasmat* > because, since; *ksharam* > the perishable; *atitah* > transcending; *aham* > I; *aksharat* > than the imperishable; *api* > even; *cha* > and; *uttamah* > superior, higher; *atah* > therefore; *asmi* > I am; *loke* > in the world; *vede* > in the Vedas; *cha* > and; *prathitah* > celebrated as; *purusha* > person; *uttamah* > the first, the best, the foremost.

Because I transcend the perishable
and am even higher than the imperishable,
I am therefore celebrated both in the world and in the Vedas
as that Ultimate Person.

Absolute Consciousness conscious of Its own existence wondrously appears as both types of persons mentioned in verse 16, and of course as all else as well.

## 19

*yo mam evam asammudho / janati purushottamam*
*sa sarva-vid bhajati mam / sarva-bhavena bharata*

*yah* > who; *mam* > Me; *evam* > thus; *asammudhah* > unconfused;
*janati* > that one regards, considers, or knows; *purusha-uttamam* > the
Supreme Person; *sah* > that one; *sarva-vit* > knowing all;
*bhajati* > that one worships; *mam* > me; *sarva-bhavena* > with every
aspect of his or her being; *bharata* > O descendant of Bharata.

**The unconfused one who thus knows Me as the Supreme Person**
**Knows all [the conclusions of the Vedas' teachings],**
**O descendant of Bharata,**
**And that one worships Me with every aspect of his or her being**
**(body, mind, intellect, and heart).**

Nine expressions of the worship mentioned here have been delineated by the sage-king Prahlada in verse 7.5.23 of the Bhagavata Purana. They are: (1) *Shravanam*, hearing devotional songs and narrations describing the qualities, pastimes, and instructions of the various incarnations of Godhead; (2) *Kirtanam*, chanting *mantras* containing the names of God (both individually [*japa*] and congregationally [*samkirtana*]), singing His/Her/Its praises, and reciting scriptural narratives concerning the Absolute; (3) *Smaranam*, remembering or meditating upon Him/Her/That; (4) *Pada-sevanam*, 'serving the feet,' connoting whole-life-oriented service in the world beginning with service to one's spiritual preceptors; (5) *Archanam*, offering ceremonial paraphernalia such as incense, lamps, flowers, etc. to representations of the Absolute; (6) *Vandanam*, offering Him/Her/That silent prayers of appreciation or supplication; (7) *Dasyam*, carrying out the instructions which one has imbibed through hearing (*shravanam*); (8) *Sakhyam*, cultivating a feeling of affectionate friendship with one's *ishtadeva* or preferred deity; and (9) *Atma-nivedanam*, dedicating one's every thought, word, and deed to Him/Her/That in complete self-surrender. As with verse 9.14 and several others previously, verses 17 through 19 here also have their application in terms of regarding Krishna as one's preferred personification of the Absolute, and hence as the natural recipient of these expressions of worship.

**20**

*iti guhyatamam shastram / idam uktam maya 'nagha*
*etad buddhva buddhiman syat / krita-krityash cha bharata*

*iti* > thus; *guhya-tamam* > most secret; *shastram* > treatise, body
of teachings; *idam* > this; *uktam* > uttered, mentioned; *maya* > by Me;
*anagha* > O blameless one; *etat* > this; *buddhva* > having awakened;
*buddhiman* > perceptive, discerning, and insightful; *syat* > one becomes;
*krita-krityah* > accomplishing one's duties, fulfilling one's purpose;
*cha* > and; *bharata* > O Arjuna, descendant of Bharata.

**This most secret body of teachings**
**has thus been disclosed by Me, O blameless one.**
**Awakening to this,**
**One becomes perceptive, discerning, and insightful, O Arjuna,**
**and one's purpose is fulfilled.**

*om tat saditi srimad bhagavad-gita / supanishatsu brahma-vidyayam / yoga-shastre*
*srikrishnarjuna samvade / purushottama-yogo nama panchadasho 'dhyayah*

From the Ambrosial Song of God —
A conversation between Krishna and Arjuna
which is a Upanishad (confidential sharing)
of wisdom-teachings regarding the Absolute
And a scripture concerning Self-realization —
Thus ends the Fifteenth Chapter entitled Purushottama-yoga,
Recognizing Divine Unicity By Way of Its Aspect As the Supreme Person.

# Chapter Sixteen

# Daivasura-sampad-vibhaga-yoga
### (Recognizing Divine Unicity By Way of Discerning Between the Angelic and Demonic Endowments)

"The peculiar thing about a boundary is that however complex and rarefied it might be, it actually marks off nothing but an inside and an outside. For example, we can draw the very simplest form of a boundary line as a circle and see that it discloses an inside versus an outside. But notice that the opposites of inside versus outside didn't exist in themselves until we drew the boundary of the circle. It is the boundary line itself, in other words, which creates the pair of opposites. In short, to draw boundaries is to manufacture opposites...and the world of opposites is a world of conflict."

"The ultimate metaphysical secret, if we dare to state it so simply, is that there are no boundaries in the universe. Boundaries are illusions, products not of reality but of the way we map and edit reality. And while it is fine to map out the territory, it is fatal to confuse the two."

"...When we see through the illusions of our boundaries, we will see, here and now, the universe as Adam saw it before the Fall: an organic unity, a harmony of opposites, a melody of positive and negative, delight with the play of our vibratory existence. When the opposites are realized to be one, discord melts into concord, battles become dances, and old enemies become lovers. We are then in a position to make friends with all of our universe, and not just one half of it." —Ken Wilber

### 1-3
*sri bhagavan uvacha:*
*abhayam sattva-samshuddhir / jnana-yoga-vyavasthitih*
*danam damash cha yajnash cha / svadhyayas tapa arjavam*

*ahimsa satyam akrodhas / tyagah shantir apaishunam*
*daya bhuteshvaloluptvam / mardavam hrir achapalam*

*tejah kshama dhritih shaucham / adroho natimanita*
*bhavanti sampadam daivim / abhijatasya bharata*

*sri bhagavan uvacha* > the glorious one (Krishna) said; *abhayam* > fearlessness; *sattva-samshuddhih* > purity of subtle essence (predominance of sattva-guna engendering clarity of the subtle body); *jnana-yoga* > the cultivation of acknowledging recognition of one's direct experience, discerning what is genuinely known from what is merely believed; *vyavasthitih* > constancy in; *danam* > generosity; *damah* > self-regulation; *cha* > and; *yajnah* > the willingness to make particular sacrifices when necessary; *cha* > and; *svadhyayah* > study and recitation of scriptural wisdom-teachings; *tapah* > austerity; *arjavam* > straightforwardness;

*ahimsa* > nonviolence; *satyam* > truthfulness; *akrodhah* > freedom from anger; *tyagah* > abandoning, giving up (surrendering); *shantih* > serenity; *apaishunam* > the absence of faultfinding; *daya* > compassion; *bhuteshu* > for all beings; *aloluptvam* > the absence of greed; *mardavam* > gentleness; *hrih* > humility; *achapalam* > freedom from restlessness;

*tejah* > vigor; *kshama* > forbearance; *dhritih* > resoluteness; *shaucham* > cleanliness; *adrohah* > the absence of malice; *na* > not; *atimanita* > the expectation of honor; *bhavanti* > these arise, these are displayed, these are found; *sampadam* > endowed with the attributes; *daivim* > of the celestials; *abhijatasya* > of those born; *bharata* > Arjuna, the descendant of Bharata.

**The glorious Krishna said:**
**Fearlessness, clarity of the subtle body,**
**Constancy in discerning what is genuinely known**
**from what is merely believed,**
**Generosity, self-regulation, austerity, and straightforwardness;**
**The study and recitation of scriptural wisdom-teachings,**
**The willingness to make particular sacrifices when necessary,**
**Nonviolence, truthfulness, freedom from anger,**
**and the absence of faultfinding;**
**Abandoning [of what is untrue] and surrendering [to what is true];**
**Serenity, compassion for all beings, the absence of greed,**
**and freedom from restlessness;**
**Gentleness, humility, forbearance, vigor,**
**Resoluteness, cleanliness, the absence of malice,**
**and freedom from the expectation of honor —**
**These are the attributes found**
**in those born with celestial endowments, O Arjuna.**

**4**
*dambho darpo 'bhimanash cha / krodhah parushyam eva cha*
*ajnanam chabhijatasya / partha sampadam asurim*

*dambhah* > hypocrisy; *darpah* > arrogance; *abhimanah* > cunning;
*cha* > and; *krodhah* > anger; *parushyam* > harshness; *eva* > certainly;
*cha* > and; *ajnanam* > a lack of wisdom; *cha* > and; *abhijatasya* > of those born;
*partha* > O son of Pritha; *sampadam* > endowed with the
attributes; *asurim* > of the demonic.

**Hypocrisy, arrogance, cunning,**
**anger, harshness, and certainly a lack of wisdom**
**Are [displayed] in those born**
**endowed with demonic attributes, O son of Pritha.**

**5**
*daivi sampad vimokshaya / nibandhaya-'suri mata*
*ma shuchah sampadam daivim / abhijato 'si pandava*

*daivi* > celestial; *sampat* > attributes; *vimokshaya* > to freedom;
*nibandhaya* > to confinement; *asuri* > demonic; *mata* > it is considered;
*ma* > do not; *shuchah* > sorrow; *sampadam* > endowed with
the attributes; *daivim* > celestial; *abhijatah* > nobly born;
*asi* > you are; *pandava* > O son of Pandu.

**The celestial attributes are considered to be conducive to freedom,**
**and the demonic traits to be confining.**
**Do not worry, O son of Pandu,**
**for you are nobly born endowed with the celestial attributes.**

**6**
*dvau bhuta-sargau loke 'smin / daiva asura eva cha*
*daivo vistarashah prokta / asuram partha me shrinu*

*dvau bhuta-sargau* > two types of created beings; *loke asmin* > in this world;
*daivah* > angelic, saintly; *asurah* > demonic; *eva* > certainly; *cha* > and;
*daivah* > angelic, saintly; *vistarashah* > in detail, extensively; *proktah* > spoken,
addressed; *asuram* > the demonic; *partha* > O son of Pritha;
*me* > from me; *shrinu* > please hear.

**There are two types of created beings in this world —**
**the angelic, and of course the demonic.**
**The angelic type has already been discussed extensively;**
**Now, O Partha, please hear from me about the demonic.**

**7**

*pravrittim cha nivrittim cha / jana na vidur asurah*
*na shaucham napi chacharo / na satyam teshu vidyate*

*pravrittim* > progressing with activity; *cha* > and; *nivrittim* > refraining
from activity; *cha* > and; *janah* > persons; *na* > not; *viduh* > they know;
*asurah* > the demonic; *na* > neither; *shaucham* > integrity; *na* > nor;
*api* > assuredly; *cha* > and; *acharah* > good behavior; *na* > nor;
*satyam* > truthfulness; *teshu* > in them; *vidyate* > it is found.

**Persons of demonic temperament cannot discern
between activities to be done and activities to refrain from.
Assuredly, neither integrity, nor truthfulness,
nor good behavior is to be found in them.**

**8**

*asatyam apratishtham te / jagad ahur anishvaram*
*aparaspara-sambhutam / kim anyat kama-haitukam*

*asatyam* > devoid of reality, devoid of truth; *apratishtham* > without a
foundational basis; *te* > they (connoting 'they say'); *jagat* > the universe;
*ahuh* > they assert, they consider; *anishvaram* > godless, without
a higher power directing; *aparaspara* > randomly, without
natural order; *sambhutam* > come together; *kim anyat* > how else;
*kama-haitukam* > caused or motivated (perpetuated) by sexual interaction.

**They say that the universe is devoid of truth,
With no [inherently ethical] basis
or any higher power directing it.
They consider that it has randomly come together
and is perpetuated "solely by sexual interaction—how else?"**

**9**

*etam drishtim avashtabhya / nashtatmano'lpa-buddhayah*
*prabhavantyugra-karmanah / kshayaya jagato 'hitah*

*etam* > this; *drishtim* > view; *avashtabhya* > holding;
*nashta-atmanah* > those 'who have lost their soul';
*alpa-buddhayah* > who are barely conscious, who are possessed
of meager intelligence; *prabhavanti* > they rise to power,
they come forth as leaders; *ugra-karmanah* > engaged in
exceedingly cruel or violent activities; *kshayaya* > for destruction;
*jagatah* > of humankind, of the world; *ahitah* > enemies.

Holding this view,
Such lost souls in a barely conscious condition
Rise to power and engage in exceedingly cruel activities
as enemies of the world bent on its destruction.

### 10

*kamam ashritya dushpuram / dambha-mana-madanvitah*
*mohad grihitva 'sadgrahan / pravartante 'shuchi-vratah*

*kamam* > desire; *ashritya* > subject to; *dushpuram* > insatiable;
*dambha* > hypocrisy; *mana* > conceit; *mada* > arrogance;
*anvitah* > accompanying; *mohat* > from delusion; *grihitva* > having
seized, having accepted; *asat* > not true; *grahan* > ideas,
concepts; *pravartante* > they set about, they forge ahead;
*ashuchi* > foul, corrupt; *vratah* > purposes.

Subject to the insatiable desires
which accompany hypocrisy, conceit, and arrogance,
And having embraced ideas which are not true,
They forge ahead with their foul purposes.

### 11

*chintam aparimeyam cha / pralayantam upashritah*
*kamopabhoga-parama / etavad iti nishchitah*

*chintam* > anxiety; *aparimeyam* > immeasurable; *cha* > and;
*pralaya-antam* > ending at the time of death; *upashritah* > clinging;
*kama upabhoga* > the enjoyment of sense-pleasures; *paramah* > primary,
highest; *etavat* > of such measure, to such a degree; *iti* > in this manner;
*nishchitah* > having formed the opinion, having concluded, being convinced.

And immeasurable anxiety clings to them
up until the very moment of death.
Convinced that the enjoyment of sense-pleasures
is paramount above all else,
They measure [their success or fulfillment] in this manner.

### 12

*ashapasha-shatair baddhah / kama-krodha-parayanah*
*ihante kama-bhogartham / anyayenartha-sanchayan*

*asha-pasha* > a trap of hopes; *shataih* > by a hundred; *baddhah* > caught;
*kama* > desire; *krodha* > anger; *parayanah* > given over to, dedicated to;
*ihante* > they strive; *kama-bhogartham* > for the purpose of enjoying
what is desired; *anyayena* > unjustly, unethically;
*artha* > wealth; *sanchayan* > accumulation.

**Caught in a trap composed of a hundred hopes,**
**Given over to desire and anger —**
**They strive to accumulate wealth by unjust means**
**for the purpose of enjoying whatever they desire.**

**13**

*idam adya maya labdham / idam prapsye manoratham*
*idam astidam api me / bhavishyati punar dhanam*

*idam* > this; *adya* > today; *maya* > by me; *labdham* > obtained;
*idam* > this (in the sense of 'this other thing'); *prapsye* > I shall acquire;
*manah-ratham* > 'on the chariot of the mind' (the connotation being
'by utilizing my mind,' 'by the power of my mind,' etc.); *idam* > this;
*asti* > there is; *idam* > this; *api* > assuredly; *me* > mine; *bhavishyati* > it
shall become; *punah* > further; *dhanam* > wealth and property.

**[The thoughts which typically arise within them are:]**
**"Today this has been obtained by me,**
**and I have determined how to acquire that as well.**
**This wealth and property is assuredly mine,**
**and more shall become mine [in the future].**

**14**

*asau maya hatah shatrur / hanishye chaparan api*
*ishvaro 'ham aham bhogi / siddho 'ham balavan sukhi*

*asau* > that; *maya* > by me; *hatah* > slain; *shatruh* > adversary, rival;
*hanishye* > I shall slay; *cha* > and; *aparan* > others; *api* > surely;
*ishvarah* > master, ruler; *aham* > I; *aham* > I; *bhogi* > enjoyer;
*siddhah* > successful; *aham* > I; *balavan* > powerful; *sukhi* > happy.

**"That adversary has been slain by me,**
**And I shall surely slay others as well.**
**I am a master...I am an enjoyer...**
**I am successful, powerful, and happy....**

## 15

*adhyo 'bhijanavan asmi / ko 'nyo 'sti sadrisho maya*
*yakshye dasyami modishya / ityajnana-vimohitah*

*adhyah* > wealthy; *abhijanavan* > born in a noble family; *asmi* > I am;
*kah* > who; *anyah* > other; *asti* > there is; *sadrishah* > resembling, similar;
*maya* > me; *yakshye* > I shall perform sacrifices; *dasyami* > I shall
give charity; *modishye* > I shall rejoice; *iti* > in this manner;
*ajnana* > nescience; *vimohitah* > those who are delusional.

**"I am so wealthy and born in such a noble family;**
**Who else can compare with me?**
**I shall perform sacrifices and give charity, and thereby rejoice."**
**In this way, they are delusional in their nescience.**

In regard to the performance of sacrifices and giving of charity mentioned
here, the implication is that it will be done ostentatiously for obtaining public
acclaim, as Krishna will confirm in upcoming verse 17.

## 16

*aneka-chitta-vibhranta / mohajala-samavritah*
*prasaktah kama-bhogeshu / patanti narake 'shuchau*

*aneka* > many; *chitta* > imaginings; *vibhrantah* > moving to and fro;
*moha* > of infatuation; *jala* > web; *samavritah* > enveloped;
*prasaktah* > strongly attached; *kama-bhogeshu* > to enjoying
sense-pleasures; *patanti* > they sink down, they descend;
*narake* > into a hellish condition; *ashuchau* > unclean, foul.

**Carried here and there by many fantasies,**
**Enveloped in a web of infatuation**
**and addicted to enjoying sense-pleasures,**
**They gradually descend into a foul, deplorable condition of life.**

## 17

*atma-sambhavitah stabdha / dhana-mana-madanvitah*
*yajante nama-yajnais te / dambhena-'vidhi-purvakam*

*atma-sambhavitah* > self-honoring, self-revering, conceited;
*stabdhah* > obstinate, rigid; *dhana* > wealth; *mana* > pride;
*mada* > intoxication; *anvitah* > accompanied by; *yajante* > they worship,
they offer; *nama-yajnaih* > with activities going by the name of 'sacrifices';

*te* > they (the demonic ones); *dambhena* > fraudulently, hypocritically; *avidhi-purvakam* > not in accordance with guidelines (known as paddhatis) previously established by sages and delineated in scriptures.

**Conceited, obstinate,**
**and intoxicated by the pride that accompanies wealth,**
**The demonic fraudulently perform activities**
**which go by the name of 'sacrifices,'**
**yet are not in accordance with previously-established guidelines.**

### 18

*ahamkaram balam darpam / kamam krodham cha samshritah*
*mam atma-para-deheshu / pradvishanto 'bhyasuyakah*

*ahamkaram* > 'I am doing,' the egoic sense of doership;
*balam* > forcefulness, aggressiveness; *darpam* > arrogance; *kamam* > desire;
*krodham* > anger; *cha* > and; *samshritah* > adhering to; *mam* > Me;
*atma-para-deheshu* > within their own body and in the bodies of others;
*pradvishantah* > hating; *abhyasuyakah* > the envious ones.

**Adhering to the egoic sense of doership—**
**To aggressiveness, arrogance, desire, and anger—**
**Such envious ones despise Me (the animating Spirit-Presence)**
**within their own body and in the bodies of others.**

### 19

*tan aham dvishatah kruran / samsareshu naradhaman*
*kshipamyajasram ashubhan / asurishveva yonishu*

*tan* > them; *aham* > I; *dvishatah* > those who hate; *kruran* > the cruel ones;
*samsareshu* > into the experiencing of sequential dreamlike states;
*nara-adhaman* > the most vile among humankind; *kshipami* > I send;
*ajasram* > repeatedly; *ashubhan* > inauspicious, malicious;
*asurishu* > into the demonic; *eva* > only; *yonishu* > into the wombs.

**Those who hate—**
**who are cruel and malicious—**
**are the most vile among humankind.**
**I repeatedly send them only into the wombs of the demonic**
**for the experiencing of sequential dreamlike states (samsara).**

**20**

*asurim yonim apanna / mudha janmani janmani*
*mam aprapyaiva kaunteya / tato yantyadhamam gatim*

*asurim* > demonic; *yonim* > wombs; *apannah* > entering; *mudhah* > those who
have gone astray; *janmani janmani* > in birth after birth (refers to body/mind
vessels); *mam* > Me; *aprapya* > not discovering, not reaching; *eva* > still;
*kaunteya* > O son of Kunti; *tatah* > thereafter; *yanti* > they proceed;
*adhamam* > the lowest; *gatim* > condition of existence.

**Entering demonic wombs**
**And still not discovering Me (their true nature)**
**in the births of one body after another,**
**Those who have thus gone astray**
**gradually proceed to the lowest condition of existence,**
**O son of Kunti.**

It has already been established in verses 5.14-15 that Krishna (Omnipresence)
"does not dispense the sweet and bitter fruits of actions" and "does not take
account of the malefic nor even the beneficent deeds of anyone whatsoever."
Moreover, as only the one Absolute exists, a literal reading of the One
sentencing any portion of Itself to eternal torment is as untenable as a person
condemning a part of his or her own body to perpetual suffering. Hence,
as "Nature proceeds spontaneously in all of this," verses 19 and 20 may be
viewed as simply representing a similar type of energetic momentum within
undivided Consciousness as was depicted in numerous prior verses up to
and including Krishna's declaration of being 'Time, the mighty destroyer
of worlds,' in 11.32.

There is also some indication from research scholars that either the author
of the Gita or leaders of the brahmin community inserted certain verses
throughout the Gita and other Hindu scriptures specifically for the purpose
of promoting law and order within Indian society at a far deeper level than
India's law-enforcement officials could ever hope to. As it has been said
about an age-old custom observed in regard to Christian ministers, "When
there's a little more fire and brimstone on the pulpit, there's a little less of
it out on the streets." Along the same lines, it is quite likely that the verses
from this point to the end of the chapter were intended to dissuade those
who would read certain teachings given in earlier portions of the Gita
and use them to justify a more self-serving and unprincipled lifestyle.

For example, in verses 42 through 53 of Chapter Two, Krishna briefly downplays the authority of the Vedas to some degree in order to establish that one's performing vital selfless action in accordance with the immediate necessity of the living present is preferable to one's mechanically adhering to concepts imbibed in the past which render one oblivious to the living present. In any case, the overall necessity of scriptural guidance is emphasized in the upcoming four verses.

**21**

*trividham narakasyedam / dvaram nashanam atmanah*
*kamah krodhas tatha lobhas / tasmad etat trayam tyajet*

*tri-vidham* > having three aspects; *narakasya* > of hellish conditions; *idam* > this; *dvaram* > entranceways; *nashanam* > destructive; *atmanah* > of oneself; *kamah* > desire; *krodhah* > anger; *tatha* > as well as; *lobhah* > greed; *tasmat* > therefore; *etat* > this; *trayam* > triad; *tyajet* > one should free oneself from, one should withdraw interested attention from.

**Desire, anger, and greed:**
**These are the three entranceways**
**which lead to hellish conditions of life.**
**Therefore one should withdraw interested attention**
**from this self-destructive triad.**

**22**

*etair vimuktah kaunteya / tamo-dvarais tribhir narah*
*acharatyatmanah shreyas / tato yati param gatim*

*etaih* > by these; *vimuktah* > given up; *kaunteya* > O son of Kunti; *tamah-dvaraih* > by the entranceways to darkness; *tribhih* > by the three; *narah* > a person; *acharati* > one behaves; *atmanah* > for oneself; *shreyah* > best; *tatah* > thereafter; *yati* > that one proceeds; *param gatim* > to the highest path (of non-return to the experiencing of the world described in verse 8.24).

**By turning away from these three entranceways**
**which lead to darkness,**
**One thus behaves in a way which is best for oneself,**
**And in due course such a person proceeds toward the highest path.**

**23**

*yah shastra-vidhim utsrijya / vartate kama-karatah*
*na sa siddhim avapnoti / na sukham na param gatim*

*yah* > who; *shastra-vidhim* > the scriptural precepts; *utsrijya* > dismissing, omitting; *vartate* > one follows a course; *kama-karatah* > created according to one's own desires; *na* > not; *sah* > that one; *siddhim* > perfection; *avapnoti* > one reaches; *na* > nor; *sukham* > happiness; *na* > nor; *param gatim* > the highest path, the supreme refuge.

**Yet one who neglects the scriptural precepts
and follows a course created according to one's own desires
Reaches neither perfection, nor happiness,
nor the supreme refuge.**

**24**

*tasmach chastram pramanam te / karyakarya-vyavasthitau
jnatva shastra-vidhanoktam / karma kartum iharhasi*

*tasmat* > therefore; *shastram* > the scriptures; *pramanam* > authority, standard; *te* > your; *karya* > proper actions to be done; *akarya* > improper actions not to be done; *vyavasthitau* > ascertaining; *jnatva* > upon knowing; *shastra-vidhana* > the scriptural precepts; *uktam* > stated, prescribed; *karma* > work; *kartum* > to perform; *iha* > here in this world; *arhasi* > you are obliged.

**Therefore, do ascertain the authoritative standard of the scriptures
regarding what is to be done and not done,
And once knowing such scriptural precepts,
you are obliged to perform your prescribed work here in this world.**

*om tat saditi srimad bhagavad-gita / supanishatsu brahma-vidyayam / yoga-shastre
srikrishnarjuna samvade / daivasura-sampad-vibhaga-yogo nama shodasho 'dhyayah*

From the Ambrosial Song of God —
A conversation between Krishna and Arjuna
which is a Upanishad (confidential sharing)
of wisdom-teachings regarding the Absolute
And a scripture concerning Self-realization —
Thus ends the Sixteenth Chapter entitled Daivasura-sampad-vibhaga-yoga,
Recognizing Divine Unicity By Way of Discerning
Between the Angelic and Demonic Endowments.

# Chapter Seventeen

# Shraddha-traya-vibhaga-yoga
### (Recognizing Divine Unicity By Way of Discerning Between the Three Types of Faith)

"When I met my Guru, he told me: 'You are not what you take yourself to be. Find out what you are. Watch the sense "I am," find your real Self.' I obeyed him, because I trusted him. I did as he told me. All my spare time I would spend looking at myself in silence. And what a difference it made, and how soon! My teacher told me to hold on to the sense 'I am' tenaciously and not to swerve from it even for a moment. I did my best to follow his advice and in a comparatively short time I realized within myself the truth of his teaching. All I did was to remember his teaching, his face, his words constantly. This brought an end to the mind; in the stillness of the mind I saw myself as I am — unbound. ...I used to sit for hours together with nothing but the 'I am' in my mind, and soon peace and joy and a deep all-embracing love became my normal state."   — Sri Nisargadatta Maharaj

"For the mind harmonized in alignment with the Way, all self-centered endeavors come to rest. Doubts and irresoluteness disappear, and a life based in true faith becomes possible. Nothing is left behind, yet neither is anything retained. All is empty, clear, and self-illumined, without the least mental effort. ...When there is a wish to immediately align with Reality in this way, all that is needed is to affirm that 'There are not two.' In this 'not-two,' everything is included and nothing is segregated. The awakened ones in all the ten directions have embraced this truth. ...The One is all things: upon realizing this, all worries about lack of perfection are finished. Faith in the Way is true nonduality, because the Nondual is the trusting mind."
—Sosan, Hsin Hsin Ming

**1**

*arjuna uvacha:*
*ye shastra-vidhim utsrijya / yajante shraddhay'-anvitah*
*tesham nishtha tu ka krishna / sattvam aho rajas tamah*

*arjunah uvacha* > Arjuna said; *ye* > those who; *shastra-vidhim* > the scriptural ordinances; *utsrijya* > dismissing, shedding; *yajante* > they worship, they offer; *shraddhaya-anvitah* > filled with faith; *tesham* > of them; *nishtha* > the basis of one's conviction or devotion; *tu* > but; *ka* > what; *krishna* > O Krishna; *sattvam* > clarity; *aho* > is it; *rajah* > coloration, intensification; *tamah* > darkness.

Arjuna inquired:
But those persons not conforming to the scriptural ordinances
who nonetheless offer worship filled with faith —
What is the basis of their devotion, O Krishna?
Is it clarity, intensification, or darkness?

**2**

*sri bhagavan uvacha:*
*trividha bhavati shraddha / dehinam sa svabhavaja*
*sattviki rajasi chaiva / tamasi cheti tam shrinu*

*sri bhagavan uvacha* > the resplendent one (Krishna) said; *tri-vidha* > of three
types; *bhavati* > it is; *shraddha* > faith; *dehinam* > of 'embodied beings' (pure
Life or Beingness manifest as a life-form); *sa* > it; *sva-bhava-ja* > born of one's
particular acquired nature; *sattviki* > predominated by the component of
sattva (clarity, luminosity, lightness, balance); *rajasi* > predominated by the
component of rajas (creation, activation, coloration, intensification);
*cha* > and; *eva* > even; *tamasi* > predominated by the component
of tamas (darkness, heaviness, inertia, dissolution); *cha* > and;
*iti* > thus; *tam* > about that; *shrinu* > please hear.

The resplendent Krishna replied:
The faith displayed in manifest life-forms is of three types,
born of their particular acquired nature —
Predominated by either clarity, intensification, or even darkness.
Please hear about that now.

**3**

*sattva-'nurupa sarvasya / shraddha bhavati bharata*
*shraddha-mayo 'yam purusho / yo yach-chraddhah sa eva sah*

*sattva-anurupa* > in accordance with the acquired nature;
*sarvasya* > of everyone; *shraddha* > faith; *bhavati* > it is;
*bharata* > O scion of Bharata; *shraddha-mayah* > composed of faith;
*ayam* > this; *purushah* > person; *yah* > who; *yat* > whatever;
*shraddhah* > faith; *sah* > that one; *eva* > indeed, just so; *sah* > that one.

Everyone expresses their faith
according to their acquired nature, O scion of Bharata.
Indeed, a person is composed of faith;
Thus, whatever is one's faith,
So also is she or he.

**4**

*yajante sattvika devan / yaksha-rakshamsi rajasah*
*pretan bhuta-ganamsh chanye / yajante tamasa janah*

*yajante* > they worship; *sattvikah* > those endowed with a predominance of clarity and balance; *devan* > celestials and avatars; *yaksha* > subtle beings who are attendants of the celestials with guardianship over nature's treasures; *rakshamsi* > unpredictable subtle beings with supernatural powers; *rajasah* > those imbued with a predominance of intensification; *pretan* > to those who are deceased; *bhuta-ganan* > the multitude of elementals; *cha* > and; *anye* > others; *yajante* > they worship; *tamasah janah* > persons shrouded in a predominance of darkness.

**Those endowed with a predominance of clarity**
**worship celestials and avatars;**
**Those imbued with a predominance of intensification**
**worship the treasure-guardians of the celestials**
**and unpredictable subtle beings with supernatural powers;**
**And others, persons shrouded in a predominance of darkness,**
**worship the deceased (disembodied spirits)**
**and the multitude of elementals (nature-spirits).**

Avatars are deities regarded as having descended from higher regions of Consciousness to interact with humankind throughout the course of Earth's history, such as Rama, Dattatreya, Buddha, and of course Krishna.

**5-6**

*ashastra-vihitam ghoram / tapyante ye tapo janah*
*dambhahamkara-samyuktah / kama-raga-balanvitah*

*karshayantah sharira-stham / bhuta-gramam achetasah*
*mam chaivantah sharira-stham / tan viddhyasura-nishchayan*

*ashastra-vihitam* > not prescribed in the scriptures; *ghoram* > violent; *tapyante* > they undergo; *ye* > those who; *tapah* > austerities; *janah* > persons; *dambha* > hypocrisy; *ahamkara* > egotism; *samyuktah* > endowed with; *kama* > desire; *raga* > an impassioned demeanor; *bala* > force; *anvitah* > attended by;

*karshayantah* > tearing up, tormenting; *sharira-stham* > situated within the body; *bhuta-gramam* > the aggregate of elements; *achetasah* > unconscious; *mam* > Me; *cha* > and; *eva* > just so;

*antah* > on the inside; *sharira-stham* > abiding within the body;
*tan* > them; *viddhi* > please know; *asura-nishchayan* > of demonic resolve.

**Those who undergo violent austerities not prescribed in the scriptures —**
**Who are suffused with hypocrisy and egotism**
**attended by desire, forcefulness, and an impassioned demeanor —**
**Who in an unconscious manner torment all the elements of the body,**
**and so also Me abiding within the body —**
**Please know such persons to be possessed of a demonic resolve.**

Krishna's words here in regard to His being tormented along with the body's
constitution may be taken as a poetic expression demonstrating the principle
of compassion inherent in pure Being. A similar statement is found earlier in
verses 4.7-8 when Krishna says that He manifests Himself for removing what
is false and produces suffering whenever there is a withering of conscious
living and Life-centered values. We may also recall "Out of compassion for
them, I destroy their darkness...." from verse 10.11.

7
*aharas tvapi sarvasya / trividho bhavati priyah*
*yajnas tapas tatha danam / tesham bhedam imam shrinu*

*aharah* > food; *tu* > but; *api* > also; *sarvasya* > of everyone; *tri-vidhah* > of three
types; *bhavati* > it is; *priyah* > preferred; *yajnah* > sacrifice; *tapah* > austerity;
*tatha* > likewise; *danam* > charity; *tesham* > of them; *bhedam* > the
distinction; *imam* > this; *shrinu* > hear now.

**But the food preferred by all is also of three types,**
**As are everyone's sacrifices, austerities,**
**and presentations of charity.**
**Hear now of the distinctions between them.**

8
*ayuh-sattva-balarogya / sukha-priti vivardhanah*
*rasyah snigdhah sthira hridya / aharah sattvika-priyah*

*ayuh* > duration of life, vitality; *sattva* > inner strength; *bala* > physical
strength; *arogya* > freedom from disease; *sukha* > joyfulness;
*priti* > satisfaction; *vivardhanah* > increasing, promoting; *rasyah* > flavorful;
*snigdhah* > unctuous; *sthirah* > substantial (connoting nourishing);
*hridyah* > agreeable, easily digestible; *aharah* > foods;
*sattvika-priyah* > dear to those predominated by clarity and balance.

Foods which promote longevity, vitality,
both inner and physical strength,
Good health, good cheer, and satisfaction,
And which are flavorful, unctuous, nourishing, and easily digestible
Are dear to those predominated by clarity.

**9**

*katvamla-lavana-'tyushna / tikshna-ruksha-vidahinah
ahara rajasasyeshta / duhkha-shokamaya-pradah*

*katu* > bitter; *amla* > sour; *lavana* > salty; *ati-ushna* > excessively hot
temperature; *tikshna* > pungent; *ruksha* > astringent, dry;
*vidahinah* > excessively hot spicing; *aharah* > foods; *rajasasya* > by
those predominated by intensification; *ishtah* > cherished;
*duhkha* > pain; *shoka* > distress; *amaya* > illness; *pradah* > causing.

Foods which are excessively hot in temperature or spicing;
Which are extremely bitter, sour, salty, pungent, or astringent;
And which cause pain, distress, and illness
Are cherished by those predominated by intensification.

**10**

*yata-yamam gata-rasam / puti paryusheetam cha yat
uchchishtam api chamedhyam / bhojanam tamasa-priyam*

*yata-yamam* > 'that which has exhausted its duration,' aged
or fermented; *gata-rasam* > flavorless; *puti* > foul-smelling, putrid;
*paryusheetam* > 'having passed a night,' stale; *cha* > and; *yat* > which;
*uchchishtam* > remnants of food eaten by others or rejected by others;
*api cha* > as well as; *amedhyam* > contaminated; *bhojanam* > food;
*tamasa-priyam* > dear to those predominated by darkness.

And foods which are aged, fermented, contaminated,
stale, flavorless, or foul-smelling,
As well as foods which are remnants partially eaten or rejected by others,
Are dear to those predominated by darkness.

**11**

*aphala-'kankshibhir yajno / vidhi-drishto ya ijyate
yashtavyam eveti manah / samadhaya sa sattvikah*

*aphala-akankshibhih* > by those not desirous of fruit (rewards);
*yajnah* > sacrifice; *vidhi* > the scriptural directives; *drishtah* > seeing,
considering; *yah* > which; *ijyate* > it is offered; *yashtavyam* > to be
worshipped, to be adored; *eva* > only, exactly; *iti* > thus;
*manah* > mind; *samadhaya* > settling; *sah* > this (the sacrifice);
*sattvikah* > predominated by clarity and balance.

**That sacrifice which is offered
by those who have no interest in rewards,
After considering the scriptural directives
and thus settling the mind solely upon That
which is to be worshipped and adored —
Such sacrifice is predominated by clarity.**

**12**
*abhisandhaya tu phalam / dambhartham api chaiva yat
ijyate bharata-shreshtha / tam yajnam viddhi rajasam*

*abhisandhaya* > aiming for, having as a goal; *tu* > but; *phalam* > fruit (rewards);
*dambha-artham* > with deception or hypocrisy in regard to the motive;
*api* > moreover; *cha* > and; *eva* > indeed; *yat* > which; *ijyate* > it is offered;
*bharata-shreshtha* > O best of the Bharatas; *tam* > this; *yajnam* > sacrifice;
*viddhi* > please understand; *rajasam* > by one predominated
by intensification or energetic distortion.

**But that sacrifice which is offered with the aim of receiving rewards,
By those who, moreover,
are deceptive or hypocritical about their motives —
Please understand this type of sacrifice
to indeed be predominated by intensification, O best of the Bharatas.**

Within the Vedas and other ancient Indian scriptures there are very specific
directions presented in regard to the process for manifesting various personal
goals. Different sacrifices are prescribed for finding a compatible mate,
gaining the ability to conceive a child, receiving protection from a perceived
enemy, traveling to the realm of one's departed ancestors, developing
mystical powers, and so forth. Here Krishna points out the distinction
between those who are honest and forthright about their intentions and those
who are not.

**13**
*vidhi-hinam asrisht'-annam / mantra-hinam adakshinam
shraddha-virahitam yajnam / tamasam parichakshate*

*vidhi-hinam* > without any scriptural guidelines; *asrishta* > not distributed; *annam* > food (especially grains); *mantra-hinam* > with no chanting of hymns or invocational prayers; *adakshinam* > with no remuneration offered (to the priests conducting the ceremony); *shraddha-virahitam* > devoid of faith; *yajnam* > sacrifice; *tamasam* > predominated by darkness; *parichakshate* > they (the sages) refer to as.

**And that sacrifice which is performed devoid of faith —**
**With no scriptural guidelines,**
**No distribution of food,**
**No chanting of hymns or invocational prayers,**
**And no remuneration offered to the officiating priests —**
**Such an affair is referred to by the sages as a display of darkness.**

**14**
*deva-dvija-guru-prajna / pujanam shaucham arjavam*
*brahmacharyam ahimsa cha / shariram tapa uchyate*

*deva* > celestials and avatars; *dvija* > the twice-born; *guru* > one's spiritual guides; *prajna* > those endowed with insight-wisdom; *pujanam* > revering; *shaucham* > cleanliness; *arjavam* > straightforwardness; *brahmacharyam* > celibacy, continence; *ahimsa* > nonviolence; *cha* > and; *shariram* > of the body; *tapah* > austerity; *uchyate* > it is said.

**Revering the celestials and avatars, the twice-born, the spiritual guides,**
**and those endowed with insight-wisdom;**
**Cleanliness, straightforwardness,**
**celibacy, and nonviolence —**
**These are said to be austerities of the body.**

*Dvija* or twice-born usually refers to one who is a member of the brahmin social class of priests and teachers, but it could also refer to anyone from any branch of society who is awake to the truth of being Brahman, pure Spirit.

**15**
*anudvega-karam vakyam / satyam priya-hitam cha yat*
*svadhyaya-'bhyasanam chaiva / vanmayam tapa uchyate*

*anudvega-karam* > not causing anxiety, not creating distress; *vakyam* > speaking words; *satyam* > truthful; *priya-hitam* > pleasing yet also beneficial; *cha* > and; *yat* > which; *svadhyaya* > recitation of scriptural texts; *abhyasanam* > as a regular practice; *cha* > and; *eva* > certainly;

*vach-mayam* > constituting speech (meaning in regard
to speech); *tapah* > austerity; *uchyate* > it is said.

**Speaking words which do not create distress —
Which are truthful, pleasing, and beneficial;
And certainly the regular recitation of scriptural texts —
These are said to be the austerities of speech.**

**16**

*manah-prasadah saumyatvam / maunam atma-vinigrahah
bhava-samshuddhir ityetat / tapo manasam uchyate*

*manah* > the mind; *prasadah* > transparency, serenity, kindness;
*saumyatvam* > gentleness; *maunam* > silence; *atma-vinigrahah* >
self-discipline; *bhava-samshuddhih* > purity of temperament,
a natural condition of purity (simplicity); *iti* > thus; *etat* > this;
*tapah* > austerity; *manasam* > of the mind; *uchyate* > it is said to be.

**And transparency, kindness, gentleness,
Silence, self-discipline,
and natural simplicity
Are thus said to be austerities of the mind.**

**17**

*shraddhaya paraya taptam / tapas tat trividham naraih
aphala-'kankshibhir yuktaih / sattvikam parichakshate*

*shraddhaya paraya* > with the utmost faith; *taptam* > practiced;
*tapah* > austerity; *tat* > this; *tri-vidham* > in three aspects;
*naraih* > by persons; *aphala-akankshibhih* > by those not desiring fruits
(rewards); *yuktaih* > by those who are attentive; *sattvikam* > predominated by
clarity and balance; *parichakshate* > they (the sages) view as, they consider as.

**These three aspects of austerity
practiced attentively with the utmost faith
by persons not desiring rewards
Are viewed by sages as austerities predominated by clarity.**

**18**

*satkara-mana-pujartham / tapo dambhena chaiva yat
kriyate tad iha proktam / rajasam chalam adhruvam*

*sat-kara* > favored treatment; *mana* > esteem; *puja* > veneration; *artham* > for the purpose of; *tapah* > austerity; *dambhena* > with hypocrisy; *cha* > and; *eva* > merely; *yat* > which; *kriyate* > it is performed; *tat* > that; *iha* > in this world; *proktam* > spoken of; *rajasam* > predominated by intensification or over-intensity; *chalam* > unstable; *adhruvam* > uncertain, fleeting.

**Austerity which is hypocritically performed**
**merely for the purpose of gaining esteem,**
**veneration, and favored treatment**
**Is spoken of in this world as being unstable and fleeting,**
**predominated by intensification.**

**19**
*mudha-grahen'-atmano yat / pidaya kriyate tapah*
*parasyotsadan'-artham va / tat tamasam udahritam*

*mudha* > confused, foolish, erroneous; *grahena* > with concepts; *atmanah* > of oneself; *yat* > which; *pidaya* > by pain, by harm; *kriyate* > it is performed; *tapah* > austerity; *parasya* > of another; *utsadana* > injuring, destroying; *artham* > with the motive; *va* > or; *tat* > that; *tamasam* > predominated by darkness; *udahritam* > it is declared to be.

**And that austerity which is performed based on foolish ideas,**
**By inflicting pain upon oneself,**
**Or with the intention of injuring others,**
**Is declared to be predominated by darkness.**

**20**
*datavyam iti yad danam / diyate 'nupakarine*
*deshe kale cha patre cha / tad danam sattvikam smritam*

*datavyam* > to be given (connotes being simply moved to give with no ulterior motive); *iti* > thus; *yat* > which; *danam* > charity; *diyate* > it is given; *anupakarine* > to one who will provide nothing in return; *deshe* > in a suitable place; *kale* > at a suitable time; *cha* > and; *patre* > to a suitable recipient (who is genuinely in need of what is being given); *cha* > and; *tat* > that; *danam* > charity; *sattvikam* > predominated by clarity; *smritam* > remembered as, regarded as.

Charity which is given because one is simply moved to give
with no ulterior motive,
At an appropriate time and place
and to a suitable recipient who will provide nothing in return,
Is charity regarded as being predominated by clarity.

**21**

*yat tu pratyupakar'-artham / phalam uddishya va punah
diyate cha pariklishtam / tad danam rajasam smritam*

*yat* > which; *tu* > but; *prati-upakara-artham* > for the purpose of obtaining
compensation or reciprocation, a service or kindness in return; *phalam* > fruit
(reward); *uddishya* > intended for, directed toward; *va* > or; *punah* > again;
*diyate* > it is given; *cha* > and; *pariklishtam* > reluctantly, unwillingly; *tat* > that;
*danam* > charity; *rajasam* > predominated by intensification;
*smritam* > remembered as, regarded as.

But that charity given
for the purpose of obtaining a favor in return —
Which is intended to bring some kind of reward,
or is given reluctantly —
Such alms are regarded as being predominated by intensification.

**22**

*adesha-kale yad danam / apatrebhyash cha diyate
asat-kritam avajnatam / tat tamasam udahritam*

*adesha-kale* > at an inappropriate place and time; *yat* > which; *danam* > charity;
*apatrebhyah* > to unsuitable recipients; *cha* > and; *diyate* > it is given;
*asat-kritam* > with mistreatment; *avajnatam* > with disrespect,
with contempt; *tat* > that; *tamasam* > predominated by
darkness; *udahritam* > it is declared to be.

And that charity which is given
at an inappropriate time and place,
To unsuitable recipients,
Disrespectfully,
Or with mistreatment of the recipient,
Is declared to be charity predominated by darkness.

### 23

*om tat sad iti nirdesho / brahmanas trividhah smritah*
*brahmanas tena vedash cha / yajnash cha vihitah pura*

*om* > "Yes, it is so" or "Be it so," the mystic syllable said in the Upanishads
to be the sound vibration which initiated the created universe; *tat* > that;
*sat* > truth, reality; *iti* > thus, as you know; *nirdeshah* > indication, designation;
*brahmanah* > of Brahman (pure Spirit, absolute Consciousness);
*tri-vidhah* > triple, threefold; *smritah* > it is recalled, it is historically recorded,
it is traditionally taught; *brahmanah* > the brahmin community of teachers and
priests; *tena* > on that account, due to that; *vedah* > the collected wisdom of
the sages collectively known as the Vedas; *cha* > and; *yajnah* > sacrificial rites,
ceremonial offerings (the acknowledgment of reciprocal caregiving between
humankind and the rest of Life described in verses 3.10-16); *cha* > and;
*vihitah* > provided, arranged, created; *pura* > in ancient times.

**"Om Tat Sat (the Source of all that is-That-absolute Reality)"—
As you know, it is historically recorded
that each of these three words [individually] represents pure Spirit;
And that from that [Source],
The Vedas, sacrificial ceremonies, and the brahmin community
were all created in ancient times.**

_____ Or: _____

**"Om Tat Sat (Yes, it is so; that is the truth)"—
It is thus traditionally taught that this three-word affirmation
refers to Brahman, absolute Consciousness,
Owing to which the collected wisdom of the sages,
The ceremonies acknowledging reciprocal caregiving,
And the community of teachers and priests
[to disseminate the wisdom and conduct the ceremonies]
Were all established in ancient times.**

### 24

*tasmad om ityudahritya / yajna-dana-tapah-kriyah*
*pravartante vidhanoktah / satatam brahma-vadinam*

*tasmat* > therefore; *om iti udahritya* > thus enunciating the syllable 'Om';
*yajna* > sacrifice; *dana* > charity-giving; *tapah* > austerity; *kriyah* > acts;
*pravartante* > they are commenced; *vidhana-uktah* > delineated in the scriptural
precepts; *satatam* > always; *brahma-vadinam* > of those who earnestly
participate in discourses about the nature of Brahman, of those
who are dedicated to realizing their true nature as pure Spirit.

Therefore, as delineated in the scriptural precepts,
The syllable 'Om' is always enunciated
at the commencement of performing any acts of sacrifice,
charity-giving, or austerity
By those who are dedicated to realizing their true nature as pure Spirit.

### 25

*tad ityanabhisandhaya / phalam yajna-tapah-kriyah*
*dana-kriyash cha vividhah / kriyante moksha-kankshibhih*

*tat iti* > in this manner saying the word 'Tat'; *anabhisandhaya* > without a view
directed toward; *phalam* > fruits (rewards); *yajna* > sacrifice; *tapah* > austerity;
*kriyah* > acts; *dana-kriyah* > acts of charity-giving; *cha* > and; *vividhah* > of
various types; *kriyante* > they are performed; *moksha-kankshibhih* > by
those who long for freedom from the illusion of separation.

In the same manner, the word 'Tat' is spoken
when performing various acts of sacrifice,
austerity, or charity-giving
By those who are not seeking material rewards,
but who simply long for freedom from the illusion of separation.

### 26

*sadbhave sadhubhave cha / sad ityetat prayujyate*
*prashaste karmani tatha / sach-chabdah partha yujyate*

*sat-bhave* > the continued prevailing of truth over falsehood;
*sadhu-bhave* > the coming into being of what is wholesome and
beneficial; *cha* > and; *sat* > the word 'Sat'; *iti etat* > this (the way of
invocation prior to performing acts) in the aforementioned manner;
*prayujyate* > it is uttered; *prashaste karmani* > in auspicious activities;
*tatha* > thus; *sat-shabdah* > the intonation of the word 'Sat'; *partha* > O son
of Pritha; *yujyate* > it is applied, it is utilized, it is pronounced.

And similarly, the word 'Sat' is uttered
To invoke a continued prevailing of truth over falsehood
and the manifesting of what is wholesome and beneficial.
Thus the intonation of 'Sat' is utilized
in conjunction with all auspicious activities, O Partha.

27

*yajne tapasi dane cha / sthitih sad iti chochyate*
*karma chaiva tadarthiyam / sad ityeva-'bhidhiyate*

*yajne* > in sacrifice; *tapasi* > in austerity; *dane* > in charity-giving;
*cha* > and; *sthitih* > constancy, stability; *sat* > the word 'Sat'; *iti* > thus;
*cha* > and; *uchyate* > it is called; *karma* > action; *cha* > and; *eva* > even;
*tat-arthiyam* > intended for that purpose; *sat* > the word 'Sat';
*iti eva* > indeed; *abhidhiyate* > it is called.

**Maintaining consistency in the performance**
**of sacrifice, austerity, and charity-giving**
**is also called 'Sat,'**
**And indeed, even actions intended for that purpose**
**are referred to as *Sat* as well.**

28

*ashraddhaya hutam dattam / tapas taptam kritam cha yat*
*asad ityuchyate partha / na cha tat pretya no iha*

*ashraddhaya* > without faith; *hutam* > the oblation poured into the sacrificial
fire; *dattam* > the gift given; *tapah taptam* > the austerity undergone;
*kritam* > an activity performed; *cha* > and; *yat* > which; *asat* > unreal,
untrue, nonexistent; *iti* > thus; *uchyate* > it is said to be; *partha* > Arjuna,
the son of Pritha; *na* > neither; *cha* > and; *tat* > that (refers to the value
of the activity performed without faith); *pretya* > hereafter, after death
(refers to the body/mind instrument of the activity's
performer); *no iha* > nor here in this world.

**But any activity —**
**The oblation poured into the sacrificial fire,**
**The charity given,**
**The austerity undergone —**
**Is said to be nonexistent (*asat*)**
**if it is performed without faith, O Arjuna,**
**Because it is of value to the activity's performer**
**neither here in this world nor in the hereafter.**

*om tat saditi srimad bhagavad-gita / supanishatsu brahma-vidyayam / yoga-shastre*
*srikrishnarjuna samvade / shraddha-traya-vibhaga-yogo nama saptadasho 'dhyayah*

From the Ambrosial Song of God—
A conversation between Krishna and Arjuna
which is a Upanishad (confidential sharing)
of wisdom-teachings regarding the Absolute
And a scripture concerning Self-realization—
Thus ends the Seventeenth Chapter entitled Shraddha-traya-vibhaga-yoga,
Recognizing Divine Unicity By Way of Discerning
Between the Three Types of Faith.

# Chapter Eighteen

---

# Moksha-yoga
## (Recognizing Divine Unicity By Way of Freedom*)
[*The Freedom To Function Via Direct Experience With Wholeness of Perception
Rather Than Via Conditioned Thought-Patterns With Fragmented Perception]

"Not wanting to experience, or wanting to keep a particular experience, creates the illusion of bondage. Until you are willing to experience anything, you will experience bondage because there will always be some mental activity generated around the desire to escape or the desire to indulge. If you are willing to experience anything, you discover that the experience of bondage is in fact illusion. The glue that holds this illusion together is the mental activity of escape or indulgence."

"Discover if you can find a limit to *being*. For this discovery, you must surrender all ideas of who you are, where you are, how you are, what you are, when you are, and more. Surrender all ideas to pure beingness and then see. The more you surrender, the more you are called to surrender. There is no landing strip where you say, 'Now I am finished with surrender.' You are called to surrender every possibility of landing—every concept of everything, every concept of *nothing*, every concept of yourself, every concept of other, and more. Obviously, this is not a surrender in defeat. It is a victorious surrender. It is a surrender to peace. The peace that *is*. Surrender does not make peace or formulate peace, but reveals the peace that *is*."

"The treasure in surrender uses everything as a signal for deeper surrender— good circumstances, bad circumstances, comfort, discomfort, beauty, and suffering. ...Surrender your identity. Surrender your suffering to that which is closer than identity, deeper than suffering."

"You may think that to surrender means losing something. In reality, all that is lost is the power of your thoughts and emotions and circumstances to dictate a point of view about the reality of life. This is victory, the most sublime victory. It cannot be understood. It cannot be imagined. It can be directly experienced, and this is your opportunity. This is your time. This is the invitation of *satsang*."   —Gangaji

**1**
*arjuna uvacha:*
*sannyasasya mahabaho / tattvam ichchami veditum*
*tyagasya cha hrishikesha / prithak keshi-nishudana*

*arjunah uvacha* > Arjuna said; *sannyasasya* > of renunciation;
*maha-baho* > O mighty-armed one; *tattvam* > truth; *ichchami* > I wish;
*veditum* > to learn; *tyagasya* > of abandonment, of giving up; *cha* > and;
*hrishikesha* > O master of the senses; *prithak* > individually,
differently; *keshi-nishudana* > O slayer of the Keshi demon.

**Arjuna said:**
**O mighty-armed one, master of the senses,**
**slayer of the Keshi demon—**
**I wish to learn the truth regarding renunciation and abandonment**
**as well as the difference between them.**

There appears to have been some uncertainty or controversy existing during
the period when the Gita was initially spoken or written in regard to usage
of the terms *sannyasa* and *tyaga* within India's *varna-ashrama* system. The four
*varnas* or vocational groups were previously defined in the notes to verse
4.13, and the four *ashramas* — spiritual stages or situations in life — are
*brahmacharya* (celibate student), *grihastha* (married student), *vanaprastha*
('forest-dweller' or recluse), and *sannyasi* (renunciate).

**2**
*sri bhagavan uvacha:*
*kamyanam karmanam nyasam / sannyasam kavayo viduh*
*sarvakarma-phalatyagam / prahus tyagam vichakshanah*

*sri bhagavan uvacha* > the majestic Lord (Krishna) said; *kamyanam* > prompted
by desire; *karmanam* > of actions; *nyasam* > setting down, dropping, resigning
from; *sannyasam* > renunciation; *kavayah* > the seer-poets; *viduh* > they
understand; *sarva* > all; *karma* > actions; *phala* > fruits (rewards);
*tyagam* > giving up; *prahuh* > they say; *tyagam* > abandonment;
*vichakshanah* > those who clearly perceive things as they are.

**The majestic Lord Krishna said:**
**The seer-poets who clearly perceive things as they are**
**understand renunciation to be resigning from any actions**
**which are prompted by desires;**
**Whereas abandonment, they say,**
**means simply giving up the fruits of all actions**
**(and not the actions themselves).**

**3**
*tyajyam doshavad ityeke / karma prahur manishinah*
*yajna-dana-tapah-karma / na tyajyam iti chapare*

*tyajyam* > to be abandoned; *dosha-vat* > full of faults, fraught with detrimental consequences; *iti* > thus; *eke* > one group, some people; *karma* > action; *prahuh* > they say; *manishinah* > thoughtful persons, philosophers; *yajna* > sacrifice; *dana* > charity-giving; *tapah* > austerity; *karma* > action; *na* > not; *tyajyam* > to be abandoned; *iti* > in this way (meaning that they think or speak in this way); *cha* > and; *apare* > others.

**Some thoughtful persons say that every action
is inherently fraught with [potentially] detrimental consequences
and should therefore be abandoned,
While others say that acts of sacrifice, charity-giving, and austerity
should not be abandoned.**

**4**
*nishchayam shrinu me tatra / tyage bharata-sattama
tyago hi purusha-vyaghra / trividhah samprakirtitah*

*nishchayam* > conclusion; *shrinu* > please hear; *me* > my; *tatra* > in this matter; *tyage* > in regard to abandonment; *bharata-sattama* > O best of the Bharatas; *tyagah* > abandonment; *hi* > certainly; *purusha-vyaghra* > O tiger among men; *tri-vidhah* > of three types; *samprakirtitah* > proclaimed, designated.

**O best of the Bharatas,
Please hear my conclusion in regard to the matter of abandonment,
As abandonment has also certainly been ascertained
to be of three types, O tiger among men.**

**5**
*yajna-dana-tapah-karma / na tyajyam karyam eva tat
yajno danam tapash chaiva / pavanani manishinam*

*yajna* > sacrifice; *dana* > charity-giving; *tapah* > austerity; *karma* > acts of; *na* > not; *tyajyam* > to be abandoned; *karyam* > to be performed; *eva* > certainly; *tat* > that; *yajnah* > sacrifice; *danam* > charity-giving; *tapah* > austerity; *cha* > and; *eva* > even; *pavanani* > purifiers; *manishinam* > of those who are wise and contemplative.

**Acts of sacrifice, charity-giving, and austerity
are not to be abandoned.
As sacrifice, charity-giving, and austerity
purify even those who are [already] wise and contemplative,
They should certainly be performed.**

**6**

*etanyapi tu karmani / sangam tyaktva phalani cha*
*kartavyaniti me partha / nishchitam matam uttamam*

*etani* > these; *api* > even; *tu* > however; *karmani* > activities; *sangam* > attachment; *tyaktva* > abandoning; *phalani* > fruits (rewards); *cha* > and; *kartavyani* > to be performed; *iti* > thus; *me* > my; *partha* > O Arjuna, son of Pritha; *nishchitam* > definitive; *matam* > opinion; *uttamam* > highest.

**However, even these activities are to be performed**
**with the abandoning of attachment**
**to receiving rewards from them.**
**This is definitively my highest opinion, O Arjuna.**

This includes the abandoning of attachment to particular details in the performance of sacrifice, austerity, and charity-giving beyond the guidelines described in verses 17.11-22. Believing ideas that "There is only one correct way to do this" or "This is the best way for everybody to do this" is simply another manifestation of egotism, yet it occurs in the guise of spirituality.

**7**

*niyatasya tu sannyasah / karmano nopapadyate*
*mohat tasya parityagas / tamasah parikirtitah*

*niyatasya* > regularly ongoing, required; *tu* > but; *sannyasah* > renunciation; *karmanah* > of actions, of duties; *na* > not; *upapadyate* > it is fitting, it is justifiable; *mohat* > impelled by bewilderment; *tasya* > of this; *parityagah* > abandonment; *tamasah* > predominated by darkness; *parikirtitah* > proclaimed.

**But renunciation of required duties**
**is not justifiable.**
**Such abandonment impelled by bewilderment**
**is proclaimed to be predominated by darkness.**

Krishna's use of the terms renunciation and abandonment interchangeably here, and once again later in verse 12, seems to indicate that he doesn't consider the difference between the words to be as important as the higher principle behind both words, which he encapsulates in verses 9 through 11.

**8**

*duhkham ityeva yat karma / kaya-klesha-bhayat tyajet*
*sa kritva rajasam tyagam / naiva tyaga-phalam labhet*

*duhkham* > difficult, troublesome; *iti* > in this manner; *eva* > merely;
*yat* > which; *karma* > duty; *kaya-klesha* > pain in the body, physical
discomfort; *bhayat* > out of fear; *tyajet* > one would abandon; *sah* > that one;
*kritva* > performing; *rajasam* > predominated by coloration or intensification;
*tyagam* > abandonment; *na* > not; *eva* > certainly; *tyaga* > of abandonment;
*phalam* > the fruit (benefit); *labhet* > one would obtain.

**And one who would abandon a duty**
**merely on account of its being difficult,**
**Or out of fear of physical discomfort,**
**Would certainly not obtain the benefit of abandonment**
**performed in such a manner predominated by intensification.**

**9**

*karyam ityeva yat karma / niyatam kriyate'rjuna*
*sangam tyaktva phalam chaiva / sa tyagah sattviko matah*

*karyam* > necessary to be done; *iti* > in this manner; *eva* > only;
*yat* > which; *karma* > duty; *niyatam* > regularly ongoing, required;
*kriyate* > it is performed; *arjuna* > O Arjuna; *sangam* > attachment;
*tyaktva* > abandoning; *phalam* > the results; *cha* > and; *eva* > indeed;
*sah* > this; *tyagah* > abandonment; *sattvikah* > predominated
by clarity; *matah* > it is considered to be.

**Yet when duties are consistently performed**
**simply because it is necessary that they be done,**
**Abandoning all attachment to the results of one's work,**
**Such abandonment is indeed considered to be predominated by clarity.**

**10**

*na dveshtyakushalam karma / kushale nanushajjate*
*tyagi sattva-samavishto / medhavi chinna-samshayah*

*na* > not; *dveshti* > one hates; *akushalam* > inauspicious,
unpleasant; *karma* > work; *kushale* > in the congenial; *na* > nor;
*anushajjate* > one is attached; *tyagi* > the abandoner, the renunciate;
*sattva-samavishtah* > fully permeated by clarity; *medhavi* > one who is
intelligent; *chinna* > severed and removed, eliminated; *samshayah* > all doubts.

**All of their doubts having been eliminated,**
**The intelligent renunciates fully permeated by clarity**
**feel no hatred for unpleasant work,**
**Nor are they attached to work which is congenial.**

**11**

*na hi dehabhrita shakyam / tyaktum karmanyasheshatah*
*yas tu karma-phala-tyagi / sa tyagityabhidhiyate*

*na* > not; *hi* > verily; *deha-bhrita* > by one carrying (affiliated with)
a body; *shakyam* > possible; *tyaktum* > to abandon; *karmani* > actions;
*asheshatah* > entirely; *yah* > who; *tu* > but; *karma* > action; *phala* > fruit;
*tyagi* > the abandoner; *sah* > that one; *tyagi* > the abandoner,
the renunciate; *iti* > thus; *abhidhiyate* > that one is known as.

**Verily, it is not even possible for one affiliated with a body**
**to abandon all actions altogether;**
**But one who abandons [both the sweet and bitter] fruits of actions**
**is known as a true renunciate.**

**12**

*anishtam ishtam mishram cha / trividham karmanah phalam*
*bhavatyatyaginam pretya / na tu sannyasinam kvachit*

*anishtam* > unwanted, disfavored; *ishtam* > cherished, favored;
*mishram* > mixed; *cha* > and; *tri-vidham* > of three types;
*karmanah phalam* > the fruits of actions; *bhavati* > it occurs, it appears;
*atyaginam* > of those who have not abandoned; *pretya* > hereafter,
after death; *na* > not; *tu* > but; *sannyasinam* > of the renunciates;
*kvachit* > at any time, any whatsoever.

**After death, three types of fruits of actions appear**
**to those who have not abandoned [their attachment to actions**
**and their results]:**
**Unwanted, cherished, and mixed.**
**But for the true renunciates**
**there are not any [fruits to be experienced] whatsoever.**

As already discussed in relation to numerous earlier verses, all dreamlike
experiences after dissociation from a body/mind vessel occur within
undivided omnipresent Consciousness, which performs no actions and
accrues no karmic reactions at any time. Therefore any renouncing of
attachment to actions and their results can also be understood to be a
manifestation of the only-existing One creatively appearing as a renunciate.

**13**

*panchaitani mahabaho / karanani nibodha me*
*sankhye kritante proktani / siddhaye sarva-karmanam*

*pancha* > five; *etani* > these; *maha-baho* > O mighty-armed one;
*karanani* > causes; *nibodha* > learn; *me* > from me; *sankhye* > in
the Sankhya system of cultivating empirical knowledge;
*krita-ante* > in conclusively ascertaining; *proktani* > taught;
*siddhaye* > for the accomplishment; *sarva-karmanam* > of all actions.

**Now learn from me, O mighty-armed one,**
**The five causes involved in the accomplishment of any action,**
**As conclusively ascertained and taught**
**in the Sankhya system of cultivating empirical knowledge.**

**14**
*adhishthanam tatha karta / karanam cha prithag-vidham*
*vividhash cha prithak-cheshta / daivam chaivatra panchamam*

*adhishthanam* > the residence, the dwelling-place (refers to the physical body);
*tatha* > as also; *karta* > the agent or apparent doer of action (the assumed self);
*karanam* > the instruments (the five knowledge-acquiring senses, the five
working senses, mind, and intellect); *cha* > and; *prithak-vidham* > of various
types; *vividhah* > manifold; *cha* > and; *prithak* > different; *cheshtah* > movement
(refers to movement of the ten life-airs throughout the body); *daivam* > that
which is provided by the celestials; *cha* > and; *eva* > certainly;
*atra* > in this matter; *panchamam* > the fifth factor.

**These are the dwelling-place (the physical body),**
**As also the agent (the imaginary 'doer' or assumed ego-self),**
**The various types of instruments (the senses, mind, and intellect),**
**The manifold different movements of life-airs throughout the body,**
**And the fifth factor in this matter,**
**That which is provided by the celestials (air, sunlight, rain, fire, etc.).**

Regarding the life-airs, there are five primary ones which have been defined
in the notes to verse 4.27, and there are also five secondary life-airs. They are
*naga* ('snakelike'), which induces belching; *kurma* ('tortoiselike'), which allows
opening and closing of the eyelids; *krikara* ('partridgelike'), which induces
hunger, thirst, and sneezing; *devadatta* ('given by the celestials'), which
induces yawning; and *dhananjaya* ('firelike'), which promotes opening and
closing of the heart valves and decomposition of the body after its death.

**15**
*sharira-vanmanobhir yat / karma prarabhate narah*
*nyayyam va viparitam va / panchaite tasya hetavah*

*sharira* > the body; *vak* > speech; *manobhih* > with the mind;
*yat* > whatever; *karma* > action; *prarabhate* > one undertakes;
*narah* > a person; *nyayyam* > suitable; *va* > either; *viparitam* > contrary;
*va* > or; *pancha* > five; *ete* > these; *tasya* > of this; *hetavah* > causes, reasons.

**Whatever action a person undertakes**
**with the body, mind, or speech —**
**Either appropriate or contrary —**
**These five are the causes.**

### 16

*tatraivam sati kartaram / atmanam kevalam tu yah*
*pashyatyakrita-buddhitvan / na sa pashyati durmatih*

*tatra* > therefore; *evam sati* > this being the actual situation;
*kartaram* > the effectuator of action; *atmanam* > oneself, the assumed
self; *kevalam* > sole; *tu* > indeed; *yah* > who; *pashyati* > one sees;
*akrita-buddhitvat* > due to incomplete perception; *na* > not;
*sah pashyati* > that one sees; *durmatih* > foolish.

**Therefore, this being the actual situation,**
**One who, due to incomplete perception,**
**foolishly views oneself as a sole effectuator of actions,**
**Truly does not see.**

### 17

*yasya nahamkrito bhavo / buddhir yasya na lipyate*
*hatvapi sa imal lokan / na hanti na nibadhyate*

*yasya* > of whom; *na* > not; *ahamkritah bhavah* > the feeling that 'I have done
this,' the egoic sense of doership; *buddhih* > understanding, perception;
*yasya* > of whom; *na* > not; *lipyate* > it is tainted; *hatva* > slaying;
*api* > although; *sah* > he; *iman lokan* > these people (on the battlefield);
*na* > neither; *hanti* > he slays; *na* > nor; *nibadhyate* > he is bound up.

**For one who is devoid of the feeling that 'I have done this' —**
**Whose perspective is not thus tainted —**
**Although slaying people on this battlefield,**
**He neither slays nor is bound up [by such actions].**

### 18

*jnanam jneyam parijnata / trividha karma-chodana*
*karanam karma karteti / trividhah karma-sangrahah*

*jnanam* > the inherent faculty of knowing; *jneyam* > the knower;
*parijnata* > that which is definitively known; *tri-vidha* > of three factors;
*karma-chodana* > the impulse which initiates or motivates action;
*karanam* > the instruments; *karma* > the capability to perform an action;
*karta* > the agent; *iti* > thus; *tri-vidhah* > of three constituents;
*karma-sangrahah* > the aggregate by which an action is effectuated.

**The knower, the known, and the faculty of knowing
are the three factors which impel the initiation of any action;
The agent, the instruments, and the capability to act
are combinedly the three constituents by which any action is effectuated.**

### 19
*jnanam karma cha karta cha / tridhaiva guna-bhedatah
prochyate guna-sankhyane / yathavach chrinu tanyapi*

*jnanam* > knowing (refers to the manner of perceiving); *karma* > action;
*cha* > and; *karta* > agent; *cha* > and; *tridha* > of three types; *eva* > just so;
*guna-bhedatah* > distinguished by their characteristics; *prochyate* > it is
explained; *guna-sankhyane* > in Sankhya's teachings about the components
of Nature, in the empirical analysis of the components of Nature;
*yathavat* > properly; *shrinu* > please hear; *tani* > these; *api* > also.

**It is explained in Sankhya's teachings about the components of Nature
That perspectives (ways of perceiving), actions, and agents
are also of three types as distinguished by their particular characteristics.
Please attentively hear of these as well.**

### 20
*sarva-bhuteshu yenaikam / bhavam avyayam ikshate
avibhaktam vibhakteshu / taj jnanam viddhi sattvikam*

*sarva-bhuteshu* > in all beings; *yena* > in which manner, whereby; *ekam* > one;
*bhavam* > existence, beingness; *avyayam* > imperishable; *ikshate* > one sees;
*avibhaktam* > undivided; *vibhakteshu* > in the various, in the manifold,
in the distinct; *tat* > that; *jnanam* > manner of perceiving, perspective;
*viddhi* > please understand; *sattvikam* > of the nature of clarity.

**That manner of perceiving
Whereby one sees one imperishable Existence in all beings,
undivided within the diversity—
You may understand that perspective
to be of the nature of clarity.**

**21**
*prithaktvena tu yaj jnanam / nana-bhavan prithag-vidhan*
*vetti sarveshu bhuteshu / taj jnanam viddhi rajasam*

*prithaktvena* > as separate; *tu* > but; *yat* > which; *jnanam* > manner of
perceiving; *nana* > different; *bhavan* > existences; *prithak-vidhan* > diffused,
arranged apart, functioning independently; *vetti* > one perceives;
*sarveshu bhuteshu* > in all beings; *tat* > that; *jnanam* > perspective; *viddhi* >
please understand; *rajasam* > of the nature of coloration or intensification.

**But that manner of perceiving whereby one sees
separate different existences in all beings,
Each of them functioning independently —
Understand that perspective
to be of the nature of coloration.**

**22**
*yat tu kritsnavad ekasmin / karye saktam ahaitukam*
*atattvarthavad alpam cha / tat tamasam udahritam*

*yat* > which; *tu* > but; *kritsna-vat* > as though it were the All or all there is or
all that matters; *ekasmin* > to one; *karye* > a thing, an object, an objective, an
effect, a situation, an occurrence; *saktam* > adhering; *ahaitukam* > senselessly,
irrationally; *atattva-artha-vat* > lacking a valid purpose, having a reason not
based upon what is real and true; *alpam* > small (connoting 'limited');
*cha* > and; *tat* > that (perspective); *tamasam* > of the nature
of darkness; *udahritam* > proclaimed to be.

**And that perspective by which one irrationally clings
to one limited thing as though it were the All,
Without any reasoning based upon what is actually true,
Is proclaimed to be of the nature of darkness.**

The clinging mentioned here refers to the investment of one's faith, energy,
and attention. In verse 20 That which is conceived as the ultimate Reality is
viewed as the undivided whole of life; in verse 21 It is conceived as being
split up and distributed throughout life; and in the present verse It is
considered to be limited to just one particular form, appearance, or manner of
being manifest by life. This includes the viewpoint that Reality is ultimately
*only* formlessness. Additionally, an alternate reading of this verse is that
that perspective by which one senselessly remains focused on one small
situation or occurrence as though it were all that mattered, for a reason not
rooted in 'seeing the bigger picture' of Reality, is declared to be of the nature
of darkness.

**23**

*niyatam sanga-rahitam / araga-dveshatah kritam*
*aphala-prepsuna karma / yat tat sattvikam uchyate*

*niyatam* > disciplined, temperate; *sanga-rahitam* > devoid of attachment,
free of obsession; *araga-dveshatah* > without inflamed longing
or aversion; *kritam* > performed; *aphala-prepsuna* > with no wish
to attain personal rewards; *karma* > action; *yat* > which; *tat* > that;
*sattvikam* > of the nature of clarity; *uchyate* > it is said to be.

**That action which is performed in a disciplined, temperate manner,**
**Without inflamed longing, aversion, or obsession,**
**And with no wish to attain personal rewards,**
**Is said to be of the nature of clarity.**

**24**

*yat tu kamepsuna karma / sahamkarena va punah*
*kriyate bahula-'yasam / tad rajasam udahritam*

*yat* > which; *tu* > but; *kama-ipsuna* > wishing to fulfill desires; *karma* > action;
*sa-ahamkarena* > with a sense of independent doership; *va* > or; *punah* > once
again; *kriyate* > it is performed; *bahula-ayasam* > with strenuous exertion,
with much trouble; *tat* > that; *rajasam* > of the nature of coloration
or intensification; *udahritam* > it is declared to be.

**But that action which is performed with a wish to fulfill personal desires,**
**With strenuous exertion,**
**Or once again, with a sense of independent doership,**
**Is declared to be of the nature of intensification.**

**25**

*anubandham kshayam himsam / anapekshya cha paurusham*
*mohad arabhyate karma / yat tat tamasam uchyate*

*anubandham* > consequences; *kshayam* > loss; *himsam* > harm;
*anapekshya* > apathetic disregard; *cha* > and; *paurusham* > capacity,
capability; *mohat* > from delusion, from unconsciousness;
*arabhyate* > it is undertaken; *karma* > action; *yat* > which; *tat* > that;
*tamasam* > of the nature of darkness; *uchyate* > it is said to be.

And that action which is undertaken
with delusion in regard to one's capacity,
Or with apathetic disregard for consequences
such as loss or harm [to oneself or others],
Is said to be of the nature of darkness.

### 26
*muktasango 'nahamvadi / dhrityutsaha-samanvitah*
*siddhyasiddhyor nirvikarah / karta sattvika uchyate*

*mukta-sangah* > freed from obsessiveness; *anaham-vadi* > not speaking
about oneself (as being the success or failure in effectuating results);
*dhriti* > stability, contentment; *utsaha* > enthusiasm; *samanvitah* > imbued
with; *siddhi* > success; *asiddhyoh* > failure; *nirvikarah* > unchanged,
equanimous; *karta* > the agent; *sattvikah* > predominated
by clarity; *uchyate* > that one is said to be.

Freed from obsessiveness and the tendency to speak about oneself,
Endowed with stability and enthusiasm
and unaffected in success or failure —
Such an agent is said to be predominated by clarity.

### 27
*ragi karma-phala-prepsur / lubdho himsatmako 'shuchih*
*harsha-shokanvitah karta / rajasah parikirtitah*

*ragi* > impassioned, driven; *karma-phala* > the fruits of action;
*prepsuh* > wishing to obtain; *lubdhah* > filled with greed;
*himsa-atmakah* > possessing an internal readiness to give physical
or psychological pain to others, possessing a nature which causes
pain for others; *ashuchih* > lacking inner purity (integrity);
*harsha-shoka-anvitah* > chained to elation and dejection;
*karta* > such an agent; *rajasah* > predominated by
intensification; *parikirtitah* > declared to be.

Driven by the wish to obtain the fruits of labor,
Suffused with greed and lacking integrity,
Enslaved by swings of elation and dejection,
And possessing an internal readiness to give pain to others
[if it is deemed necessary in order to achieve objectives] —
Such an agent is declared to be predominated by intensification.

**28**

*ayuktah prakritah stabdhah / shatho naikritiko 'lasah*
*vishadi dirgha-sutri cha / karta tamasa uchyate*

*ayuktah* > inattentive, careless; *prakritah* > crude, rough-hewn;
*stabdhah* > obstinate; *shathah* > deceitful; *naikritikah* > mean-hearted;
*alasah* > lazy; *vishadi* > melancholy; *dirgha-sutri* > procrastinating;
*cha* > and; *karta* > agent; *tamasah* > predominated by
darkness; *uchyate* > that one is called.

**And one who is careless, crude, obstinate,**
**deceitful, mean-hearted, lazy,**
**And prone to melancholy and procrastination**
**Is called an agent predominated by darkness.**

**29**

*buddher bhedam dhritesh chaiva / gunatas trividham shrinu*
*prochyamanam asheshena / prithaktvena dhananjaya*

*buddheh* > of perception, of comprehension, of intelligence;
*bhedam* > the distinction; *dhriteh* > of the application of will (either
willfulness or willingness); *cha* > and; *eva* > indeed; *gunatah* > in relation
to the components of Nature; *tri-vidham* > of three types;
*shrinu* > now hear; *prochyamanam* > explained; *asheshena* > fully;
*prithaktvena* > individually; *dhananjaya* > O winner of wealth.

**Hear also now, O winner of wealth —**
**Fully and individually explained —**
**The distinctions between the three types of intelligence**
**and application of will**
**in accordance with the components of Nature.**

**30**

*pravrittim cha nivrittim cha / karyakarye bhayabhaye*
*bandham moksham cha ya vetti / buddhih sa partha sattviki*

*pravrittim* > proceeding forward; *cha* > and; *nivrittim* > desisting,
withdrawing; *cha* > and; *karya* > actions which are to be performed;
*akarye* > actions which are not to be performed; *bhaya* > that which is
threatening or dangerous; *abhaye* > that which is not dangerous or a cause
for fear; *bandham* > contraction and limitation; *moksham* > release and
expansiveness; *cha* > and; *ya* > which; *vetti* > it knows; *buddhih* > intelligence;
*sa* > this; *partha* > O son of Pritha; *sattviki* > of the nature of clarity.

[The intelligence that knows] which actions are to be performed
and which ones are not to be performed;
When to move forward and when to stop;
When there is actual danger threatening
and when there is no genuine cause for fear;
As well as what creates [the feeling of] contraction and limitation
and what creates [the felt sense of] release and expansiveness —
Such intelligence is of the nature of clarity, O son of Pritha.

### 31

*yaya dharmam adharmam cha / karyam chakaryam eva cha*
*ayathavat prajanati / buddhih sa partha rajasi*

*yaya* > by which; *dharmam* > ethical, rightful; *adharmam* > unethical, unjust;
*cha* > and; *karyam* > actions which are to be performed; *cha* > and;
*akaryam* > actions which are not to be performed; *eva* > certainly; *cha* > and;
*ayatha-vat* > incorrectly; *prajanati* > it understands; *buddhih* > intelligence;
*sa* > this; *partha* > O son of Pritha; *rajasi* > of the nature of intensification.

That intelligence which has an incorrect understanding
of what is to be done and what is certainly not to be done —
Of what is rightful and what is unjust —
Is intelligence of the nature of intensification, O Partha.

### 32

*adharmam dharmam iti ya / manyate tamasavrita*
*sarvarthan viparitamsh cha / buddhih sa partha tamasi*

*adharmam* > unrighteous; *dharmam* > righteous; *iti* > thus; *ya* > which;
*manyate* > it perceives, it considers; *tamasa* > by nescience; *avrita* > covered
over, permeated; *sarva-arthan* > all things; *viparitan* > turned around,
the opposite way; *cha* > and; *buddhih* > intelligence; *sa* > this;
*partha* > Arjuna, the son of Pritha; *tamasi* > of the nature of darkness.

And that intelligence which is permeated by nescience
and thus perceives all things in an opposite way —
Considering what is unrighteous to be righteous —
Is of the nature of darkness, O Arjuna.

### 33

*dhritya yaya dharayate / manah-pranendriya-kriyah*
*yogena-'vyabhicharinya / dhritih sa partha sattviki*

*dhritya* > by the application of will; *yaya* > by which;
*dharayate* > one restrains, one directs; *manah* > the mind;
*prana* > vital breath; *indriya-kriyah* > the functions of the senses;
*yogena* > by raja-yoga practice; *avyabhicharinya* > by undeviating;
*dhritih* > application of will; *sa* > this; *partha* > O son of Pritha;
*sattviki* > of the nature of clarity.

**That application of will by which one restrains and directs**
**the functions of the mind, senses, and vital life-airs**
**through undeviating raja-yoga practice**
**Is of the nature of clarity, O son of Pritha.**

**34**

*yaya tu dharma-kamarthan / dhritya dharayate'rjuna*
*prasangena phala-'kankshi / dhritih sa partha rajasi*

*yaya* > by which; *tu* > but; *dharma* > duties; *kama* > desire, pleasure;
*arthan* > motives, wealth; *dhritya* > by application of will; *dharayate* > one
maintains; *arjuna* > O Arjuna; *prasangena* > with eagerness, with
addiction; *phala-akankshi* > hoping for or expecting the fruits
of work; *dhritih* > application of will; *sa* > this; *partha* > O Arjuna,
son of Pritha; *rajasi* > of the nature of intensification.

**But that application of will by which one maintains one's duties**
**for the sake of wealth and pleasures,**
**Eagerly anticipating the fruits of one's labor,**
**Is of the nature of intensification, O Arjuna.**

**35**

*yaya svapnam bhayam shokam / vishadam madam eva cha*
*na vimunchati durmedha / dhritih sa partha tamasi*

*yaya* > by which; *svapnam* > sloth, the state of dreaming; *bhayam* > fear;
*shokam* > lamentation; *vishadam* > despair; *madam* > arrogance, intoxication;
*eva* > certainly; *cha* > and; *na* > not; *vimunchati* > one gives up, one detaches
from; *durmedha* > one who is dull-minded or slow-witted;
*dhritih* > application of will; *sa* > this; *partha* > O son of
Pritha; *tamasi* > of the nature of darkness.

**And that application of will**
**By which one who is dull-minded does not give up sloth,**
**fear, lamentation, despair, and of course arrogance,**
**Is of the nature of darkness, O Partha.**

Lamentation is generally associated with one's memories about the past, and this is here distinguished from despair, which is generally associated with what one imagines will occur in the future. What is particularly interesting is that Krishna is saying that these conditions are actually being willfully maintained by the one described in this verse; that it requires conscious effort to sustain an unhappy state of mind.

### 36-37

*sukham tvidanim trividham / shrinu me bharatarshabha*
*abhyasad ramate yatra / duhkhantam cha nigachchati*

*yat tad agre visham iva / pariname 'mritopamam*
*tat sukham sattvikam proktam / atmabuddhi-prasadajam*

*sukham* > happiness; *tu* > but; *idanim* > now; *tri-vidham* > of three types; *shrinu me* > hear from me; *bharata-rishabha* > O best of the Bharatas who possesses bull-like strength; *abhyasat* > by practice, by repetition; *ramate* > one delights in; *yatra* > in which; *duhkha-antam* > the end of suffering; *cha* > and; *nigachchati* > one approaches, one arrives at;

*yat* > which; *tat* > that; *agre* > at the beginning, at first; *visham iva* > like poison; *pariname* > upon evolving, upon ripening, upon transforming; *amrita-upamam* > comparable to nectar; *tat* > that; *sukham* > happiness; *sattvikam* > of the nature of clarity; *proktam* > it is stated; *atma-buddhi* > one's own mental/intellectual faculty, one's own power of forming and retaining concepts or notions, one's own faculty of understanding; *prasadajam* > born of serenity.

**But now hear from me about the three types of happiness,**
**O best of the Bharatas.**
**That which delights one [in due course] by way of cultivation,**
**and through which one arrives at the end of suffering —**
**Which seems like poison at first,**
**but upon ripening is comparable to nectar —**
**That happiness is declared to be of the nature of clarity,**
**born of the stillness of one's mental/intellectual faculty.**

The statement here recalls some similar expressions in the sixth chapter, such as in verses 6.20-21 where we find: "In that place where all fabrications born of thoughts come to rest...one feels perpetual happiness...."; and in 6.27: "The yogi whose mind is tranquil...indeed encounters the highest happiness."

### 38
*vishayendriya-samyogad / yat tad agre 'mritopamam*
*pariname visham iva / tat sukham rajasam smritam*

*vishaya* > the range of sense-experience, the objects of the senses;
*indriya* > the senses; *samyogat* > from the contact; *yat* > which; *tat* > that;
*agre* > at the beginning, at first; *amrita-upamam* > resembling nectar;
*pariname* > over the course of time, in the end, upon undergoing
transformation; *visham iva* > like poison; *tat* > that; *sukham* > happiness;
*rajasam* > of the nature of intensification; *smritam* > recollected as.

**That which is experienced**
**as a result of the senses coming into contact with their objects —**
**Which at first resembles nectar,**
**but over the course of time becomes like poison —**
**That is recollected as happiness of the nature of intensification.**

### 39
*yad agre chanubandhe cha / sukham mohanam atmanah*
*nidralasya-pramadottham / tat tamasam udahritam*

*yat* > which; *agre* > at the beginning, at first; *cha* > and; *anubandhe* > as an
uninterrupted sequence, at the conclusion; *cha* > and; *sukham* > happiness;
*mohanam* > deluding; *atmanah* > oneself; *nidra* > sleep; *alasya* > laziness;
*pramada* > negligence, carelessness, intoxication; *uttham* > derived from;
*tat* > that; *tamasam* > of the nature of darkness; *udahritam* > declared.

**And that happiness which is self-deluding**
**throughout its entire duration, beginning to end —**
**Which is derived from sleep, laziness, negligence, and carelessness —**
**Is declared to be of the nature of darkness.**

### 40
*na tad asti prithivyam va / divi deveshu va punah*
*sattvam prakritijair muktam / yad ebhih syat tribhir gunaih*

*na* > not; *tat* > that; *asti* > there is; *prithivyam* > on the Earth; *va* > either;
*divi* > in the heavenly strata of Consciousness; *deveshu* > among the celestials;
*va* > or; *punah* > even; *sattvam* > being in existence; *prakriti-jaih* > born of
Nature; *muktam* > free; *yat* > which; *ebhih* > from these; *syat* > it can be;
*tribhih gunaih* > from the three components of Nature.

There is no being in existence —
Either here on Earth,
or even among the celestials in the heavenly realm —
Who is free from these three components born of Nature.

**41**

*brahmana-kshatriya-visham / shudranam cha parantapa*
*karmani pravibhaktani / svabhava-prabhavair gunaih*

*brahmana* > the teachers and priests; *kshatriya* > the royal administrators and
warriors; *visham* > farmers and merchants; *shudranam* > craftspeople, skilled
laborers, and life-assistants; *cha* > and; *parantapa* > O subduer of foes;
*karmani* > activities, duties; *pravibhaktani* > individually allocated; *svabhava* >
own natural disposition, own acquired nature; *prabhavaih* > by being present
in, by springing out of, by being derived from; *gunaih* > by the characteristics.

O subduer of foes, the work-responsibilities
of the brahmins (teachers and priests),
Kshatriyas (royal administrators and warriors),
Vaishyas (farmers and merchants),
and shudras (craftspeople, skilled laborers, and life-assistants)
Are individually allocated in accordance with the characteristics
exhibited in each person's own particular acquired nature.

**42**

*shamo damas tapah shaucham / kshantir arjavam eva cha*
*jnanam vijnanam astikyam / brahma-karma svabhavajam*

*shamah* > calmness; *damah* > self-discipline; *tapah* > austerity;
*shaucham* > cleanliness, integrity; *kshantih* > patience, forbearance;
*arjavam* > simplicity; *eva* > indeed; *cha* > and; *jnanam* > higher knowledge,
wisdom; *vijnanam* > discernment, realization; *astikyam* > faith in a Reality
beyond thought and sensory experience; *brahma* > of the priests and teachers;
*karma* > actions (in the sense of characteristics actively exhibited);
*svabhava-jam* > born of their own acquired nature.

Calmness, self-discipline, austerity, integrity,
Forbearance, simplicity, wisdom, discernment,
And faith in a Reality beyond thought and sensory experience
Are the actively exhibited characteristics of the priests and teachers
born of their own acquired nature.

**43**

*shauryam tejo dhritir dakshyam / yuddhe chapyapalayanam*
*danam ishvara-bhavash cha / kshatram karma svabhavajam*

*sauryam* > courage; *tejah* > powerful strength; *dhritih* > steadfast
resolve; *daksyam* > skillfulness; *yuddhe* > in conflict, in combat;
*cha api* > as well as; *apalayanam* > not fleeing; *danam* > generosity;
*ishvara-bhavah* > a majestic disposition reflecting the ability for
leadership; *cha* > and; *kshatram* > of the royal administrators and
warriors; *karma* > actions (in the sense of characteristics actively
exhibited); *svabhava-jam* > born of their own acquired nature.

**Courage, powerful strength, steadfast resolve, skillfulness,**
**As well as generosity, not fleeing from conflicts,**
**and a majestic disposition reflecting the ability for leadership**
**Are the actively exhibited characteristics of the royal administrators**
**and warriors born of their own acquired nature.**

The words *yuddhe chapyapalayanam,* 'as well as not fleeing from conflicts,'
appears to be a friendly little elbow in the ribs from Krishna to Arjuna.
One could easily imagine Krishna slightly smiling and softly clearing his
throat before speaking those particular words.

**44**

*krishi-gorakshya-vanijyam / vaishya-karma svabhavajam*
*paricharyatmakam karma / shudrasyapi svabhavajam*

*krishi* > agriculture; *go-rakshya* > cow protection; *vanijyam* > trade;
*vaishya* > of the farmers and merchants; *karma* > occupation, work, activity;
*svabhava-jam* > born of one's own acquired nature; *paricharya-atmakam* >
consisting of dedicated service; *karma* > occupation, work, activity;
*shudrasya* > of the craftspeople, skilled laborers, and life-assistants;
*api* > also; *svabhava-jam* > born of one's own acquired nature.

**Agriculture, cow protection, and trade**
**are the occupations of the farmers and merchants,**
**Born of their natural proclivities;**
**And the work of dedicated service**
**rendered by the craftspeople, skilled laborers, and life-assistants**
**Is also born of their own acquired nature.**

Although there are a number of Gita commentaries which present Krishna as establishing — and here reaffirming — an Indian caste system based on the family one is born into, in the previous three verses we find him repeatedly using the term *svabhavajam*, 'born of one's acquired nature,' rather than *jatijam, kulajam, gotrajam*, or any other term which would indicate birth in a particular family. It also bears noting that although the *shudras* are often exclusively depicted as 'the servant caste,' there are actually no members of any of the four sections of human society who are *not* servants of society in their own ways. The brahmins serve by providing general education and spiritual guidance; the *kshatriyas* serve by providing protection and maintaining law and order; and the *vaishyas* serve by providing food and all other necessary commodities. In this way, everyone participates in a serving capacity for the good of the whole society. A few Gita commentators classify craftspeople as *vaishyas* rather than *shudras*, and this can certainly be accommodated as well since countless artists also promote and sell their own artistic creations.

### 45

*sve sve karmanyabhiratah / samsiddhim labhate narah*
*svakarma-niratah siddhim / yatha vindati tach chrinu*

*sve sve* > each to his or her own; *karmani* > in activities, in occupational duties; *abhiratah* > fulfilled, contented; *samsiddhim* > complete success, perfection; *labhate* > one finds, one meets with; *narah* > a person; *sva-karma* > one's own allocated activities or work-responsibilities; *niratah* > devoted to; *siddhim* > success, perfection; *yatha* > how; *vindati* > one finds; *tat* > that; *shrinu* > please hear.

**A person who is content with his or her own particular occupation discovers perfection.**
**Please hear how one devoted to one's own allocated activities finds such perfection.**

### 46

*yatah pravrittir bhutanam / yena sarvam idam tatam*
*svakarmana tam abhyarchya / siddhim vindati manavah*

*yatah* > from whom; *pravrittih* > arising, appearing, proceeding; *bhutanam* > of living beings; *yena* > by whom; *sarvam* > all; *idam* > this (the world); *tatam* > pervaded; *sva-karmana* > by one's own occupational activities; *tam* > Him; *abhyarchya* > worshipping; *siddhim* > perfection; *vindati* > one finds; *manavah* > 'descended from Manu (an ancient king),' a human being.

**By worshipping Him [or Her] from whom all living beings appear
and by whom all of this (the world) is pervaded,
A human being finds perfection
through his or her own occupational activities.**

It is recorded in the Bhishma Parva section of the Mahabharata, section 6.23, that on the eve of the battle at Kurukshetra Arjuna offered beautiful prayers to the Divine Mother aspect of the One for receiving Her blessings of protection and victory, having been directed to do so by Krishna Himself.

### 47
*shreyan svadharmo vigunah / paradharmat svanusthitat
svabhava-niyatam karma / kurvan napnoti kilbisham*

*shreyan* > preferable; *sva-dharmah* > one's own occupational duty; *vigunah* > imperfectly, incompletely; *para-dharmat* > than duties prescribed for others; *su-anusthitat* > well performed; *svabhava-niyatam* > established in accordance with one's own acquired nature; *karma* > activity, work; *kurvan* > doing; *na* > not; *apnoti* > one incurs, one meets with; *kilbisham* > fault, guilt, offense.

**Performing one's own occupational duties deficiently
is preferable to performing another's duties excellently.
By performing work established in accordance
with one's own acquired nature,
one commits no fault.**

The first line of this verse reiterates the principle stated in verse 3.35, and once again refers to taking up the work of someone with an altogether different acquired nature.

### 48
*sahajam karma kaunteya / sadosham api na tyajet
sarvarambha hi doshena / dhumenagnir ivavritah*

*sahajam karma* > the performance of one's natural work; *kaunteya* > O son of Kunti; *sadosham* > defective; *api* > even; *na* > not; *tyajet* > one should abandon; *sarva-arambhah* > all undertakings; *hi* > indeed; *doshena* > with defects; *dhumena* > with smoke; *agnih* > fire; *iva* > just as; *avritah* > abounding with, invested with.

One should not abandon one's natural duty, O son of Kunti,
even if its performance is flawed.
Indeed, all undertakings are attended by flaws,
just as fire abounds with smoke.

### 49

*asakta-buddhih sarvatra / jitatma vigata-sprihah*
*naishkarmya-siddhim paramam / sannyasena-'dhigachchati*

*asakta-buddhih* > whose mental/intellectual faculty is free from attachment;
*sarvatra* > in all cases, everywhere; *jita-atma* > whose sense of being a separate
self has been overcome; *vigata-sprihah* > whose longings have disappeared;
*naishkarmya-siddhim* > the perfection of non-action, the perfection of
freedom from the consequences of action; *paramam* > supreme;
*sannyasena* > by renunciation; *adhigachchati* > one discovers.

One whose mental/intellectual faculty
is free of attachment in all situations,
Whose sense of being a separate self has been overcome
and whose longings have disappeared,
By such renunciation discovers the supreme perfection of non-action.

As explained in Chapter Five, 'non-action' does not refer to physical
inactivity, but rather to the recognition that the body/mind vessel is not
an independent doer of actions and cause of their results, as indicated by
the word *jitatma* herein.

### 50

*siddhim prapto yatha brahma / tathapnoti nibodha me*
*samasenaiva kaunteya / nishtha jnanasya ya para*

*siddhim* > perfection; *praptah* > having arrived at; *yatha* > how;
*brahma* > Brahman, pure Spirit; *tatha* > thus; *apnoti* > one reaches;
*nibodha* > now learn; *me* > from Me; *samasena eva* > just summarily,
very succinctly; *kaunteya* > O son of Kunti; *nishtha* > culmination,
consummation; *jnanasya* > of higher knowledge;
*ya* > which is; *para* > supreme.

Now learn from me just summarily, O son of Kunti,
How one who has arrived at such perfection
thus reaches [the recognition of being] pure Spirit,
Which is the supreme culmination of higher knowledge.

### 51-53
*buddhya vishuddhaya yukto / dhrityatmanam niyamya cha*
*shabdadin vishayams tyaktva / raga-dveshau vyudasya cha*

*viviktasevi laghvashi / yata-vak-kaya-manasah*
*dhyanayoga-paro nityam / vairagyam samupashritah*

*ahamkaram balam darpam / kamam krodham parigraham*
*vimuchya nirmamah shanto / brahma-bhuyaya kalpate*

*buddhya* > with mental/intellectual faculty; *vishuddhaya* > completely clear; *yuktah* > endowed; *dhritya* > constancy; *atmanam* > oneself; *niyamya* > restraining, regulating; *cha* > and; *shabda-adin* > beginning with sound; *vishayan* > the objects of the senses (as listed in the notes to verse 13.5); *tyaktva* > resigning, relinquishing; *raga* > inflamed longing; *dveshau* > hatred, aversion; *vyudasya* > indifference to, letting go of; *cha* > and;

*vivikta-sevi* > dwelling in a private place, visiting secluded places; *laghu-ashi* > eating moderately; *yata* > restrained, regulated; *vak* > speech; *kaya* > body; *manasah* > in relation to the mind; *dhyana-yoga-parah* > devoted to the practice of meditation; *nityam* > continually; *vairagyam* > dispassion; *samupashritah* > supported by, resting upon;

*ahamkaram* > the egoic sense of doership; *balam* > aggressive force; *darpam* > conceit; *kamam* > lust; *krodham* > anger; *parigraham* > grasping or possessiveness (generally meant in regard to objects, property, and relationships); *vimuchya* > shedding, detaching from; *nirmamah* > 'not mine,' disinterest in self-referencing; *shantah* > serene; *brahma-bhuyaya* > for the realization of being Brahman or pure Spirit; *kalpate* > one is fit, one is prepared.

**Being endowed with a completely clear mental/intellectual faculty,**
**Consistently regulating oneself,**
**Relinquishing [obsessions in regard to] the objects of the senses**
**beginning with sound;**
**Letting go of inflamed longings and aversions,**
**Visiting secluded places,**
**Eating moderately,**
**Exercising self-restraint of the body, mind, and speech;**
**Shedding the egoic sense of doership as well as aggression,**
**conceit, lust, anger, and possessiveness;**
**Ever devoted to a practice of meditation supported by dispassion;**
**Disinterested in self-referencing, and thus serene —**
**Such a one is fit for the realization of being pure Spirit.**

Again, disinterest in self-referencing is characterized by recognizing the futility of investing energetic attention in the maintenance of an imaginary self-identity composed of nothing more than memories of past experiences.

### 54

*brahma-bhutah prasannatma / na shochati na kankshati*
*samah sarveshu bhuteshu / mad-bhaktim labhate param*

*brahma-bhutah* > fully embodying the realization of being pure Spirit; *prasanna-atma* > whose expressed self is clear or pure; *na* > neither; *shochati* > one laments; *na* > nor; *kankshati* > one longs for; *samah* > equal, impartial; *sarveshu* > toward all; *bhuteshu* > among sentient beings; *mat-bhaktim* > loving devotion to Me; *labhate* > one meets with, one finds, one attains, one gains; *param* > the highest.

**Fully embodying the realization of being Brahman,**
**One whose expressed self is transparent**
**neither longs for nor laments for anything.**
**Equal and impartial toward all sentient beings,**
**such a one discovers the highest loving devotion to Me.**

### 55

*bhaktya mam abhijanati / yavan yash chasmi tattvatah*
*tato mam tattvato jnatva / vishate tad-anantaram*

*bhaktya* > by loving devotion; *mam* > to Me; *abhijanati* > one comes to perceive or recognize; *yavan* > how great, to what extent; *yah* > who; *cha* > and; *asmi* > I am; *tattvatah* > in truth; *tatah* > thereupon, then; *mam* > Me; *tattvatah* > in truth (here connoting 'in fullness' or the full truth rather than just one aspect of truth); *jnatva* > knowing; *vishate* > one enters into, one settles into; *tat-anantaram* > very soon thereafter.

**By such loving devotion to Me,**
**One comes to perceive the extent of My glories**
**and who I am in truth.**
**Upon knowing Me fully,**
**One settles into [the embodying of that truth] very soon thereafter.**

In verse 50 we find that the culmination of higher knowledge (*nishtha jnanasya*) is the realization of being pure Spirit (*brahma tathapnoti*). In verse 54, Krishna states that the realized *jnani* who is *prasannatma* ('clear' — of all self-identification, including that of being a *jnani*) discovers *mad-bhaktim labhate param,* the highest loving devotion for Him. This recalls Krishna's words in verses 2 through 7 of Chapter Twelve wherein He says that although the tribulation is greater along the way for those whose minds are attached to the Unmanifest, those who worship His form and those who focus upon His formless aspect both reach realization of Him who is the all-inclusive Absolute. We can also trace some similarity in application to what Krishna mentions in verse 5.4 about those who cultivate empirical knowledge and those who perform selfless work, that "Even one of these paths practiced wholeheartedly yields the fruit of both."

Again here, as previously in verse 7.3, the word *tattvatah* signifies 'in fullness,' as the one being spoken about had already realized the most fundamental truth in the preceding verse (*brahma-bhutah*). The greatness or glories mentioned here which are perceived in such a one's fullness of realization have been summarily described throughout the Gita's Chapters Seven through Eleven and Fifteen, and have been elaborated upon considerably in later writings such as the Puranas. The tenth book of the Bhagavata Purana specifically depicts the life-story of Krishna. And the word *vishate* may also be read as 'one enters into,' following along the lines of verse 11.54, where we find: "By way of unalloyed devotion, one can enter into the truth (*tattvena praveshtum*) whereby I am able to be seen and known...."

**56**

*sarva-karmanyapi sada / kurvano mad-vyapashrayah*
*mat-prasadad avapnoti / shashvatam padam avyayam*

*sarva* > all; *karmani* > activities; *api* > but even; *sada* > always;
*kurvanah* > doing; *mat-vyapashrayah* > trusting in Me;
*mat-prasadat* > by My grace; *avapnoti* > one reaches;
*shashvatam* > eternal; *padam* > home; *avyayam* > imperishable.

**But even by one's simply engaging in all activities**
**with implicit trust in Me at all times,**
**By My grace one reaches one's eternal imperishable home**
**(both while still with the body,**
**and at the time of dissociation from the body).**

In this verse, Krishna, speaking from the standpoint of the Absolute, offers considerable solace to Arjuna and any others who might feel a bit discouraged upon hearing the formidable list of apparent prerequisites for Self-realization presented in verses 51 through 54. It is actually sometimes the case in certain schools of Zen and other spiritual traditions that the practices given to students are deliberately formulated in such a way that the student gradually arrives at realizing the ego's complete inability to be a doer/achiever. One comes to the point of deeply feeling: "I honestly can't do this. It's hopeless; I'm not going to attain enlightenment by my strenuous personal efforts." That moment is a crossroads within Consciousness, so to speak, insofar as the way in which one's attention moves from there will very likely determine how *all* of life — not just spiritual life — is perceived and viscerally experienced for at least some time to come. Attention may either go the way of entertaining ideas which evoke feelings of dejection and self-deprecation, or go the alternate way of viewing the illusory self's 'failure' as an extremely valuable opportunity for authentic wholesale surrender, which Krishna begins suggesting here and consummates in verse 66.

**57**

*chetasa sarva-karmani / mayi sannyasya mat-parah*
*buddhi-yogam upashritya / mach-chittah satatam bhava*

*chetasa* > by the mental/intellectual faculty, by the heart; *sarva-karmani* > all activities; *mayi* > in Me; *sannyasya* > renouncing, completely entrusting; *mat-parah* > regarding Me as the Absolute; *buddhi-yogam* > the recognition or application of one universal Intelligence functioning throughout all of life; *upashritya* > relying solely upon; *mat-chittah* > observing Me [in/as all that is], with attention upon Me, attending Me, with Me in the heart; *satatam* > always; *bhava* > be.

**[Therefore,] regarding Me as the Absolute,**
**Internally entrusting all activities to Me,**
**And relying solely upon the functioning**
**of one universal Intelligence throughout all of life,**
**Remain ever attending Me within your heart.**

*Mach-chittah* has some very useful and profound multiple connotations here. (1) 'Observing Me' or 'with attention upon Me': "Consider Me, the only-existing Reality, to be ever-present, appearing as yourself and all else which is perceived in all directions, including the space in which all things appear. Gently relax into and stabilize in that perspective." (2) 'With Me in the heart' or 'attending Me': "Consider Me to be your *ishtadeva*, your preferred deity or valued ideal of Spirit in personification. Adore Me and live in service to Me as your heart is moved to do so, also from the perspective of My being ever-present within you and within all that is." (3) 'With attention upon Me' or 'attending Me': "I am pure Awareness. Simply allow your attention to be as I am — completely free, open, whole, and all-inclusive — without narrowing, limiting, or confining your attention to any self-referenced perspective. Or better still, notice what is always open and all-inclusive without even any *allowing* involved."

Although the second interpretation above would of course be considered the most fitting for Arjuna specifically, the third reading also has a relevant application in his immediate situation on the battlefield. Arjuna's limited perspective from the standpoint of being a member of a certain family is, after all, what initially caused him to throw down his bow, refusing to participate in the endeavor to get the exploitative members of that family out of their positions of power. Therefore his relinquishing that contracted viewpoint for embracing a holistic one would bring the clarity that although he may not be thrilled about the idea of fighting with his relatives, he is still obliged to act in the best interest of all regardless of his personal likes and dislikes.

### 58
*mach-chittah sarva-durgani / mat-prasadat tarishyasi
atha chet tvam ahamkaran / na shroshyasi vinankshyasi*

*mat-chittah* > observing Me [in/as all that is], with attention upon Me, attending Me, with Me in the heart; *sarva* > all; *durgani* > difficulties, impediments; *mat-prasadat* > by My grace; *tarishyasi* > you will cross over, you will pass through; *atha chet* > but if; *tvam* > you; *ahamkarat* > due to the sense of being an independent doer of actions; *na shroshyasi* > you will not listen; *vinankshyasi* > you will be utterly lost, you will be ruined.

**By attending Me within your heart,
you will pass through all difficulties by My grace.
But if, considering yourself to be an independent doer of actions,
you do not heed [My counsel], you will be ruined.**

Krishna here accentuates the connection between genuine spirituality and very basic practicality by reminding Arjuna about the natural repercussions that would inevitably come as a result of his turning away from performing his prescribed duty as a warrior in a crisis situation. They would have their impact on his entire experience of life, as elaborated in verses 33 through 36 of Chapter Two: "For all time to come people will dishonor you when speaking about you....you will come to be regarded as insignificant...," etcetera, which for Arjuna would be 'worse than death' (2.34).

### 59

*yad ahamkaram ashritya / na yotsya iti manyase*
*mithyaisha vyavasayas te / prakritis tvam niyokshyati*

*yat* > if; *ahamkaram* > the egoic sense of personal doership; *ashritya* > taking
a stance in, taking shelter in; *na yotsye* > "I shall not fight"; *iti* > thus;
*manyase* > you think; *mithya* > futile; *eshah* > this; *vyavasayah* > resolve;
*te* > your; *prakritih* > acquired nature; *tvam* > you; *niyokshyati* > it will compel.

**If, taking a stance in personal doership,**
**you think: "I shall not fight!",**
**This resolve of yours will be futile,**
**Because your acquired nature [as a kshatriya]**
**will compel you [to exhibit that nature].**

### 60

*svabhavajena kaunteya / nibaddhah svena karmana*
*kartum nechchasi yan mohat / karishyasyavasho 'pi tat*

*svabhava-jena* > born of your own acquired nature; *kaunteya* > O son of Kunti;
*nibaddhah* > fettered by, turned towards, dependent upon; *svena* > by your
own; *karmana* > by the actions; *kartum* > to do; *na* > not; *ichchasi* > you wish;
*yat* > which; *mohat* > from confusion; *karishyasi* > you will do;
*avashah* > unwillingly; *api* > even; *tat* > that.

**O son of Kunti,**
**That which, out of confusion, you do not wish to do,**
**You will do anyway, even unwillingly,**
**Being turned towards actions born of your own acquired nature.**

### 61

*ishvarah sarva-bhutanam / hrid-deshe'rjuna tishthati*
*bhramayan sarva-bhutani / yantra-'rudhani mayaya*

*ishvarah* > the Lord, God; *sarva-bhutanam* > of all sentient beings,
all life-forms; *hrit-deshe* > 'in the region of the heart,' as the core essence;
*arjuna* > O Arjuna; *tishthati* > that one abides; *bhramayan* > causing to move,
animating; *sarva-bhutani* > all the figures animated by omnipresent Being;
*yantra* > instrument, mystical diagram, energy-pattern appearing as the
universe; *arudhani* > riding upon; *mayaya* > by the wondrous
mystical power of the Absolute, by the divine Potency (Shakti)
which miraculously produces all perceivable phenomena.

God abides as the core essence of all life-forms, O Arjuna,
And the wondrous mystical power of this omnipresent Being
animates all the [otherwise hollow, inanimate] figures
which ride upon the energy-pattern appearing as the universe.

In a great many translations of the Gita, this verse is rendered presenting
God as 'moving all living beings as though they were puppets mounted
on a rotating carousel.' In such a depiction, however, it's essential to clearly
recognize that puppets are not the oppressed captive victims of a puppeteer.
God, undivided infinite Being, is all that is *living*, and all the other 'beings' are
not 'living' at all. With or without a living puppeteer, puppets are merely
lifeless material objects in regard to which there can never be a serious
conversation about their bondage or freedom.

### 62

*tam eva sharanam gachcha / sarva-bhavena bharata*
*tat-prasadat param shantim / sthanam prapsyasi shashvatam*

*tam* > in Him (Absolute Truth); *eva* > alone; *sharanam gachcha* > go for refuge;
*sarva-bhavena* > with all aspects of being, wholeheartedly; *bharata* > O scion
of the Bharata dynasty; *tat-prasadat* > by His grace; *param* > supreme;
*shantim* > peace; *sthanam* > abode, home; *prapsyasi* > you will
reach, you will meet with; *shashvatam* > eternal.

**[Therefore,] wholeheartedly take refuge in Him alone,
O scion of the Bharata dynasty;
For by His grace you will reach the supreme peace
of your eternal home.**

### 63

*iti te jnanam akhyatam / guhyad guhyataram maya*
*vimrishyaitad asheshena / yathechchasi tatha kuru*

*iti* > thus; *te* > to you; *jnanam* > knowledge; *akhyatam* > informed,
communicated; *guhyat* > than the secret; *guhyataram* > more secret; *maya* > by
me; *vimrishya* > having pondered, having deliberated upon; *etat* > this;
*asheshena* > fully; *yatha ichchasi* > as you wish; *tatha* > thus; *kuru* > do.

**I have thus imparted to you that knowledge
which even among secrets is more secret still.
Having fully pondered this,
you may then do as you wish.**

**64**

*sarva-guhyatamam bhuyah / shrinu me paramam vachah*
*ishto 'si me dridham iti / tato vakshyami te hitam*

*sarva-guhya-tamam* > the most secret of all; *bhuyah* > again; *shrinu* > listen;
*me* > My; *paramam* > highest; *vachah* > instruction; *ishtah* > beloved;
*asi* > you are; *me* > by Me; *dridham* > strongly, closely; *iti* > as you know;
*tatah* > therefore; *vakshyami* > I shall speak; *te hitam* > for your benefit.

**But listen once again to My highest instruction,**
**which is the most secret of all.**
**As you know, you are dearly beloved by Me,**
**and therefore I shall repeat it for your benefit.**

**65**

*manmana bhava madbhakto / madyaji mam namaskuru*
*mam evaishyasi satyam te / pratijane priyo 'si me*

*man-manah* > with attention focused upon Me; *bhava* > be;
*mat-bhaktah* > wholeheartedly devoted to Me; *mat-yaji* > sacrificing
for Me; *mam* > to Me; *namaskuru* > bow in homage; *mam* > to Me;
*eva* > just so; *eshyasi* > you will come; *satyam* > sincerely, honestly, faithfully;
*te* > to you; *pratijane* > I promise; *priyah* > dear; *asi* > you are; *me* > to Me.

**With wholehearted devotion to Me,**
**Focus your attention upon Me,**
**Sacrificing for Me and bowing in homage to Me.**
**Thus you will come to Me;**
**I sincerely promise you this, for you are dear to Me.**

The first two-thirds of this verse reiterates Krishna's exhortation to Arjuna
in verse 9.34, and the two different readings of *madyaji* ('sacrificing for Me')
and *mam evaishyasi* ('you will come to Me') have been discussed in the
accompanying notes there. Such perspectives, which would apply to the
phrase *mam evaishyati* in upcoming verse 68 as well, are not mutually
exclusive, as those who have realized their true nature are certainly not
exempt from the experience of being in Krishna's or any deity's abode,
either while still affiliated with the present body or after dissociation from it.

**66**

*sarva-dharman parityajya / mam ekam sharanam vraja*
*aham tva sarva-papebhyo / mokshayishyami ma shuchah*

*sarva-dharman* > all general religious instruction; *parityajya* > abandoning;
*mam* > in Me; *ekam* > alone; *sharanam vraja* > take refuge; *aham* > I;
*tva* > you; *sarva-papebhyah* > from all sins, from all misfortunes;
*mokshayishyami* > I shall release; *ma shuchah* > do not grieve.

**Abandoning all general religious instruction,**
**Take refuge in Me alone.**
**I shall release you from all sins**
**[which you feared you would be guilty of**
**by participating in the battle here];**
**You need not grieve.**

As discussed in the notes to verse 2.40, Arjuna was deeply concerned
about being responsible for transgressing several religious injunctions by
participating in the battle at Kurukshetra. When he was a young boy he had
learned that *ahimsa*, nonviolence, is one of the foremost tenets among all
Vedic and yogic principles, and Krishna indeed confirms this to be true in
verses 13.7, 16.2, and 17.14. Therefore, in this verse and verily throughout
his entire Gita discourse, Krishna conveys the sense of: "Yes, Arjuna, there
*are* general instructions strongly emphasizing nonviolence, forbearance,
and forgiveness, and this is unquestionably the *dharma* to be observed in all
routine, day-to-day life situations. However, this situation at Kurukshetra is
not in the category of routine affairs. This is an extenuating circumstance, an
emergency, and so to adhere to a particular set of formally established rules
in such a crisis would represent a fundamentalist type of expression—
machinelike unconsciousness completely oblivious to what is vitally needed
in the moment for the benefit of all involved. Something different is presently
called for, for the sake of all the citizens who, as we speak, are being ruled by
exceedingly cruel men whose reign is not serving the best interests of the
world-community.

"I know you haven't forgotten what happened when I myself went to the
Kauravas' court as an emissary of peace attempting to avert this war by
negotiating an agreement with Duryodhana and his supporters. He would
not accede to even discussing the matter. Although the *kshatriya*'s code
of ethics clearly states that an ambassador on a mission of proposing
reconciliation is never to be harmed or abducted, he nonetheless ordered
his men to seize me and hold me as a hostage in order to possess yet another
unlawful advantage over you and your brothers. Of course, he could not
capture me, as I am a master of all mystic potencies, but his attempt to do so
in such a dishonorable fashion informed us that pacifism would not be an
option for us on this particular occasion.

"I know you also remember how Duryodhana and his men usurped the kingdoms of you and all of your brothers by deceitful means in the dice-game, and how they prepared a house of combustible materials for all of you to stay in so that they could set fire to it and murder you during the night as you slept. As these are the very same men who are currently in power ruling over provinces with millions of citizens, Life Itself has ordained that they be removed from their positions, their madness brought to an end in this very place for the greater good of all. That is therefore the prevailing standard of *dharma* at this present moment. Once Duryodhana and his supporters have been removed from power and the need of the whole has been met, then the general principles of routine *dharma* are reinstated, so to speak, to be carefully observed. Universal Intelligence, which is alive and dynamically flowing with boundless unconditional love, naturally moves in this way, decreeing that the rules can change in an instant in such an emergency as we are presently faced with. It can be said that such love is above law, or that such love is the highest law. So from the broader perspective, we may wish to consider whether it may be far less loving and a far greater act of violence to just leave greedy assassins in power for generations to come.

"Since nothing can be separate from the totality of life, it is a certainty that you (the life-form of Arjuna) will be utilized as an instrument of Totality in one manner or another. If within that instrument there is availability for what is called for right now, then there will accordingly be a particular flow of experiences for you in the time to come. If instead of availability there is avoidance—even avoidance that is scripturally supported—then it is inevitable that there will henceforth be a very different flow of experiences for you, for it is known by all that you have been extensively trained to act as a dutiful *kshatriya*. Whatever decision is made, however, you have My complete assurance that by your courageous trusting of your own true nature as the Absolute, and the surrendered relaxing of your acquired nature into alignment with that Reality, there's not the slightest possibility of your experiencing whatever you had imagined to be the result of 'sinning.'" In this way, Krishna's use of the words *ma shuchah* here also convey the sense of "Have no fear; you needn't worry about that."

**67**

*idam te natapaskaya / nabhaktaya kadachana*
*na chashushrushave vachyam / na cha mam yo 'bhyasuyati*

*idam* > this; *te* > by you; *na* > not; *atapaskaya* > to one who performs no austerities (refers to self-discipline, not harsh asceticism); *na* > not;

*abhaktaya* > to one who is not devoted; *kadachana* > at any time;
*na* > not; *cha* > and; *ashushrushave* > to one who does not wish to hear,
to one who performs no service; *vachyam* > to be said; *na* > not;
*cha* > and; *mam* > Me; *yah* > who; *abhyasuyati* > one who shows
contempt toward, one who speaks ill about.

**This [confidential advice] is not to be divulged by you at any time
to those without self-discipline,
Nor to those who are not devoted [to higher truth];
Also not to those who are without a serving disposition,
or do not wish to hear My words, or who show contempt for Me.**

A substantial portion of the Gita's teachings — about karma-yoga, Sankhya,
meditation, and devotion in a general sense — were for the most part already
accessible throughout most sections of Indian society by the time of the Gita's
recital; yet verses 56 through 66 of this chapter are considered to be especially
confidential. In all likelihood the prohibitions here in regard to sharing their
message were issued because it was apprehended that persons predominated
by the lower components of nature might use Krishna's statements therein
for pursuing self-centered interests in the name of 'abandoning all religious
instruction for taking refuge in Krishna alone.'

### 68
*ya idam paramam guhyam / mad-bhakteshvabhidhasyati*
*bhaktim mayi param kritva / mam evaishyatyasamshayah*

*yah* > who; *idam* > this; *paramam* > supreme; *guhyam* > secret; *mat-bhakteshu* >
to My devotees; *abhidhasyati* > one will impart; *bhaktim* > loving devotion;
*mayi* > to Me; *param* > highest; *kritva* > performing; *mam* > to Me;
*eva* > alone; *eshyati* > that one will come; *asamshayah* > undoubtedly.

**[But] one who imparts this supreme secret to My devotees
Performs the highest act
of loving devotion to Me,
And will undoubtedly come to Me alone.**

### 69
*na cha tasman manushyeshu / kashchin me priya-krittamah*
*bhavita na cha me tasmad / anyah priyataro bhuvi*

*na* > not; *cha* > and; *tasmat* > than that one; *manushyeshu* > among humankind;
*kashchit* > anyone; *me* > to Me; *priya-krit-tamah* > performing an activity
more cherished, pleasing, or valued; *bhavita* > that one shall be;

*na* > not; *cha* > and; *me* > of Me; *tasmat* > than that one; *anyah* > another; *priya-tarah* > more dear, more pleasing, more valued; *bhhuvi* > in the world.

**No one among humankind**
**performs an activity more pleasing to Me than that one,**
**Nor shall any other in this world**
**be more dear to Me.**

### 70
*adhyeshyate cha ya imam / dharmyam samvadam avayoh*
*jnana-yajnena tenaham / ishtah syam iti me matih*

*adhyeshyate* > one will study; *cha* > and; *yah* > who; *imam* > this;
*dharmyam* > rich with virtues, virtue-evoking; *samvadam* > conversation;
*avayoh* > of ours; *jnana-yajnena* > by the sacrifice of cultivating
true wisdom (through scriptural study vide verse 4.28);
*tena* > by that one; *aham* > I; *ishtah* > worshipped; *syam* > will be;
*iti* > thus; *me* > My; *matis* > conviction, view.

**And one who studies this virtue-evoking conversation of ours**
**Will be worshipping Me**
**through the sacrifice of cultivating true wisdom;**
**This is My view.**

### 71
*shraddhavan anasuyash cha / shrinuyad api yo narah*
*so 'pi muktah shubhan lokan / prapnuyat punya-karmanam*

*shraddha-van* > full of faith; *anasuyah* > without envy,
without discontent, without complaint; *cha* > and; *shrinuyat* > one
would hear; *api* > even; *yah* > who; *narah* > a person; *sah* > that one;
*api* > also; *muktah* > liberated; *shubhan* > auspicious, joyous,
fortunate; *lokan* > worlds; *prapnuyat* > one reaches;
*punya-karmanam* > of those whose activities are pure.

**Even the person who simply hears it**
**with great faith and without complaint**
**Is also liberated [in due course, after first] reaching the auspicious worlds**
**of those whose activities are pure.**

This verse recalls the path of light described in verse 8.24.

**72**
*kachchid etach chrutam partha / tvayaikagrena chetasa*
*kachchid ajnana-sammohah / pranashtas te dhananjaya*

*kachchit etat* > has this; *shrutam* > been heard; *partha* > O son of Pritha;
*tvaya* > by you; *eka-agrena* > with singularly-focused attention;
*chetasa* > with the mind; *kachchit* > has it; *ajnana* > the tendency to
ignore what is innately known and to ignore the recognition of what
is not actually known but merely believed; *sammohah* > confusion;
*pranashtah* > dispelled; *te* > your; *dhananjaya* > O winner of wealth.

**O son of Pritha, has this been heard by you**
**with singularly-focused attention of mind?**
**Have your confusion and your tendency to ignore**
**[the recognition of what is truly known and truly not known]**
**been dispelled, O winner of wealth?**

**73**
*arjuna uvacha:*
*nashto mohah smritir labdha / tvat-prasadan mayachyuta*
*sthito 'smi gata-sandehah / karishye vachanam tava*

*arjunah uvacha* > Arjuna said; *nashtah* > lost; *mohah* > confusion;
*smritih* > remembrance; *labdha* > gained, found; *tvat-prasadat* > by your grace,
by your kindness; *maya* > by me; *achyuta* > O infallible one; *sthitah* > abiding,
settled; *asmi* > I am; *gata* > gone; *sandehah* > with doubts; *karishye* > I am
prepared to act; *vachanam* > counsel, instruction; *tava* > your.

**Arjuna said:**
**My confusion is gone,**
**And I have regained remembrance [of my true nature]**
**by your kindness, O infallible one.**
**Settled as I now am with all doubts gone,**
**I am prepared to act according to your counsel.**

It bears noting that upon awakening to Self-realization, Arjuna did not say:
"Well, now that I clearly perceive the illusoriness of this world, it's even
clearer than ever before that I certainly don't need to fight in this war
that's about to begin here. So let's turn this chariot around and head for
the Himalayas." This may help in putting to rest the erroneous notion
sometimes voiced that all those who awaken to absolute truth immediately
become apathetic towards absolutely everything and promptly begin

disregarding all responsibilities in the world. Such a response to spiritual awakening is certainly possible and has admittedly been demonstrated from time to time, yet such occurrences are rarities and not foregone conclusions.

### 74
*sanjaya uvacha:*
*ityaham vasudevasya / parthasya cha mahatmanah*
*samvadam imam ashrausham / adbhutam roma-harshanam*

*sanjayah uvacha* > Sanjaya said; *iti* > thus; *aham* > I;
*vasudevasya* > Krishna, the son of Vasudeva; *parthasya* > Arjuna,
the son of Pritha; *cha* > and; *maha-atmanah* > the great expression of the
Spirit-Self, the great-hearted one; *samvadam* > conversation; *imam* > this;
*ashrausham* > I have heard; *adbhutam* > wonderful, extraordinary;
*roma-harshanam* > causing the hairs to stand on end.

**Sanjaya said:**
**Thus have I heard the conversation**
**between Krishna and the great-hearted Arjuna.**
**So wondrous was it**
**that it causes my hair to stand on end.**

### 75
*vyasa-prasadach chrutavan / etad guhyam aham param*
*yogam yogeshvarat krishnat / sakshat kathayatah svayam*

*vyasa-prasadat* > by the grace of Vyasa; *shrutavan* > one who has heard;
*etat* > this; *guhyam* > mysterious; *aham* > I; *param* > highest;
*yogam* > the science of Self-recognition; *yoga-ishvarat* > from the
Lord of Yoga; *krishnat* > from Sri Krishna; *sakshat* > directly;
*kathayatah* > communicating; svayam > Himself.

**By the grace of [my spiritual preceptor] Vyasa**
**I have heard this highest and most mysterious science of Self-recognition**
**Communicated directly by Sri Krishna,**
**the Lord of Yoga Himself.**

The science of Yoga is called mysterious because in many ways it functions in a way which is exactly the opposite of what the rational mind would expect. One example of this is the tendency of spiritual awakenings to occur when one is not seeking for them.

### 76

*rajan samsmritya samsmritya / samvadam imam adbhutam*
*keshav'-arjunayoh punyam / hrishyami cha muhur muhuh*

*rajan* > O king (Dhritarashtra); *samsmritya samsmritya* > remembering
again and again; *samvadam* > conversation; *imam* > this;
*adbhutam* > wonderful, extraordinary; *keshava* > Krishna,
who possesses splendid hair; *arjunayoh* > and Arjuna;
*punyam* > auspicious; *hrishyami* > I am thrilled with joy;
*cha* > and; *muhuh muhuh* > at every moment.

**O king, remembering again and again**
**this extraordinary, auspicious conversation**
**between Krishna and Arjuna,**
**I am thrilled with joy at every moment.**

### 77

*tach cha samsmritya samsmritya / rupam atyadbhutam hareh*
*vismayo me mahan rajan / hrishyami cha punah punah*

*tat* > that; *cha* > and; *samsmritya samsmritya* > repeatedly remembering;
*rupam* > the form; *ati-adbhutam* > beyond magnificent; *hareh* > of Krishna,
who removes all miseries; *vismayah* > amazement; *me* > my; *mahan* > great;
*rajan* > O king; *hrishyami* > I experience waves of rapture;
*cha* > and; *punah punah* > again and again.

**And repeatedly remembering**
**that exceptionally magnificent [universal] form of Krishna,**
**My amazement is great, O king,**
**and I experience waves of rapture again and again.**

### 78

*yatra yogeshvarah krishno / yatra partho dhanurdharah*
*tatra srir vijayo bhutir / dhruva nitir matir mama*

*yatra* > wherever; *yoga-ishvarah* > the Lord of Yoga, the supreme master of
the science of Self-realization, the supreme master of all mystic abilities;
*krishnah* > Krishna; *yatra* > wherever; *parthah* > Arjuna, the son of Pritha;
*dhanuh-dharah* > the wielder of the bow, the archer; *tatra* > there; *srih* > good
fortune, prosperity; *vijayah* > victory; *bhutih* > well-being; *dhruva* > assured,
enduring; *nitih* > judiciousness; *matih mama* > my opinion, my conviction.

Wherever there is Krishna,
the supreme master of Self-realization and all mystic abilities —
And wherever there is Arjuna, the wielder of the bow —
There too will unfailingly be victory,
Prosperity,
Well-being,
And judiciousness;
This is my firm conviction.

Throughout the Gita, Sanjaya had from time to time infused his narration with some subtle encouragements to King Dhritarashtra to try to put an end to the war on its tenth day, and the Gita's final verse certainly represents the pinnacle of Sanjaya's noble endeavors.

*om tat saditi srimad bhagavad-gita / supanishatsu brahma-vidyayam*
*yoga-shastre srikrishnarjuna samvade / moksha-yogo namashtadasho 'dhyayah*

From the Ambrosial Song of God —
A conversation between Krishna and Arjuna
which is a Upanishad (confidential sharing)
of wisdom-teachings regarding the Absolute
And a scripture concerning Self-realization —
Thus ends the Eighteenth Chapter entitled Moksha-yoga,
Recognizing Divine Unicity By Way of Freedom.

# A Closing Offering To Sri Krishna
by Sajohn Daverly

1. I offer wholehearted homage unto You, the supreme poet Sri Krishna, who are the ocean containing the immortal ambrosia of the Bhagavad-Gita. Within the Gita, Sanjaya narrates to King Dhritarashtra how, as Arjuna's affectionate friend, You acted as both his most humble chariot driver and his most gracious spiritual advisor. Yet this really comes as no surprise, as You are the dearmost friend of *all* sentient beings.

2. Arjuna fell into great despair upon seeing all of his relatives and friends on the battlefield of Kurukshetra, yet after his historic conversation with You, he not only became relieved of his sorrow, but he awakened to his true nature. This is also not surprising, for although You are timeless, You are the one Awakener in all teachers throughout time, such as Gorakhnath, Adi Shankara, Jnaneshvara, and Sri Chaitanya.

3. You begin your Gita recitation by describing the nature of the Spirit-Self as the only constant amidst all the things of the world which constantly come and go, just as in a previous age You disseminated the brilliant science of Sankhya in Your appearance as the peerless sage Kapila. By wholehearted reception of Your life-renewing teachings, one feels as if one has received *shaktipat* (energetic transmission).

4. You then speak about the body/mind system being a clear channel for universal Intelligence (*buddhi-yukta*), the principle by which one may recognize that one is always already the unimaginably serene presence of Awareness. This is also not surprising, as You are the infallible, ever-flowing fountain-source of all perfect insight-wisdom and realization who later returned to once again reestablish dharma in the world as Siddhartha Gautama Buddha.

5. After that You speak about selfless action, exhorting Arjuna to conquer desire, that thief which steals one's attention away from Self-realization. Dearest friend, this seems a bit ironic, for are You not also a thief who steals away the minds of all by Your inexpressibly charming pastimes in Vrindaban with relations such as Your mother Yashoda, Your friends the cowherd boys, and Your beloved Sri Radha?

6. You then speak about the direct knowing of truth, and all the different kinds of sacrifices that truth-seekers make in earnestly trying to access that knowing. In like manner, You previously emitted spiritual illumination in all directions in Your appearance as the rapture-entranced sage Dattatreya, whose timeless teachings have been preserved in the Upanishads, the Puranas, and other revealed scriptures.

7. In the next portion of Arjuna's *satsang* with You, You speak about renunciation. You previously demonstrated one type of that in Your pristine incarnation as Sri Rama by leaving an extraordinarily opulent lifestyle and taking up residence in the Dandakaranya Forest for fourteen years. By doing so, You, Sita, Lakshman, and Hanuman dispelled a great many malefic energies influencing the world at that time.

8. Following thereafter, You instruct Arjuna in the science of meditation, just as throughout time You instructed countless sages, renunciates, yogis, and devotees in Your various manifestations of Shiva. Again and again, homage unto You, Lord Krishna, who are Yogeshvara, the master of mysticism who effortlessly creates, maintains, and withdraws all the myriad universes simply by Your *being*.

9. Ultimately, Your message in the Gita is that surrender on the inner battlefield is completely the opposite of what it is on a conventional battlefield of the world — it requires the greatest courage rather than cowardice, and ushers in the greatest fulfillment rather than suffering. May Your nectarous teachings serve to assist all those who wish to discover such courage and fulfillment within themselves.

# Govindashtakam
## by Adi Shankaracharya

**1**

*satyam jnanam anantam nityam anakasham paramakasham*
*gostha-prangana-ringana-lolam anayasam paramayasam*
*maya-kalpita-nana-karam anakaram bhuvanakaram*
*kshamaya natham anatham pranamata govindam paramanandam*

Let there be respectful obeisance to Govinda (Krishna, chief of the boys tending to the cows), who is the personification of supremely joyous contentment. He is the direct knowing of that truth which is continuous and unlimited in scope, like an uttermost sky which does not even have the elemental sky [as a defining limitation]. Although [as a child] He appeared to be greatly troubled as He restlessly moved here and there in the courtyard and the cow-shed, He is completely free from all affliction. He is both formless as well as with form, including all the manifold different forms of the universe created by His own divine potency. There is no refuge [necessary] for Him who is the enduring refuge [for all beings].

**2**

*mritsnam atsiheti yashoda-tadana-shaishava-santrasam*
*vyadita-vaktralokita-lokaloka-chaturdasha-'lokalim*
*loka-traya-pura-mula-stambham lokalokam analokam*
*lokesham paramesham pranamata govindam paramanandam*

Let there be respectful obeisance to Govinda, who is the personification of supremely joyous contentment. As a child, He trembled in terror of being hit by His mother Yashoda when she accused Him of eating clay. Yet as He is the Supreme Lord of all the worlds, when He opened His mouth she beheld the fourteen planetary systems — both this world and those beyond — within Him. He is the ancientmost foundational support of the three worlds* which, although unseen, is the light [of Awareness] by which all things are seen.

* The fourteen planetary systems are situated within 'the three worlds,' universal regions or dimensions of Consciousness known as *bhur* (earthly), *bhuvah* (astral), and *svah* (celestial).

**3**

*trai-vishtapa-ripu-viraghnam ksheeti-bharaghnam bhava-rogaghnam*
*kaivalyam navanitaharam anaharam bhuvanaharam*
*vaimalya-sphuta-cheto-vritti-visheshabhasam anabhasam*
*shaivam kevala-shantam pranamata govindam paramanandam*

Let there be respectful obeisance to Govinda, the personification of supremely joyous contentment who slays all the heroic adversaries of the three worlds. He removes the burdens of the Earth and 'the disease of becoming' (the illusion of becoming a limited separate self). Although He is the singular Absolute which eats nothing whatsoever, He also eats fresh butter, and ultimately consumes the entire world (at the time of universal dissolution and renewal). Though He casts no reflection, He appears as a distinctly reflected light in the clarity of an open, expanded mind. He is that unalloyed peace which promotes all auspiciousness.

**4**

*gopalam bhu-lila-vigraha-gopalam kula-gopalam*
*gopi-khelana-govardhana-dhrita-lila-lalita-gopalam*
*gobhir nigadita-govinda-sphuta-namanam bahu-namanam*
*gopi-gochara-duram pranamata govindam paramanandam*

Let there be respectful obeisance to Govinda, the personification of supremely joyous contentment who in His pastimes on Earth tended to cows in the form of a cowherd boy within a community of cowherding people. He sported with the milkmaids of that community and was cherished by all the cowherders as He enacted the pastime of holding up a hill in the village of Govardhana, 'the place where cows are nourished and exhilarated.' Those cows could be heard distinctly calling out the name 'Govinda!' to that one with innumerable names who went a great distance from His sphere of activities with the milkmaids (such as to Dvaraka*).

* A city founded by Krishna on the west coast of India where he ruled as king for many years of his adult life. Dvaraka is over 800 miles from Vrindaban in northern India where Krishna grew up and lived as a youth until the age of 16.

**5**

*gopi-mandala-goshthi-bhedam bhedavastham abhedabham*
*shashvad gokhura-nirdhutoddhat-dhuli-dhusara-saubhagyam*
*shraddha-bhakti-grihitanandam achintyam chintita-sad-bhavam*
*chintamanim ahimanam pranamata govindam paramanandam*

Let there be respectful obeisance to Govinda, the personification of supremely
joyous contentment. He whose 'state' [as the Absolute] is that of simultaneous
oneness and differentiation playfully delights in creating differences
(arguments) in the areas where the milkmaids congregate. He considers it His
good fortune to continually have the grey-colored dust [of Vrindaban] raised
upwards and alighting upon Him via the hooves of the galloping cows. He
receives great joy from the faith and loving devotion of those who meditate
upon Him, the Inconceivable, as the ever-abiding Reality. Indeed, He displays
qualities similar to those of a wish-fulfilling gemstone (philosopher's stone).

**6**

*snana-vyakula-yoshid-vastram upadayagam uparudham*
*vyaditsantir atha dig-vastra hyupadatum upakarsantam*
*nirdhuta dvaya-shoka-vimoham buddham buddher antah-stham*
*satta-matra-shariram pranamata govindam paramanandam*

Let there be respectful obeisance to Govinda, the personification of supremely
joyous contentment. While His young maiden friends were completely
occupied with bathing [in the river Yamuna], He playfully took all of their
clothing and climbed up into a tree [on the riverbank], offering to return the
clothing of every girl who [came out of the water and] approached the tree.
Both sorrow and confusion are driven away from those who perceive Him
abiding within as awake [universal] Intelligence. His body is composed of
nothing other than pure Being.

**7**

*kantam karana-karanam adim anadim kalam anabhasam*
*kalindi-gata-kaliya-shirasi muhur muhuh sunrityantam*
*kalam kala-kalatitam kalitashesham kali-doshaghnam*
*kala-traya-gati-hetum pranamata govindam paramanandam*

Let there be respectful obeisance to Govinda, the personification of supremely
joyous contentment who is the beautiful cause of all causes, the beginningless
beginning of all, both dark-blue-colored and without color as well.

He went into the Yamuna river to confront the Kaliya serpent in the water, and suddenly, on the spur of the moment, He began jubilantly dancing [on the serpent's hoods]. For a certain period of time He appears as time, but at the same time He surpasses time, leaving it behind entirely. [Similarly,] after all else has been defined, He remains [as the Indefinable]. It is He who is the cause of the movement of the three periods of time (past, present, and future), and it is also He who removes the ill effects of the age of discord (Kali-yuga).

8

*vrindavana-bhuvi vrindaraka-gana-vrindaradhyam vande 'ham*
*kundabhamala-manda-smera-sudhanandam suhrid-anandam*
*vandyashesha-maha-muni-manasa-vandyananda-pada-dvandvam*
*vandyashesha-gunabdhim pranamata govindam paramanandam*

Let there be respectful obeisance to Govinda, the personification of supremely joyous contentment. I praise He who, dwelling in Vrindaban, is worshipped by Vrindadevi (one of the leaders among the milkmaids) as well as by the leaders of the hordes of celestials. His soft, relaxed smile is like a garland of jasmine flowers, the sweetness of which delights all of His jubilant friends. The minds of the great inspired sages ever dwell upon Him with wholehearted veneration and blissful adoration of His two lotus feet. All of His qualities are fully praiseworthy.

9

*govindashtakam etad adhite govindarpita-cheta yo*
*govindachyuta madhava vishno gokula-nayaka krishneti*
*govindanghri-saroja-dhyana-shudha-jala-dhauta-samastagho*
*govindam paramanand'-amritam antah-sthah sa samabhyeti*

This Govinda is also known as Achyuta, the infallible one; Madhava, the very embodiment of springtime; Vishnu, the all-pervasive one; Gokula-nayaka, the foremost jewel in the necklace of Gokula ('the village where cows reside'); and of course, Krishna. Thus, whoever reads or recites these eight verses in praise of Govinda, installing Him within the sanctuary of one's heart and meditating on the lotus feet of this cow-tending lad, has all of his or her iniquities and suffering cleansed away by the poem's relief-giving waters. Such a one draws near to [the perceiving of] Govinda, who is the imperishable supremely joyous contentment situated within [all forms of life].

# References

Chapter One
Swami Vivekananda: From *The Complete Works of Swami Vivekananda*, Vedanta Press, Hollywood, CA. Reprinted by arrangement with the Ramakrishna Vedanta Society, Boston, MA.

Sri H.W.L. Poonja: Material excerpted from the book *The Truth Is* © 1995, 1998, 2000 Prashanti de Jager and Yudhisthira by Red Wheel/Weiser, LLC, Newburyport, MA and San Francisco, CA, www.redwheelweiser.com.

Chapter Two
Baba Hari Dass: From *Fire Without Fuel: The Aphorisms of Baba Hari Dass*, © 1986 Sri Rama Publishing, Santa Cruz, CA. Reprinted with the author's permission.

Chapter Three
Piet Hut: Used with the author's permission. www.ids.ias.edu/~piet/index.html.

Ramesh S. Balsekar: From *Sin & Guilt: Monstrosity of Mind* by Ramesh S. Balsekar, edited by Susan Waterman and published by Zen Publications, Mumbai, India.

Chapter Five
Roy Eugene Davis: From *Life Surrendered In God: The Kriya-Yoga Way of Soul Liberation* by Roy Eugene Davis, © 1995 CSA Press, Lakemont, GA. Reprinted with the author's permission.

Chapter Six
Adyashanti: Transcription © 2012 Open Gate Sangha, Campbell, CA. Used with the author's permission.

Chapter Seven
Isaac Shapiro: From *It Happens By Itself: Satsang With Isaac* by Isaac Shapiro, © 2001 by Luechow Press, Haiku, HI. Reprinted with the author's permission.

Chapter Ten
Shunryu Suzuki: From *Zen Mind, Beginner's Mind*, by Shunryu Suzuki.
Protected under the terms of the International Copyright Union. Reprinted
by arrangement with Shambhala Publications, Inc., Boston, MA.
www.shambhala.com.

Sri Anandamayi Ma: From *Ma Anandamayi Lila: Memoirs of Hari Ram Joshi*
by Hari Ram Joshi, © 1974 Shree Shree Anandamayee Charitable Society,
Calcutta, India.

St. Therese of Lisieux: From *Poems of St. Teresa, Carmelite of Lisieux, Known
As The 'Little Flower of Jesus,'* translated by S. L. Emery, © 1907 Carmelite
Convent. Reprinted with permission from Christian Classics Ethereal Library,
Calvin College, Grand Rapids, MI.

Chapter Eleven
Tukaram: From *Your Head In the Tiger's Mouth* by Ramesh S. Balsekar, edited
by Blayne Bardo and published by Zen Publications, Mumbai, India.

Chapter Twelve
Rumi: From *A Garden Beyond Paradise: The Mystical Poetry of Rumi*, translated
by Jonathan Star and Shahram Shiva, © 1992 Bantam Books, New York, NY.

Chapter Thirteen
Princess Hemalekha: From *Tripura Rahasya: The Mystery Beyond the Trinity*,
translated by Swami Sri Ramanananda Saraswathi and published by T.N.
Venkataraman, © Sri Ramanasramam, Tiruvannamalai, India.

Sri Ramana Maharshi: From *Erase the Ego* by Sri Ramana Maharshi, compiled
by Swami Rajeshwarananda, © 1996 Bharatiya Vidya Bhavan, Mumbai-
400 007, India.

Chapter Fourteen
Ramprasad: From *Mother of the Universe: Visions of the Goddess and Tantric
Hymns of Enlightenment* by Lex Hixon, © 1994, p. 187. Reproduced by
permission of Quest Books, the imprint of The Theosophical Publishing
House (www.questbooks.net).

Chapter Fifteen
Sri Ramakrishna: From *The Gospel of Sri Ramakrishna*, translated by Swami
Nikhilananda (New York: Ramakrishna-Vivekananda Center of New York,
1942), pp. 191, 217, 370.